KNOWING THE ADVERSARY

KNOWING THE ADVERSARY

LEADERS, INTELLIGENCE, AND ASSESSMENT OF INTENTIONS IN INTERNATIONAL RELATIONS

Keren Yarhi-Milo

PRINCETON UNIVERSITY PRESS

PRINCETON AND OXFORD

Library of Congress Cataloging-in-Publication Data
Yarhi-Milo, Keren, 1978–
Knowing the adversary : leaders, intelligence, and assessment of
intentions in international relations / Keren Yarhi-Milo.
pages cm — (Princeton studies in international history and politics)
Summary: "States are more likely to engage in risky and destabilizing actions such as military build-ups and preemptive strikes if they believe their adversaries pose a tangible threat. Yet despite the crucial importance of this issue, we don't know enough about how states and their leaders draw inferences about their adversaries' long-term intentions. Knowing the Adversary draws on a wealth of historical archival evidence to shed new light on how world leaders and intelligence organizations actually make these assessments. Keren Yarhi-Milo examines three cases: Britain's assessments of Nazi Germany's intentions in the 1930s, America's assessments of the Soviet Union's intentions during the Carter administration, and the Reagan administration's assessments of Soviet intentions near the end of the Cold War. She advances a new theoretical framework—called selective attention—that emphasizes organizational dynamics, personal diplomatic interactions, and cognitive and affective factors. Yarhi-Milo finds that decision makers don't pay as much attention to those aspects of state behavior that major theories of international politics claim they do. Instead, they tend to determine the intentions of adversaries on the basis of preexisting beliefs, theories, and personal impressions. Yarhi-Milo also shows how intelligence organizations rely on very different indicators than decision makers, focusing more on changes in the military capabilities of adversaries. Knowing the Adversary provides a clearer picture of the historical validity of existing theories, and broadens our understanding of the important role that diplomacy plays in international security."— Provided by publisher.
Includes bibliographical references and index.
ISBN 978-0-691-15915-7 (hardback) — ISBN 978-0-691-15916-4 (paperback) 1. Intelligence service. 2. International relations. 3. World politics—20th century. 4. Great Britain—Foreign relations—1936–1945. 5. Great Britain—Foreign relations—Germany. 6. Germany—Foreign relations—Great Britain. 7. United States—Foreign relations—1945–1989. 8. United States—Foreign relations—Soviet Union. 9. Soviet Union—Foreign relations—United States. 10. Detente. I. Title.

JF1525.I6Y37 2014

327.12—dc23

2014000415

British Library Cataloging-in-Publication Data is available

This book has been composed in Minion Pro

Printed on acid-free paper.

Printed in the United States of America

1 3 5 7 9 10 8 6 4 2

*To my mother, Dvora Yarhi, and
the memory of my father, Moshe Yarhi*

CONTENTS

ACKNOWLEDGMENTS

I could not have written this book without the support and guidance of several remarkable individuals. Robert Jervis was my academic adviser when I was an undergraduate student at Columbia and my first professor of international relations. He is the reason I chose to enter graduate school and become a political scientist. His tremendous knowledge of history, rigorous mind, and enthusiasm for teaching and mentoring were so inspiring. He has been a constant source of support, and his advice has always proven to be extremely useful. It is clear, to me at least, that his intellectual impact on my thinking is evident in every page of this book. Barbara Farnham and Dick Betts encouraged me to pursue a PhD, and helped me to think critically even as an undergraduate student, and Ian Lustick challenged me from the beginning of graduate school to think untraditionally about traditional topics in political science. Daryl Press's own work provided a great motivation, and his criticism and suggestions were always invaluable. Edward Mansfield—thank you for your vote of confidence in me and keeping me on track. I cannot overstate Avery Goldstein's contribution to this project. Avery is the epitome of a great mentor. I certainly could not have gone through graduate school, let alone finish my dissertation, if it were not for his emotional support and substantive comments. He is one of a kind, and everyone who knows him seems to share this feeling. I can only wish to be as good a mentor to my students as he has been to me.

I want to thank my friends at the University of Pennsylvania. Ryan Grauer, Dan Miodownik, Bill Petti, Sarah Salwen, Kaija Schilde, and Matt Tubin, have made the process of writing the dissertation that provided the platform for this book so pleasant and rewarding. It is hard to imagine surviving graduate school without them. The Olin Institute for Strategic Studies and the Belfer Center for Science and International Affairs at Harvard University offered great opportunities to develop my ideas and finish the dissertation. I am grateful to Mike Glosny, Michael Horowitz, Yev Kirpichevsky, Steve Rosen, Elizabeth Saunders, Paul Staniland, Caitlin Talmadge, and Alex Weisiger, who all carefully read and commented on earlier drafts of this project.

Princeton University has provided an excellent setting to complete the revisions on the book manuscript. I am so lucky to have had the opportunity to receive inputs from such a diverse, high-quality set of scholars. A special thanks to Joanne Gowa, Aaron Friedberg, Gary Bass, Christina Davis, John Ikenberry, Andy Moravcsik, Robert Keohane, Kris Ramsay, David Carter, and Jake Shapiro. Thomas Christensen read multiple versions of this book and always had original suggestions on how to improve it. Chuck Myers and Eric Crahan of Princeton University Press were always encouraging and supportive of the project, thereby making this process quite enjoyable and pleasant.

Outside Princeton, several individuals have encouraged me to challenge myself. For their valuable advice and comments I thank Richard Betts, Jonathan Caverley, Charles Glaser, Todd Hall, Jack Levy, Sean Lynn-Jones, Jonathan Mercer, Yaacov Vertzberger, and Bill Wohlforth. I apologize to those I may have forgotten.

Alex Lanoszka, Omar Bashir, and Lamis Abdelaaty provided superb research assistance. Teresa Lawson worked with such dedication and attention to the manuscript, helping me find the right words and tone. Her outstanding editing improved the manuscript significantly. I could not have brought this book to the finish line without the aid of these individuals.

I am also grateful for the financial and academic support that I received for this project from several institutions, including the Graduate School of Arts and Sciences at the University of Pennsylvania, the Browne Center for International Politics at the University of Pennsylvania, the Smith Richardson Foundation, the Olin Institute for Strategic Studies at Harvard University, the Belfer Center for Science and International Affairs at Harvard University, the Saltzman Institute of War and Peace Studies at Columbia University, Duke University's Triangle Institute for Security Studies, and the Morris Abraham Foundation. I owe a special thanks to the Center for International Security Studies at the Woodrow Wilson School of Public and International Affairs, Princeton University, for sponsoring my book workshop.

Finally, I could not have asked for a better support system. Ariel, my husband, has been a constant source of strength and humor. His love, encouragement, and patience made this whole ordeal possible as well as enjoyable. I simply adore you and cannot thank you enough. Jonathan and Daniel, my amazing boys, always helped by lifting my spirits even when things did not progress as expected. While keeping me on my toes, they make sure I have my priorities straight. I love you more than you can imagine! My family and friends in New York and Israel also deserve special thanks for their understanding along with encouragement to keep going. To my sister, Tali, and nephews, Ori and Shachar—thank you for being so supportive and simply awesome. To my in-laws, Roni and Elisheval Milo—I will forever be indebted for your love, encouragement, and generosity. To Inbal, Tal, Zehavit, Karin, Adi, Talia, Avital, Keren, Efrat, and Vicky—thank you for your support and entertainment throughout these years, and being so patient with me during the times I was buried under piles of documents. To Rhona, Ruty, Jessica, Gopi, Jackie, Julie and Carol—my gratitude for being so amazing at what you do, thereby allowing me to concentrate on what I needed to accomplish.

This book is dedicated to my wonderful parents, Dvora and Moshe Yarhi. My father, even while dying, made efforts to ask about the status of the book and whether the publisher had decided to extend a contract. When he passed, he knew that the book I had been working on so hard would come out. No one could wish for more loving, supportive, and dedicated parents. Even if it meant leading my life far from them, they gave me the assistance and confidence to pursue my dreams.

Introduction

The question of how policy makers gauge their adversaries' intentions remains fundamental to international relations theory and world affairs. Given states' uncertainty about each other's motives and types, and their incentives to misrepresent these factors, the task of determining another country's foreign policy plans is extremely difficult. This is not to argue that decision makers cannot gather potentially valuable information about their adversary's intentions. On the contrary, decision makers face information overload, with large amounts of "noise" compounded by deliberate attempts at deception. An overabundance of simultaneous signals carrying contradictory messages often leaves the decision maker unable to determine which to believe. This book shows that a number of outcomes are affected by decision makers' judgments regarding which indicators are credible: the conclusions decision makers will reach about the adversary's intentions, the reasoning they will provide to others in explaining their assessments, and the foreign policies they will choose to adopt. The complexity and variability of this phenomenon is demonstrated by the fact that during the three different historical episodes examined in this book, decision makers within the same administration—as well as the intelligence apparatus serving them—rarely agreed on what constituted a credible indicator of intentions. Observing the same behavior by the adversary, they drew different inferences about the informative value of the information on hand and what it signified regarding the adversary's long-term foreign policy plans. These differences were rooted not in personal idiosyncrasies, but rather reflect distinct, systematic patterns that challenge much of the current theoretical literature on costly signaling.

Discovering how observers infer the long-term intentions of their adversaries, and specifically, how a state's leaders and its intelligence apparatus—the bureaucracy that is explicitly tasked with assessing threats—gauge the enemy's foreign policy intentions, has important theoretical implications for different schools of thought in the international relations literature. Moreover, this question has historical significance and policy relevance. If British decision makers had understood the scope of Nazi Germany's intentions for Europe during the 1930s, for example, the twentieth century might have been much different. Today, predicting the future policy behavior of potential adversaries remains as critical as ever.

A Brookings report from March 2012 illustrates the significance of this question in contemporary international relations: "The issue of mutual distrust of long-term intentions . . . has become a central concern in U.S.-China relations."[1] US and Chinese officials' statements confirm this attitude. In a January 18, 2012, interview, US ambassador to China Gary Locke said, "I think that there is a concern, a question mark, by people all around the world and governments all around the world as to what China's intentions are."[2] Some observers have found China's recent actions along its coastal waters and maritime periphery particularly alarming. Others have worried that the "limited information" China has provided about "the pace, scope, and ultimate aims of its military modernization programs" raises "legitimate concerns regarding its long-term intentions."[3] Statements by Chinese officials indicate that Beijing, similarly, views recent US policies as a "sophisticated ploy to frustrate China's growth."[4] It is not clear, however, what concrete data either government is using to justify its adversarial stance and fear of the other's long-term intentions. Undoubtedly, current assessments of the degree of threat to US interests of a rising China—or for that matter, a possibly nuclear armed Iran or resurgent Russia—depend on the indicators observers use to derive predictions about the intentions of these countries.

Little empirical work identifies which indicators decision makers and intelligence organizations use or ignore when making such assessments.[5] For instance, disputes among US intelligence professionals over alleged Soviet military capabilities dominated debates on the Soviet threat throughout the Cold War, yet there has been little empirical examination of the extent to which calculations of force levels or military balances shaped US political decision makers' assessments of Soviet intentions. Examining how leaders assess intentions could also shed light on the sources of change in adversarial relations and longstanding rivalries. What prompts changes in how leaders perceive the intentions of their adversaries? What factors, for example, best explain the change in Ronald Reagan's beliefs about the intentions of the Soviet Union under Mikhail Gorbachev? Can these types of indicators usefully be compared to those that led members of the Carter administration to reevaluate Soviet objectives in the late 1970s, or those that Neville Chamberlain used to reassess Adolf Hitler's intentions in 1939? Finally, understanding the processes and biases that affect how a state's leaders and intelligence apparatuses read others' signals of intentions, and exploring how a state's own behavior shapes others' understanding of its intentions, can inform useful advice to policy makers on how to deter or reassure an adversary more effectively.

THE SELECTIVE ATTENTION THESIS AND ALTERNATIVE HYPOTHESES

This book addresses these gaps in the literature by advancing and testing a framework I call the selective attention thesis, and compares it to three promi-

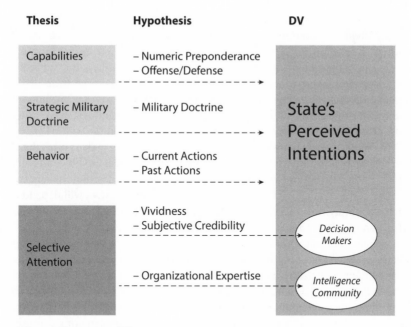

Figure 1. Summary of Theses

nent existing explanations of perceived intentions: the capabilities thesis, strategic military doctrine thesis, and behavior thesis.

Drawing on insights from information processing and organizational theory, the selective attention thesis posits that the ways in which decision makers form judgments about intentions differ from those of the intelligence community. Individual perceptual biases and organizational interests and practices are likely to shape what types of indicators are regarded as informative signals of the adversary's intentions as well as how these actors interpret such information about intentions. Put differently, the manner in which rationality is bounded varies across individuals and organizations as a function of psychological and organizational biases.

The selective attention thesis offers three key hypotheses: the vividness hypothesis and subjective credibility hypothesis pertain to the inference process of decision makers, and the organizational expertise hypothesis seeks to explain how a state bureaucracy—specifically, its intelligence organization—processes information about intentions (see figure 1).

The vividness hypothesis posits that decision makers tend to rely on kinds of information that are particularly vivid, even if "costless." Vividness refers to the "emotional interest of information, the concreteness and imaginability of information, and the sensory, spatial, and temporal proximity of information." This hypothesis is rooted in affective decision-making models, which predict that vivid information will receive greater weight than its evidentiary value warrants.[6] Vivid information, especially when received in face-to-face communications, is believed to be especially informative or, in Robert Jervis's terminology, a signal that is hard to manipulate (an "index").[7] This hypothesis predicts that decision makers will rely on personal impressions acquired from private interactions with the adversary's leadership, or from the adversary's response to their own litmus tests, to derive conclusions about its intentions, even though this information may be costless and therefore less credible.

The subjective credibility hypothesis posits that decision makers often debate the significance of or entirely ignore what scholars consider credible indicators of intentions. In fact, my research shows that individual decision makers vary in their responses: which indicators they regard as informative will depend on their own individual theories and expectations about the adversary's behavior. This hypothesis is rooted in cognitive (unmotivated) decision-making models, which posit that in order to avoid the cognitive expense of reevaluation, decision makers discount or misinterpret disconfirming evidence rather than change their preexisting beliefs.[8] This essentially means that decision makers tend to downplay or ignore information (even "costly" signals) about the adversary's intentions when it is inconsistent with their prior images and beliefs, and tend to pay inordinate attention to information (whether costly or cheap) that is consistent with their beliefs. Put differently, decision makers would "perceive what they expect to be there."[9] In addition, this hypothesis draws on the idea that decision makers have varying theories about the link between certain actions and underlying characteristics. Decision makers who strongly believe in the influence of regime type on foreign policy behavior, for example, will attend to indicators of the adversary's domestic institutions and norms to infer its intentions, and will ignore or discount informative indicators that do not pertain to regime type characteristics.[10] In sum, the subjective credibility hypothesis claims that decision makers' selection and interpretation of signals will be influenced by their own theories and preexisting stances toward the adversary. Accordingly, changing their perceptions about the adversary's intentions is likely to be difficult as well as unresponsive even to costly signals. Yet a change in beliefs about intentions is not impossible. It tends to occur under a particular set of conditions, such as when a specific experience is too vivid or salient to be ignored, too unambiguous to be discounted, or so directly in conflict with a decision maker's expectations that it becomes cognitively cheaper to abandon that belief instead of trying to tolerate the inconsistency.[11]

The organizational expertise hypothesis uses insights from information processing in organizations. It posits that the organizational context in which intelligence analysts operate makes them attend to different indicators than those used by decision makers. Organizational missions and goals channel attention, and affect the selection of information. In intelligence organizations, collecting and analyzing data on the adversary's military inventory typically receives priority for a variety of reasons. Military power is the sine qua non for strategic attack, which intelligence organizations are charged with preventing by early detection. Further, military inventories are relatively easy to track and monitor over time; they are tangible and thus quantifiable, and can be presented in a quasi-scientific way to decision makers. Intelligence organizations develop substantial knowledge about these material indicators, which they then use to make predictions about the adversary's intentions. This is not to argue that intelligence organizations only know how to count the number of missiles and divisions. Rather, this hypothesis posits that because analyzing intentions is one central issue with which intelligence organizations are explicitly tasked, and since there is no straightforward or easy way to predict the adversary's intentions, a state's intelligence apparatus has strong incentives to apply the relative expertise it has to the task of estimating others' intentions. This relative expertise frequently comes in the form of careful empirical analysis of components of the adversary's military capabilities. Consequently, as a collective, intelligence organizations tend to analyze the adversary's intentions through the prism of its military arsenal. Nevertheless, unlike the capabilities thesis, the organizational expertise hypothesis sees the logic of relying on capabilities as stemming from bureaucratic and practical reasons pertaining to intelligence organizations.[12]

THE COMPETING THESES

The capabilities thesis draws on the logic of several realist theories. It examines how different measurements of the adversary's military capabilities and significant changes in its armament policies—such as unilateral reductions in its military capabilities—give clues to its intentions.[13] The strategic military doctrine thesis argues that an adversary's military doctrine, military training patterns, and strategic thought reveal information about its political and military intentions. The behavior thesis posits that particular types of noncapabilities-based actions by an adversary—such as withdrawing from a foreign military intervention or joining a binding international organization—are used to draw conclusions over its intentions.

All three competing theses share two issues. First, they draw, explicitly or implicitly, on the costly signaling approach, which emphasizes the role of information as a key influence on state behavior.[14] This approach contends that states strategically undertake actions that are costly in order to convey information regarding their interests and intentions to other states. According to this view, in gauging others' intentions, observers should only attend to those actions that are costly because they either involve an expenditure of significant resources that cannot be recovered ("burning money") or severely constrain a state's future decision making ("tying hands").[15] The basic logic of this approach is that any actor, regardless of whether it has benign or malign intentions, could engage in behavior that costs nothing, thereby offering no credible information about its likely plans.[16] Cheap talk should, therefore, be ignored, and produce no effect on the perceivers' belief about the interests or intentions of the other state.[17] Second, all three theses—at least as they have been presented by international relations scholars—presume that the state makes its assessments about the adversary's intentions as if it were unitary. That is, they do not look for significance in differences between decision makers and intelligence organizations in the *types* of signals they focus on to reach their conclusions about intentions.[18]

CASES

This book tests all four theses using three cases: British assessments of the intentions of Nazi Germany in the period leading to World War II; US assessments of Soviet intentions under the administration of President Jimmy Carter; and US assessments of Soviet intentions in the years leading to the end of the Cold War during the second administration of President Reagan. These cases exhibit important within-case variation in both the independent and dependent variables, allowing evaluation of the relative influence of various indicators of intentions on assessments. They also control for a number of key variables. Each concerns a democratically elected administration that is engaged in interstate communications with a nondemocratic great power adversary. A prior history of militarized disputes (at varying levels of violence) characterized each of these adversarial relationships. Moreover, even setting aside their historical significance, these cases are crucial because of the theoretical debates they generated. Carter's changing assessments of Soviet intentions marked the collapse of détente, leading observers to debate the evolution of his foreign policy. Analysts also dispute the extent to which revised understandings of Soviet intentions drove US foreign policy as the Soviet Union was collapsing.[19] A new wave of research has revisited the conventional wisdom regarding Chamberlain's policy of appeasement.[20]

The analysis shows that our current approaches are insufficient to explain the patterns observed in the empirical analysis. Decision makers draw divergent meanings and interpretations depending on their theories, expectations, and needs. They sometimes attend to costless actions while ignoring costly ones. Organizational affiliation and role matter; intelligence officials consistently refer to different types of indicators of intentions than do political decision makers. Put together, differences in inference processes among decision makers as well as between them and the state's intelligence community may lead to consistent divergence in interpretations of that adversary's intentions.

SIGNALING AND PERCEPTIONS IN INTERNATIONAL RELATIONS THEORIES

Realists actively debate the question of what role information about others' intentions should play in the strategic choices of states. Realist scholars have advanced propositions, implicit or explicit, about the sources and effects of assessments about intentions. Offensive realists such as John Mearsheimer argue that because intentions are both difficult to discern with confidence and liable to change, cautious decision makers must always assume the worst about their adversaries' intentions and formulate policies on the basis of relative material indicators alone.[21] Defensive realists also emphasize the role of material capabilities in a state's calculus. In contrast to offensive realists, however, they reject a worst-case analysis of intentions, and contend that assessments of others' intentions should play a significant role in state's decisions on whether to adopt competitive or cooperative policies toward another state.[22] Based on insights grounded in the security dilemma, defensive realists have thus identified a key role for signals about intentions in inducing cooperation even under anarchy. They maintain that by adopting certain reassuring armament policies and foregoing actions that may appear threatening to others, states can effectively communicate their benign intentions and desire for cooperation. Drawing on Jervis's work on cooperation under the security dilemma, defensive realists have examined how a state's decisions to deploy offensive or defensive weapon systems, and adopt offensive or defensive military doctrines, may provide important information to others about its interests and intentions.[23] A large literature explores the offense-defense balance along with the ways in which the quality, not just the quantity, of certain weapons can affect how states perceive each other's intentions and consequently interact with each other.[24]

Building on Thomas Schelling's insights on credibility, Jervis's study on the logic of images, and work in economics on market signaling, international relations scholars have asserted that "informative" behaviors are those that distinguish different "types" of actors.[25] Thus, when gauging whether another country is an expansionist or status quo power, leaders should look only at those state actions that cannot readily be faked. Some actions that are costly for one "type" of state (e.g., a revisionist one) to undertake may not be equally costly for another (e.g., a status quo state). Costly and therefore informative actions include those actions that place greater constraints on a state's ability to alter its own policies in the future, such as by giving up armaments or joining a binding treaty organization. Statements of peaceful intent, by contrast, constitute "cheap talk" because either an expansionist leader or statesperson who is committed to peace or war could make such a statement if it would be to their state's advantage.

Using this basic intuition, rationalist security dilemma scholars such as Charles Glaser and Andrew Kydd have proposed various avenues for a security-seeking state to signal its nonaggressive stance, including arms control agreements (especially those reducing offensive capabilities), unilateral shifts toward a more defensive military posture, and unilateral and broad reductions of military forces. The cost of such signals is rooted in the possibility that the other side is genuinely aggressive.[26] Although costly changes in a state's military policy and capabilities have been most salient in this literature on signaling, other types of nonmilitary-based actions have also been recognized as important. Due to some types of international institutions' "unique ability to impose costs on states," neoinstitutionalists have emphasized the instrumental role of international institutions in allowing states to distinguish those with benign intentions from those that are aggressive. Constraints imposed by certain institutions, for example, could decrease or limit a state's power; states with benign intentions are more likely to accept such constraints. Accordingly, by joining an international institution, a state signals that it does not intend to pursue aggression in the near future, contributing to others' belief that its intentions are benign.[27]

These rationalist approaches underlie much of the signaling literature. Some scholars have also used psychological literature to explain how actors assess threats and discern information. In particular, psychological approaches to interstate communication focus predominantly on how actors' beliefs, background roles, cognitive limitations, and interests shape how they process information about intentions. Utilizing individual-level psychological variables, this literature in international relations has explored how various psychological biases and heuristics (shortcuts) can lead decision makers to mistaken judgments.[28] Analysts have thus attributed bad decisions, as Jonathan Mercer notes, "to the need for cognitive consistency, improper assimilation of new data to old beliefs, the desire to avoid value trade-offs, groupthink, idiosyncratic schemas, motivated or emotional bias, reliance on heuristics because of cognitive limitations, incorrect use of analogies, the framing of information, feelings of shame and humiliation, or a miserable child-hood."[29] To date, however, this research program has yet to offer an integrated theory of misperceptions. The rationalist and psychological approaches discussed above provide a platform for addressing the questions guiding this book, but this basis leaves a number of significant theoretical gaps.

First, both the rationalist approaches to signaling and psychological literature on the sources of perceptions and misperceptions have essentially looked at the same transaction from two sides. The ability of states to signal their intentions and influence others' impressions effectively depends on how actors perceive these signals.[30] Surprisingly, there has been little attempt to study these twin aspects of interstate communication together.[31] As Janice Stein and Raymond Tanter correctly argue, "We do not know enough about the conditions that promote effective signaling and reasonably accurate perception of threat."[32] More recently, Jervis observed that "if signaling theories are arcane, perceivers who have not read the literature will draw inferences differently, which means that the theory will neither describe the thoughts of perceivers nor prescribe the signalers' behavior. A theory of signaling then requires a careful investigation of how signals are perceived."[33] This study attempts to bring together these two literatures by examining whether and under what conditions observers understand concepts such as costly signals; to what degree they associate such actions with credibility; and how exactly observers' theories, predispositions, and impressions shape what indicators of intentions they will find informative.

Second, some rationalist approaches to signaling typically assume that in reading others' intentions, states can be envisioned as unitary actors. This simplification has several advantages, but it precludes us from examining why and to what extent individual decision makers, elites, and bureaucracies may read and interpret the adversary's intentions differently from one another. Indeed, if we find that different perceivers infer intentions differently, then there may not be a satisfactory way of aggregating divergent preferences for policies to satisfy all individuals. If the selective attention thesis is correct, furthermore, then we might observe persistent divergence among individual decision makers as well as between them and the state's intelligence community as to how to read and interpret the adversary's intentions. In other words, notwithstanding the existence of multiple costly actions and similar access to information by all observers, there may be no convergence toward a single view attributable to the state as a whole of its adversary's intentions.

This book, then, relaxes the unitary actor assumption and explores two *types* of perceivers. First, at the individual level, I examine how decision makers gauge intentions. I concentrate on the primary decision maker (i.e., the prime minister or president) and their closest advisers on issues of foreign policy. Second, at the organizational level, I analyze how the intelligence community estimates the adversary' intentions in its collective assessments. A state's intelligence apparatus is explicitly tasked with estimating threats, and policy makers often use its estimates to justify or reject various defense and foreign policies. Despite the centrality of these organizations, little scholarship exists on how intelligence organizations assess the intentions of the adversary.[34] Thus, this study tries to open the black box of the unitary state to examine different types of filters that decision makers and bureaucracies use to understand as well as interpret others' signals of intentions.

Third, some of the implications and hypotheses found in existing rationalist approaches to signaling have not been adequately tested. One reason for this gap lies in the normative and prescriptive nature of some of the existing rationalist work on signaling. As Glaser explains, a rationalist theory of signaling asks how a state would signal or infer intentions if its decision makers were to behave rationally or optimally. Although they provide important insights into how decision makers *should* behave to achieve their goals given the constraints they face, such theories' explanatory power may be limited when decision makers fail to act rationally.[35] Indeed, a substantial and diverse literature in international relations establishing that leaders rarely act rationally raises doubts about the empirical validity of these rationalist approaches. The assumptions that undergird some of the rationalist approaches should be questioned, given the ambiguity that is frequently associated with interpreting behavior. Jervis points out that while "behavior may reveal something important about the actor, often it is not clear exactly what is being revealed, what is intended to be revealed, and what others will think is being revealed."[36]

This study tests the core insights of various contending approaches to signaling against a variety of primary and secondary sources. These tests allow us to look at the extent of the gap between the rational baseline of how leaders should behave and the empirical record of how they actually behave, and discuss its significance. We can also evaluate the casual mechanism that is so central to the arguments found in the current literature regarding the informative value of different types of signals. It may be that changes in actor's perceptions of the adversary's intentions are not due to the impact of costly signals, for instance. Tracing these inference processes may also reveal which *types* of costly signals actors tend to use or ignore. After all, observers often must interpret not just one but rather multiple signals. Some of these signals may suggest that the adversary's intentions are becoming more benign, while others may indicate the opposite. Formal models are usually silent as to which costly signals perceivers are likely to notice and which they are likely to ignore. The empirical analysis of this book not only tests and modifies existing theories but also helps generate new theoretical claims about how different actors assess intentions.

Finally, the crisis-bargaining literature has only recently examined the role of costless communication in shaping conflict processes and outcomes.[37] This study is not specifically concerned with how states assess others' resolve during crisis. Yet ascertaining the intentions of an adversary at a given time—and specifically, how committed it is to changing the status quo—can have significant implications for a state's determinations regarding the other's resolve in crisis situations. If decision makers view the adversary as an unlimited expansionist for whom coercive statecraft would not change its foreign policy objectives, then a corollary judgment is that the adversary is highly resolved. Examining differences in how decision makers assess intentions and respond to perceived levels of resolve might therefore offer critical clues as to how likely they are to enter into crises with the adversary.

It is important to note what is outside the scope of this study. First, this study is primarily concerned with the perceptions of an adversary's long-term political intentions, because these are likely to affect a state's own foreign policy and strategic choices.[38] The distinction between short- and long-term assessments is important, because during crises and war, observers are likely to focus on questions that are distinct from those that normally inform their assessments of an adversary's intentions. Second, this exploration is not concerned with whether decision makers or intelligence organizations identified the intentions of their adversaries correctly. Although a significant question, it is a complicated one. Such judgments would require that we first establish what the leaders of Nazi Germany and the Soviet Union during the periods examined here actually believed their own intentions to be at the time. Rather, I ask a narrower question: How were assessments of intentions derived from the information available? Third, this book does not seek to discover all the sources of states' foreign policy and defense planning. It concentrates on the sources of assessments about intentions. Finally, this study does not attempt to address fully the conditions under which leaders' beliefs change. The focus here is on the indicators that leaders and intelligence organizations tend to privilege or ignore in their assessments of political intentions, how actors' subjective theories influence their expectations, and how organizational practices shape the ways in which different observers see signals of intentions as informative. I return to all these points in the book's concluding chapter.

SUMMARY OF FINDINGS

The three competing theses of costly signals—the capabilities, strategic military doctrine, and behavior theses—fail to explain the systematic differences between the analytic lenses used by decision makers and intelligence communities to infer the adversary's intentions. They also do not explain persistent differences among decision makers as to what types of actions they each perceive as informative. For example, in the mid- to late 1970s and 1980s, US decision makers and the US intelligence community disagreed on the USSR's intentions, and analyzed these intentions through different analytic lenses. Prime Minister Chamberlain and other British officials held differing opinions of Germany's long-term plans before the outbreak of World War II. Such differences were not rooted in personal idiosyncrasies but rather reflect distinct, systematic patterns that can be explained by the selective attention thesis. In the rest of this section, I summarize the findings from the historical record that support my arguments.

British decision makers during the interwar period and US decision makers in two different administrations all gave the greatest weight to indicators associated with the noncapabilities-based behavior of their adversaries when estimating their political intentions. Yet contrary to the expectations of the behavior thesis, decision makers within each administration diverged in what costly actions by the adversary they categorized as credible and did not restrict their focus exclusively to costly actions when gauging intentions. Consistent with the logic of the vividness hypothesis, decision makers often relied on costless information when it was conveyed in ways that were highly salient and vivid. They repeatedly used private insights about the adversary's intentions acquired from personal interactions with its leaders to infer the adversary's intentions and justify their assessments. Furthermore, as the selective attention thesis predicted, variations in decision makers' expectations about intentions influenced what they categorized as credible signals of intentions: those who had initially held relatively more bellicose views of the adversary categorized more of the adversary's actions as credibly signaling hostile intentions, compared to those who had initially held relatively more dovish views, and vice versa.

The capabilities thesis performs poorly in explaining how decision makers assess intentions, but it more accurately reflects the inference process of intelligence communities. Specifically, changes in the adversary's military capabilities did not by themselves alter decision makers' perceptions of adversaries' political intentions. Privately, decision makers only rarely linked the adversary's capabilities to their interpretations of its political intentions, even in cases when employing such evidence would have bolstered their contentions. In contrast, the adversary's military capabilities served as the most significant indicator on which the intelligence communities based their perceptions of intentions in all three cases. This pattern is consistent with the predictions of both the capabilities and selective attention theses. In most cases, however, intelligence assessments about political intentions had only marginal effects on the perceptions of civilian decision makers. Civilian actors chiefly relied on their own personal observations and private insights from meetings with their counterparts.

Finally, evidence suggests that decision makers did not use the adversary's military doctrine as an indicator of its intentions. Intelligence organizations found it difficult to agree on the nature of the adversary's military doctrine, and frequently debated what inferences, if any, about the adversary's intentions could be drawn from its military doctrine. Thus, support for the strategic military doctrine thesis is also weak.

The Plan of the Book

Chapter 1 provides the theoretical framework for the book's arguments. It defines what this study seeks to explain, and outlines the theoretical foundations of the selective attention thesis and three competing ones: the capabilities, strategic military doctrine, and behavior theses.

The empirical section of the book comprises three case studies, each in three chapters. The first case analyzes British assessments of Nazi Germany's intentions during the interwar period (1934–39). Chapter 2 outlines the predictions generated by each of the four explanations about perceived intentions, and tracks changes in Germany's capabilities, its military doctrine, and actions during this time. Chapter 3 draws on documents in the British National Archives to examine the evolution of the views held by key British decision makers about Germany's intentions, the indicators they used to make inferences about the nature and scope of Hitler's intentions, and the policies they advocated that reflected their assessments. Chapter 4 discusses the analysis provided by the British intelligence community during the same period.

The second case looks at US perceptions of Soviet intentions during 1977–80, the years leading to the collapse of détente. Chapter 5 lays out the relevant predictions of the alternative theses about how states should assess intentions. Using evidence from US archives and interviews with former US decision makers, chapter 6 explores how well each of the alternatives explains how President Carter, National Security Advisor Zbigniew Brzezinski, and Secretary of State Cyrus Vance assessed the intentions of the Soviet Union during the Carter administration. Utilizing evidence from declassified National Intelligence Estimates (NIEs) and Special National Intelligence Estimates (SNIEs) as well as interviews with former US intelligence analysts, chapter 7 tests the theoretical predictions against the collective estimates of the US intelligence community during the same period.

The third case analyzes how US decision makers and the US intelligence community reached conclusions about Soviet intentions during Reagan's second term as president. Chapter 8 discusses US perceptions of Soviet military capabilities, military doctrine, and behavior between 1985 and 1988. It derives predictions from the selective attention thesis as well as the three competing theses to predict how observers would assess intentions. Chapter 9 then uses newly declassified documents, open sources, and interviews to assess how President Reagan, Secretary of State George Shultz, and Secretary of Defense Casper Weinberger evaluated various indicators of Gorbachev's intentions. Chapter 10 focuses on the US intelligence community, and explores how the preparers of the NIEs and SNIEs on the Soviet threat reached their conclusions about Gorbachev's intentions during the period prior to the end of the Cold War.

The concluding chapter of the book, chapter 11, summarizes the empirical evidence, explains the significance of the findings for both theory development and contemporary international politics, and suggests important avenues for further research.

Theories of Intentions and the Problem of Attention

THE ADVERSARY'S INTENTIONS: WHAT PERCEPTIONS MATTER?

In this study, perception of an adversary's intentions refers to the set of beliefs held by observers in a state about its adversary's foreign policy goals (political intentions) with regard to changing or maintaining the status quo, and to a lesser extent, about the adversary's inclination to use military force to achieve these objectives (military intentions).[1] This study is primarily concerned with the perceptions of an adversary's long-term intentions, since these are likely to affect a state's own foreign policy and strategic choices.[2] Further, this study examines peacetime assessments of intentions between adversaries. Thus, in all the periods I analyze, the perceiving state has already defined the other country as one of its main sources of threat.

While perceived political intentions can range anywhere along a continuum from benign to hostile, I simplify matters by dividing such intentions into five ideal-type categories based on the degree to which the enemy is believed to have the determination required to revise the status quo and the extent of its revisionist intentions.[3] These categories are: unlimited expansionist, limited expansionist, unlimited opportunistic, limited opportunistic, and status quo powers.

Expansionist Intentions, Limited or Unlimited

An adversary is perceived to have expansionist intentions if it is believed to have a strong determination to expand its power and influence beyond its territorial boundaries. Expansionism could consist of an active plan to achieve a hegemonic international position (unlimited expansionist) or effect a change in the distribution of power that while significant, is more limited in scope (limited expansionist). Such an adversary is perceived as difficult to deter, as it is believed to actively and consistently seek to revise the status quo, and its leadership is believed to place a high priority on achieving its revisionist political goals (whether limited or unlimited in scope). Outside observers may therefore view it as unconstrained and extremely dangerous.

Opportunistic Expansionist Intentions, Limited or Unlimited

A state that is perceived to be opportunistic is believed to desire a favorable change in the distribution of power, whether limited or unlimited in geographic scope, but is not believed to be actively seeking change. Rather, the enemy is viewed as having a moderate level of determination to change the status quo; it may have contingent plans to seize revisionist opportunities, but is currently not willing or capable of acting on its revisionist goals when the cost of doing so appears to be high.[4] While expansionist and opportunistic states differ only in their determination to execute their revisionist designs, such a distinction is significant for those who are trying to gauge intentions and formulate a responsible policy toward their adversary. A state that faces an opportunistic adversary must hedge against the possibility that this adversary will act on contingent plans to expand. A state may thus pursue coercive diplomacy against this type of adversary, combining threats to dissuade the adversary from taking advantage of opportunities as well as offering assurances if the adversary maintains the status quo. Facing an adversary determined on expansion, however, requires assertive balancing and confrontational policies, or even force—if a country has the means—aimed at denying the adversary its revisionist objectives.[5]

Status Quo Intentions

The perception of an adversary's intentions as essentially supportive of the status quo does not entail a normative belief that the status quo is morally just, only a strategic belief that the adversary seeks "preservation" versus "aggrandizement."[6] We should expect to see that those state decision makers who perceive their adversary's intentions as oriented toward the status quo will support this belief with arguments that the adversary is mainly interested in maintaining its current position in the international system, and that it is unlikely to create or take advantage of opportunities to expand its power as well as influence.

In addition to political intentions, I also examine perceptions of military intentions—that is, whether the adversary is perceived as likely to use military force to support its political goals or is instead more likely to rely on nonmilitary means, such as the use of verbal or written propaganda, political subversion, and economic assistance or sanctions.[7]

THE SELECTIVE ATTENTION THESIS

The point of departure of the selective attention approach I develop and test in this book is that individual decision makers and bureaucratic organizations, such as the state's intelligence community, process information differently.

Civilian decision makers are human beings, and their selection and interpretation of signals will be influenced by their own theories, needs, and expectations. Meanwhile, the organizational context in which intelligence analysts operate along with the organizational mission of a state's intelligence apparatus channel attention and affect the selection of information as well as the preference for certain interpretations. In light of these inherent differences between the two sets of perceivers, I offer a set of hypotheses as to how these different actors assess the adversary's intentions.

How Do Decision Makers Infer Intentions?

Information about intentions is often complex, ambiguous, and subject to manipulation and deception, thereby requiring much interpretive work. Cognitive limitations in processing innumerable stimuli, coupled with the need to distinguish usefully and correctly between credible signals and meaningless noise, require the use of some inference strategies or shortcuts (heuristics). These simplified models of reality frequently have the unintended effect of focusing perceivers' attention toward certain pieces of information, or indicators, of the adversary's intentions and away from others. Building on some prominent insights from psychology on information processing and attitude change, I offer two hypotheses, which are not mutually exclusive—the vividness and subjective credibility hypotheses—to explain how vivid information as well as decision makers' theories, expectations (unmotivated biases), and needs (motivated biases) shape what indicators of intentions they will attend to and value as credible.[8]

THE VIVIDNESS HYPOTHESIS

At the heart of the vividness hypothesis is the idea that people give inferential weight to information in proportion to its vividness. Vividness refers to the "emotional interest of information, the concreteness and imaginability of information, and the sensory, spatial, and temporal proximity of information."[9] Recent work in psychology and political science has shown that our emotional responses shape the certainty of our beliefs and preferences for certain choices.[10] This finding dovetails with earlier work on information salience.[11] As Eugene Borgida and Richard Nisbett classically argued, "There may be a kind of 'eyewitness' principle of the weighing of evidence, such that firsthand, sense-impression data is assigned greater validity."[12] In the words of Chaim Kaufmann, "Information that is highly salient (vivid, concrete, immediate, emotionally interesting or exciting) will receive greater weight than its evidentiary value warrants. . . . People pay more attention to, and are more influenced by, especially salient information than less vivid information."[13] Accordingly, information about intentions that is vivid, personalized, and emotionally involving is more likely to be remembered, and hence to be disproportionately available for influencing inferences. Conversely, studies have shown that information that lacks vividness, such as information that is abstract, colorless, and less concrete, is more likely to be neglected or ignored.[14]

Two forms of vivid information are emphasized in this study: decision maker's impressions from personal interactions with members of an adversary's leadership, and a decision maker's perception of the adversary's response to a litmus test that they believed they have communicated to the adversary. An adversary's failure to comply with such a test can be expected to result in perceptions of hostile intentions; behavior that appears to pass the test (even if it is not, in fact, meant by the adversary as a response to it) is similarly vivid information that is, I predict, likely to result in perceptions of more benign intentions.

I argue that these practices contain affective reactions to vivid stimuli, occurring automatically, and influencing decisions and judgments. As such, this inference process may be more or less rational depending on the extent to which decision makers are analytic and deliberative in how they use vivid information to infer intentions. At the same time, more recent discoveries in neuroscience have shown that the reliance on affect and emotion is a quicker, easier, and more efficient way to navigate in a complex, uncertain, and sometimes-dangerous world. Or as Antonio Damasio explains, rationality is not only a product of the analytic mind but the experiential mind as well.[15] That is, without the ability to reference emotion, people remain incapable of making so-called rational decisions. Viewed in this way, there is little value in debating whether the use of personal impressions from personal meetings or litmus tests are fully rational, as various studies demonstrate that affect is a strong conditioner of preference whether or not the cause of that affect is consciously perceived.[16]

Decision makers can and frequently do treat personal impressions, garnered from personal observations of the behavior of their adversary's leaders in summit meetings or private conversations, as highly salient indicators of those leaders' sincerity. Consequently, they view these opportunities as providing important evidence about the intentions of their adversary. The affective nature of personal impressions of the adversary's behavior, being both personal and personally felt, makes them more likely to be treated as highly salient information. Such impression formation reduces cognitive burdens, given that individuals can quickly form and later invoke established stereotypes rather than having to assimilate a wide variety of complex, abstract information. Consider, for example, the comments President George W. Bush made in reference to the intentions of the Russian leader Vladimir Putin following their 2001 meeting: "I looked the man in the eye. I found him to be very straightforward and trustworthy. We had a very good dialogue. I was able to get a sense of his soul."[17] Bush is certainly not the only world leader to draw on personal impressions to judge the sincerity of his counterparts. Indeed, notable figures such as

Winston Churchill, Anthony Eden, and Franklin Roosevelt were all strongly influenced by their personal impressions of Joseph Stalin.[18] Churchill at one point even stated, "Poor Neville Chamberlain believed he could trust Hitler. He was wrong. But I don't think that I am wrong about Stalin."[19]

Decision makers' attentiveness and responsiveness to this kind of information has a certain justification and confers occasional advantages. Interpersonal interaction provides a setting in which leaders exchange information not only through the content of what they say but also via a myriad of other channels. These include facial expressions, attitude, body language, tone of voice, and even unconscious movements or reactions. "When an actor is able to directly observe one of his adversaries he will . . . scrutinize those presumably uncontrolled aspects of personal behavior that are indices to the adversary's goals, estimate of the situation, and resolve."[20] Robert Frank has asserted that emotional predispositions—as evidenced through cues in expression, voice, and posture, for instance—supply real information about intentions.[21] Because these behaviors are not fully under the individual's control, they help us as human beings distinguish "cooperators" from "defectors." The adversary's emotional behavior in these circumstances is, according to Jervis, a signal that is hard to manipulate and accordingly could be perceived as inextricably linked to the adversary's intentions, or what Jervis calls an index.[22]

Impressions derived from private meetings, however, can be misleading and potentially risky. Alexander Groth notes that most politicians tend to be overconfident about their own ability to judge others and as such may be too tempted to use their personal impressions as credible information about intentions. This is most risky in instances where the adversary chooses to be deceitful and is skillful at it.[23] Thus, personal encounters can produce impressions based on certain behavioral indicators of our interlocutor that are retained not only as explicit assessments but also as affective evaluations. Such impressions form the intuitive basis for negative or positive judgments about others' intentions. These feelings are not objective facts; nevertheless, they do form a type of subjectively experienced information. Further, these impressions are not static; during the process of interaction we continuously and unconsciously update the affective impressions we have of the adversary based on negative or positive experiences.[24]

It is difficult to forecast exactly what behavior leaders will pay attention to and what impressions they will take away from meetings with their counterparts. By their very nature, personal impressions are contingent on highly personal and contextual factors. I hypothesize, though, that personal impressions of the adversary's behavior will likely influence assessments of intentions under three conditions. First, all else being equal, leaders institutionally endowed with the power to make independent judgment calls will have more discretionary freedom to draw on their own personal impressions in making decisions. Conversely, should leaders perceive their counterparts to be under strong institutional constraints and hence relatively powerless, they may give their personal impressions of those counterparts less weight. Second, situations where information is scarce, ambiguous, or contradictory can push leaders to rely on personal impressions for lack of other sources. Leaders may also fall back on instinctual personal impressions in situations when they experience reduced cognitive processing capacity—for instance, due to crisis-induced stress.[25] Third, certain leaders' personal attributes may also play a role. Leaders highly confident of their own judgment, and distrusting or dismissive of bureaucratically produced assessments, will be more likely to draw on their own impressions. Actors with strong preconceptions or prejudices about their opposite numbers may be slower to adjust their explicit evaluations in response to personal interactions.[26]

Yet we should not anticipate that personal interactions will always cause leaders to infer intentions. Much depends on the strength of a decision maker's impressions of their counterpart. At times, a decision maker could meet with the adversary's leader but not come away with significant impressions, either positive or negative, of the leader's characteristics or sincerity, and as a result may not rely on personal interactions to draw inferences about the adversary's intentions.

In addition to personal impressions, decision makers may perceive the adversary's response to their litmus test as informative of intentions either because they have their theories about what indicators are good predictions of intentions or because of the "egocentric" bias, by which people tend to exaggerate the causal significance of their own actions and discount the importance of other factors, thereby overestimating the linkages between their own actions and the behavior of others.[27] Such a predilection for decision makers to see themselves as the central point of reference when they explain particular actions of their adversaries can produce a significant emotional response, making an adversary's behaviors in such situations highly salient information from the observer's perspective. The three primary decision makers I consider in the cases—President Carter, President Reagan, and Prime Minister Chamberlain— all exhibited this egocentric bias, each believing that certain positive or negative actions by his adversary were a direct response to his own actions.

Egocentric bias might be especially salient to inferring intentions when a decision maker believes that they have communicated to the adversary, through private or public channels, what kind of actions they would expect the adversary to undertake to reveal its intentions. An adversary's reluctance or refusal to respond to such litmus tests may have an especially personalized and negative emotional effect on the observing decision makers.[28]

The egocentric bias might also work in the converse direction: an adversary's actions that seem to be responsive to the proposed litmus test could be seen as a especially salient reassuring signal from the perspective of the observer, since they will likely attribute the adversary's actions to their own prior behavior even if the adversary decided to undertake these actions for unrelated reasons.

This mechanism can also be linked to what is known as the self-serving at-tribution bias; according to this phenomenon, when the adversary acts in ac-cordance with our wishes, we are prone to overestimate the degree to which we are responsible for its behavior, either because it enhances our self-esteem or because we discount the role of unknown influences.[29] In sum, the adversary's actions, particularly when the observer has set up a test, are likely to be viewed by the observing decision maker as a personal response, leading the latter to give those actions disproportionate weight in their assessments of the adversary's intentions. We should thus expect decision makers to give special attention to those of an adversary's actions that seem to respond, whether fail or pass, to a litmus test, especially if the decision maker has personally communicated the test to the adversary.

In anticipating the effects of personal impressions or litmus tests on percep-tions of intentions, the observer's initial beliefs about the adversary's intentions also matter. "How I perceive your signal is strongly influenced by what I already think of you. Even what might seem to be the clearest signals will make no im-pression if the perceiver's mind is made up."[30] As such, in line with the cognitive consistency principle, this hypothesis predicts that all else being equal, those decision makers who hold more hawkish views about the adversary's intentions will be slower to change their beliefs on receiving vividly positive information (and quicker when the information is negative) than those who hold more dov-ish views of that adversary.[31]

Finally, studies on the role of vividness have shown that in the absence of personal experience or firsthand knowledge, decision makers are keener to rely on concrete anecdotal information that contains vivid description, and more reluctant to rely on evidence that is abstract, colorless, and objective—such as changes in measurements of the adversary's weapon inventory or its doctrinal manuals—even if that objective-evidence could be regarded as "extremely reli-able."[32] This kind of information is not nearly as engaging as the vivid, salient, and often emotion-laden personal responses of leaders to their opponents.[33] As we will see in the empirical cases, most intelligence reports that estimate the threat posed by the adversary could be described as relatively colorless. For example, US assessments of the Soviet Union frequently included statisti-cal summaries of Soviet military capabilities, and British strategic assessments of the German threat were similar. According to this thesis, we should expect decision makers to ignore or discount such reports even when their evidentiary base is strong.

THE SUBJECTIVE CREDIBILITY HYPOTHESIS

A psychology-based theory of attention offers a more nuanced understanding of credibility than that supplied by game-theoretical accounts, although some of its predictions may overlap with some rationalist approaches that take variations in prior beliefs seriously.[34] The subjective credibility hypothesis posits that both the existence and meaning of credibility depend on the perceiver's expectations about the links between the adversary's behavior and the adversary's underlying characteristics.[35] Hence, how much attention is paid to costly actions will hinge on observers' theories and expectations about their adversary.

This hypothesis is rooted in models of unmotivated decision making. According to these models, cognitive mechanisms such as "attention to confirming evidence, denial, source derogation and biased assimilation of contradictory evidence buffer beliefs from refutation."[36] This is especially the case when we are dealing with an observer's core beliefs about the nature of the adversary's intentions. Thus, when a state is already believed to be hostile, contrary indications that would be seen as informative in other contexts are likely to be ignored, dismissed as propaganda ploys, or interpreted as signs of the adversary's weakness.[37] Since this study deals with assessments of an adversary's intentions, all the decision makers studied start out by holding negative images of the other, mistrusting its actions, and attributing to it some degree of malign intentions.

Similar to some rationalist models, the subjective credibility hypothesis begins with the assumption that observers are likely to vary in their prior degree of distrust toward a single adversary, and the extent to which they believe its intentions are hostile.[38] This variation in decision makers' beliefs explains some differences in whether and when decision makers will view a particular costly action as credible. Specifically, those decision makers who already hold hawkish views about the adversary's intentions are unlikely to perceive its costly reassuring actions as credible signals of benign intentions, and consequently such signals will not necessarily change their perceptions of their adversary's intentions. In comparison, those who hold relatively less hawkish views of the adversary's intentions are less likely to see reassuring signals as necessarily contradicting their existing beliefs. They therefore are more likely to use them as informative evidence of more benign intention. Conversely, hawks are likely to be responsive to costly actions by the adversary that indicate malign intentions, because these would be consistent with their existing beliefs about the adversary's intentions. They might regard even ambiguous information as consistent with their beliefs, and at times will use such evidence to confirm these beliefs. When faced with hostile actions, then, hawks are likely to be quicker in attributing more malign intentions to the adversary in comparison to doves within the same administration.

Nevertheless, unlike some game-theoretical models of signaling, the subjective credibility hypothesis predicts that the differences in observers' beliefs about the adversary's intentions are not simply a function of different access to information. Notwithstanding the presence of informative signals and shared information about such signals, some individuals may not change their beliefs about the adversary's intentions at all, and as such, convergence toward a common interpretation of intentions among observers who have similar access to information will not take place. Put differently, even when faced with multiple public and costly signals of reassurance, some observers may continue to reason, for example, that the adversary's actions are intended to deceive observers into believing it harbors no malign intentions, so as to take advantage of their cooperative policies. Others may believe that the adversary's reassuring signals have arisen from economic or domestic political needs, and therefore should not be seen as informative signals of more benign foreign policy goals.[39]

Related to the notion that beliefs shape expectations about the adversary's intentions, decision makers' expectations are also influenced by their individual theories about the relationship between the adversary's behavior and underlying characteristics. As Jervis points out, different observers will interpret even costly behavior differently, "because some of them saw a certain correlation while others either saw none or believed that the correlation was quite different." Accordingly, if, for instance, a decision maker believes in the logic of diversionary war, they are likely to pay attention to indicators of social unrest, believing them to be informative evidence that the adversary's leadership is about to embark on a revisionist foreign policy. In the eyes of such a decision maker, social unrest serves as an index of intention—one that the adversary is unlikely to be able to manipulate to project a false image. Others within the same administration, however, may not share this diversionary-war theory, and so not treat social unrest as an informative indicator of future intentions.[40] It is, indeed, difficult to predict what theory a decision maker holds when assuming office, and the aim of this study is not to test this proposition empirically. Rather, I note that decision makers' expectations influence what information they attend to and ignore, and both preexisting beliefs and individual theories shape these expectations.

A few clarifications about the subjective credibility hypothesis are in order. First, the importance of prior beliefs in assimilating new information is central to both psychological and most rationalist approaches that take prior beliefs seriously. Yet one crucial prediction that distinguishes some rationalist models from the selective attention thesis has to do with whether perceivers with identical prior beliefs and uncertainty will be equally affected by the new information revealed by costly signals. The subjective credibility hypothesis highlights that observers with similar priors and identical access to information about costly signals may disagree on what signals should be perceived as credibly revealing intentions. We should therefore not necessarily expect to observe convergence among decision makers with respect to the existence and interpretation of these indicators, irrespective of the actual sincerity (or truthfulness) of these signals.[41] Likewise, we should expect to see instances where observers find no connection between particular indicators of behavior and the adversary's intentions, despite the fact that outside observers would categorize these indicators as important or costly. In fact, under purely rationalist (Bayesian) updating, disconfirming data should always lead to some belief change, or at least to low-ered confidence in existing beliefs.[42] In contrast, under the subjective credibility hypothesis, we should expect to see some decision makers who refuse to revise their beliefs even when confronted with valuable and costly information. This might be due to the existence of a strong confirmation bias, the colorless nature of the information, or a mismatch between the adversary's behavior and a deci-sion maker's theories about what type of signals reflect intentions.[43]

Organizational Information Processing and Intelligence Communities

The organizational context in which intelligence analysts operate makes them different kinds of perceivers than are civilian decision makers. Organizational missions and goals are known to channel attention and affect the selection of information as well as the preference for certain interpretations. Intelligence organizations' estimates about the adversary's intentions reflect the expertise these organizations have developed in the cultivation of the organizational goal. Since it is often the case that the primary mission of intelligence is to forewarn of hostile action, these organizations tend to devote the most time and energy to the collection, production, and analysis of information about the adversary's military inventory. In addition, capabilities information is frequently quantifi-able and therefore lends itself to quasi-scientific analysis. Expertise about these quantifiable aspects of the adversary's military arsenal is then used to derive predictions about the adversary's intentions.[44]

THE ORGANIZATIONAL EXPERTISE HYPOTHESIS

Intelligence analysts are unlike most types of civilian decision makers. Intel-ligence analysts operate in a formal, professional, and institutionalized orga-nization that is part of a bureaucracy.[45] Bureaucratic-organizational processes shape the selection and evaluation of information. Attention to information is strongly affected by how organizational goals and standard operating proce-dures to realize them are defined as well as specified.[46] One of the most signifi-cant goals, if not the governing objective, of any intelligence organization is to guard against a surprise attack. In other words, the most significant failure an intelligence organization could be blamed for is a failure to warn. This mission can shape the organization's tasks of searching for, collecting, interpreting, and disseminating information. Since any attempt by the adversary to launch an attack would require that it first have the capability to do so, the most prudent practice for any intelligence organization is allocating resources to monitor the capabilities, latent or current, of existing or potential adversaries. This biases the organization's search for information and its processing in predictable ways.

Moreover, military inventories are a convenient target for data collection and can be easily tracked over time. As Mark Lowenthal writes:

This is particularly true of deployed conventional and strategic forces, which are difficult to conceal, as they tend to exist in identifiable garrisons and must exercise from time to time. They also tend to be garrisoned or deployed in large numbers, which makes hiding them or masking them impractical at best. The regularity and precision that govern each nation's military make it susceptible to intelligence collection.[47]

Military arsenals also are tangible in the sense that they can be quantified and presented in a quasi-scientific way to decision makers. Indeed, much of the intelligence that was produced about the Soviet Union, for example, was statistical. The US intelligence community devoted great time and energy to monitoring and reporting the size of Soviet material capabilities, defense spending, and so on, while disregarding intangibles such as the cohesion of the Soviet state or depth of support for its leadership among the general population and satellite states.

Over time, the enactment of preestablished routines can create myopia. As described in Graham Allison's organizational process model, behavior at one time, t, becomes only marginally different from behavior at $t-1$ or $t+1$. That is, standard operating procedures followed in the hiring practices, training, and socialization of intelligence analysts may lead members of the community to emphasize their expertise about the adversary's material capabilities in support of judgments about its intentions. Intelligence analysts responsible for writing strategic assessments that reflect the sociocognitive style of the intelligence community as a whole are likely to highlight the information that receives the most salience within the organization.[48]

The extensive monitoring of the adversary's military inventory both creates expertise and narrows focus. To use Isaiah Berlin's metaphor, intelligence experts can be characterized as hedgehogs.[49] A review by Phillip Tetlock of experts' style of reasoning notes that "the intellectually aggressive hedgehogs knew one big thing and sought, under the banner of parsimony, to expand the explanatory power of that big thing to 'cover' new cases."[50] The intelligence communities in the United States during the Cold War and in Britain during the interwar period appear to have relied on their expertise about their adversary's capabilities to address questions pertaining to its political intentions. Furthermore, expertise can create a reluctance to adjust assessments in response to new information. In comparison to nonexperts, Tetlock found that hedgehogs were less likely to change their beliefs, did not update their views in a manner consistent with rationalist updating rules, and were less inclined to entertain dissonant scenarios that undercut their own beliefs and preferences. As a result, they were less equipped to adapt to rapidly changing environments.[51]

This analysis involves certain assumptions and qualifications. For one, there is no doubt that intelligence organizations develop expertise on a variety of issues pertaining to the adversary that go beyond the adversary's military inventory and calculations of the balance of forces. I argue, though, that since a coordinated intelligence assessment will often draw on the shared knowledge of the organizations and their standard practices, we are more likely to see information about capabilities advanced as the primary influence on their assessments of intentions. Second, this hypothesis tells us nothing about what kinds of conclusions intelligence agencies, individual analysts, or the heads of that bureaucracy will reach about the adversary's intentions. This hypothesis instead only pertains to the collective intelligence products. Its only claim is that in such assessments, the adversary's capabilities are likely to be the predominant influence on the assessments of long-term political intentions.

It is reasonable to assume that some intelligence agencies or individuals will be more biased than others toward overestimating the adversary's capabilities, because of their parochial organizational interests or own beliefs, and will therefore reach more alarming conclusions about its intentions. For instance, the US Defense Intelligence Agency (DIA) or military service intelligence agencies may be more likely to reach alarming conclusions about the adversary's capabilities than, say, the State Department's Bureau of Intelligence and Research (INR), because more alarming conclusions justify bigger budgets and forces that will bolster the essence along with the prestige of the DIA or military services. Nonetheless, the organizational expertise hypothesis is agnostic about the effects of such calculations on assessments of intentions at the level of particular intelligence agencies. Rather, I contend that at the level of coordinated estimates, intelligence agencies would tend to rely more on capabilities due to their specific knowledge and expertise, although different agencies might differ in their estimates of the adversary's capabilities.[52]

The State's Assessments in the Selective Attention Thesis

In light of the differences between decision makers and intelligence organizations in how they assess the adversary's intentions, what can we expect to observe about the assessment of intentions of the observing state? Although this book does not attempt to develop a statist theory of intention, several important observations follow from the selective attention thesis that are worth highlighting.

First, given the significant differences between the two sets of observers, and the differences in the kinds of indicators each appears to prefer, there is no reason to believe that their assessments of the adversary's intentions should converge over time. Indeed, disagreements or tensions between civilian decision makers and the intelligence community over the adversary's long-term intentions are likely to take place. Such discrepancies can appear in situations in which the adversary's military policies do not match its diplomatic behavior as subjectively viewed by the key decision makers Alternatively, we may see either convergence or a simultaneous change in the same direction between decision makers and the intelligence community in their assessments of adversary's intentions in cases where the adversary's military capabilities are changing in the same direction as its diplomatic behavior. The factors producing the change in the assessments, according to this thesis, would differ depending on whether the observer is a decision maker or intelligence community. Unsatisfied with the assessments of their intelligence community, decision makers may choose to ignore such assessments, attempt to provide better guidance to intelligence officers as to how to improve intelligence analysis, or manipulate the intelligence by politicizing it.[53]

Second, although decision makers and intelligence organizations can agree to disagree about the adversary's long-term political intentions, all else being equal, changes in the primary decision maker's assessment of intentions are more likely than changes in intelligence estimates about intentions to lead to changes in the state's policies.[54] After all, intelligence organizations do not have the mandate to prescribe (or criticize) policy options for the decision makers, and intelligence is subordinate to policy in that its activities are intended to serve the policy makers. I do not claim that the scope of bureaucratic action and importance are epiphenomenal to the president's or prime minister's own preferences. Intelligence input may have some effect on policies by influencing the views of members of Congress to gain policy support, and in cases of information leaks, even shaping the public's views of the nature and magnitude of the threat.

Third, all else being equal, significant changes in the assessment of intentions by the primary decision maker (the president or prime minister) should have greater causal impact on changes in the state's policies than changes in advisers' assessments. At the same time, the more cohesive the assessment of the adversary's intentions among the key decision maker and their closest advisers, the stronger the impact that changes of assessments of intentions should have on the state's collective policies. To be sure, as I point out later in this chapter, assessments of intentions are just one factor influencing a state's policy toward its adversary. We therefore cannot expect the primary decision maker's assessment of intentions to precisely mirror the contours and changes in the policies at the aggregate level. Rather, we should probe whether changes in this decision maker's assessment of intentions affected the polices advocated or rejected, and whether the changes in such assessments resulted from variables associated with the selective attention thesis or from those highlighted by the alternative theses outlined below.

COMPETING THEORIES OF INTENTIONS

Drawing on insights from the international relations literature, I develop three alternative explanations of how observers assess an adversary's intentions.[55]

Each of these theses postulates a specific causal relationship between specific sets of indicators and observers' resulting assessments of intentions.[56]

The Capabilities Thesis

The capabilities thesis posits that observers infer an adversary's intentions from different indexes of its current military power in predictable ways. This thesis draws on several realist theories—such as Mearsheimer's theory of offensive realism, the offense-defense theory of defensive realism, and other rationalist approaches to the security dilemma—whose common denominator is the idea that both a country's military capabilities and its armament policies reveal and significantly shape its intentions.[57]

REALIST THEORIES

Mearsheimer's theory of offensive realism posits that governments are unlikely ever to be certain about others' intentions, and that intentions are fluid and can easily change; as a result, decision makers in an anarchic international system must assume the worst about other states' intentions.[58] An implicit assumption in offensive realist theory is that observers should anticipate not only that another state will strive to maximize its power but also that this power could be fully utilized to support aggressive designs. Thus, an adversary's level of threat is essentially a function of its power. As a result, even if observers do not, or should not, concern themselves with assessments of others' intentions per se, they do inevitably draw inferences about intentions from capabilities: a state with a powerful military arsenal will necessarily be perceived as having aggressive intentions. The scope of its expansionist designs, its particular military intentions, and the time frame in which it is expected to execute its plans are, according to this theory, subject only to the constraints of material capabilities.[59]

In contrast to offensive realists, defensive and other rationalist realist approaches contend that states can effectively signal intentions.[60] According to these interpretations, states can reduce (or increase) the severity of the security dilemma by revealing information about their intentions through various types of costly signals. Launching a military buildup that provides a military advantage larger than would be required to maintain the status quo, for instance, could signal hostile intentions, because a revisionist state is more likely than a status quo one to require such military advantages; exhibiting military restraint that limits a state's military advantage relative to its adversary should be taken as a costly signal of that state's benign intentions.[61]

In addition to purely numerical changes in military forces, scholars have also highlighted the distinctions between offensive or defensive forces as a potentially important way for states to signal their intentions, giving rise to what has become known as the offense-defense theory.[62] One of the causal claims of the offense-defense theory holds that when offensive and defensive weapons are distinguishable, states can both more easily signal their own peaceful intentions and more quickly recognize others' aggressive intentions. If the strategic uses of weapons are clear, and defense is more cost-effective than offense, states will convey hostile intentions if they deploy mainly offensive rather than defensive weapons. When offense has an advantage, the deployment of defensive forces is an especially costly reassuring signal of benign intentions; a state would have to make a comparatively larger investment in defensive military forces to offset the advantages that offensive forces confer on its prospective adversaries. In cases where either the defensive or offensive advantage is extreme, or when offensive and defensive weapons are indistinguishable, the usefulness of weapons deployments as a signal of intentions is greatly reduced.[63]

While the logic of the theory is clear, the operationalization and measurement of its key concepts are difficult.[64] Typically, though, offensive weapons have been associated with systems designed to seize territory or destroy assets. Technologies that enhance the mobility of military forces are claimed to contribute more to offense than defense. Weapons that enable the blocking of attacking forces, often by exploiting innovations that enhance firepower, tend to be seen as defensive. In the nuclear realm, most offense-defense theorists have argued that the nuclear revolution has created a world of deterrence dominance in which offense and defense are distinguishable.[65] Under conditions of mutual assured destruction, deployment of counterforce weapons, including weaponry designed to diminish the deterrent effectiveness of retaliation, will be viewed as a grab for military advantage and thus seen as a signal of potentially offensive intentions.[66] Countervalue capabilities, on the other hand, while offering no defensive advantage and threatening horrific destruction, are viewed as simply increasing the redundancy of one's retaliatory capabilities rather than signaling malign intent.[67]

DERIVING HYPOTHESES FROM THE CAPABILITIES THESIS

The preceding analysis allows us to generate two hypotheses about the relationship between an adversary's military capabilities and the other state's perceptions of its intentions. The first hypothesis, which I term *numerical preponderance*, posits that an observer will infer an adversary's intentions from a combination of perceived trends in the quantity of its military capabilities—greater or lesser—and a comparison of its capabilities relative to those of the observer. This combination of absolute and relative measures of capabilities produces four possible perceptions of an adversary's intentions. Given the premise that intentions follow from capabilities, a balance of capabilities that favors the adversary should be associated with more hostile intentions. Under these conditions of military superiority favoring the adversary, a build up of the adversary's forces contributes to more alarming inferences about its intentions. A reduction in the adversary's capabilities will be perceived as a sign of restraint, and thus as a reassuring signal that encourages inferences of less hostile intentions. Where the adversary is perceived as weaker, the logic is similar. A less powerful adversary will be viewed as less likely to take aggressive actions; such an inference will be updated if significant increases in the adversary's material capabilities appear to be larger than what is required for defending the status quo. In any of these cases, the more substantial the reduction of or increase in the adversary's military capabilities, the more substantial the change in the assessments of intentions.

Based on the logic of defensive realism, and especially offense-defense theory, the *offense-defense hypothesis* posits that when offensive and defensive forces are distinguishable, observers will infer intentions from the character of the weapon technology that the adversary is developing or deploying. Under conditions of defense or deterrence dominance, the decision to devote resources to offensive or counterforce weapons signals hostile intentions. Under conditions of offense dominance, the decision to devote resources to defensive weapons signals benign intentions.[68]

Since this study is concerned with how intentions are *perceived*, the relevant assessments of trends in military capabilities, their relative size, and their type are analyzed from the perspective of the observers who are monitoring their adversary. Thus, in each of the case studies I examine official estimates, both classified and declassified, that detail contemporary assessments of the military balance, and the perceived balance between offense and defense by various domestic actors.[69]

The Strategic Military Doctrine Thesis

The strategic military doctrine thesis posits that observers infer intentions from the adversary's military doctrine. Some defensive realists and offense-defense scholars have pointed out that because it provides a set of ideas about how to employ the instruments of military power, a state's military doctrine is likely to be seen as a valuable indicator of intentions. As Barry Posen writes, "Military doctrines and capabilities are hard to hide, but the political intentions that lie behind the military preparations are obscure. This being the case, in watching one another, states tend to focus on military doctrines and military capabilities" as opposed to political intentions. Posen notes, for example, that Arab states have inferred "malign intent from the offensive military doctrine of the Israel Defense Forces."[70] Few scholars, however, have investigated empirically whether and under what conditions a state's military doctrine is used in inferring the political or military objectives of an adversary. Therefore, I next develop the strategic military doctrine thesis and its key variables.

The strategic military doctrine thesis explains how offensive, defensive, and deterrent doctrines reveal information about an adversary's long-term political and military intentions.[71] Offensive doctrines aim to disarm an adversary by destroying its military capabilities. They often call for early and massive or even preemptive attacks.[72] Defensive doctrines, in contrast, aim to deny an adversary the objectives it seeks.[73] Deterrence doctrines aim to punish an aggressor, so as to raise the adversary's costs without regard for reducing one's own.[74] The distinction between deterrent and offensive nuclear doctrines has usually focused on what the doctrine targeted. Declaratory public statements issued by states, patterns in their deployment of forces, and the ways they plan for the contingency of war can help distinguish between deterrent and offensive nuclear doctrines.

According to the offense-defense theory, the nuclear revolution created a world of deterrence dominance where offensive capabilities are easily recognized. Under the logic of offense-defense theory, nuclear deterrence doctrines, with their emphasis on countervalue retaliatory capabilities, should increase a state's sense of security without threatening the security of its adversary. In contrast, the offense-defense theory considers a war-fighting doctrine, with its stress on counterforce capabilities and damage limitation, to be offensive, possibly revealing hostile intentions.[75] Because the nuclear revolution created the opportunity to forgo offense and embrace a relatively unthreatening deterrence doctrine, the reasoning goes, developing a war-fighting nuclear doctrine appears especially provocative. Counterforce targeting along with strategies aimed at controlling escalation and protecting the homeland would appear as "clearly 'optional' 'offensive capabilities'—that go beyond those required for deterrence—and are therefore more likely to communicate malign intentions than if they were necessary for deterrence."[76]

DERIVING THE STRATEGIC MILITARY DOCTRINE HYPOTHESIS

According to the logic of the offense-defense theory, offensive conventional or nuclear doctrines are expected to increase the probability that others will perceive that country as having aggressive intentions. Conversely, adopting deterrent nuclear doctrines, or deterrent or defensive conventional ones, are expected to be seen as indicators of benign intentions.

The Behavior Thesis

While the previous two theses are concerned with an adversary's behavioral choices—actions relating to the development and deployment of military force—the behavior thesis posits that certain kinds of nonmaterial-capabilities-based actions are useful in revealing information about intentions. This study considers the relationship between some behavioral indicators—entering and exiting from binding international institutions, creating and dismantling democratic domestic institutions, signing and reneging on arms control agreements, and engaging in military conquests, interventions, and withdrawals—and assessments of intentions.[77] Common to all is the idea that these actions reveal something about the adversary's intentions, because undertaking them requires the adversary either to sink costs or commit itself credibly by tying its own hands.[78] Following a consideration of these indicators, I offer two hypotheses pertaining to the temporal proximity of the behavioral action in relation to assessments of intentions, which I term the *current actions* and the *past actions hypotheses*.

DOMESTIC AND INTERNATIONAL INSTITUTIONS

The decision to join binding international institutions can be an important way for states to reduce the severity of the security dilemma and associated difficulty of determining other states' intentions.[79] Some international institutions are believed to be particularly effective at imposing costs on participants, and as such can allow states to distinguish other states with benign intentions from those that are aggressive.[80] Constraints imposed by such binding institutions, it is argued, typically decrease or limit states' military power, and states with benign intentions are more likely to accept such constraints. Thus, by joining such international institutions a state signals that it probably does not intend to pursue aggression in the near future. An institution's usefulness as a source of signals about intentions depends on institutional characteristics, such as "the nature of enforcement (centralized, decentralized, or none), the effects of external or internal veto points on state decision making, and its ability to affect member states' domestic political institutions."[81] Moreover, the decision to withdraw from a binding institution may be interpreted as an alarming signal that indicates the state's intentions are becoming more malign.

According to democratic peace theorists, a potential adversary's domestic institutions can also influence another state's perceptions about its intentions. This work asserts that decision makers in liberal democracies "understand the intentions of foreign liberal democracies, and that those intentions are always pacific toward fellow liberal democracies."[82] The general implication is that democracies draw inferences about other states' intentions based on the nature of their domestic institutions.[83] Two explanations link democratic political institutions and others' assessments of intentions. The first highlights the role of institutional checks and balances in constraining the ability of leaders to initiate aggressive wars. A second explanation points to the transparency of democratic institutions, which allows foreign observers to draw accurate inferences about a democratic state's intentions more easily.[84] Hence, the democratic peace theory suggests that a state should view a shift in its adversary's domestic political institutions from authoritarian to democratic as a credible signal that its intentions are becoming more benign.[85]

FOREIGN MILITARY INTERVENTIONS AND TERRITORIAL CONQUESTS

Foreign military interventions in, or territorial conquests of, weaker states are another crucial behavioral signal. A state's decision to spill blood and treasure in order to change the status quo in a weaker state or exert control over it is a costly, and hence credible, signal of other aggressive intentions. According to Kydd, states with hostile intentions usually "want to dominate, if not conquer and annex their surroundings. They may wish to fill power vacuums and establish protectorates and client states as far as their power will reach."[86] A state that militarily intervenes in or conquers a country outside its sphere of influence is likely to be judged by others as having hostile intentions. Conversely, the signaling scholarship tells us that a state's decision to refrain from intervening militarily or unilaterally withdraw from an ongoing intervention can be useful reassuring signals of more benign intentions.[87]

ARMS CONTROL AGREEMENTS

Scholars have long debated the usefulness of arms control agreements in signaling intentions and fostering cooperation between adversaries. Glaser argues that when offense and defense are distinguishable, arms control agreements—especially those that limit offensive deployment and contain adequate verification agreements—provide a reassuring signal of benign intentions. An aggressive state that planned on expanding its power and influence would be reluctant to sacrifice military advantages as well as subject its military facilities to significant and intrusive monitoring.[88]

In the case of arms control agreements, the capabilities and behavior theses can intersect, as both types of signals ultimately deal with the relationship between a state's military policy and others' assessments of its intentions. Yet it may be possible to differentiate the signing of arms control agreements as a behavioral signal of intentions from indicators associated with the capabilities thesis. First, if the capabilities thesis is correct, a change in perceived intentions should occur only when the implementation for the agreement results in an actual decrease in the adversary's capabilities. If the behavior thesis is correct, perceived intentions should shift earlier, even as soon as the arms control agreement is signed. Second, if the capabilities thesis is correct, we should see that policy makers refer to the actual change in capabilities as the impetus for a change in their perceptions of the adversary's intentions. If the behavior thesis is correct, though, we would expect to see references by policy makers to the action of signing the agreement as a critical factor. Still, this does not exclude the possibility that observers may interpret signing an arms control agreement as evidence of both a change in military capabilities and a behavioral signal of intentions.

CURRENT AND PAST ACTIONS

Scholars have emphasized the importance of past actions in the formation of reputations. Led by Schelling, Cold War theorists contended, for example, that a failure to stand firm in response to limited Communist probes against peripheral interests would invite increasingly aggressive moves against increasingly central concerns.[89] A number of influential analyses of historical crises nonetheless found relatively little evidence that leaders paid much attention to adversaries' past actions.[90] These studies were mainly concerned with assessing the impact of past actions on current assessments of resolve. In this study, however, I test whether, and to what extent, leaders rely on the adversary's past costly actions to infer long-term political and military intentions. If leaders use historical analogies and depend on "lessons of the past" to form current judgments about intentions, then we should observe leaders referring to the adversary's past actions—even under a different leadership whose intentions might have been different from those of the current leadership—in their statements and writings about the current intentions of the adversary.[91]

DERIVING HYPOTHESES FROM THE BEHAVIOR THESIS

If certain kinds of noncapabilities-based actions may be perceived as credible indicators of intentions, either because of the sunk cost mechanism or hand-tying effects they have, and if the timing of these actions matters, this suggests two hypotheses. The current actions hypothesis posits that observers focus most closely on particular costly actions taken by an adversary if it is still under the same leadership. Observers should not regard actions that are "cheap" as informative, and thus cheap actions are not seen as credible signals of intentions. To capture the logic of costly signals, I operationalize the past actions hypothesis narrowly and suggest that we should expect observers to infer the current intentions of the adversary from its past costly behavioral signals under an adversary's previous leadership.[92] Put differently, the only important distinction between the two hypotheses is whether the costly actions were taken during the adversary's current or previous leadership. This distinction, I believe, allows us to probe whether perceived intentions are leader specific.

OBSERVABLE IMPLICATIONS FROM THE THESES

Several observable implications follow from the insights of the theses. The three alternative theses, for starters, all draw on essentially rationalist statist theories of international relations in the sense that they prescribe and can even explain the behavior of states that act rationally. As such, they are not designed to tell us much about how often states actually act according to these rational imperatives.[93] Second, the three theses assume states to be unitary actors. They accordingly do not attempt to theorize about differences among observers regarding the types of indicators they heed in assessing intention. Overall, however, we should expect to see shifts in perceived intentions covary with shifts in the adversary's capabilities, strategic military doctrine, and behavior. Over time we should also observe convergence among observers in terms of how they assess the adversary's intentions as a result of costly changes in the variables that each thesis identifies as critical. For example, in Kydd's theory, "*convergence on correct beliefs is more likely than convergence on incorrect beliefs*. That is, although the learning process is noisy and prone to errors of all kinds, beliefs over time and on average are more likely to converge towards reality than to diverge from it. As can be noted, the selective attention thesis does not expect observers to converge on their assessments about intentions, and divergent interpretations among decision makers as well as between decision makers and intelligence communities may coexist and persist over time. Third, in the reasoning invoked to support assessments of intentions expressed in private statements and reports, observers are expected to refer to the same set of factors emphasized in each of the three theses. We should, finally, also be able to observe correlations between an individual decision maker's statements about their perceptions of the adversary's intentions and the policies that they advocate toward the adversary.[94]

The selective attention thesis has several observable implications that are different from those suggested by the previous three theses. First, from the perspective of information processing, civilian decision makers and intelligence communities are different kinds of perceivers; the particular kinds of evidence about the adversary's intentions they heed will therefore reflect differences in individual-level biases and organizational processes. Accordingly, each set of actors will support its reasoning by referring to different indicators of intentions. The complexity of integrating multiple indicators into a unitary assessment of the adversary's intentions also encourages a motivational bias toward relying predominantly on a single indicator.[95] This is because "a single dominant indicator as a decisive input into judgment . . . simplifies the whole process of searching for and evaluating information," as Yaacov Vertzberger notes, and thus the risk that "multiple indicators will produce inconsistency and a need for choice between alternative incongruent action orientations, with a resultant value trade-off, is preempted and avoided."[96] This implies that rather than relying on various indicators of intentions simultaneously, an observer is likely to focus attention on just one set.[97]

The observable implications of the selective attention thesis overlap to a certain extent with those suggested by the capabilities thesis. Indeed, both place high value on the adversary's capabilities as a gauge of political intentions. But the logic that drives the reliance on capabilities is different: from the perspective of the realist logic underlying the capabilities thesis, it is the anarchic nature of the international system that forces states to focus on the adversary's military capabilities. From the vantage point of the costly signaling argument, it is the informative value of the signal that catches the attention of observers. This differs from the organizational logic that guides and shapes these organizations' convictions about what kind of knowledge they can and must produce with confidence, precision, and regularity. Some differences also exist in the observable implications that follow from the capabilities thesis and organizational expertise hypothesis. Most significantly, while the capabilities thesis predicts that both decision makers and the intelligence community will follow the logic that "intentions are reflected in capabilities," the organizational expertise hypothesis is only applicable to the inference process of intelligence communities, not individual decision makers.

In addition, there are some similarities between the predictions of the behavioral signals thesis and the selective attention thesis in the case of civilian decision makers. Once again, however, the mechanisms as well as the observable implications in some instances appear to be different. In the case of the behavior thesis, *all* perceivers are expected to recognize the costs that are associated with an adversary's undertaking certain noncapabilities-based actions and change their beliefs about the adversary's actions accordingly. In contrast, if the selective attention thesis is true, we would expect to see decision makers differ in the indicators to which they attend in their assessments of intentions, based on the vividness of the information presented to them and their subjective reading of the credibility of various signals.

Table 1 summarizes the differences in the observable implications of the three alternative theses—the capabilities, strategic military doctrine, and behavior theses—along with those offered by the selective attention thesis.

The Cases

To evaluate the explanatory power of the theses discussed above, I employ the comparative historical case study method. The universe of potential cases for this study includes all pairs of state adversaries. Within this population, I selected the British assessment of Germany's intentions prior to World War II (1934–39), US assessments of Soviet intentions during the years leading to the collapse of détente (1976–80), and US assessments of Soviet intentions during the final years of the Cold War (1985–88). These three cases provide multiple observations on several dimensions, since each one comprises several temporal periods. I analyze the observations of two groups in each period—the decision makers and intelligence organization—and offer a detailed evaluation of the

Table 1 Summary of Predictions

	Capabilities Thesis	Military Doctrine Thesis	Behavioral Signals Thesis	Selective Attention Thesis
Do observers vary in how they assess the adversary's intentions?	Not necessarily	Not necessarily	Not necessarily	Yes, decision makers and the intelligence community will vary in the indicators they rely on
What are the key variables guiding observers' assessments of intentions?	Costly changes in quantity and type of the adversary's military capabilities	Perceived orientation of the adversary's military doctrine	Costly current or past noncapabilities-based actions by the adversary	For decision makers: vivid or salient information that addresses what they subjectively judge as credible — For intelligence community: information in which they have the most expertise, which in most cases will pertain to the adversary's military capabilities
When do assessments about intentions change?	In response to costly changes in the perceived quantity and type of the adversary's military capabilities	In response to changes in the perceived orientation of the adversary's military doctrine	With the undertaking of particular costly actions	For decision makers: in response to vivid or salient information and a subjective reading of credible (even if costless) indicators — For intelligence community: slow response to changes in the perceived military capabilities of the adversary

What does the state's assessment of intentions reflect?	Convergence among observers over time in response to changes in the adversary's military capabilities	Convergence among observers over time in response to changes in the adversary's military doctrine	Convergence among observers over time in response to changes in the adversary's costly actions	No single view of adversary's intentions; possible to have divergence of assessments among decision makers as well as between decision makers and intelligence community
How do observers reason their assessments of intentions?	By referring to the quantity or type of the adversary's military capabilities	By referring to the orientation of the adversary's military doctrine	By referring to the current or past behavior of the adversary that was costly	For decision makers: by referring to information that they perceive as vivid or credible; they will discuss personal impressions from meetings with leaders, including the adversary's compliance with litmus tests / For intelligence community: by referring to information on which they have the most expertise, which in most cases is likely to be about the adversary's military capabilities
What policies will be advocated?	Consistent with changes in the adversary's military capabilities	Consistent with changes in the adversary's military doctrine	Consistent with changes in the adversary's costly actions	Consistent with information that is vivid and subjectively credible / For intelligence community: policies will not be advocated

inference processes of a number of different individual decision makers. Each case thus supplies a number of data points.

The cases were selected according to several criteria. First, the cases represent differing values of the dependent variable—the perception of the adversary's intentions—and whether the adversary was becoming more or less hostile. Both the British-German interaction in the 1930s and US-Soviet relations in the late 1970s tell a story of an evolution toward a more malign interpretation of the adversary's intentions, while US-Soviet interaction in the late 1980s tracks the process by which Soviet intentions were perceived as becoming more benign. My analysis of all three episodes focuses on how the intentions of a country's principal adversary were inferred. The stakes involved in voicing opinions about the adversary's intentions in such cases are likely to be high, and as such, statements about the adversary's intentions are more likely to reflect the true beliefs of the observer. Second, to test the propositions offered by the selective attention thesis, I examine how the primary decision makers—President Carter, President Reagan, and Prime Minister Chamberlain along with their senior advisers—varied in their initial assessments of the enemy, after personal meetings with the adversary's leadership.

Third, the values of the key independent variables derived from the competing theses on capabilities, doctrine, and behavior also vary within and between the cases. Both the initial level of the adversary's capabilities relative to those of the observer and magnitude of change in the adversary's capabilities during the period of interaction vary across the cases. Given this, both Cold War cases assume relative equality in military capabilities between the superpowers, with a moderate increase (in 1976–80) or decrease (1985–88) in Soviet capabilities during the interaction period. The interwar case, in contrast, starts with a German military that was far inferior to the British one, followed by a period during which an unprecedented increase in German military capabilities ultimately changed the balance of power between the two powers. The interwar case should thus be seen as an especially good one to test the capabilities thesis, as the dramatic increase in German military capabilities and shift in the balance of power should have led observers to focus on this indicator as a signal of intentions. Moreover, military doctrine also varies across the cases. Soviet military doctrine was perceived as generally offensive or counterforce oriented during the 1970s, and as becoming more defensive in nature toward the late 1980s. While British observers did not understand the specifics of the German blitzkrieg doctrine during the 1930s, they clearly perceived Germany's doctrine to be offensive in nature during the years leading up to World War II. The cases also provide variation on both the types of costly actions the adversary was undertaking as well as the direction in which such actions should have influenced perceived intentions. These include military interventions and withdrawals, entering and exiting from binding international institutions, creating and dismantling democratic domestic institutions, and signing and reneging on arms control agreements. In particular, the end of the Cold War can be seen as an easy test for the behavior thesis as Gorbachev undertook what scholars have categorized as a series of costly actions of reassurance, including a withdrawal from Afghanistan and willingness to accept the conditions of the INF Treaty. Gorbachev's costly actions should have had a significant influence over observers' perceptions. Finally, in all three cases the primary decision makers— Chamberlain, Carter, and Reagan—and their respective advisers differed to various extents in the initial enemy image each held during the period prior to the one I analyze. Further, in each case all decision makers had equal access to information about the adversary's costly behavior and military capabilities.

A final criterion for the selection of cases was the accessibility of archival material. Both the quantity and quality of archival documents used to evaluate the competing explanations are excellent for the episodes dealing with British-German interaction and the collapse of détente, and are quite good in the case of the Cold War's end.

One potential criticism of this case selection is that each of my cases examines how a Western democracy assesses the intentions of a nondemocratic adversary. While including assessments by nondemocratic countries would strengthen the research design plus might also allow us to evaluate how countries like China, Iran, or North Korea draw inferences about the intentions of the United States, there are two important advantages to looking at Western democracies. For one, the quantity and quality of available data are sufficiently rich as to provide a reasonable examination of what decision makers and intelligence analysts discussed, wrote, and thought when they inferred the intentions of their adversaries. This has allowed me to reach conclusions about these processes and test the relative importance of competing explanations with greater confidence. Second, from a theoretical standpoint, there is no a priori reason to believe that decision makers in nondemocratic countries infer intentions differently from those in democratic states. Whether the dynamics shown in this study are in fact applicable to totalitarian, Communist, or theocratic states is nevertheless an empirical question of significance, and worth investigating as information becomes available.

MEASUREMENT AND METHODOLOGY

To evaluate the competing explanations, in each case I coded both the independent and dependent variables—the perceptions of an adversary's political and military intentions—based on the measurement criteria outlined below. I then used two different methods of causal analysis: within-case congruence procedures, which looked at the fit between the theses' predictions along with the continuity or changes in perceived intentions, and the fit between a decision maker's statements about intentions and the policies each advocated; and process tracing to examine the reasoning invoked to support assessments of intentions, and changes in such assessments. Below, I look at the method used to code the relevant variables as well as the causal relationship between different explanatory variables and perceived intentions.

I used standardized questions as a template to code the dependent and independent variables plus evaluate the causal relationship between them in the empirical chapters. The first set of questions helps identify the key players and centrality of an adversary's intentions during the period in question. Questions of interest include: Which decision makers were closest to the primary decision maker (the president or prime minister) or had the most influence on issues pertaining to foreign policy? How much did the documents available discuss the intentions of the adversary?[99] General questions pertaining to the intelligence community include: What sort of coordinated assessments did the intelligence community produce at the time? To what extent did the intelligence community deal with (or was tasked with exploring) the intentions of that particular adversary?

The next set of questions was intended to capture the nature and evolution of the discourse on perceived intentions. As a first step, I measured the perceptions of the adversary for each of the key decision makers prior to and at the beginning of each period that I analyzed.[100] I am not concerned with how and why decision makers' beliefs about the adversary's intentions were formed prior to assuming office, as the objective of this study is to examine how and why these beliefs change during the interaction with the adversary while these individuals are in office. For the intelligence community, the baseline for perceived intentions was coded on the basis of the most recent intelligence assessments issued prior to the period that I analyzed. For each of these perceivers, I determined whether the political intentions of the adversary were perceived as status quo, opportunistic, or expansionist, and whether their aims were viewed as limited or unlimited. I also asked whether observers believed that the adversary would use military force to achieve its political objectives. Finally, I looked to see whether there was a consensus among decision makers or among intelligence agencies about the adversary's intentions over time.

After I derived predictions for each of the four theses, I determined the congruence between the independent and dependent variable. To that end, I first tracked the degree to which change in the perceived adversary's military capabilities and its military doctrine as well as its costly actions covaried with changes in perceived intentions. I did the same for the variables that constituted the selective attention thesis. How many interactions, for example, did a specific decision maker have with the leadership of the adversary? What impressions did the decision maker express? Did the latter's intentions change following these meetings? Second, I examined the fit between the predictions of each of the theses and the conclusions reached about intentions over time: Was the time and direction of change in perceived intentions congruent with the predictions of the selective attention thesis or those of any of the three alternative theses? Was there a fit between a decision maker's baseline beliefs about intentions and their understanding of different actions by the adversary over time? The same questions were then applied to the texts of collective assessments issued by the intelligence community. Were there changes in the NIEs about intentions following a change in any of the indicators analyzed here? The congruence test alone cannot confirm or disconfirm the competing theses, nor can it help settle which of the hypothesized causal mechanisms is most consequential. But the congruence procedure is nonetheless important as an initial step to check whether the observed outcomes are consistent with the predictions of each thesis. It also helps establish a framework for process tracing.

In the fourth set of questions, I identified the causal process by evaluating the reasoning and evidence that observers invoke to support their assessments of an adversary's intentions. For instance, if assessments of the adversary's military capabilities were used to infer its intentions, I expected to find some evidence that decision makers and intelligence agencies referred to the adversary's military forces, the balance of power, or trends in the adversary's weapons development when gauging its intentions. General discussions about the adversary's capabilities, doctrine, and actions, or personal interactions with its leadership, were treated as irrelevant if they were not associated with assessments of the adversary's intentions. This evidence about reasoning also allowed for tracking, to some extent, of whether and why an observer focused on particular evidence, but did not change their views about the adversary's intentions as a result. Equivalent questions were used to probe the reasoning provided in the collective assessments of the intelligence community. Variations in the reasoning used by the decision makers and intelligence community served as potentially important evidence for the selective attention thesis.

In tracing processes, I evaluated policies that decision makers advocated toward the adversary. Since intelligence estimates are neither intended nor designed to support or reject particular policies, this test is applied only to the documents capturing the views of civilian decision makers. First, I look at policies advocated by the leading decision makers. While the menu of policy options is determined by a variety of factors, we should generally see decision makers adopting more competitive or confrontational policies toward an adversary when they believe its intentions are becoming more hostile.[101] Conversely, when a decision maker perceives an adversary's intentions as relatively more benign, this should lead them to advocate hedging policies that emphasize cooperation with and reassurance of the adversary.[102] A mismatch between a decision maker's statements about the adversary's intentions and the nature of the policies they advocate or reject raises doubts about those statements. At the same time, policies may be advocated for a variety of reasons unrelated to assessments of intentions (including, for instance, considerations of domestic politics). By taking a close look at the timing of these policies and the reasoning that decision makers express to justify them, though, we might be able to gauge the role a decision maker's perceptions of intentions played in shaping their policy choices.

I then provide a brief examination of the congruence between changes in beliefs about intentions and the policies that were adopted at the collective level, as opposed to those advocated by individual decision makers. By looking at the evolution in an administration's overall policies, we might be able to assess the importance of perceived intentions in shaping the state's policies. If we found that intentions do not affect policies, then studying the sources of perceived intentions would have little relevance for how states really behave. But if a change in decision makers' perceptions of intentions corresponds to a change in policies, and if the timing of and reasoning expressed for the shift in policies point to the significance of perceived intentions, we can reject the null hypothesis that perceived intentions do not affect policies.[103]

The methods of inquiry outlined above introduce two methodological issues that are worth noting.[104] First, it is difficult to determine the sincerity of decision makers' statements about the reasoning behind their assessments concerning the adversary's intentions. For several reasons, however, it seems doubtful that decision makers have deliberately misrepresented the indicators they relied on. The observers in the empirical cases were consistent in the thought process they cited to support their assessments of the adversary's intentions. That is, they did not shift between categories of indicators but rather attended to a particular set of indicators through the period I analyze. More important, they rarely mentioned other indicators even when those could have been rhetorically useful. This research nonetheless supplements these private assessments with other types of evidence (such as interviews and references to other policies decision makers advocated) to evaluate the reliability of decision makers' statements about how and why they perceived their adversaries' intentions. Still, it is possible that decision makers themselves have failed to understand how they reached conclusions about the adversary's intentions because cognitive processing of this kind is beyond the reach of conscious thought.[105] If so, observers may have listed the reasons they sincerely believed drove their assessments even if their assessments were actually shaped by other indicators. Although this phenomenon might be plausible, I find little evidence to support it in my empirical analysis.[106]

A second concern stems from the asymmetry in power between civilian decision makers and the intelligence community. As Lowenthal puts it, "Policymakers can exist and function without the intelligence community, but the opposite is not true."[107] This basic asymmetry might allow policy makers to manipulate or politicize intelligence for their own political needs.[108] In the context of this study, this presents a methodological challenge—namely, civilian decision makers' assessments of the adversary's intentions and their overall policy preferences may significantly affect the intelligence community's estimates of that adversary's objectives. If this were the case, an examination of the intelligence community's coordinated assessments would not necessarily capture the community's inference process but instead would reflect the administration's beliefs and policy agendas.[109]

To deal with this problem in the empirical studies, I use a variety of methods and sources. I probe whether fluctuations in intelligence estimates can be explained by either the explanatory variables (that is, the adversary's capabilities, military doctrine, or costly behavior), or availability of new information. A temporal correlation between such exogenous variables and intelligence estimates would somewhat counter implications of politicization. The absence of such alternative explanations for significant changes in intelligence estimates —or the failure to update intelligence estimates despite changes in these exogenous variables—might indicate that intelligence was politically biased.[110] These measures are not perfect and certainly cannot disprove the influence of politicization. But as we will see—at least in the two Cold War episodes I examine—intelligence estimates about Soviet intentions were not correlated with the perceptions of key decision makers. This implies that even if there were attempts to influence intelligence, these were unsuccessful. The analysis of the interwar period is more challenging, since the conclusions of British intelligence appear to have been somewhat correlated with Chamberlain's policy of appeasement. My review of a wealth of primary documents, though, allows me to trace the evolution in British intelligence to changes in strategic calculations and especially assessments (however flawed they retrospectively turned out to be) about the evolving balance of power during this period.

***

Appendix I summarizes the predictions of the theses. The next three chapters use the hypotheses described in this chapter to explore the efforts by Britain's leaders and its intelligence community to predict the intentions of Hitler's Germany in the years leading to World War II.

CHAPTER 2

Indicators of Nazi Germany's Intentions and the Coming of World War II, 1934–39

In hindsight, Nazi Germany's ambitious intentions were always obvious: Hitler's stated objectives in *Mein Kampf* correlated with the horrific actions later committed by Nazi Germany during the Second World War. British decision makers were clearly wrong to hold benign views of Nazi Germany, and were especially wrong in thinking that some concessions could satisfy Nazi Germany's geopolitical appetite. Nevertheless, viewing their error as resulting from mere naïveté is anachronistic and misleading. An active debate took place during the 1930s among British decision makers and government agencies as they struggled to assess the nature and scope of Nazi Germany's foreign policy aims for continental Europe and beyond.

These three chapters revisit the discussions over the German threat during the period prior to the outbreak of World War II. Unlike many other studies of this period, the efficacy of British policies toward Germany at the time is not assessed, nor is the extent to which British policy makers were correct in drawing the inferences that they did about the German threat then.[1] Rather, the next three chapters examine only the question of what indicators of German intention Britain's decision makers and its intelligence community used as well as ignored when they sought to infer the long-term intentions of Nazi Germany. This chapter tracks changes in British perceptions of Nazi Germany's capabilities, military doctrine, and behavior from 1934 to 1939. It then derives case-specific predictions for the selective attention, capabilities, strategic military doctrine, and behavior theses, and delineates how the expectations of the selective attention thesis and its hypotheses diverge from those offered by the three competing theses. Chapter 3 tests these predictions against the inference processes of several key British decision makers, especially Prime Minister Chamberlain, Foreign Secretary Eden, and Eden's successor as foreign secretary, Lord Halifax, and chapter 4 does the same for the British intelligence community.

In the next section of this chapter, I outline the hypotheses of the selective attention thesis and point out its predictions for this case. I then derive predictions for each of the competing theses.

THE SELECTIVE ATTENTION THESIS

The selective attention thesis expects British decision makers to be influenced by their own theories about the adversary and by vivid information when assessing German intentions. This thesis expects British intelligence to use a different inference process when estimating intentions than did British decision makers.

The Vividness Hypothesis

The vividness hypothesis predicts that positive impressions from personal interactions with counterparts will lead a decision maker to view the adversary's intentions in a less threatening way. For example, Germany's positive response to British decision makers' litmus tests would engender a more benign interpretation of Germany's intentions. During the interwar period, the three principal decision makers I analyze—Chamberlain, Eden, and Halifax—met personally with the German leadership, including Hitler himself. They each derived impressions about Germany as a whole from their interactions with the leaders of the German Nazi Party. Chapter 3 describes these interactions in greater detail.

Chamberlain met with Hitler in three private meetings during September 1938 in the midst of the second crisis over the Sudetenland. The evidence indicates that although Chamberlain emerged with mixed impressions about Hitler's personality, he felt that "it was impossible not to feel impressed with the power of the man," and was well pleased with the first meeting. Despite difficult exchanges between the two leaders during the second and third meetings at Bad Godesberg, the British prime minister reported that "a relationship of confidence had grown between himself and the Fuhrer." Chamberlain formed the impression that he could trust Hitler.[2]

Eden had two series of official meetings with Hitler before he took office as foreign secretary. At their first meeting in February 1934, Eden probed Hitler's willingness to accept a British proposal to bring Germany back into the Disarmament Conference, whose objective had been to reduce the level and pace of armament as well as states' possession of offensive weapons. The records indicate that in this meeting, Hitler made a strong and favorable impression on Eden, who found Hitler a "surprise." In conversation, the führer was "quiet, almost shy with a pleasant smile. Without doubt the man has charm." Eden believed he had established an immediate rapport with Hitler on the basis of their wartime experiences.[3] Eden's second series of meetings with Hitler took place on March 25 and 26 in the same year. This time, Eden joined Foreign Secretary John Simon to probe Hitler's positions on armament limitation, Austrian independence, and an air pact with Britain. Eden recorded his impressions, noting that "Hitler was definitely more authoritative and less anxious to please than a year before. At this second interview, I was almost unfavorably impressed by Hitler's personality."[4]

In November 1937, Halifax traveled to Germany to meet with the Nazi leadership to gauge Hitler's future plans in Europe and examine the degree to which a comprehensive agreement could be reached with Germany. On that trip, Halifax met with Joseph Goebbels, Hermann Göring, and the führer. On his return, Halifax shared his insights with members of the cabinet. Halifax could "not help but like" Goebbels, and found himself entertained by Göring. He also found Hitler to be charismatic and "very sincere."[5]

In addition to personal interactions, the vividness hypothesis examines the links between litmus tests and the adversary's behavior. It posits that decision makers will attend more to actions that they themselves had called for when setting tests. Chamberlain, Eden, and Halifax all sought to test Germany's intentions during this period. All assigned importance to the results of one litmus test in particular: a questionnaire carefully formulated by the British Cabinet in April 1936. They hoped for clear responses from Hitler on four specific questions: whether Germany was ready for "genuine treaties"; whether Hitler drew a distinction between the Third Reich and the German people—that is, Germans living outside the Third Reich's territorial boundaries; whether Germany now intended to respect the existing territorial and political status of European states except insofar as they might subsequently be modified by free negotiation or agreement; and whether Hitler was prepared for nonaggression pacts with Soviet Russia, Latvia, and Estonia. From the perspective of the British Cabinet, particularly Eden, negative responses to these questions would indicate that Hitler's policy was aggressive. Positive responses would suggest his willingness to reach a bargain with Britain.

In sum, the vividness hypothesis posits that decision makers regard personal interactions with their counterparts and responses to litmus tests as credible indicators. These components provide especially vivid and salient information on which officials are often likely to rely to infer an adversary's intentions. If the vividness hypothesis is accurate, then Chamberlain, Eden, and Halifax should have linked their assessments of Germany's intentions explicitly to their impressions of the Nazi leadership during these personal interactions as well as the German leadership's compliance with or rejection of the actions proposed in Britain's litmus tests.

The Subjective Credibility Hypothesis

The subjective credibility hypothesis emphasizes the role of an individual's personal needs and his or her expectations about the adversary in the interpretation of that adversary's behavior. This hypothesis postulates that those decision makers who held more negative images of Germany by or before 1934 should have been more likely to categorize Germany's subsequent costly hostile actions as credible signals of its expansionist intentions. Conversely, decision makers with more favorable views of Germany should have been more likely to discount the significance of these actions and express doubts that the intentions behind them were hostile. Furthermore, the subjective credibility hypothesis would not expect British decision makers necessarily to focus on costly indicators of intentions but rather to rely on various pieces of information that they subjectively judged to be credible.

Evaluating personal attitudes toward Germany in early 1934 is a challenging task in part because beliefs about Nazi Germany were only beginning to form. A combination of primary documents, secondary literature on the background of some of these individuals, and their own memoirs and biographies help to establish a crude measure of baseline beliefs. The permanent undersecretary at the Foreign Office, Robert Vansittart, was well known for his extremely negative image of Germany. He was accused of being a Germanophobe. Even before Hitler's rise, he wrote that German history was a "continuum," and saw the "Wilhelmine, Weimar, and Nazi eras as extensions of Prussian history and, more specifically, the continuation of Prussian military values and traditions."[6] On the other end of the spectrum, the British ambassador to Germany, Nevile Henderson, held considerably more benign views of Germany. Henderson's writing suggests he believed there was no reason why Germany should perpetually constitute a threat to Britain. Indeed, Henderson was critical of French attempts to contain Germany after World War I. He also accepted the territorial claims that the Nazis made in the 1930s, in part because he believed Britain should take the role of independent arbitrator in European affairs. His public speeches similarly had a pro-Nazi overtone; he was quoted as saying that Britain should put less stress on the Nazi dictatorship and suggested that England could learn some useful lessons from Germany.[7]

In view of these patterns, the subjective credibility hypothesis would predict that Vansittart would categorize German actions as credible signals of malign intentions and discount reassurance actions as cheap talk. He should have updated his beliefs to recognize the expansionist nature of Germany's intentions much earlier than other decision makers. Henderson, by contrast, would be predicted to remain quite skeptical about the informative value of many of Germany's hostile actions, and would have updated his beliefs about Germany's intentions only at a later time. Eden and Halifax as well as Chamberlain fall between these two extremes. They shared similar views of Germany's intentions by 1934, and would be expected to have changed their stances about the expansionist nature of Germany's intentions in response to their own subjective judgments of what constituted credible signals of intentions.

The Organizational Expertise Hypothesis

The British intelligence community during the 1930s considered its primary mission to be monitoring the progress of German militarization and predicting the speed and scale of German rearmament.[8] These estimates were particularly significant from 1934 onward, as the British government embarked on a policy of selective rearmament. All three service intelligence organizations placed a premium on collecting and analyzing information pertaining to trends in the German military arsenal. For example, the air intelligence branch's approach to gathering intelligence on the German Luftwaffe, according to Wesley Wark, "was reductive and carried with it all the benefits and costs of simplicity. The future German air menace was to be measured in terms of numbers of first-line aircraft." As a result, Wark explains, "a great deal of emphasis was to be placed on quantitative long-range predications."[9] Similar practices characterized the work of British army intelligence, as it, too, believed that numerical trends in German rearmament provided a good guide to the pace of future army expansion. The Chiefs of Staff (COS) and service intelligence reports on the German threat are littered with charts comparing the forces of Germany with those of the Allies, thereby indicating that British intelligence closely monitored the German arsenal. Forecasts of changes in the military balance of power in Europe were also central to the Strategic Appreciation reports by the COS.

The organizational expertise hypothesis would expect British intelligence to rely on its assessments about German military capabilities when addressing questions pertaining to Germany's political and military intentions. In contrast to the capabilities thesis that I discuss below, the organizational expertise hypothesis does not expect British decision makers, in their analysis of German intentions, to have adopted a similar inference process.[10]

THE CAPABILITIES THESIS

During the period under study (1934–39), Britain observed significant increases in Germany's military capabilities. Accordingly, Britain believed that the balance of power with Germany changed in Germany's favor around 1936. This section reviews trends in British perceptions of the German Luftwaffe, army, and navy, and the European balance of power.

The German Luftwaffe

In early 1934, Britain's Air Intelligence Directorate noted that the German air force, already in violation of the Treaty of Versailles, had more than doubled in size between February 1933 and February 1934. Until 1936, however, the Air Ministry believed that the pace of German air force rearmament was shaped by the dictates of efficiency and professionalism. That suggested that what Britain was seeing was a moderate pace of rearmament.[11] When Hitler announced in March 1935 that Germany had achieved equality in air strength with Britain, British civilian leaders and the Air Ministry concluded that he was, whether

SOUR STRAWBERRY
Sativa
THC 21.9%
CBD 0.1%
CBG 2.2%

perately or not, overestimating the Luftwaffe's air strength. The declara-
, though, prompted the Air Intelligence Directorate to update its figures on
rate of expansion of the German air force. The directorate had previously
predicted that the Luftwaffe would reach thirteen hundred aircraft by October
1936. After Hitler's March 1935 announcement, the air staff believed that the
German Air Ministry had accelerated the pace of rearmament and asserted,
therefore, that Germany would probably have fifteen hundred aircraft by April
1937. This was the same size, the British estimated, as the French air force.[12] The
air staff also suggested that efficiency considerations would not dictate further
expansion of the Luftwaffe after April 1937.

As British intelligence on the German air force improved, the Air Ministry
revised its estimates. In September 1936, the air staff concluded that Germany
sought to establish not just parity but also air superiority over France. Indeed,
"every element of the air intelligence picture as it developed from the autumn
of 1936," writes Wark, "suggested the increasing striking power and numerical lead of the Luftwaffe over other European air forces."[13] The year 1936 thus
stands as a turning point in Britain's intelligence assessments of Germany's
air strength. From 1937 to 1939, the air staff reported acceleration in German
air force expansion. In February 1937, the COS estimated that Germany "will
probably be as far ahead of Great Britain [in numbers of aircraft] in 1937 as she
will ever be." Yet that report concluded that Great Britain was still "considerably
superior in first-line strength . . . [with] an exceptional advantage where long-
range bombers, which are of particular value for exploiting the initiative in air
warfare, are concerned."[14] Five months later, however, the COS projected that
the Luftwaffe would obtain superiority over Britain in both first-line planes and
bombers by 1939.[15] During this period, the Air Intelligence Directorate made
worst-case assumptions about the future rate of German air expansion, and its
estimates grew increasingly pessimistic about the evolving balance of power.
This thinking colored British assessments of the potential threat of German
bombing, especially against Britain, in the event of war.

In early 1939, there was speculation as to whether Germany was approaching the limit of its peacetime rearmament effort, as it had nearly exceeded the
capacity of the German economy. Although lower than the British had expected
in late 1938, the estimated Luftwaffe strength was still superior to the combined
total strength of the British and French air forces.[16] In a memo dated February
15, 1939, the British air attaché concluded:

> The rapid growth of the German air force since 1935 is a very remarkable achieve-
> ment, and there is nothing to show that an end to the expansion is yet in sight. I have
> no information that shortage of labour or of raw materials have yet proved limiting
> factors, but most of the new factories are now almost in full production, and it seems
> to me that any further marked increase in output is unlikely. . . . The formation of

new units may be expected to continue steadily, but, unless there is some radical change in conditions, it seems impossible that there can be any further rapid expansion in the strength of Germany's air force.[17]

Britain appeared unlikely to be able to offset the German advantage; "it seems doubtful whether for some time it will be possible to equal the German output, much less make up lost ground."[18]

The German Army

British perceptions of the German army also changed dramatically in 1936. Before that year, the War Office (unlike the Foreign Office) did not see the German military's rate of growth as threatening. It interpreted the army's expansion as defensive. From 1936 onward, though, British estimates concluded that the German army was readying for total war.

Although British observers realized early on that Germany was increasing its military capabilities, they underestimated both the scope and nature of the German rearmament program during the first two years of the Nazi regime (1933–34).[19] The indicators were thought to point "to Germany's present preparations being entirely defensive."[20] In March 1935, however, Hitler introduced conscription and declared that the new German army would number thirty-six divisions (five hundred thousand troops).[21] Consequently, in 1936, the War Office revised its estimates about the rate of growth of the German buildup. It concluded that there would undoubtedly be further expansion and that the German Army was being readied for total war. Throughout 1936, British intelligence continually increased its projections of expected German army divisions.[22] In February 1937, the COS Committee concluded that the army of Germany "is likely to have a marked superiority" over that of France by 1939, and that the British army, even after its projected expansion, was "not likely to outweigh the importance of [Germany's] numerical advantage over France."[23]

On March 20, 1938, the COS concluded that the strength of Germany's peacetime army had been increased by the motorization of four of the thirty-six infantry divisions, the creation of additional tank battalions and motorized machine gun battalions, increases in the tank strength of the armored divisions, and the formation of one or more new independent "Light Brigades." The report also saw no evidence of slowdown in the rate of production of armaments for the army. Thus, by January 1942, "but not before, [Germany would be able] to mobilize the maximum land forces of which the national man-power and economy is capable."[24] In July 1938, the German army's strength was further increased by incorporation of Austrian units following the Anschluss.[25] The War Office stated that Germany continued to build up its military capabilities. In January 1939 and again in July, the Industrial Intelligence Center and War Office "called attention to significant increases in the fighting strength of the

Germany army."[26] By then, the British expected the German army to continue its expansion and Germany to progress toward war readiness.

The German Navy

The British Admiralty did not perceive the German navy as a threat during the 1930s. Neither the scale nor pace of German naval rearmament was, in its view, significant. Britain saw the Naval Agreement between Britain and Germany as a constraint. The danger from Germany was considered secondary to the threat from the Japanese Navy.

In 1933, the German Navy was small and unimpressive. In 1935, the British Naval Intelligence Division (NID) reported that Germany was seeking to rebuild its U-boat (submarine) fleet. The NID could not predict in detail what kind of naval force Germany intended to build, but the assumptions at the time were that Germany would not attempt to build a fleet that would challenge British power and that Hitler would be willing to sign an agreement to limit the strength of the German Navy. Indeed, in March 1935, Hitler announced that Germany would enter into a Naval Agreement with Britain and would agree to limit its fleet to 35 percent of the size of the Royal Navy. After the Naval Agreement was signed, British intelligence reported that Germany was in compliance with it.[27] In February 1937, the COS reported that France and Great Britain had many more capital ships than Germany, including six aircraft carriers, a naval platform possessed by neither Germany nor Italy. The naval balance of power was thus heavily in their favor. Reports in November 1937 outlined the numerical superiority of France and Britain in other respects, such as the number of cruisers, destroyers, and submarines.

Between 1935 and 1939, the British Admiralty believed in the restraining power of the Naval Agreement. Its faith rested on the conviction that Germany was abiding by its terms. The British Admiralty assumed that Germany's potential for a far greater navy was constrained by the agreement.[28] Given this, Germany's unilateral announcement in December 1938 that it was seeking parity in submarines came as a surprise. It was followed by an even more alarming German announcement in April 1939 renouncing the Naval Agreement. Despite growing anxiety in 1939 over Germany's rising naval strength, Britain continued until the war's outbreak to believe in its naval superiority over Germany.

The Military Balance of Power

British perceptions of the overall European military balance of power shifted in 1936 as well. From 1935 to 1939, the COS provided four Strategic Appreciations that summarized the military and economic threat from Germany. The first report, submitted to the cabinet in October 1935, concluded that despite German buildup, the Allies would have ground, air, and naval superiority until

1939.[29] The next COS report, issued in October 1936, was described by Wark as a "painful reevaluation of German military strength . . . by the service intelligence departments" that gave a "picture of a militarized, totalitarian Germany" already fully mobilized in peacetime. Specifically, Wark noted that "both the War Office and the Air Ministry had abandoned their early projections of limited German rearmament and had begun to measure German capabilities in terms of [Germany's] vast manpower and industrial potential." The report concluded that while Britain and France would continue to enjoy a naval advantage through 1939, Germany was likely to have overall "superiority over the Allies during the first 24 weeks" of a war due to the accelerated rate of expansion of the German Army.[30] During the Czechoslovakian crisis, the COS offered a somber picture of the European balance of power: "Germany will have an advantage in respect to pre-war preparedness. Our naval forces will be greatly superior to those of the Germans . . . [but] the German army will be numerically superior to the combined British and French armies. Germany seems likely to possess a marked advantage over the allies in air striking power."[31]

The final Strategic Appreciation before the outbreak of war was released in February 1939. The picture had worsened for the Allies, with Germany and Italy enjoying great superiority in ground and air forces. Nevertheless, the report also emphasized other factors such as air defense, population morale, and latent economic strength, whose combined effect gave grounds for greater British optimism about the future balance of power in Europe.[32] As Norrin Ripsman and Jack Levy observe, British confidence was also increased by quantitative and qualitative developments in British military capabilities, such as "closing the gaps in the coastal defense of the British Isles, expanding the bomber force of the Royal Air Force (RAF) to enable it to conduct offensive air operations against Germany, and improving the Royal Navy to the point where it could conduct operations in both the Mediterranean and in home waters."[33] Overall, however, the reports remained unequivocal that the total balance of power favored Germany.

Summary of Predictions

Britain's perception of German military capabilities and the overall balance of power varied over time. First, from 1933 to 1935, Britain saw Germany's military buildup as defensive in nature and moderate in pace. The military balance of power "was expected to show comfortable margins of superiority for the Allies in all three dimensions of warfare—air, land, and sea." In fall 1936, British intelligence and military establishments revised their assessments. The rapid rate of Germany's military expansion was seen as unprecedented. Reports suggested that the military balance of power now favored Germany.[34] From the perspective of the numerical preponderance hypothesis, this evidence should have led to a more hostile British view of German intentions, especially after

1936; both British decision makers and the intelligence community should, according to this theory, have based their assessments of Germany's intentions on trends in German military capabilities.

British observers clearly thought the offense-defense balance in Europe favored the defense. Strategic belief in defensive efficacy shaped Britain's buckpassing behavior during the interwar period, according to Thomas Christensen.[35] Germany's build up of its offensive capabilities, especially after 1936, should have led British observers to regard these efforts as costly signals of offensive intentions, per the offense-defense hypothesis. Based on the capabilities thesis, we would expect both British decision makers and the intelligence community to refer to the offensive or defensive nature of the German buildup in their deliberations over German intentions.

THE STRATEGIC MILITARY DOCTRINE THESIS

Germany's military doctrine under Hitler was more offensively oriented and more innovative than in earlier years. It was designed to achieve, as Posen argues, "a campaign of limitless, if opportunistic, aggression."[36] This doctrine used a distinct combination of fast-paced air and armor aimed directly at the adversary's command, control, communication, and intelligence functions. Known as blitzkrieg, this doctrine was designed to "unravel" an enemy army with armored penetration deep into its rear areas through infiltration tactics and flanking movements by both infantry and armor. Germany used the blitzkrieg doctrine during World War II, but historians are divided on when and how much Hitler provided political support to advocates of the new military doctrine prior to the Second World War.[37] It is also unclear exactly when the German army adopted blitzkrieg as its official doctrine.[38]

Prior to the war, British observers did not develop a coherent view of Germany's blitzkrieg doctrine. There was a general consensus that Germany's military doctrine at the time was offensive, but available documents reveal that the British intelligence community was divided about its nature. This was especially true after 1937, when intelligence about German armored forces became available. Some in the British intelligence community, including the British military attaché in Berlin, Colonel Frederick Hotblack, reported that the German High Command was debating armor doctrine in early 1937. Advocates for the deployment of armored vehicles for warfare beyond Germany's eastern boundaries were gaining support from Hitler. By mid-1937, after witnessing a German training exercise, Hotblack reported the great speed at which the German armored divisions could advance in the initial phase of war. He argued that the German army was determined to develop a rapid offensive strategy. At the same time, German tactical simulations led Hotblack to conclude that at least for the present, "the doctrine for the use of the new weapons has not been worked out, nor, of course, have all the troops yet had time to learn to use them." Hotblack indicated that cooperation between the German Luftwaffe and army was not highly developed. The British government was convinced that the Luftwaffe was designed chiefly for the strategic bombing of Great Britain.[39] This was due to the assumption that governed all British war planning during this period: that Germany was most likely to go for a quick victory through a knockout blow from the air against Britain's strategic assets.[40]

By mid-1938, the War Office for the first time "had managed to identify all the elements of what was becoming Germany's blitzkrieg method—the triad of armored spearhead, speed of advance, and air support."[41] Not all members of the British intelligence community focused on those components. For instance, the new British military attaché in Berlin, Colonel Noel Mason-Macfarlane, emphasized conventional elements of German army doctrine as the main instruments of a surprise attack, including strategic bombing and infantry divisions, which relied on slow horse-drawn transport.[42] The historical evidence indicates that the British intelligence community was not able to pull together a coherent view of Germany's military doctrine prior to the outbreak of war in September 1939.[43] Most important, as F. H. Hinsley remarks, "in the extant records there is no sign that the War Office circulated any study of the possibility that the German Army would use armored Blitzkrieg methods though evidence to this effect was certainly coming in."[44] Uncertainty about Germany's military doctrine was perhaps understandable, as the blitzkrieg doctrine evolved further after German experience in the Polish and French campaigns of 1939–40.[45]

Summary of Predictions

Despite the lack of a comprehensive understanding of the particulars of the blitzkrieg, the British intelligence community clearly and consistently perceived Germany's land and air doctrine as offense oriented. All the available evidence of British war plans assumed Germany would be the aggressor. The British expected the German army to launch an initial offensive attack to secure a quick victory, and predicted that the German Luftwaffe would be used independently and immediately to try for a knockout blow against Britain. British strategists believed at the time that a defensive strategy had the advantage over an offensive one, especially in land warfare. According to the strategic military doctrine thesis, the offensive nature of Germany's military doctrine under conditions of perceived defense dominance should have led British policy makers to perceive Germany's intentions as hostile between 1934 and 1939, and we should expect to find evidence that both Britain's decision makers and its intelligence apparatus based their assessments of German intentions at least in part on their beliefs about Germany's military doctrine.

The Behavior Thesis

The behavior thesis tests how costly actions by Germany affected how Britain perceived its intentions. During this period, Germany engaged in a series of costly actions, both hostile and reassuring. Determining what, objectively, constitutes a costly behavior signal is not always straightforward. Here, I provide a list of international actions that fit the criteria set by other scholars and that received at least some attention by British perceivers. Out of about a dozen actions that are defined here as costly, two hostile actions were especially prominent: the remilitarization of the Rhineland in 1936 and the invasion of Czechoslovakia in 1939. In both, Germany explicitly used military threats and applied military force outside the boundaries of the Reich. Nonetheless, as we will see, because Hitler was employing costly actions of reassurance along with hostile ones, deriving clear predictions about when British perceptions should have changed according to the behavior thesis is a challenge and might be subject to interpretation. After 1936, however, the majority of Germany's costly actions seem to have been aimed at changing the status quo and thus were not reassuring in nature.

Hitler withdrew from both the Disarmament Conference and League of Nations in 1933, less than a year after becoming Germany's chancellor. Yet in 1934, Germany signed a ten-year nonaggression pact with Poland—a move designed to reassure Europe of Germany's peaceful intentions.[46] Another significant reassuring action was the British-German Naval Treaty, which Germany signed in June 1934. The treaty limited the German fleet to 35 percent of the number of Britain's surface craft and 45 percent of its submarines.

German troops remilitarized the Rhineland on March 7, 1936. This breach of the Treaty of Versailles represented Nazi Germany's first use of military force outside the boundaries of the Reich. Hitler's action in the Rhineland was costly not because it entailed the mobilization of German forces but instead because it risked armed conflict with France and Britain, and therefore should have been seen as an action that only a country with revisionist intentions would be willing to take.[47] In July 1936, Austria and Germany signed an agreement in which Germany recognized the full sovereignty of Austria, and the latter recognized itself as an ethnically German state. The Austrian government promised to act accordingly in its general policy and its policy toward Germany in particular.[48] Germany's actions during 1937 again exhibited a mix of aggressive and reassuring costly actions, but the hostile actions outweighed the reassuring ones. In January 1937, Hitler repeated his demand for the return of German colonies, while claiming that Germany was ready to guarantee the inviolability of Belgium and the Netherlands.[49] But in May, alarming reports arrived at the British Foreign Office that Hitler planned to embark on a limited military adventure in Czechoslovakia or Austria.[50] The announcement of the Anschluss with Austria followed in March 1938.[51] Between March and August, tensions over the

Sudeten territories increased. In September, as German military action against Czechoslovakia appeared imminent, Chamberlain flew to Berchtesgaden to meet with Hitler. Britain, France, Germany, and Italy signed the resulting Munich Agreement in September, agreeing to transfer the Sudetenland, and Britain and France guaranteed Czechoslovakia's newly drawn boundaries against external aggression. Czechoslovakia had little choice but to accept the Munich Agreement. On October 1, 1938, German troops occupied the Sudetenland.

In January 1939, Germany demanded a political reunion of the city of Danzig with the Reich, offering in return a guarantee of Poland's economic interests. Hitler followed this with a conciliatory speech before the Reichstag on January 30, declaring that Germany had no territorial claims on England and France except for the return of German colonies. Around the same time, though, British decision makers were receiving intelligence reports suggesting that Hitler was contemplating an attack in the West within months or even weeks. Germany's behavior toward Czechoslovakia in the following months raised even greater concern among British decision makers. On February 28, Germany replied to a British and French query by stating it could not guarantee Czechoslovakia's frontiers because conditions within the country as well as its relations with its neighbors were still far from satisfactory. Finally, on March 13, Germany presented an ultimatum to Czechoslovakia, demanding that its government dismiss several ministers suspected of being anti-Nazi. German troops occupied Czech territory on the following day.[52]

In the next month, Hitler responded to Chamberlain's announcement that Britain and France would defend Poland against German aggression by renouncing the 1935 Anglo-German Naval Agreement.[53] Germany and Italy then signed a formal treaty of military alliance on May 22. This was followed by further German efforts to balance against the Western Allies, culminating in a nonaggression treaty with Russia in August. On September 1, 1939, in spite of the British and French guarantee, German troops invaded Poland, triggering the British-French guarantee.

Summary of Predictions

The preceding review indicates that during this period, Germany took several costly international actions that worried British decision makers.[54] Especially alarming were Germany's withdrawal from the League of Nations and Disarmament Conference, militarization of the Rhineland, Anschluss with Austria, public threats to use force in the crises over the Sudeten territories, and invasion of Czechoslovakia. From the perspective of the current actions hypothesis, such actions should have led British observers to perceive Germany's intentions as increasingly hostile. But concurrent reassuring actions by Germany, such as signing a Naval Agreement with Britain in 1935 and its willingness to sign nonaggression treaties with several of its neighbors, somewhat blunted the effects of the hostile signals on British assessments of German intentions. From 1936 onward, however, the majority of Germany's actions were hostile, not reassuring. Two such actions should have been considered especially informative: the remilitarization of the Rhineland, which was the first time Germany used its military force outside the Reich, and Germany's invasion and occupation of Czechoslovakia in March 1939, in which it explicitly reneged on the agreement reached in Munich. These actions should have conveyed a clear message, according to the current actions hypothesis. Overall, the current actions hypothesis tells us to expect that Britain's decision makers and intelligence community would consider Germany's costly actions as indictors of hostile intentions, and would update their beliefs accordingly. We should expect both sets of actors to refer to those costly actions when explaining their assessments of Germany's intentions, and ignore or dismiss noncostly actions.

Emphasis on past actions suggests that British perceptions of Germany from 1934 to 1939 were shaped by costly actions that had been undertaken by Germany well before Hitler's ascendance to power in January 1933. In this context, Germany's hostile behavior in the period leading up to and during World War I should be expected to have served as a reference point.[55]

✳✳✳

In the next chapter, I examine what indicators British decision makers used to reach their conclusions about Germany's intentions and the degree to which we find support for the selective attention thesis as well as the three competing theses. The subsequent chapter assesses the inference process of the British intelligence services as reflected in their coordinated strategic reports.

CHAPTER 3

British Decision Makers' Perceptions
of Nazi Germany's Intentions

This chapter uses primary documents to examine the analytic lenses that several key British decision makers used to evaluate Nazi Germany's intentions between 1934 and 1939.

This chapter analyzes the views of the key decision makers most responsible for the formulation of Britain's foreign policy toward Germany during this time. The views expressed by two of the three British prime ministers in the period under study receive less attention: neither James Ramsay MacDonald (June 1929–June 1935) nor Stanley Baldwin (June 1935–May 1937) was greatly involved in issues of foreign policy. Starting in 1933, MacDonald's health significantly declined. Baldwin was reluctant to intervene in foreign affairs, other than to establish broad guidelines, and his deteriorating health during summer 1936 also made him less available and interested. The foreign secretary who served under him during most of his tenure, Eden, thus enjoyed a remarkable degree of latitude in the conduct of foreign policy. In addition to Eden, I focus on Prime Minister Chamberlain (May 1937–May 1940) and Eden's successor as foreign secretary, Halifax (February 1938–December 1940), who were both intimately involved in the formulation of British foreign policy.[1] In addition, this section explores—albeit not in depth—the reasoning used by Foreign Office senior members, whose reports about Germany's intentions were discussed at length in cabinet meetings. They include Permanent Undersecretary of Foreign Affairs Vansittart, his successor Alexander Cadogan, and the two British ambassadors to Berlin, Eric Phipps and his successor, Henderson, all members of the Foreign Office.

The analysis that follows is based largely on over ten thousand primary documents from the British National Archives as well as a large collection of documents from the Foreign Office published in the series *Documents on British Foreign Policy, 1919–1939* (herein *DBFP*). Specifically, I rely on the following types of sources: the collection of minutes from all meetings of the British Cabinet (CAB 23 series) and the memorandums circulated to the members (CAB 24 series); the minutes, memorandums, and reports produced by cabinet committees and subcommittees that dealt with assessments of the German threat, such as the Cabinet Committee on Foreign Policy (CAB 27 series), the Committee on German Rearmament, the Cabinet Committee on Germany (CAB 27), and the Defence Requirements Committee (CAB 16); correspondence among senior officials in the Foreign Office available in the *DBFP* collection; private papers from the office of the prime minister (PREM) along with memoirs and letters written by its officials; and secondary literature on this period as well as memoirs and biographies of the key decision makers involved.

The evidence in this chapter strongly supports the selective attention thesis along with the vividness and subjective credibility hypotheses that are derived from it, adequately supports the behavior thesis's current actions hypotheses, and only weakly supports the capabilities and strategic military doctrine theses. The empirical support for the three competing theses is therefore mixed. While Hitler's costly actions played a relatively important role in the inference process of *some* decision makers, indicators associated with the capabilities or strategic military doctrine and Germany's past actions were less central to the process of inferring Hitler's political intentions.

Changes in Statements about German Intentions over Time

Germany as the "Ultimate Potential Enemy" (1934)

Hitler took power in January 1933. Shortly thereafter, the British Foreign Office warned the cabinet that the Disarmament Conference involving members of the League of Nations was likely to fail because Germany refused to accept further reductions of and restrictions on its military. On May 16, the Foreign Office released a memo tallying alarming internal developments within Germany, including the militarization of German society and abundant evidence of accelerating rearmament, illegal under the Treaty of Versailles that ended World War I. It stated that the German government was pursuing "a point of preparation, a jumping off point from which she can reach solid ground before her adversaries can interfere." The Foreign Office perceived that Germany was determined to produce a "very large reserve of personnel who will require little further training to take their places in the armed forces of the country on the outbreak of war." This memo predicted "a European war in four or five years' time." It argued that public speeches by German officials left no doubt about Germany's dissatisfaction with the status quo, even if the specific plans of the German government were still difficult to gauge. Yet it concluded that "Germany needs peace until she has recovered such strength that no country can challenge her without serious and irksome preparations."[2] Simon, the foreign secretary, warned the cabinet one year later that German aggression would take place in stages:

[An Anschluss] would be her first move in a general policy of the reassertion by force, if necessary, of her international position—a policy of which German rearmament, German domination of Central Europe, and the eventual recovery of the Polish Corridor are the other principal objectives. . . . In any case Germany would become the dominant force in the Danube Basin, preparatory to trying out her strength elsewhere.[3]

The cabinet did not share Simon's alarming views. In an attempt to probe Germany's willingness to return to the Disarmament Conference, Eden, then newly appointed as lord privy seal, traveled to Berlin to meet with Hitler. Eden believed in the power of private interactions. He expected that he and Ambassador Phipps would "discover whether the German demands are in truth exorbitant, as I anticipate, or reasonable. If the former, the sooner British public opinion wakes up to the fact the better. If the latter we shall then have something definite upon which to work." Eden's visit left him with a favorable impression of Hitler. He reported on his interactions with the führer in great detail, describing him as a "shy man" with a "pleasant smile." These meetings led him to believe that Germany wanted peace in order to concentrate on solving its internal problems and that it must be permitted an element of "defensive security." Eden concluded of Hitler, "I find it very hard to believe that the man himself wants war. My impression is much more that this country has plenty to do internally to be thus pre-occupied for five years to come."[4] While Hitler's proposals on armaments reduction pleased Eden, Foreign Secretary Simon was less enthusiastic. Simon later reported that Hitler's proposals for the immediate legalization of the German air force and other concessions had "put us in a position of great embarrassment." Prime Minister MacDonald said to Eden, "We should not allow Germany to dump its confidence upon us in order to use us for its own policy. Hitler should know at once that his proposals in substance and in method of handling are unacceptable."[5]

A month later, Britain officially declared Germany its "ultimate potential enemy." A comprehensive report issued in February 1934 by the Defence Requirements Committee (DRC) stated that Britain's " 'long range' defense policy must be directed" against Germany. The DRC (an ad hoc subcommittee of the CID) first met in November 1933, following Hitler's announcement of Germany's withdrawal from the conference of the League of Nations.[6] The DRC's role was to prepare Britain to address its "worst deficiencies" in defense. The first comprehensive DRC report marked a fundamental shift in Britain's assessments of threat and its defense policy. It warned of the possibility of war in five years, and considered Germany, not Japan, Britain's primary adversary.[7] News that Germany had signed a nonaggression pact with Poland on January 26, which Hitler presented as evidence of his peaceful intentions, brought about a renewed discussion in the DRC over Germany's intentions. At the ninth meeting of the DRC in January 1934, Vansittart asserted that if Hitler were sincere—a proposition that he himself did not believe—the German-Polish pact provided Germany a "great increase in strength," both domestically and strategically. Domestically, Hitler was now perceived as stronger than his political opponents on the Right. Strategically, it freed "Germany's eastern flank, so allowing them if they wished to throw their weight in other directions." The pact caused Vansittart to revise his thoughts on the order of priority in Germany's aims. Previously, he believed that Germany would go after Austria first, then Poland, then the return of her colonial empire. Hitler's January 26 announcement, however, caused him to believe that Germany's demand for a colonial empire "would step up into the second place of Germany's priorities" or that Germany might turn to Czechoslovakia, although it was still too soon to "fix any firm date" for that.[8] The DRC's first comprehensive report, in February 1934, reached conclusions that echoed Vansittart's view of Germany's political agenda, although its military proposals were much more in line with the priorities of the COS. The report stated clearly that the danger from Germany was increasing:

> Her permanent system, with its full complement of armaments and trained reserve, has not yet taken shape, though it is rapidly doing so. Surrounded by armed and suspicious neighbours she is not at present a serious menace to this country, but within a few years will certainly become so. It will, indeed, be impossible to have any confidence in German gestures to the outside world so long as every German act at home belies them. In her case we have time, though not too much time, to make defensive preparations.[9]

For the rest of the year, Britain's decision makers debated whether Germany should be prevented from rearming.[10] Some cabinet members, such as the secretary of state for India, Samuel Hoare, argued that the DRC exaggerated the threat from Germany.[11] Simon responded that while Germany was not a threat to Britain today, "the methods adopted by Hitler and his friends were often menacing." Because "the fact remained that [Hitler] had two and a half million people enrolled in these forces," "his methods of appealing to his own people might easily result in a menacing situation." The DRC report, Simon said, should not be read as indicating that Germany was threatening Britain today "but that her method tended in a menacing direction."[12] Simon believed that Hitler's next steps would be "to create abroad an impression of the peaceful nature of German foreign policy and thereby, if possible, further to divide the remnants of the war coalition" as well as free himself "of foreign complications until he has effected the constitutional and administrative reorganization of the German Reich and the unification of German politics and thought."[13] Vansittart expressed an even more alarming view, claiming that there was continuity in Germany's aspirations and intentions since World War I. "There is no doubt whatever of the ultimate intentions of Germany. . . . In the place of the men of Weimar, there are now men whose ultimate aims are much of the same, but whose radically different methods may at some future date precipitate an international conflict." Vansittart warned that the new Reich would include "all the Germans in Europe (. . . not only Austria, but South Tyrol, Memel, Czechoslovakia, Eupen, Malmedy, Luxemburg, Slesvig, [and] German Switzerland)." This time, though, Germany was not likely to "repeat the mistake of fighting all her enemies at once. She must single out the most dangerous in turn, and attack him with all her forces." Much like Simon and Phipps, Secretary Vansittart also believed that Germany's policies would change in stages. The first stage would be one of "internal reform, regrouping of the population, and general training of the race." The second stage, which he termed the "expansionist phase," would begin when the increased population, artificially stimulated, required more land. Like the DRC report, Vansittart concluded that there was no "*immediate* danger." Yet he maintained that "the Germans are too competent, and matters are now moving too fast, to make a long estimate a safe one."[14]

The Ministerial Committee, dominated by Chamberlain (as the secretary of the exchequer), ultimately endorsed the DRC recommendation. Its discussions began treating Germany as the principal menace.[15] Nevertheless, Hitler's military intentions and strategies were the subject of speculation in the Ministerial Committee, and committee members debated Britain's defense plans to counter the German threat. Chamberlain claimed that he had always believed that "Germany would take on first one country, and then the other, that she would come to us last." He thought Britain would only have to take on Germany by itself after Germany conquered France. Concerned about Britain's ability to carry out its continental commitment and the threat of German air power, Chamberlain (backed by Simon and Hoare) emphasized the British air force, placing it above the army in importance.[16]

Stalemate and a Breakthrough (January–June 1935)

It was by no means evident to Britain's decision makers how to proceed. With so much uncertainty about Germany's intentions (and motives) and in the absence of a clear policy, they resorted to a renewal of personal contacts. The government dispatched Eden and Simon to probe Hitler's willingness to participate in a series of multilateral security pacts. Eden's views changed significantly following this round of meetings with Hitler. In contrast to his past observations, this time he found Hitler "authoritative" but was overall impressed "most unfavorably by him." This meeting changed Eden's stance about Germany's intentions and the possibility of coming to terms with Germany: "The essential question seems to be does a basis now exist for a general European settlement? A year ago I believe there was such a basis, but it is exceedingly difficult to maintain that it exists now." He explained that "Germany's demands on land and sea, in respect of neither of which is there any sign of abatement, seem to make an agreement impossible."[17] Simon warned that "Hitler had a tremendous sense of grievance," not against Britain, but against others, "which he held closely and was accustomed to ventilate with extreme vigour."[18] He reported that Germany was "determined to go her own course in rearmament; that she expects in time to get all Germans within her borders, including Austria; that she does not fear isolation and has no intention of joining in collective security."[19] Hitler's March 1935 announcement of his intention to build up the German air force and reintroduce compulsory military service, in combination with the tone of his remarks before Simon and Eden, generated British pessimism about the chance of any progress with Germany.[20]

British decision makers were slightly more encouraged when Germany signed a bilateral Naval Agreement in June 1935. The Naval Agreement allowed Germany to build a navy 35 percent the size of the British surface navy. British officials signed this agreement not because they perceived Germany's intentions to be benign but instead because they thought Germany intended to build a fleet regardless of Britain's stance. It was better to agree formally to limit such a fleet at the lowest obtainable level, especially since the German government stated that it would regard this as a "final and permanent" agreement. British decision makers (especially the British Admiralty) accepted the agreement, believing that Germany would never voluntarily accept so low a limit in the future.[21]

A few months later, in November 1935, the DRC's third report to the cabinet cautioned that Czechoslovakia and Austria were "threatened at a date not yet assignable." Germany's restless desire for expansion and demand for colonies presented great difficulties in establishing friendly relations on a durable basis. Nevertheless, the report indicated that the establishment of such a relationship with Germany continued to be in Britain's interest. It stated that Hitler "on several occasions affirmed his desire for friendly relations, and by concluding the recent Naval Agreement he had given to it some practical expression."[22]

The Prelude to the Rhineland Crisis (January–February 1936)

By 1936, British decision makers had concluded that Germany desired to expand its power and influence, but had no definitive answers about the reasons underlying Germany's expansionism, the scope of Germany's ultimate ambitions, or its determination to achieve these aims. On January 17, Eden circulated a memo asserting that Hitler's policy since 1933 had followed "along definite and pre-ordained lines"—that is, "the destruction of the peace settlement and re-establishment of Germany as the dominant power in Europe." Hitler would seek to achieve this, first, "internally, through the militarisation of the whole nation in all its aspects"; and second, externally, by "economic and territorial expansion so as to absorb as far as possible all those of German race who are at present citizens of neighbouring States, to acquire new markets for German industry and new fields for German emigration, and to obtain control of some of the sources of those raw materials at present lacking in Germany."

Eden thought that "the form and direction of this expansion" was "the one still doubtful factor in Germany's plans for the future."[23]

Although he saw Germany's expansionism as reaching back to 1933, Eden perceived a more recent change in Germany's confidence and determination to pursue its revisionist intentions. He surveyed Germany's foreign policy aims as stated in speeches made by German officials between May 1934 and January 1936. This study was circulated to the cabinet in February 1935. Eden said that these "scarcely leave us room to doubt that the rearmament of Germany is not being carried out for nothing or without a purpose. We can hardly avoid the conclusion that it is being carried out because in the words of General Göring, 'there are sometimes extraordinary deaf partners' in the [German] diplomatic Council Chamber who can only 'be aroused by the powerful voice of guns.'" Eden pointed to a change in Germany's stated objectives: before Germany announced rearmament plans in March 1935, German officials had said that their foreign policy aspirations were "strictly limited," and that Germany desired only equal rights in armaments and a fair settlement of the Saar question, which centered on whether the highly industrial former Prussian province would belong to France or Germany. But "after the decree of March 1935 reintroducing Conscription the German leaders began to speak differently." They emphasized the need to reverse treaties, reclaim German colonies, and restore Germany's place in the sun.[24]

Phipps was similarly growing more pessimistic about Hitler's ambitions. He judged that at least in the short term, Hitler wished to reach a friendly understanding with England. "Should [his] approaches to England fail," Phipps said, Hitler "may embark on a campaign to reconcile France and Germany. If he fails in this in turn, he will revise his policy fundamentally. He may even turn to Russia or Japan or decide to plough a lonely furrow."[25] Nevertheless, by late 1935, even those who saw Germany as determined to pursue its aggressive designs by military means did not envision that Germany would seek territorial expansion beyond certain parts in Central and Eastern Europe.[26]

The Rhineland Crisis and Its Aftermath (March–December 1936)

On March 7, the German Army reoccupied the Rhineland while Germany's leaders invoked their interest in collective security and called for a German return to the League of Nations (Hitler had pulled his country out of the organization in 1933). The British Cabinet had known of Hitler's complaints about the demilitarized zone in the Rhineland long before Germany took military action. In January 1936, the Foreign Office had acknowledged that this issue "must now be regarded as one of the questions of the hour: and that the issue is really whether the zone will be re-occupied by agreement or whether it will be occupied in a brusque and sudden manner."[27]

Hitler's actions led some in the Foreign Office to reassess their beliefs about Germany's intentions. On March 8, Eden described Hitler's actions as "alarming" because of "the fresh confirmation which it affords of the scant respect paid by German Governments to the sanctity of treaties." He concluded the memo to the cabinet by stating, "We must be prepared for [Hitler] to repudiate any treaty even if freely negotiated (a) when it becomes inconvenient; and (b) when Germany is sufficiently strong and the circumstances are otherwise favourable for doing so."[28] Due to the growing strength of Germany, however, Eden urged the cabinet to try to come to terms with the country as long as Hitler was "in the mood to do so." Ambassador Phipps was pessimistic; a few days after the crisis, he believed the chances of war were higher than one in ten.[29] Likewise, Vansittart expressed alarm that while Germany was perhaps sincere in wanting peace in Western Europe, he was "somewhat surer that they do not ultimately desire peace in Central and Eastern Europe." Germany's actions should, Vansittart cautioned, teach Britain that German assurances could not be taken at face value. A change of heart in Germany would be nothing less than a "miracle." Vansittart concluded, "Nothing that is really going on inside Germany, nothing that is being said or taught there, gives at present any sign of more than the ephemeral sincerity of which we have all along recognised Hitler to be capable."[30]

Other decision makers, though, did not consider that Hitler's actions revealed any new information about his intentions. Uncertainty about the scope and extent of his determination to revise the status quo led Eden to declare before the cabinet that Britain must demand "complete clarity" about Germany's intentions. Consequently, the cabinet formulated a questionnaire to explore Germany's terms for a comprehensive settlement and sought assurances as to its commitment not to change the status quo in Europe by other means than free negotiations. The questionnaire served in Eden's eyes as a litmus test. A negative response from Hitler would indicate the aggressive nature of his policy, whereas a positive response would serve as evidence of Hitler's commitment to reach a settlement by peaceful means. The prospects for success were remote from the start. Hitler's refusal to reply led members of the Foreign Office to conclude that Hitler "does not desire any negotiations and that he is merely playing for time."[31]

During this period, reports arrived at the Foreign Office that the Nazi Party was "bent on conquering Czechoslovakia and Roumania [sic] and annexing Austria; hoping for an alliance with Hungary and Yugoslavia with whom they would divide the territorial gains; and [the Nazi Party] was talking wildly of undermining and overthrowing the Soviet Government, establishing a Fascist Russian dictatorship in Moscow and forming a Russo-German alliance." While the German Army was seeking time to rearm, Hitler and his advisers were believed to be "pressing for more speed."[32] Eden also reported on alarming domestic developments within Germany, such as the youth "being imbued with the idea of expansion both east and west," and the fact that there was "really no moderate party in Germany." He wrote, "We should not be under any illusion as to the aims that underlie German policy. The Germany of to-day (and, I fear, to-morrow, in view of the forces of miseducation which are perverting her youth) has no intention of respecting the integrity of her smaller neighbours, no matter what paper she may sign." Yet Eden insisted that this reading of Germany's intentions should not "make any difference to our intention to probe and explore Herr Hitler's offers."[33]

Eden's pessimism was greater after a visit to Germany. He noted that since the Nazi Party had taken over the military, this allowed Hitler to "act when and where he pleases." German remilitarization seemed to be all-encompassing, "on a scale only hitherto heard of in the USSR." He was troubled by the Germans' determination "to carry out their Eastern expansion programme in spite of all comers," as they perceived the menace from Bolshevism to be great.[34] Influenced by these observations, Eden warned the cabinet in July that "he could give no guarantee of the certainty of peace even during the present year."[35]

The Colonial Question and European Appeasement (January–April 1937)

Secretary Eden opened the first cabinet meeting of 1937 by stating that it "was likely to be a critical year in Foreign Affairs." It looked as though this year Germany would choose between a "policy alternatively of co-operation or foreign adventure."[36] Reports of Germany's shortages in raw materials and foreign currency indicated an opportunity to "actively influence Hitler in the direction of adopting the moderate course."[37] Other reports at the Foreign Office concluded that Hitler would not attempt any adventures in Central and Eastern Europe as long as he could not be sure that Britain would stand "aloof." This reading of Germany's plans meant that Britain had some time. Eden added, "If the Germans feel that she cannot achieve such wonderful relations with us as to free them for aggression elsewhere, they may once more modify their policy."[38]

Around the same time, the German minister of economics, Hjalmar Schacht, reported that Hitler was willing to consider accepting colonial concessions in return for a German promise of peaceful behavior. Schacht's report led British decision makers to reexamine Britain's policy on colonial transfers. Eden believed that consideration of this question should follow only after Britain received certain assurances from Germany, which could not be "merely eye-wash"; Britain must require "outward and visible signs" of "a definite change of political orientation in Germany."[39] Eden reminded members of the Committee on Foreign Policy that Hitler had not expressed a willingness to conclude any general pact but instead had maintained his refusal to return to the League of Nations.[40] Vansittart similarly questioned whether Hitler would give up his expansionist designs. He wrote in January, "I don't know how we could ever be sure that Hitler was a genuine convert to an idea so greatly at variance with his present aims and professions."[41] In late March, Vansittart added, "I do not now at all believe that the Germans of 1937 would pay any adequate European price for only this small retrocession," referring to Britain's willingness to transfer the French colonies of Togoland and Cameroon to Germany. "Indeed

I think she is bound for European expansion anyway, unless quite other factors now combine to deter her."[42] Chamberlain, however, was more hopeful. He believed Germany would genuinely consider a full and final settlement in return for African colonies. As the internal situation in Germany was "steadily deteriorating," Chamberlain was optimistic that Hitler might now be prepared "to go a long way to reach a complete settlement."[43] Chamberlain explained the rationale for changing the current British policy on the issue of transfer of colonies:

> It will, I think, be admitted that the general situation in Europe is such that we cannot afford to miss any opportunity of reducing the international tension. The present rulers of Germany and Italy have been organizing their nations systematically for war: but they justify their measures to their people on the ground that they are surrounded by enemies that they have no alternative means of self-preservation. . . . It is difficult for a dictator to climb down publicly, but Herr Hitler's last speech contains certain definite assurances in regard to the peaceful intentions of Germany, and Dr. Schacht's approaches, which have been made with the approval of Herr Hitler, cannot be regarded as anything but an invitation to a general discussion.

> Any Government which turned down this invitation without at least exploring the possibilities sufficiently to make sure that there was no possible basis of improvement in the international atmosphere would incur a very heavy responsibility. Even a slight improvement in the international atmosphere may lead gradually to a general détente whereas a policy of drift may lead to a general war.[44]

Throughout this period, German officials continued to reassure British decision makers in private conversations of Germany's peaceful intentions, its defensive motivation for militarization, and the necessity of obtaining colonies for both economic and status reasons.[45] Hitler himself had promised the British ambassador that "the era of surprise was over," and that "any further steps would only be taken after most mature reflection and consideration."[46] Some members of the Foreign Office were far from reassured. Orme Sargent, supervising undersecretary for the Central European Department, cautioned in April that the era of surprise was likely to be reopening soon. Vansittart added that "most of the really unpleasant [surprises] are still in posse."[47]

The Chamberlain Cabinet and Foreign Office (May–December 1937)

On May 28, 1937, Chamberlain succeeded Baldwin as prime minister. Henderson replaced Phipps as Britain's ambassador to Berlin around the same time. Henderson's belief in the sincerity of stated German aims, willingness to accept the territorial claims declared by the Nazis in the 1930s, conviction of the success of the appeasement policy, and strong personal relations with German officials quickly made the new ambassador Chamberlain's confidant, but also a target of ridicule and criticism within the Foreign Office.

Disturbing reports arrived at the Foreign Office during this time regarding Hitler's intentions to exploit the possibility of a war between Italy and Britain in order to occupy Czechoslovakia, Austria, and Hungary. As Sargent put it, "The old Road to the East and Bagdad was once again being spoken of."[48] Some officials questioned these reports. Henderson said in early July that he was "disinclined to believe in the reality of Germany's aggressive intentions against Great Britain unless and until she goes back on the Naval Agreement." Such a step, Henderson continued, would make it "quite certain what her [Germany's] ultimate intentions are. Otherwise, risk though there be, it has got to be faced, and we have got to trust her."[49] Henderson angered senior officials in the Foreign Office when he claimed that it was not Germany's intention to divide England and France; he said that Germany wanted to "induce Great Britain to disassociate herself, not from France, but from the French system of alliances in Central and Eastern Europe." A number of statements by German officials had convinced Henderson that the colonial question for Germany was only secondary. Since, as he believed, its primary objective was to attain a free hand in the East, Henderson argued that Germany would abide by any agreement with Britain and France that was "limited to the West." Germany's reservations, Henderson concluded, were "in respect of Central and Eastern Europe where she feels that her future lies by means of realization of aspirations which are in her opinion vital to her well-being, legitimate and not in conflict with any direct British interest."[50] Henderson argued that there was no need to adopt "a panicky mood" because of the recent reports about Hitler's immediate plans in Central and Eastern Europe. Dire prophecies would be self-fulfilling: any fervor would lead Germany to believe that overthrowing the government of Austria or Czechoslovakia was simply expected of it. According to Henderson, the reality was that Hitler had calmed down and "the tension of ten days ago had been followed by a definite détente."[51]

Henderson saw Germany's intentions as opportunistic overall, but he did see Hitler as determined to change the status quo in Central and Eastern Europe, if possible through nonmilitary means, and thought Hitler's policy was motivated by "legitimate and natural" aspirations. In his words, Germany's foreign policy was "guided by circumstances and opportunity." In fact, he asked, "If Germany is blocked from any Western adventures . . . have we the right to oppose German *peaceful* expansion and evolution in the East?" Henderson did not define what he meant by peaceful, but the rest of his memo indicates that he was willing to accept a dramatic change in the status quo in Central and Eastern Europe.[52] He was influenced by General Göring's candid remarks about Germany's goals in Central and Eastern Europe. Göring saw the Anschluss with Austria as inevitable. Poland, Göring continued, "could be solved with no difficulty." He declared that the Italian Tyrol was not part of German aspirations. Göring reassured Henderson that the stronger Germany got, the more restraint it would show. He was even willing to state what Germany's aims did not include: "[Germany] could definitely say that she desired nothing in the West, nor in the South, nor in the North. Nor did she want any single thing which Great Britain possessed." Henderson took Göring's statements at face value.[53]

In November 1937, Chamberlain sent Halifax to Berlin in an attempt "to convince Hitler of our sincerity and to ascertain what objectives he had in mind." Halifax gave detailed reports of his conversations with Hitler and other leading German officials, and Chamberlain declared the trip a success. Still, Chamberlain was concerned about Hitler's increased determination to revise the status quo in Central and Eastern Europe, despite his ostensibly peaceful intentions overall toward Britain and other parts of Europe. In a personal letter to his sister Ida dated November 26, Chamberlain summarized his perceptions of Germany's intentions:

> Both Hitler and Goering said repeatedly and emphatically that they had no desire or intention of making war and I think we may take this as correct at any rate for the present. Of course they want to dominate Eastern Europe; they want as close a union with Austria as they can get without incorporating her in the Reich, and they want much the same things for the *Sudetendeutsche*.[54]

To the cabinet, Halifax said that Germany wanted friendly relations with Britain and that he had no policy or immediate plans to change the status quo as the Germans were "too busy building up their country, which was still in a state of a revolution." Nevertheless, Halifax expected German officials to continue with "beaver-like persistence in pressing their aims in Central Europe, but not in a form to give others cause—or probably occasion—to interfere." Unlike Henderson, Eden and Halifax believed that the colonial question "loomed larger than before in the minds of the Germans." Germany did not want to "connect Central Europe with the Colonial issue," as Hitler was basing the colonial claims on grounds of fairness and equity. This was an important distinction, Eden concluded, because Britain's policy was premised on the notion that this sort of quid pro quo was possible to achieve. Chamberlain agreed, though he still believed that Britain should push to obtain "some satisfactory assurance that [Germany] did not mean to use force in Eastern Europe." That, to Chamberlain, was a more crucial point.[55]

The Anschluss and Sudeten Crisis (March–July 1938)

On March 12, 1938, the German 8th Army marched into Austria. While Hitler's desire to incorporate Austria into Germany had been known to British decision makers, the timing and manner of the annexation of Austria took the British Cabinet by surprise.

There was some evidence beforehand that Hitler had intended to act. On March 3, Henderson had met with Hitler, and reported to the cabinet that "the German Government appeared to be set head-on to achieve their desiderata in Central Europe and did not want to tie their hands by talks, and still less by undertakings to ourselves."[56] There had been no signs that action was imminent though.[57] In Chamberlain's eyes, Hitler's actions in Austria were "most distressing and shocking." They represented "a typical illustration of power politics."[58] Both the cabinet and Foreign Policy Committee believed that there was nothing Britain could have done to prevent the Anschluss, however disillusioning the takeover was. It was thought best to avoid "giving the impression [to the British public] that the country was faced with the prospect of war within a few weeks."[59]

The Anschluss itself and Germany's behavior during this crisis signified different things to different decision makers. In Henderson's eyes, this action revealed important clues about the führer's character, intentions, and future behavior. He wrote that Hitler's actions "brought home to us with greater force than ever before—since Austria is Hitler's first adventure outside the actual frontiers of the Reich itself—how precarious is to-day the peace of the world when it rests in the hands of a single fanatical and unbalanced individual whose reactions are arbitrary and personal."[60] Other officials reasoned that if Hitler spoke and acted on his intentions, then there was little doubt that Hitler's attention would now turn to the Sudeten territories in Czechoslovakia. But only the minister of the coordination of defense asked whether Germany wished to absorb the whole of Czechoslovakia. Chamberlain replied:

> It might be rash to forecast what Germany would do, but at the same time the seizure of the whole of Czechoslovakia could not be in accordance with Herr Hitler's policy, which was to include all Germans in the Reich but not to include other nationalities. It seems most likely . . . that Germany would absorb the Sudeten German territory and reduce the rest of the Czechoslovakia to a condition of dependent neutrality.[61]

In the same meeting, Halifax attributed to Hitler similarly limited objectives, but thought that if these objectives could not be achieved through peaceful means, Germany would use force against Czechoslovakia.[62]

Just after the Anschluss, the cabinet received a somber report from the COS that it would be "extremely difficult for Britain to effectively exercise any military pressure against Germany in time to save Czechoslovakia." It warned of not just "a limited European war only, but of a world war." In its current stage of rearmament, Britain was not ready for a war.[63] Yet Halifax did not think the situation required Britain to issue a deterrent threat to Germany. "The need for a deterrent commitment rested on the assumption that when Germany secured the hegemony over Central Europe she would then pick a quarrel with France and ourselves."[64] Halifax did not believe that assumption was justified. In a memo circulated to members of the Foreign Policy Committee in mid-March, Halifax expressed his views about the scope of Hitler's long-term intentions and their implications for near-term British policy:

> It may well be true that Germany's superiority in arms may be greater a year or two hence than it is now, but this is not a good argument for risking disaster now. The

ground upon which it is sought to justify the undoubted risk which we should be assuming is that unless we make a stand now, Germany will march uninterruptedly to hegemony in Europe, which will be but a first step towards a deliberate challenge to the British Empire. There is much force in this argument, and yet it may well be based upon a more confident prediction of future events than the experience of history will support. . . . It cannot be contended that the future is not black, but there is at least an element of uncertainty in our diagnosis, and on the strength of that uncertainty we might at least refrain from embarking on the more hazardous courses.

On the other hand, the fact must be faced that we are now witnessing the beginning of Germany's penetration of Central Europe, which, if not checked, will culminate in her establishing more or less complete domination of that part of Europe. It may be foreseen that this in its turn will lead to the isolation of Great Britain and France in Western Europe, with all the consequent loss of influence, prestige, and even security.[65]

Halifax maintained that if Britain were able to conclude an agreement between Germany and the Czechoslovakian government over the Sudeten territory, then Germany would "have less reason to risk the hazards of war."[66] Chamberlain was persuaded by Halifax's conclusions, as he at the time also did not believe that Hitler intended to use military force. "If Germany could obtain the desiderata by peaceable methods," he argued, "there was no reason to suppose that she would reject such a procedure in favour of one based on violence."[67]

In June, questions surfaced as to whether Germany might desire more than the recovery of the Sudeten territory. According to the British ambassador in Prague, "There is ample evidence for the view that the German Government does not consider the settlement of the Sudeten Germans as their real objective." Halifax did not believe that Hitler's intentions were to occupy the whole of Czechoslovakia. Rather, he thought that Germany had defensive motivations for any actions beyond the Sudeten territories because of the security arrangements Czechoslovakia had with the USSR and France.[68] Influenced by the reassuring reports he had received from Henderson, Chamberlain also believed that Germany was not contemplating any action in the immediate future. In mid-July, he cautioned cabinet members not to give "too much credence to unchecked reports from non-official sources. He himself had seen His Majesty's ambassador to Berlin, who gave an account of the attitude of the Nazi government that was not discouraging."[69]

Chamberlain's Personal Diplomacy (August–November 1938)

By summer 1938, views of Hitler's long-term political intentions differed within the British leadership. There was uncertainty as to Hitler's likelihood of using military force against Czechoslovakia:

One view . . . was that Herr Hitler, against the advice of the Army and of the moderate party, was determined to intervene by force.

The alternative view was that, while Herr Hitler was determined to get the Sudeten German question settled this year, he had not yet made up his mind to use force for this purpose. He was, however, determined to have everything ready. . . . This was the view of [Henderson,] our Ambassador [to Berlin].

The evidence was not clear-cut. Henderson's reasoning—that Hitler did not have malign intentions toward France, that Hitler was not an extremist but rather that people in his close circle were, and that his military preparations were largely defensive—resonated with both Halifax and Chamberlain.[70]

Against this background, Chamberlain decided to meet with Hitler to settle the Czechoslovakian problem. The first meeting took place at Berchtesgaden on September 14. Hitler demanded self-determination for the Sudeten Germans, but promised to refrain from hostilities until after Chamberlain had consulted with the British Cabinet. Furthermore, Chamberlain was also reassured by Hitler's assertion that the boundary with Poland was "definitely fixed," renunciation of any claim to Alsace-Lorraine, and statement that he had signed the Naval Agreement with Britain because he believed that there would be no war between the two countries. Following that meeting, Chamberlain informed his cabinet that he had "formed an opinion that Herr Hitler's objectives were strictly limited."[71] Chamberlain also reported his belief that Hitler was sincere in saying he only wanted the return of the Sudeten Germans and "did not wish to include Czechs in the Reich." With that accomplished, Hitler claimed, he would be satisfied. The cabinet meeting protocol concluded, "The Prime Minister said that the impression left on him was that Herr Hitler meant what he said. . . . It was clearly of the utmost importance to make up one's mind whether the inclusion of the Sudeten Germans in the Reich was the end at which Herr Hitler was aiming or only a beginning. This was a matter on which one could only exercise one's judgment. The Prime Minister's view was that Herr Hitler was telling the truth."[72]

Probed in September about Hitler's intentions beyond Czechoslovakia, Chamberlain answered again that he "was satisfied that Herr Hitler was speaking the truth when he said that he regarded this [Sudeten] question as a racial question. He was also satisfied that Herr Hitler regarded the terms offered as his last word, and that if they were rejected he [Hitler] would fight."[73] On September 22, Chamberlain flew to Bad Godesberg, and learned that Hitler wanted immediate occupation of the Sudeten territories and would not guarantee Czechoslovakian borders until other German claims to repatriate territories containing German-speaking communities were satisfied. Hitler threatened military invasion of the Sudetenland on September 28. These additional demands shocked and surprised Chamberlain, who rejected them and found the meeting "most unsatisfactory." The next evening they met again. Chamberlain failed to convince Hitler to soften his demands. On September 23 and 24, Hitler reassured Chamberlain that he was interested only in the Sudetenland, but still demanded the cession of the Sudetenland by October 1 and a military occupation endorsed by a plebiscite before November 25, 1938. Shortly thereafter, Czechoslovakia rejected these terms. Chamberlain suggested a conference of representatives of Britain, Czechoslovakia, France, Germany, and Italy; Hitler then offered to postpone his move into Czechoslovakia by twenty-four hours. Hitler invited Chamberlain, Italian leader Benito Mussolini, and French prime minister Edouard Daladier to Munich on September 28; no Czechoslovakian representative attended. The four leaders agreed to cede the Sudetenland to Germany. Britain and France guaranteed Czechoslovakia's new boundaries. Chamberlain and Hitler signed a pledge for future consultation. Czechoslovakia had little choice but to accept the Munich Agreement. On October 1, 1938, German troops occupied the Sudetenland. Less than six months later, German forces would invade and occupy Czechoslovakia's capital city, Prague.

On hearing Hitler's inflated demands in Godesberg, Halifax's perceptions of Hitler's intentions shifted. From that point on, Halifax and Chamberlain disagreed on what Hitler wanted to accomplish through negotiation with Britain. Following Chamberlain's meeting with Hitler, Chamberlain received a telegram from Halifax warning that "a great mass of people" believed that Hitler's terms were unjust and should not be accepted. Halifax now shared Cadogan's concern that Chamberlain had been too quickly influenced by Hitler's assurances: "Alec . . . I came to the conclusion that you were right."[74] Halifax was not reluctant to voice his disagreement with Chamberlain publicly. Before the cabinet, he admitted that "he had found his opinion changing" and "was not sure that their [his and Chamberlain's] minds were still together at one." He "could not rid his mind of the fact that Herr Hitler had given us nothing and that he was dictating terms, just as though he had won a war but without having to fight." He said that "as long as Nazi-ism lasted, peace would be uncertain. For this reason he did not feel that it would be right to put pressure on Czechoslovakia to accept" the demands made by Hitler in Godesberg.[75] Halifax's reaction surprised Chamberlain, who said, "Your complete change of view since I saw you last night is a horrible blow to me."[76]

Halifax and Cadogan were not alone in criticizing Chamberlain's confidence that Hitler had but limited ambitions. First Lord of the British Admiralty Duff Cooper found it "difficult to believe that self determination of the Sudeten Germans was Hitler's last aim," and referred to statements that Hitler had previously made "to the effect that he had no intentions of attacking Austria or Czechoslovakia" as evidence that his promises were "quite unreliable." He maintained that Germany's aspirations were far greater and at some point Germany might "make some attempt" on Britain's colonies. The president of the Board of Trade and lord president of the council both voiced similar assessments.[77] The latter explained his lack of trust in Hitler's assurances, citing their contradictions in a number of public declarations of territorial claims in Europe made by Hitler or other German officials since 1935. The secretary of state for the colonies expressed doubts as to Chamberlain's optimism regarding the scope of Hitler's objectives and credibility he assigned to his verbal assurances. The lord privy seal stated that "after looking at Herr Hitler's record and his intentions as set out in his writings, it was impossible to have any confidence in him. If what was now asked for was conceded, he would only ask for more later."[78]

The Goal of World Supremacy (December 1938–April 1939)

In early 1939, some British decision makers significantly reassessed their estimates of Hitler's ultimate intentions. A new reading of Germany's intentions —in which Hitler was seen as able and willing to attack in the West, and in which his ultimate plans were viewed as nothing less than world domination— became the predominant interpretation within the Foreign Office and cabinet. The seeds of this new perception can be traced to a series of intelligence reports from clandestine sources. These indicated that by signing the Munich Agreement, Hitler had to change his earlier plans, which had been to conquer Czechoslovakia and then invade Romania. Hitler was said to blame Chamberlain for depriving him of this adventure and gaining the enthusiasm of the German people for peace.

Beginning in November 1938, Halifax gave the Foreign Policy Committee a series of reports, which concluded that since the Munich Agreement, Hitler had become "increasingly anti-British and that his intention was to work for the disintegration of the British Empire and, if possible, for the domination of the world by the German nation."[79] As of mid-November, however, there was not enough evidence, according to a Foreign Office memo, to indicate what sort of action Hitler would take. Chamberlain noted there was "no suggestion that Herr Hitler contemplated any immediate aggressive action."[80] Despite Chamberlain's expressed doubts about several pieces of political intelligence that had sparked these alarms, he agreed to take action in response. None of his statements indicated a dramatic change in his perceived intentions or the abandonment of appeasement. Still, it was clear by then, as Wark puts it, that "the moral-code of the Chamberlain-Hitler declaration had apparently been dishonoured by Hitler, who was showing too little interest in Anglo-German friendship, peace, and consultation."[81]

On December 20, the Foreign Office published a memo drawn up on special instructions from Cadogan.[82] It described Hitler as a person acting on "sudden intuition," whose characteristics included "fanaticism, mysticism, ruthlessness, cunning, vanity, moods of exaltation and depression, fits of bitter self-righteous resentment, and what can only be termed a streak of madness." These made the task of predicting his next move especially daunting. But the section of the report dealing with Hitler's aims leaves no doubt that the Foreign Office's assessment of Germany's intentions had been transformed:

The aims of Herr Hitler and the regime are, in their broadest sense:

a. The attainment of supremacy in Europe
b. World supremacy

Hitherto (a) has been spoken of amidst the inner Party circles, but . . . thoughts are now turning more seriously to (b).

Steps to the attainment of supremacy in Europe—apart from the inevitable recovery, when convenient, of lost territory in Eastern and Northern Europe—include:

1. The establishment of German political and economic hegemony over the whole of Central and S.E. Europe, on the "Vassal State" principle. . . .
2. The bringing, through the disintegration of the Soviet regime, of a large part of South Russia within Germany's political and economic orbit. . . .
3. The application of the "Vassal State" principle, in greater or lesser degree, to the Baltic and other Northern States, and also to Belgium and Holland;
4. Substantial concession in Spain.[83]

Nazi expansion for Lebensraum (living space) would be toward the "Ukraine and further East in Russia." German aims outside Europe were now said to include:

1. The recovery of all lost Colonial possessions, or the obtaining of a satisfactory equivalent in overseas territory;
2. A privileged position in areas under Japanese control in China;
3. The formation of an ideological front with Islam, whereby Germany shall acquire great influence in the Arab and Moslem [sic] world, bringing with it markets and the means of embarrassing Britain;
4. The establishment of strong German influence in South America.[84]

As for Germany's objectives in Western Europe, the report concluded that "it stands out unmistakably that *in the eyes of Herr Hitler and of the majority of the Nazi Party. . . . Great Britain is Enemy No. 1.*"[85] The Foreign Office believed that in sum, while the eastward drive was "the order of the day . . . Herr Hitler is *incalculable,* even to his intimates. He is capable of throwing the machine he has created, regardless of settled policy and on his own initiative, in *any* direction at short notice. He can personally precipitate a conflagration, whatever the consequences to his regime may be."[86]

By the end of 1938, though, Foreign Office officials had identified a pattern in Hitler's behavior: his policies revealed a well-planned expansionist design that was unlimited in its scope.

There have hitherto been two distinct stages in the attainment of German aims. The first was concerned with the removal of the servitudes of the peace treaties within the boundaries of the post-war Reich. During this period we saw the rearmament of Germany and the reoccupation of the Rhineland. . . . The consequent accession of strength enabled Herr Hitler to embark on the second stage, namely, the union of all Germans in "Grossdeutschland." It is true that certain German pockets still remain outside the Reich, but these are considered so insignificant and their eventual incorporation so easy that they need not be considered. . . .

It is the general conviction in Germany to-day that Herr Hitler is now about to embark on the third stage of his programme, namely, expansion beyond the boundaries of the territories inhabited by Germans. How exactly this is to be achieved is the subject of much speculation. One thing is certain: Nazi aims are on a grandiose scale, and there is no limit to their ultimate ambitions.[87]

Thus the year 1939 opened with a heightened sense of concern. Additional reports arrived in mid-January indicating more clearly that Hitler intended to act contrary to the Munich Agreement. It was "unfortunately no longer possible to assume that there is no likelihood of Germany 'coming West' in 1939." Foreign Office officials concluded that there was "incontrovertible evidence" that Hitler was "seriously considering the possibility of a direct attack on Great Britain and France during the next few months—perhaps during the next few weeks." For the first time, the report acknowledged that Hitler was "barely sane, consumed by insensate hatred for this country, and capable both of ordering an immediate aerial attack on any European country and of having his command instantly obeyed."[88]

Chamberlain was still skeptical of the conclusions the Foreign Office reached in its reports about Hitler's intentions. He noted before the cabinet that "he had been alarmed at the contents of certain telegrams from Berlin."[89] Yet there was still a sense of "considerable uncertainty" since Britain was dealing with "a man whose actions were not rational." Halifax reported that Hitler "may decide that the moment is propitious for dealing an overwhelming blow at the Western Powers. This was held to be always the ultimate object, but some reports indicate that he may judge the moment opportune now to achieve it before the rearmament of those Powers may have deprived him of the advantage which he now possesses over them."[90] To support his assessments, Halifax circulated a memo by Cadogan arguing that consistent with his writings in *Mein Kampf*, Hitler would first "acquire control over the resources of eastern and southeastern Europe, and then, thus reinforced, turn against the West."[91] Cadogan was skeptical that Hitler would deliberately engage himself on both fronts simultaneously. He predicted that Hitler's attack in the West "might be by way of direct (and perhaps completely surprise) air attack on this country, or it might be by way of invasion of Holland."[92] Still, Halifax was uncertain whether Hitler had committed himself to attacking the West; this doubt made the task of formulating a coherent foreign policy especially difficult, but the need to act was apparent. Cadogan commented, "We cannot guess what Hitler will decide—much less can we guess at the probable outcome of his decision. We can only prepare for the worst shocks."[93] Frustrated with the situation, Halifax pointed out that British officials were all "moving in a mental atmosphere much like that surrounding a child in which all things were possible and impossible, and where there were no rational guiding rules."[94]

During the month of February, Chamberlain was slightly less anxious for several reasons. For one, there was Hitler's Reichstag speech on January 30, in which he made a conciliatory reference to a "long peace." Chamberlain viewed this as a direct response to his earlier appeal to Hitler to declare his peaceful intentions. Second, Chamberlain believed that "the peace side of the balance" was given weight by Germany's economic troubles, public opinion in Germany that "was alarmed by the prospect of war," and Britain's increased confidence in its own military. The third factor that fueled Chamberlain's optimism in February and early March was a series of reassuring reports from Ambassador Henderson, who returned to Berlin in mid-February skeptical about the credibility of the intelligence reports that had generated the war scare. In January, he declared that "Herr Hitler does not contemplate any adventures at the moment and all stories and rumors to the contrary are completely without real foundation."[95] The German people, he added a month later, wanted peace "just as much as and even more than ourselves," and Henderson argued that Hitler was "not going to disappoint them if he can help it."[96] Only a few days before Hitler occupied Czechoslovakia, Henderson wrote that "even if [Hitler] does dream of unlimited expansion he cannot but be influenced by the reflection that a further advance is dangerous before the consolidation of his latest gains."[97] He believed that Hitler's objectives in the next two years were limited for the most part to the occupation of "Memel, Danzig and colonies, and the complete subordination of Czecho-Slovakia politically and economically to Germany." Henderson explained that talk of German advances into Holland, Romania, Switzerland, and the Ukraine should be regarded as "premature."[98] Chamberlain relied on Henderson's reassuring reports. In a meeting with the US ambassador Joseph P. Kennedy Sr., he reported that "Hitler and [Joachim von] Ribbentrop are so far from hatching schemes against us [that they are] searching round for some means of approaching us without the danger of a snub."[99] He suggested to the US ambassador that the "only hope of doing business with Hitler is to take him at his word," and "it was by no means certain that the word will be kept, but up to date he [Chamberlain] had no reason personally to disbelieve it."[100]

Chamberlain's optimism regarding the state of Anglo-German relations on the eve of the German invasion of Czechoslovakia as well as his excessive reliance on Henderson's reports contributed to the growing split between the prime minister and his foreign secretary. Halifax was visibly annoyed at Chamberlain when the latter did not consult him before delivering an encouraging press briefing on March 9 about foreign affairs. He did not share Chamberlain's view that European tensions were then decreasing. In fact, shortly after Munich,

Halifax came to the conclusion that Hitler was both able and willing to use force against Britain and its allies in the coming months.[101]

The German Invasion of Czechoslovakia (March 1939)

The war scare of late 1938 and early 1939 led members of the British Cabinet to understand that Germany's intentions might not be limited. Germany's occupation of Czechoslovakia in mid-March 1939 provided clear proof that Hitler sought more than just the reintegration of all Germans within his Third Reich. Hitler had larger objectives in mind. As Wark explains, "The nature of the German action against Czechoslovakia was a stark and unwelcome confirmation of the warning contained in political intelligence reports after Munich. That was simply a product of the fact that unwelcome intelligence had come true with such lightning speed and finality. The inevitable gap between acceptance of intelligence warnings and complete belief was closed by Hitler's action in March."[102]

The significance attached to the German invasion was stated in a Foreign Office report written in late March:

> The absorption of Czecho-Slovakia has clearly revealed Germany's intentions. It marks the first departure from the Nazi racial theory, under which the reason to suppose that the treatment applied to Czecho-Slovakia will be extended to other countries in Europe, notably Roumania [sic] and Poland.[103]

Likewise, on March 16, Halifax said in a cabinet meeting that he considered the military occupation of Czechoslovakia "significant" since "this was the first occasion on which Germany had applied her shock tactics to the domination of non-Germans." He pointed out that "Germany had deliberately preferred naked force to the methods of consultation and discussion"—an attitude completely inconsistent with the Munich Agreement.[104] In a conversation with Henderson, Halifax made a similar statement: "The conclusion which everybody in this country and far outside it would draw must be that [the German government] had no great desire to establish good relations with this country, that they were prepared to disregard world opinion and were seeking to establish a position in which they could by force dominate Europe and if possible the world."[105] Cadogan noted that the invasion was an act confirming Vansittart's alarmist views and debunking Henderson's optimistic reports, calling the latter "completely bewitched by his German friends."[106] Halifax argued that while it was impossible to anticipate where Germany would attack next, "the real issue was Germany's attempt to obtain world domination" and it was "in the interest of all countries to resist. . . . Otherwise we might see one country after another absorbed by Germany."[107]

Chamberlain agreed, but with marked reluctance. On March 15, in a speech before the House of Commons, he defended the Munich Agreement. He declared that he would not be deflected from his efforts "to substitute the method of discussion for the method of force in the settlement of differences."[108] On March 17, however, he delivered a relatively hostile speech that he regarded as "a challenge to Germany on the issue [of] whether or not Germany intended to dominate Europe by force."[109] Chamberlain stated explicitly that Hitler's ultimate objectives would be revealed by Germany's next action:

> It followed that if Germany took another step in the direction of dominating Europe, she would be accepting the challenge. A German attempt to dominate Roumania [sic] was, therefore, more than a question [of] whether Germany would thereby improve her strategic position: it raised the whole question [of] whether Germany intended to obtain domination over the whole of South Eastern Europe.[110]

By March 18, he stated in a cabinet meeting that "he had now come definitely to the conclusion that Herr Hitler's attitude made it impossible to continue to negotiate on the old basis with the Nazi regime. . . . No reliance could be placed on any of the assurances given by the Nazi leaders." Chamberlain reiterated these assertions on March 19, declaring, "If Germany showed signs that she intended to proceed with her march for world domination, we must take steps to stop her by attacking her on two fronts."[111]

In sum, during the 1930s, British decision makers had determined early on that Hitler's intentions were revisionist. Less clear, and thus more open to disagreement, were the scope of his revisionist intentions, determination to pursue his revisionist goals, inclination to use military force, and desire to maintain peaceful relations with Britain. The pattern of convergence toward a more alarming interpretation of German intentions, in its broader sense, is theoretically consistent with all three competing theses. For example, Germany's early aggressive behavior inspired some change in British decision makers' assessments of its intentions. Still, the observed differences among the British decision makers pose important challenges to the three alternative theses. British decision makers frequently debated whether Germany's costly actions revealed its intentions. Eden and Chamberlain, for instance, drew significantly different inferences from German actions in the Rhineland about Hitler's intentions. There is also evidence to suggest that the process of updating views did not follow from changes in Germany's capabilities, doctrine, or costly actions but instead turned more on costless indicators. Finally, it seems that the most significant change in perceptions by British decision makers, apart perhaps from Chamberlain and Henderson, occurred *prior* to the invasion of Prague.

Reasoning about Nazi Germany's Intentions

British decision makers were rarely explicit about the indicators that informed their beliefs about German intentions.[112] Yet some patterns are apparent in the historical record. Germany's actions, both international and domestic, served as primary indicators. In early assessments, the militarization of German society caught the attention of British observers, as did Germany's withdrawal from binding international institutions and bilateral agreements as well as its diplomatic and military behavior in numerous crises. Germany's actions in the Rhineland and Czechoslovakia were also seen as crucial pieces of evidence by a range of British officials. The first revealed Hitler's untrustworthiness and his inclination to repudiate treaties. The second showed a flagrant reversal of his personal commitment to Chamberlain and a clear break from Nazi "racial" justifications for Germany's demands. British litmus tests were focused almost exclusively on changes in German behavior rather than in its military capabilities or doctrine.[113] While the evidence clearly shows the centrality of some behavioral signals, British decision makers varied in what actions they categorized as credible, and in the inferences they drew from them about intentions. As the subjective credibility hypothesis predicts, those decision makers who initially held beliefs that Germany's intentions were warlike tended to categorize more of Hitler's actions as malign indicators. As the vividness hypothesis posits, during critical times British decision makers relied on their personal impressions of German officials. Chamberlain, Eden, Halifax, Henderson, and Phipps tried to use personal diplomatic channels expressly to gauge the intentions of the German leadership. Their impressions at times contradicted the record of past German actions. Even so, some, especially Chamberlain and Henderson, chose to base their assessments on these positive impressions, especially—though not only—when these confirmed their already-existing beliefs. Contrary to the expectations of the behavior thesis, British decision makers throughout this period relied heavily on cheap talk: Hitler's writings, public statements, and private assurances were all taken as important indicators of Germany's plans by some members of the Foreign Office and cabinet, while other decision makers were skeptical about the credibility of these assurances. The behavior thesis cannot explain why certain people, notably Chamberlain and Henderson, regarded this costless information as reliable. Overall, then, the reasoning evidence strongly supports the subjective credibility and vividness hypotheses of the selective attention thesis, adequately supports the current actions hypothesis of the behavior thesis, and weakly supports the capabilities thesis, the strategic military doctrine thesis, and the past actions hypothesis of the behavior thesis.

Reasoning in Early Assessments

British decision makers looked to a variety of indicators for their early assessments of Germany's intentions. Several costly actions in 1934 signaled Germany's dissatisfaction with the status quo. Germany's withdrawal from the Disarmament Conference and League of Nations, its ten-year nonaggression pact with Poland, the buildup of its military forces far in excess of those permitted by the Treaty of Versailles, and the militarization of its society all raised the possibility that Germany might threaten Britain in the future.[114] As the DRC report of February 1934 noted, "It will, indeed, be impossible to have any confidence in German gestures to the outside world as long as every German act at home belies them."[115] Vansittart told cabinet members that the German threat to Britain could be seen in "a continuous and daily stream of German oration, broadcast, literature, and teaching."[116] Dozens of Foreign Office memorandums produced in 1934 reported on the militarization of German society and dominance of the Nazi Party.

None of these indicators revealed to British decision makers how determined Hitler was to pursue his revisionist objectives nor pointed to the scope of his objectives. To Phipps and Vansittart, though, public statements made by German officials provided important clues. In April 1934, for example, Vansittart urged British decision makers to "listen to the Germans themselves—beginning with the official ones," who were "giving us more specific warnings than ever we had before 1914." Like Phipps, Vansittart based his assessment of both the scope and manner of German expansionism on Hitler's own writings:

> Let us turn to the 1925 edition of "Mein Kampf." The foundation of Herr Hitler's faith is that man is a fighting animal. Pacifism is therefore the deadliest sin. The German race, had it been united in time, would now be master of the globe. The new Reich must therefore include all the Germans in Europe (This would mean not only Austria, but South Tyrole, Memel, Czechoslovakia, Eupen, Malmedy, Luxemburg, Slesvig, German Switzerland). . . . Germany's lost provinces can only be regained by force of arms. But Germany must not repeat the mistake of fighting all her enemies at once. She must single out the most dangerous in turn and attack him with all her forces.[117]

Vivid information and litmus tests played significant roles as well. Consistent with the vividness hypothesis, Eden inferred German intentions from his personal meetings with Hitler. Following their meeting in 1934, Eden expressed great skepticism that Hitler desired to engage in war, and as a result, he disbelieved that Germany's intentions writ large were hostile. His insights were directly drawn from his favorable impressions of the führer. In a letter to his wife, Eden confessed, "I rather liked him," and concluded that the führer did not want war. The personal bond of having served in World War I, Eden reported, brought the two together. "Poor man . . . he was badly gassed by us and blind in consequence for three months." Eden's positive meeting was described by Basil Newton, of the British Embassy in Berlin, as a "distinct success. Eden and Hitler liked one another and were impressed by each other's good intentions."[118] In contrast, Eden's unfavorable impressions from his second set of meetings with Hitler in March 1935 led him to question his earlier assumptions about Hitler's intentions and, on his return, advocate a different approach to dealing with Germany. Not just Hitler's statements but also his tone and behavior contributed to Eden's assessment. Eden noted Hitler's "whole tone and temper very different to a year ago, rearmed and rearming with the old Prussian spirit very much in evidence." British Foreign Office diplomat Lord William Strang, who attended both of Eden's meetings with Hitler, similarly remarked, "At the meeting in 1934 Hitler had been out to please. By the time that Sir John Simon and Mr. Eden visited him in 1935 his mood had changed. Though he still did not rave or rant, his manner was abrupt and his tone at times verging [sic] on the truculent while his voice took on a strident or guttural note and his gestures betrayed an ill-concealed exasperation."[119]

As soon as Germany's dissatisfaction with the status quo became clear, British decision makers employed a litmus test to probe the scope and nature of Germany's intentions. They were explicit about what they expected Germany to do in order to demonstrate its benign intentions, although different decision makers placed different weight on the importance of each action. Some believed that the signing of the Naval Agreement was considered a credible indicator in that "the Germans have, by the Naval Agreement, renounced all hope of recovering the colonies by force. They hope to recover them by working on public opinion in this country."[120] Other significant tests proposed by the British were Germany's return to the League of Nations and Disarmament Conference, its accession to an Eastern Pact of mutual assistance with its eastern neighbors, and a declaration that it respected Austrian integrity and independence.[121]

Germany's military buildup alone was insufficient to reveal Germany's long-term political intentions. For instance, in November 1934, Prime Minister MacDonald noted before the Foreign Policy Committee that "German rearmament was not merely of a defensive nature." To support this assessment, however, MacDonald referred not to the offensive nature of Germany's weapons but instead to Germany's domestic behavior. He observed that "evidence was accumulating from many quarters showing the German Government were training their people to march; that they were producing the physical means which would enable them to take offensive action against their neighbors, and that, hard though it was for us to say so, Germany had become war-minded again."[122] Foreign Secretary Simon stated in the cabinet that it was not Germany's current capabilities that constituted the threat but rather Hitler's "methods of appealing to his own people" that might "easily result in a menacing situation."[123] Simon similarly asserted in July 1934 that Hitler's ability to control the opposition in his country indicated that "Germany was getting back to the attitude of before 1914, with Prussian and military influence at the top."[124] Indicators that pointed to the militarization of German society, not simply changes in German military capabilities per se, set off alarm bells suggesting that Germany intended to revise the status quo.[125]

In sum, prior to 1936, British reasoning about German intentions drew from varied sources, including costly and noncostly German actions, public statements and writings, vivid information, and litmus tests. The support for the three competing theses is weak, while the evidence is stronger for the two hypotheses of the selective attention thesis, vividness and subjective credibility.

Costly Actions, Cheap Talk, and Reasoning during the Crisis Years

Evidence of British reasoning from 1936 to 1938 provides strong support for the selective attention thesis but only mixed support for the three alternative ones. During that period, British decision makers sought to assess how determined Hitler was to change the status quo in Central and Eastern Europe, and whether he would use military force to do so.

Some decision makers, such as Eden and Vansittart, regarded Hitler's reoccupation of the demilitarized zone in the Rhineland and withdrawal from the Locarno Treaty of 1925 as credible indications of hostile intentions. The reoccupation suggested that Hitler was willing to use Germany's military power to change the status quo; the withdrawal was "alarming because of the fresh confirmation which it affords of the scant respect paid by German Government to the sanctity of treaties."[126] Nevertheless, these actions allowed for a variety of interpretations about Hitler's intentions. Even Eden and Vansittart felt it was necessary to propose a new test of Germany's intentions:

> What he [Eden] would ask Hitler to say would be that, having stated that he wanted to negotiate a series of new pacts as a basis for peace in Europe, he would, as a proof of his intentions, withdraw all his forces from the Rhineland over and above the troops necessary for a symbolic occupation. In addition, pending the conclusion of the new pacts, for the regularization of the situation, he should not reinforce the "symbolic" troops, nor build fortifications in the demilitarized zone. . . . If Herr Hitler would do this he would be doing something to help us in working for a peaceful settlement.[127]

Eden relied greatly on personal observations from his visit to Germany in July. The degree of militarization of society and behavior of the Nazi Party convinced him that "time was very short."[128] Phipps, too, reached important conclusions about Germany's aims through personal insight. In April, he inferred that Germany's aims included expansion both to the West and East, partially due to the observation that Hitler's public "renunciation of Alsace-Lorraine has not reached the schools. On the contrary, they are teaching that it is as much 'terra irredenta' as any other German territories." Further, citing passages from the textbooks read by Hitler youth, Phipps observed that German students "have been told that war will occur in 1937 or 1938 and that Germany will regain her pre-war might and assimilate all Europe."[129] Eden took such observations seriously. He sent these reports to the cabinet with an accompanying note that Britain "should not be under any illusion as to the aims that underlie German policy." Germany, he wrote, "has no intention of respecting the integrity of her smaller neighbors, no matter what papers she may sign."[130]

British decision makers also focused, to a surprisingly large extent, on Germany's public declarations and the writings of its officials. This contrasts with the expectations of the behavior thesis and is consistent with the subjective credibility hypothesis of the selective attention thesis. Senior Foreign Office officials looked to Hitler's statements in *Mein Kampf* as evidence of Germany's intentions to expand in Central and Eastern Europe. The Foreign Office also voiced the logic that the public renunciation of any claim to Alsace-Lorraine should be viewed as credible: "Hitler has unilaterally and *publicly* renounced any claim to Alsace-Lorraine. If we except Schleswig, the only other possible territorial danger point in the West lies in the two small provinces of Eupen and Malmedy. If Hitler is really prepared similarly to abandon *publicly* all claim to these districts, such action may be very much to our advantage."[131]

Eden and members of the Foreign Office also monitored the evolution in tone and substance of speeches by German ministers between 1934 and 1936. They saw this progression as credible proof of a change in Germany's plans. Specifically, in a memo circulated to the cabinet in early 1936, Eden notes that up until January 1935, Hitler and his colleagues had repeatedly stated that Germany's intentions were merely to "live in peace and happiness." During this period, German officials renounced the use of military force to achieve their goals. Following the events of March 1935, however, "the German leaders began to speak somewhat different[ly]. They spoke of a necessity to revise international treaties, the right to 'take what they need for their existence,' and of Germany's intentions to 'recover her place in the sun.'" Eden added that German officials had become more confident in their country's military might and expressed their preference for Germany to "rely on guns" rather than on institutions such as the League of Nations. Eden also pointed out that declarations concerning Germany's desire for colonies, although not new, had became "more frequent" since March 1935.[132] British officials viewed the written word as credible, even though the inferences they drew about Germany's future plans were at times altogether different. In October 1936, Phipps concluded from a passage from *Mein Kampf* that "there is no reason to believe that Herr Hitler is now prepared to revise this dictum, to abandon his aspirations in Europe, and to be satisfied, even for a measurable period, with colonies." Moreover, Phipps saw Hitler's bellicose written and published words as more credible than his spoken assurances of peaceful intentions or his signature on the Naval Agreement.[133] Henderson cited *Mein Kampf* to conclude, by contrast, that Hitler viewed Russia, not Britain, as his primary enemy.[134] Even following the Anschluss, Henderson admonished other British officials that in trying to discern Hitler's future behavior they should look at Hitler's own statements and writings:

> What is the German programme in Czechoslovakia which Herr Hitler is determined to carry through with this characteristic obstinacy? The answer may be read clearly in his own statements and in the reports from the Embassy during the last five years. On every page of "Mein Kampf" Herr Hitler writes: "The German nation possesses no moral right to the development of colonial policy so long as it is not able to in-

clude its own sons in a common State." The first point of the Party programme reads: "We demand, on the ground of the right of self-determination of all peoples, the union of all Germans in a Greater Germany."[135]

Henderson concluded from this that "any material advance beyond those limits [of the Sudeten territories], except so far as colonies are concerned . . . is in fact, not only [merely] hypothetical but contrary to Hitler's own doctrine of nationality and of a pure German race."[136] Henderson admitted in this memo, however, that "during the last five years German intentions have often been deliberately veiled by a smoke screen, and there have been many statements which do not tally with those quoted above. But it may be regarded as certain that the latter represent the fixed line of German policy and the world will have no reason to express surprise when Herr Hitler . . . attempts to translate his words into deeds."[137]

Foreign Office officials discounted Germany's verbal assurances.[138] In his last memo as ambassador to Berlin, Phipps said that he was no longer certain that Germany would follow the line of policy outlined in *Mein Kampf*. Hitler's book had suggested that Germany should seek friendly relations with Britain, but as Phipps wrote, "some Nazi Party extremists have already come to the conclusion that the effort to reconcile England has failed and that the threat of force must be used to coerce her." Nevertheless, he concluded, "to abandon the principles laid down in *Mein Kampf* is a decision which will not be lightly taken [by Hitler] and for which, incidentally, the time is not yet ripe."[139]

In sum, the evidence suggests that the modest change that occurred in the minds of some British decision makers during 1936 is most consistent with the vividness and subjective credibility hypotheses. While the current actions hypothesis of the behavior thesis is partially consistent with this inference process, British decision makers diverged considerably from the predictions of this thesis. They repeatedly relied on noncostly actions, specifically German public declarations of intentions and reassurance, and vivid information to assess Germany's intentions. In debating the credibility of Germany's costly actions, they drew different inferences about Germany's future behavior.

The Role of Personal Impressions and the Reasoning of the Appeasers

As uncertainty about Hitler's intentions increased, British officials relied even more on personal interactions with German officials to gauge Germany's foreign policy. Chamberlain, Halifax, and Henderson, who were closely tied to appeasement policy, evaluated Germany's commitment to revisionist intentions in Europe and Hitler's inclination to use military force largely through vivid impressions along with other kinds of costless information.

A series of meetings between Halifax and a number of top German officials in November 1937 provided crucial pieces of vivid information about Germany's plans. Hitler, Göring, Goebbels, and Konstantin von Neurath were all present. Reporting afterward to the cabinet, Halifax repeatedly referred to his "impressions" of his three-hour-long meeting with Hitler. His conclusion was that "the Germans had no policy of immediate adventure. They were too busy building up their country, which was still in a state of revolution." Halifax drew these conclusions about Germany's future behavior not only from what Hitler or Göring had said but also from how they behaved during their meetings. In his diary, Halifax described his meeting with Hitler:

> I can quite see why he is a popular speaker. The play of emotions, sardonic humour, scorn, something almost wishful—is very rapid. But he struck me as very sincere, and as believing everything he said. . . . As to the political value of the talk, I am not disposed to rate this very high. . . . There was little or nothing he wanted from us and he felt time to be on his side.

Halifax also described his impressions of Göring at length. Göring had reassured Halifax that "under no circumstances shall we use force." Halifax was "immensely entertained" by meeting Göring. Even knowing about Göring's ruthless behavior during the 1934 political purge known as the Night of the Long Knives, Halifax found him an "attractive personality."[140] Halifax was similarly impressed with Goebbels: "I had expected to dislike him intensely—but didn't. I suppose it must be some moral defect in me." He noted, "I couldn't rather help out but like the little man."[141]

Chamberlain, like Halifax, believed that the meeting provided a good occasion to gauge the intentions of the German leadership. In a letter to his sister Ida, Chamberlain remarked that he saw Halifax's meetings as a form of the test that the British Cabinet had tried unsuccessfully to use earlier: "What I wanted Halifax to do was convince Hitler of our sincerity and to ascertain what objectives he had in mind and I think that both of these objects had been achieved." Chamberlain regarded the visit as "a great success" in which Hitler and Göring were reassuring in stating that they "had no desire or intention of making war." He thought that the British government should take this as correct at any rate for the present.[142] Both Halifax and Chamberlain stressed the former's personal impressions when discussing Germany's intentions with various French officials. Chamberlain said to the French prime minister, "The Chancellor had completely changed his view on this subject since Mein Kampf was written. The question of amour-propre played a great part in the German mind. Until Germany regained colonies, her self-respect would not be restored, and she would not enjoy full equality."[143]

Henderson, too, relied greatly on private assurances, personal impressions, and litmus tests. In November 1937, he concluded after one conversation with Göring that Germany had modified its attitude about Central and Eastern Europe and had become more "colonial minded." Henderson was "altogether convinced" that Britain should seize the opportunity to approach Germany again.[144] Halifax also was impressed with these assurances. He made the case to the French government that an agreement between Germany and Czechoslovakia was now attainable, based on the "solemn assurances" recently given by Göring to the Czechoslovakian minister in Berlin as well as in the private interviews between Henderson and German officials.[145] Henderson also used the Naval Agreement as a litmus test. He viewed Germany's adherence to the Naval Agreement, which placed Germany in an inferior position relative to Great Britain, as a credible indicator of Germany's intention to maintain good relations with Britain and that it would not want to risk war with it. In July 1938, Henderson stated, "I am very disinclined to believe in the reality of Germany's aggressive intentions unless and until she goes back on the Naval Agreement."[146]

Until the eve of the crisis over Czechoslovakia, Chamberlain relied greatly on private assurances and personal impressions to interpret Hitler's intentions. The prime minister genuinely believed that he could trust the latter's personal assurances that he had no intention of occupying the rest of Czechoslovakia if an agreement could be reached over the Sudeten territories. In a private letter to his sister, dated September 19, 1938, Chamberlain wrote, "I had established a certain confidence which was my aim and on my side and in spite of the hardness & ruthlessness I thought I saw in his face I got the impression that here was a man who could be relied upon when he had given his word."[147]

To the cabinet, Chamberlain claimed that he had established "some degree of personal influence over Herr Hitler." He "was satisfied that Herr Hitler would not go back on his word once he had given it" to Chamberlain. That discussion of Hitler's intentions was summarized as follows:

> The crucial question was whether Herr Hitler was speaking the truth when he said that he regarded the Sudeten question as a racial question which must be satisfied and that the object of his policy was racial unity and not the domination of Europe. . . . The Prime Minister believed that Herr Hitler was speaking the truth.[148]

Like Halifax, Chamberlain was attuned to Hitler's expressive signals, and perceived them as sincere and nonmanipulated. In a letter to his sister Hilda, Chamberlain commented, "Hitler's appearance and manner when I saw him appeared to show that the storm signals were up. . . . Yet, these appearances were deceptive. His opening sentences when we gathered round for our conference were so moderate and reasonable that I felt instant relief."[149] In a letter to Ida, he wrote, "I did not see any trace of insanity but occasionally he [Hitler] became very excited and poured out his indignation against the Czechs." Chamberlain claimed that "Hitler was at my disposal."[150] His strong belief in his ability to read Hitler's intentions was received with some skepticism by cabinet members, who saw Hitler's record of breaking promises as more credible evidence of his intentions. They specifically cited Hitler's past public declarations, following the incorporation of the Rhineland, that he no longer had any territorial ambitions as well as his previous promises not to utilize military force to achieve his political goals. Some ministers wanted to demand that Hitler signal his benign intentions through peaceful deeds. In addition to stating his views in the cabinet meeting, the secretary of the Board of Trade wrote a personal letter to Chamberlain, expressing doubts as to the prime minister's interpretation of Hitler's intentions. "I am afraid that I remain profoundly skeptical of Nazi promises and shall do so until I see peaceful words accompanied by peaceful deeds."[151] Even Halifax and Cadogan were surprised by Chamberlain's willingness to believe Hitler's assurances. They were concerned that the prime minister was staking too much on his instincts and impressions.

Some might argue that Chamberlain was suffering from a motivated bias: in seeking to avoid war, he saw what he wanted to see. From this perspective, invoking his personal impressions was instrumental, intended simply to convince members of his cabinet to support his policy; it did not genuinely represent his inference process. If Chamberlain had simply been driven by a motivated bias, though, he would have cited any and all confirming evidence such as the fact that Hitler's actions up to that point were consistent with only limited revisionist goals. But Chamberlain did not use that line of reasoning. Rather, he put a priority on his own observations as valid proof and explicitly linked his assessments of Hitler's sincerity primarily to his personal impressions.

From Limited to Unlimited Revisionism

Prior to December 1938, British officials saw Hitler as a dictator with limited expansionist aims who was willing to use any means—including military power—to achieve the return of Germans into the Reich. Nevertheless, as explained in more detail in chapter 6, beginning in spring 1938, intelligence reports suggested that Hitler would not limit his use of military force to the East. Indeed, it was now reported that Hitler was likely to attack in the West. The British Foreign Office had confidence in these sources.[152] Halifax found it "remarkable" that there was "one general tendency that was running through all the reports," and so it was "impossible to ignore them," especially "in view of the character and proved reliability of many of the informations."[153] Germany's actions corroborated the evidence presented in these intelligence reports. For example, Germany's renewed relations with Poland's foreign minister, Colonel Józef Beck—and the impression that the latter was no longer afraid of Hitler—provided an important clue that Germany was now aiming to attack in the West rather than in the East; so did Germany's support for Italy's claims against France.[154] Activity in Germany itself provided Foreign Office officials with further evidence that Hitler was contemplating an attack in the West, and soon. Vansittart reported that "railway repair shops in the West have been instructed urgently to repair all railway lines," while "old men and women were now being used in the armaments industry." This information helped to change his mind about the scope of Hitler's intentions. He now believed that "the odds are at even in regard to Hitler's attack falling first on the West."[155] Other domestic developments that were "symptomatic of [Hitler's] frame of mind" included "the persecution of the Jews and the press campaign against England."[156] Cadogan wrote in his diary that "Hitler's open atrocities against the Jews in the autumn of 1938 certainly deeply impressed Chamberlain. . . . Of course Halifax was no less shocked."[157]

Henderson did not share this sense of alarm, dismissing the intelligence information as exaggerated or altogether untrue. He reasoned that the Anschluss with Austria and incorporation of the Sudeten Germans could be explained by Hitler's limited objective of bringing all Germans into the Reich. Henderson invoked this line of reasoning in early March:

> It must not be forgotten that a principle of Nazism in its present form is purity of race. Austria and the Sudeten lands, where all were pure Germans, and where, even in the former case, the majority of the inhabitants were, in principle, in favour of Greater Germany, is one thing, and countries in which such a majority is non-existent quite another. One is too apt to believe that, because the one happened, the other must equally be contemplated.[158]

He continued as late as March 9, 1939, to rely on personal assurances given by Hitler. Henderson wrote to Halifax that "as an individual, he [Hitler] would be as likely to keep it [his word] as any other foreign statesman," and that Hitler "would probably honour his signature with Britain—as long as Britain remained even comparatively [well] disposed to Germany."[159] Chamberlain and Halifax were not certain what Hitler's next steps would be, but by that time they both advocated not reading too much into Hitler's public speeches and private assurances, concluding that these justified "no relaxation of our precautions."[160] Yet, as noted earlier, Chamberlain's actions in February and early March 1939 show that he still relied heavily on Henderson's reassuring reports, and was more optimistic than Halifax about the future of Anglo-German relations.

The German invasion of Czechoslovakia on March 15 debunked Henderson's Nazi racial-unification theory. Chamberlain and Halifax viewed this action as conclusive proof that Hitler's assurances could not be trusted. As Chamberlain put it on March 18, "No reliance could be placed on any of the assurances given by the Nazi leaders."[161] Even Henderson, who believed as late as March 9 that he could count on the Nazi dictator's word, admitted that this was no longer the case. A Foreign Office memo dated March 29, 1939, stated unequivocally that "the absorption of Czecho-Slovakia has clearly revealed Germany's intentions. It marks the first departure from the Nazi racial theory."[162]

In debates prior to the Prague invasion, decision makers who already saw Germany's intentions as hostile trusted intelligence reports that indicated a change in the scope of Germany's aspirations, while those who had not updated their beliefs prior to March 1939 continued to rely on personal assurances that

Germany's intentions were limited in scope. The German invasion of Czecho-slovakia, unlike any previous German actions, served as a credible behavioral signal even for those who put stock in private conversations. But this German invasion was informative, not only because of its cost or because it presumably allowed British decision makers to clearly distinguish what type of intentions Germany had. Perhaps more important, this action was both vivid and emo-tionally significant for Chamberlain and his supporters. Hitler had explicitly reneged on his personal assurances to Chamberlain, and in doing so humiliated the prime minister and gave others reason to doubt his judgment. Chamber-lain wrote to his sister Hilda, "As soon as I had time to think, I saw that it was impossible to deal with Hitler, after he had thrown all of his assurances to the wind."[163] After the invasion of Czechoslovakia, Chamberlain genuinely worried about the "possibility of a surprise air attack" on Britain. "With this fanatic, you can't exclude entirely the conception," and while "it all sounds fantastic and melodramatic . . . I cannot feel safe with Hitler."[164]

BRITISH POLICIES TOWARD NAZI GERMANY

The sources and implications of British policy during this period have received much attention from historians and political scientists.[165] This study does not seek to address the factors that shaped these policies but instead is designed to achieve a more limited objective. If the first two sections of this chapter ac-curately describe the beliefs of British decision makers about Nazi Germany's intentions, then the policies advocated by these decision makers should be con-sistent with these beliefs. If there is not consistency between statements about intentions and policies advocated by individuals, we should infer that the state-ments about intentions were either insincere or not important.

This chapter also seeks to review the evolution in British policies at the col-lective level. In this section, the aim is to probe whether there is a correlation between assessments of intentions and policies. The presence of such a correla-tion should not lead us to conclude that perceived intentions were the most important cause, nor that they constituted the only factor that shaped British policies. Rather, the presence of such a correlation allows us to be somewhat more confident in dismissing the null hypothesis—that perceptions of a foe's intentions do not affect policies toward it.[166]

The evidence reveals that, notwithstanding differences among key British decision makers in their perceptions about Germany's intentions, between 1934 and 1939 most advocated a mixture of policies aimed at achieving both a military and diplomatic balance against the German threat while attempting to reach an agreement with Germany. Balancing was initially manifested in a pol-icy of limited rearmament. This reflected Britain's growing recognition of Hitler's revisionist aims and the related expectation that the two countries would be at war within five to seven years. The policy usually labeled appeasement reflected Britain's primary objective of avoiding another war while it lacked sufficient resources to fight and win.[167] Appeasement was consistent with the dominant British perceptions of Hitler's intentions at the time: Hitler's limited objectives of conquering certain regions in Central and Eastern Europe were reasonable, if not morally right; there was uncertainty about Hitler's determination to pursue his aggressive designs; and Germany's expansionism stemmed largely from economic need. Appeasement included return of some of Germany's previously owned colonies in an effort to convince Hitler to give up his territorial ambitions in Central and Eastern Europe.

Yet cabinet members and the Foreign Office disagreed, especially following the German remilitarization of the Rhineland, about the rationale for pursing this dual policy, the relative emphasis that should be placed on rearmament versus diplomacy, and what this policy could realistically achieve. Those who held relatively more hawkish views about Germany, including Vansittart and some members of the Foreign Office, also believed that appeasement was necessary to buy time for Britain to rearm. They opted for a change in policy as soon as Britain was strong enough to challenge Germany effectively. They were skeptical that offering concessions to Germany would genuinely dissuade it from pursuing its revisionist aims and pushed for a stronger emphasis on increasing the pace of rearmament. Chamberlain, Halifax, and Henderson, who viewed Germany's intentions as relatively more benign, did not doubt that Germany was unsatisfied with the status quo, but held it possible to reach a genuine peace settlement with Germany by offering concessions. In their view, war was not inevitable. While believing in the importance of rearmament, these decision makers wished to avoid antagonizing Germany and sought to buy time to make Britain's deterrent threat more credible in the future.

Following the reports in November and December 1938 warning of an imminent German attack in the West, British officials increasingly doubted Chamberlain's optimism and seriously questioned his policies. The British decision to shift to deterrence and containment was reinforced by Hitler's military occupation of Prague in March 1939 along with the accompanying realization that Hitler's political intentions were unlimited in scope. Germany, they now believed, posed a direct threat to Great Britain's security. Moreover, the hope of achieving peace through diplomacy began to be seen as futile after Hitler explicitly reneged on his assurances. Finally, both the British public and COS had become more optimistic about the British prospects of countering as well as resisting Germany. A combination of increases in British arms production and potential weaknesses in the German air machine gave the military authorities more confidence in Britain's ability to withstand a German attack and prevail in a prolonged war.[168]

My argument is more or less consistent with what diplomatic historians call the revisionist interpretation of the sources of appeasement.[169] In this interpretation, British decision makers were aware of Hitler's expansionist intentions, but external conditions coupled with domestic, political, and economic constraints significantly limited British policy options. The revisionist stance is that Britain's appeasement policy endured as long as its leaders thought that Germany had only limited plans to revise the status quo in areas that were not deemed vital to the British Empire's security and as long as the balance of military power continued to constrain Britain's military options. Revisionist accounts that portray Chamberlain as certain and confident about the true nature and scope of Hitler's intentions are not, however, entirely correct. There is evidence that Chamberlain vacillated between interpretations. What is clear is that Chamberlain was highly influenced by vivid information and selectively attended more to information that did not cast doubt on the usefulness of his preferred policy. The egocentric bias, the salience-vividness bias, and Chamberlain's motivated defensive avoidance all pushed him to adhere to his existing assessment of Hitler's intentions even during late 1938. It took a significant and vivid external event as well as Halifax's alternative interpretation of Hitler's intentions to produce a change in Chamberlain's beliefs.[170] Chamberlain changed his policies with his beliefs; he explicitly linked this shift to the realization that Germany's actions in Czechoslovakia revealed that Hitler's intentions were indeed unlimited and his threat of using military force against Britain was real. But Chamberlain's new policy did not mean that he had ceased to believe he could dissuade Hitler from acting on his plans.

Limited Armament and the Origins of Appeasement (1934–35)

Britain embarked on a mixed policy of balancing and diplomacy in 1934. This policy was consistent with the widely held belief that Germany would soon act by force to revise the status quo. Fierce debates took place, though, about whether the German threat was greater than that posed by Japan to British colonies in Southeast Asia. The first DRC report in February 1934 and the Ministerial Committee on Disarmament agreed on the need to balance against the German threat. The preferred mode of balancing was internal, through military buildup, rather than external, via alliances. The cabinet accorded strategic and budgetary priority to the Royal Air Force in order to maintain parity with Germany in bombers, improve deterrence, and safeguard Britain from air attack if deterrence failed.[171] The policy known as limited liability, which discouraged the use of British troops on the European continent, was also pursued by the cabinet until March 1939. This policy reduced the need to devote resources to building up the army. This choice reflected the perception that Germany did not intend to strike in the West and that Britain would not be asked to repeat its

Great War continental commitment. It also reflected Britain's limited resources for rearmament.

Alongside British defense policies, government officials believed that Britain should actively pursue a policy of engagement with Germany. The cabinet felt it appropriate to start settlement negotiations with Germany because it believed Germany's revisionist intentions were limited. The objective was to persuade Germany to return to the League of Nations and Disarmament Conference, and dissuade it from pursuing its objectives in Europe by force. Appeasement was perceived as the only viable policy that could buy time for Britain to rearm while seeking to satisfy Germany's perceived grievances.

Although most British policy makers subscribed to a policy mixture of military balancing and diplomatic negotiations, divisions existed within both the cabinet and Foreign Office. Alarmed by Hitler's actions, tone, and behavior during their private meetings in March 1935, Eden became convinced that Germany's intentions were not reasonable, and that it could only be contained if Britain, France, and Italy presented a common front. Eden's recommendations to establish security agreements were supported by Vansittart and Ralph Wigram, the head of the Central Department in the Foreign Office. In contrast, most cabinet members, including Simon, Chamberlain, and Prime Minister MacDonald, thought that Hitler had fixed and limited goals. Short of war, they saw little point in attempting to deter or contain him through military alliances.[172] Early disagreements between Eden, then the lord privy seal, and Secretary of State Simon also surfaced during this period. Despite their differences, both sides believed that Britain should accelerate its rearmament programs in order to deter future German aggression.

During much of 1935, members of the Cabinet Committee agreed that some concessions to Germany were unavoidable, but they differed on the form, scope, and nature of them.[173] Their differences hinged on what they perceived as Germany's motivation for expansion. The Foreign Office offered two perspectives. First, Germany's expansionism really reflected "the lust for power of an essentially domineering and rapacious people." This perception assumed that Germany could overcome its economic crisis without expansion. Therefore, Britain should not only refrain from assisting Germany in any way but also "make it increasingly difficult for her to 'expand' at all, in the belief that we shall all have to fight her one day, and that any concessions will only weaken our position when the fatal day arrives." The second interpretation claimed that Nazism was merely a "symptom" of Germany's aspirations, whereas the cause was its economic distress.[174] Eden, who was more pessimistic about Hitler's intentions, asserted that Germany's economic situation might encourage Hitler to "launch his people on some foreign venture as the only means that remain to him to distract their attention from the failure of his policy at home." Britain should "assist Germany's economic recovery, thereby easing the strain upon the

German rulers, and making an outbreak less likely." Nevertheless, Eden recognized that no one could be certain that "if, in fact, we do make efforts to improve Germany's economic position, her rulers will not use the advantage they may gain in future prosecuting their rearmament and preparing their nation for war." Thus, he cautioned, no concessions should be given to Germany merely to keep it quiet. Significant and costly concessions should be made only as part of a final settlement that included further arms limitations along with Germany's return to the League of Nations.[175]

The Rhineland Crisis and Growing Skepticism in the Foreign Office

After the militarization of the Rhineland in March 1936, senior officials in the British Foreign Office debated Hitler's ultimate objectives. Sargent, Wigram, and Vansittart questioned the possibility of any comprehensive agreement with Germany short of accepting its hegemony in Europe. These assessments widened the gulf between the Foreign Office and Eden, on the one hand, and other members of the cabinet, on the other hand, about the prospects of reaching a settlement with Germany in the long run. Indeed, the British Cabinet was more inclined toward and even optimistic about seeking a comprehensive settlement with Germany after the Rhineland crisis. Efforts to establish better relations with Germany were fiercely debated within the Foreign Office. Sargent and Wigram argued that Britain had three policy choices. The first one was termed a "policy of drift": Britain would refrain from intervening in continental affairs and hope that a compromise could be reached with Germany, or that the threat of League sanctions would restrain Germany from further expansion. A second choice entailed the "encirclement of Germany" through a British alliance with France and Russia. The Foreign Office described these as options of "negation and despair." It favored the third option, "Britain's traditional policy of coming to terms with Germany." In this scenario, Britain would discourage German military expansion in Central and Eastern Europe, while allowing for German cultural and economic penetration in those regions. Britain would also return Germany's colonies. This approach, it was argued, would remove German grievances by peaceful means.

Nevertheless, members of the Foreign Office could not agree on the scope of the concessions Britain should offer. Edward Hallett Carr and Owen O'Malley of the Foreign Office urged allowing Germany a free hand in Central and Eastern Europe, since that area was not of vital interest for Great Britain. Sir Laurence Collier of the Foreign Office thought that Britain should not be drawn into any discussions of either colonial claims or German ambitions in Central and Eastern Europe; instead, he believed, the scope of proffered cooperation with Germany should be much narrower, to include only conversations about an air pact and other specific matters. Vansittart hoped that a colonial deal would convince Germany not to pursue expansion in Central and Eastern Europe. His writings suggest that he was pessimistic about the long-term success of a colonial deal, but believed that such concessions were needed in order for Britain to regain time to rearm. At the conclusion of one memo, he wrote,

> What we can do is to gain time, hoping against hope that there may be some change of heart or system in Germany, or—with better ground—that we and our League associates may within a respite of x years . . . grow to a position where defense can make attack too hopeless to be worthwhile. But no member of the League had embarked on this course in time, and Germany will be ready before the League. This is the whole essence of the future. That gap in time had somehow to be bridged. Would not a colonial restitution, as part of a reasonable and comprehensive settlement, reached in collaboration with France, and concluded at Geneva, justifiable in any case, be doubly so if no other bridging material can be devised?[176]

Eden echoed the rationale of his deputy Vansittart for a dual policy of rearmament and diplomacy.[177] Both pushed for presenting Hitler with a series of questions designed to discover German conditions for a settlement. But dissimilar views about the scope of Hitler's intentions at the time led to repeated disagreements between the foreign secretary and his deputy about the sincerity of Germany's assurances to limit its expansionist goals to Central and Eastern Europe. Eden and Vansittart both pressed for an accelerated rate of armament. As Eden explained, the only way to restrain Germany from pursuing its expansionist goals "will be that the collective strength of the potential victims should be twice as great in spirit and in truth, and not only on paper." Eden noted, "We are, in the matter of most armament and all munitions, already weaker than Germany. Moreover, owing to the late date of starting our own reequipment . . . , it is now inevitable that Germany will be ready for aggression long before we and the League can be ready for defense." Eden recommended that Britain hasten its rearmament while keeping open the option of reaching some modus vivendi with Germany.[178] The cabinet agreed with Eden. Britain's key strategic goal was to stall Germany until Britain could pose a credible deterrent threat or engage in a major war.

After the Rhineland crisis, Eden grew increasingly worried that coming to terms with Germany might be impossible. Both Eden and Vansittart became even more reluctant to endorse a policy of "economic and financial help" to Germany in return for a general political settlement. As Vansittart stated, "It is of the prepared war that I am afraid, & justifiably so, seeing that Germany has embarked on 4 such within living memory. Until we can be quite sure that she has forever renounced her evil ways, we must be extremely cautious in strengthening her at the expense of ourselves."[179] Eden nonetheless continued to assert that neither the British public nor its military capabilities supported a change in policy, and therefore Britain's policy "ought to be framed on the basis that we could not help Eastern Europe."[180] Amid reports that Germany was considering another adventure in Europe, cabinet members discussed what policies Britain could adopt. Some argued that Hitler had to be "told that there was a definite limit beyond which we could not allow him to go." The unfortunate fact that Britain at the time "had neither the means nor the heart" to stop Hitler put an end to that debate in the cabinet.[181] British decision makers realized that Germany's increased power and its behavior meant that a general European settlement was no longer attainable in Central and Eastern Europe.[182] In June, the Plymouth Committee on the Transfer of a Colonial Mandate to Germany presented its final report, opposing surrender of any colonies to Germany as part of a political settlement:

> In short, though Germany would undoubtedly obtain certain advantages from the return of her former colonies, these advantages would, we think, be much smaller than she expects. Her amour-propre, though perhaps not her ambitions, would be satisfied. . . . She might well advance reasons not very different from those now put forward to show that it was imperative for her, as a Great Power claiming a place in the sun, to have more, better and larger colonies.[183]

Toward the end of 1936, Vansittart and other Foreign Office officials believed that the Germans were not "necessarily going—and staying—East," and questioned the notion that war was avoidable. Vansittart concluded that an agreement with Germany was no longer possible unless Britain would accept German hegemony in Europe.[184] Eden had moved closer to Vansittart's position, but he had not definitively concluded that an agreement was "unobtainable." Rather, he maintained, we "must continue to aim at the general agreement. . . . It may be that it is unobtainable, but it is we who must prove this, by making an effort to obtain it."[185] Chamberlain and Halifax, however, continued to believe that an agreement with Germany could be achieved and war averted. Notwithstanding these differences, by the time Chamberlain became prime minister in May 1937, all key decision makers subscribed to the idea of a dual policy of rearmament and negotiation (appeasement). All shared some uncertainty about the scope of Germany's intentions and its level of commitment to changing the status quo. It is important not to exaggerate the differences between the policies that Chamberlain advocated and those advocated during this period by other members of his cabinet, including Eden and members of the Foreign Office. But differences did exist, and different decision makers saw the dual policy as motivated by and aimed at different goals. Those who were more concerned about Germany's determination to pursue its aggressive designs thought that the rationale for appeasement was mainly to buy time to rearm. Others who saw Germany's intentions as less alarming regarded this dual policy as justifiable on moral grounds or believed that these territories were not vital to British interests. Still others saw the dual policy as a pragmatic form of hedging that reflected uncertainty about how determined Hitler might be to execute his plans in Central and Eastern Europe.

Chamberlain's Version of Appeasement (May 1937–March 1939)

In mid-1937, the British Cabinet, now headed by Chamberlain, modified the existing policy by explicitly adopting the concept of limited liability, which rested on a narrow definition of British interests in Europe and a rejection of alliance diplomacy. This meant that Britain would rely primarily on internal balancing (especially building up the Royal Air Force) and would continue vigorous pursuit of an Anglo-German détente. The abandonment of alliance diplomacy angered those at the Foreign Office who believed that Britain must work closely with France and Russia to counter the growing Nazi threat. During this period the Foreign Office and particularly Eden grew increasingly disillusioned about the prospects of achieving a peace settlement in Europe. They were thus uneasy about Chamberlain's initiatives. Consequently, Chamberlain regarded Eden as an obstacle to an agreement with Germany and Italy, as the latter pushed to accelerate the pace of British rearmament and cautioned against acquiescing to the demands of any dictator. Chamberlain saw these views as too alarmist and rigid. In July, he recorded his frustrations with the Foreign Office: "I believe the double policy of rearmament and better relations with Germany and Italy will carry us safely through the danger period, if only the F.O. will play up."[186] Soon after, Eden resigned.

With the appointments of Henderson as ambassador to Berlin and Halifax as foreign secretary as well as the removal of Vansittart from the post of deputy, Chamberlain had a Foreign Office more in line with his approach. He wanted the Foreign Office to "hold the situation" until at least 1939. This implied maintaining sufficiently friendly relations with Germany to convince Hitler to refrain from using force in Central and Eastern Europe, while keeping Germany guessing about Britain's response to any German attack in the East.[187] Chamberlain's cabinet refused to provide any clear statements about Britain's interests in the region; it would not state what Britain would do in case of a German attack on either Austria or Czechoslovakia.[188] As Chamberlain explained to the French ministers, if Germany used only peaceful means to change the status quo in Austria and Czechoslovakia, the public in Britain would not support any forcible intervention on behalf of either country.[189] He concluded that his government "could certainly not go so far as to state what their [British] action would be in the event of an attack."[190] Some in the Foreign Office, including Strang, wanted Chamberlain to make a clearer deterrent warning to Germany against undertaking any military action to change the status quo. Others, like Henderson, believed that in order to improve relations with Germany and achieve tranquillity in Europe, "at a minimum" Britain had to "concede so far as Central and Eastern Europe is concerned."[191]

The Anschluss was not a defining moment for Chamberlain, yet the methods Germany used convinced him that rearmament and defensive alliances were necessary.

It is perfectly evident surely now that force is the only argument Germany under-
stands and the 'collective security' cannot offer any prospect of preventing such
events until it can show a visible force of overwhelming strength backed by the determination to use it. . . . Heaven knows I don't want to get back to alliances but if
Germany continues to behave as she has done lately she may drive us to it.[192]

There was nothing new in Chamberlain's policy decision following the Anschluss, because he believed that these actions revealed nothing new about
Germany's intentions. Chamberlain and Halifax still perceived Hitler's intentions as opportunistic and limited in scope. The COS reports circulated to the
cabinet on the eve of the crisis in March 1938, which made it abundantly apparent that Britain was simply unprepared for war, led Chamberlain and Halifax to
conclude that it was impossible for Britain to extend a commitment to defend
Czechoslovakia. Any deterrent threat would not be perceived as credible by
Germany. With the recognition that a confrontational policy was not yet possible as well as not necessarily needed, Chamberlain's cabinet continued to rely
on personal diplomacy.

The Turning Point (1939)

Intelligence reports in winter 1939 that Germany had made plans to attack
in the West generated uncertainty and confusion. Members of Chamberlain's
cabinet, including Halifax, increasingly began to suspect that Germany's intentions were unlimited in scope. The recognition grew that Britain had no choice
but to discard the limited liability stance that had characterized Chamberlain's
version of appeasement. Chamberlain's cabinet embraced a series of moves to
exhibit its continental commitment. In January, Chamberlain went to Rome to
try to disrupt Mussolini's attachment to Hitler, but this attempt at rapproche-
ment with Italy failed. The cabinet concluded that the British public would not
support granting Italy any significant concessions. Second, the cabinet decided
that any German invasion of Holland would automatically cause Britain to
declare war. Third, Britain announced in February that it was committed to
guaranteeing France's borders: any attack on France would automatically mean
war with Great Britain. Staff talks were also initiated between the British and
French military establishments. Fourth, the cabinet agreed to create a full-scale
continental army of thirty-two divisions. Four new battleships, a battle cruiser,
and an aircraft carrier were ordered to augment the five battleships and five
aircraft carriers already being built. All these steps were taken before Germany
invaded Czechoslovakia.

With the fall of Czechoslovakia came the realization that the worst-case scenario portrayed by various intelligence sources was taking shape. Chamberlain's
cabinet took additional steps to contain Germany. Shortly after the invasion,
Britain extended its guarantee of military support to Greece, Romania, and

Turkey. In April, the government announced a guarantee to defend Poland. It introduced a system of limited conscription to increase the size of the army—a move unprecedented in British peacetime history.[193] On August 25, the British Parliament ratified an Anglo-Polish mutual defense treaty with the hope that this would dissuade Hitler from executing his expansionist objectives.

The invasion of Czechoslovakia united the Foreign Office. Those who had previously sympathized with Germany's demand to bring all Germans back into the Reich now believed that Germany had more grandiose intentions. They too began to urge the British Cabinet to abandon active appeasement. A passage from Cadogan's diary dated March 20, 1939, spells out the rationale for a shift in policy:

> These are awful days. The crisis is worse, really, than last September, but the public don't [sic] know it. It's more critical and more imminent, and more acute. And I'm afraid we have reached the crossroads. I always said that, as long as Hitler could pretend he was incorporating Germans in the Reich, we could pretend that he had a case. If he proceeded to gobble up other nationalities, that would be the time to call "Halt!" That time has come.[194]

The link between a revised assessment of Germany's intentions following its actions in Czechoslovakia and the adoption of a harder-line policy was expressed by Chamberlain at a cabinet meeting on March 18:

> The Prime Minister said that up till a week ago we had proceeded on the assumption that we should be able to continue our policy of getting on to better terms with the Dictator Powers, and that although those powers had aims, those aims were limited. We had all along had at the back of our minds the reservation that this might not prove to be the case, but we had felt that it was right to try out the possibilities of that course.

> On the previous Wednesday, German actions in Czechoslovakia had only just taken place. He [Chamberlain] had now come definitely to the conclusion that Herr Hitler's attitude made it impossible to continue to negotiate on the old basis with the Nazi regime. This did not mean that negotiations with the German people were impossible. No reliance could be placed on any of the assurances given by the Nazi leaders.[195]

The process of shifting the emphasis in Britain's policy away from appeasement was not an easy one for Chamberlain. During late 1938, Chamberlain had questioned the intelligence that warned of a possible German attack on the West. He clearly preferred the reassuring reports from Henderson. Even after the Prague invasion, his change in policy required significant persuasion. Halifax, his close confidant, had adopted an alternative interpretation of Hitler's intentions since the Godesberg meeting, and helped Chamberlain recognize the invasion of Prague as a significant change in Germany's behavior and intentions.[196] As biographer Adam Roberts notes, "It is inconceivable that a guarantee would have been given to Poland had Halifax not been Foreign Secretary." Without Halifax's input, the prime minister "could have been able to view Prague as a setback instead of being forced to see it as a major reversal."[197] A recent historiography of Chamberlain argued that the Prague invasion signified a watershed for Chamberlain only in terms of his method and approach to dealing with Hitler rather than in his broader strategic conception. Those in his circle reported that "his heart is not really in this new policy [the Polish guarantee] which has been forced upon him by Hitler." There is evidence to suggest that Chamberlain continued to work toward a peaceful settlement between Germany and Poland. Yet Chamberlain's recognition that Hitler's intentions might be unlimited and extend to an attack on Britain were matched by a significant shift toward a clear policy of containment, although the shift did not necessarily mean that diplomacy was abandoned altogether.[198] The policy change was made possible by several other factors as well, including a COS report that was more optimistic about the British military's capacity to challenge Germany effectively along with British public opinion favoring a bold, determined policy to stop Hitler.[199]

CONCLUSION

In light of the evidence presented in this chapter, the support for the capabilities, military doctrine, and behavior theses is mixed. Solid support exists for the current actions hypothesis of the behavior thesis, but only to the extent that certain costly German actions were significant in shaping the views of *some* decision makers. These costly actions included Germany's withdrawal from the League of Nations and Disarmament Conference in 1934, and its actions in a series of crises over the Rhineland, Austria, the Sudetenland, and Czechoslovakia. Domestic behavior such as the militarization of German society also drew political attention. There is little support for the strategic military doctrine thesis, capabilities thesis, or past actions hypothesis of the behavior thesis. This is not to say that Germany's prior military capabilities, doctrine, or actions during the First World War were unimportant in the eyes of British decision makers but instead that these were not the primary indicators that British decision makers used to assess Hitler's intentions. British decision makers rarely, if ever, discussed Germany's military doctrine in their deliberations about Germany's political intentions. To be sure, Germany's rearmament program played a crucial role in alerting British decision makers to the rising threat and dictating the menu of policy options available. As in Cold War cases, trends in Germany's military buildup were not used as the primary indicator from which inferences about Germany's political intentions were made.

The historical evidence provides strong support for the selective attention thesis and significant evidence against the three competing theses. The ways in which British decision makers understood German intentions were shaped by their theories, expectations, and needs. There was little agreement on what constituted a credible indicator of German intentions. Those who initially held more hawkish views of Germany's intentions also considered much of its costly behavior as giving informative indicators of hostility. By contrast, those who saw Germany's intentions as less hostile continued to dismiss even those costly actions that might have revealed its expansionist intentions.

Moreover, decision makers relied to a substantial degree on costless information. Vivid indicators were seen as particularly informative. In several instances, specifically on the eve of the Munich Agreement, Chamberlain clearly ignored the history of Germany's past actions and instead based his judgment of Hitler's intentions on evidence he gleaned from three personal interactions with Hitler. This information was far from costly, but it was vivid and hence salient. Chamberlain used it as a credible indicator of Hitler's political intentions. The strongest evidence in support of this assertion can be found in Chamberlain's public and private reasoning during the crises, especially during the German invasion of Czechoslovakia. Nor was Chamberlain alone in relying on his personal impressions and private assurances. Eden, Halifax, and Henderson also drew important inferences from their interactions with German officials. Simply put, private assurances and personal impressions had powerful influences on the reasoning of nearly all the British decision makers. This chapter thus offers strong support in favor of both the subjective credibility and vividness hypotheses derived from the selective attention thesis.

***

The next chapter examines the analytic lenses through which the British intelligence community evaluated Nazi Germany's intentions during the same time period.

CHAPTER 4

The British Intelligence Community's Assessments of Nazi Germany's Intentions

This chapter reviews assessments of the British intelligence community about the nature and scope of Germany's foreign policy plans along with its perceptions of Germany's willingness to use military force. The purpose here is to track the evolution in the stated beliefs of Britain's intelligence community about Germany's intentions and evaluate how well the predictions of the theses set forth in chapter 2 fit the evolution in perceived intentions. This chapter also describes the reasoning behind the intelligence community's conclusions. As we will see, the evolution of the British intelligence community's collective assessments is most consistent with the predictions of the capabilities thesis and organizational expertise hypothesis of the selective attention thesis.

The analysis is based largely on primary documents from the British National Archives. It draws on all the available intelligence reports circulated to the cabinet during the period under study as well as reports related to the issue of intentions released by the most significant COS committees. The main focus is on the coordinated COS reports and memorandums, because these represent the integrated analysis of all three military service intelligence agencies: army intelligence, air intelligence, and navy intelligence.[1] As such, they provide a guide to the evolution of perceptions of the German threat by the British intelligence community.[2]

Concentrating on COS reports presents an important limitation to the analysis of German political intentions due to the division within the British system between military and political intelligence. Because the Foreign Office (and Secret Intelligence Service [SIS] under its control) had a monopoly on political intelligence, such intelligence was separated from the general run of military and economic intelligence, and generally was not integrated into the assessment of the community as a whole. The Foreign Office jealously guarded its information and was typically unwilling to share with the other intelligence organizations. Until March 1939, the COS simply incorporated a summary of the world situation provided by the Foreign Office into its Appreciation Reports. With the growing realization of the need for coordination beyond the service departments in 1938, the Foreign Office became more involved in drafting the Strategic Appreciation Reports.[3] This division of labor within the British intelligence community complicates the analysis of COS assessments of political and military intelligence. Nevertheless, several COS reports did include conclusions and explanations about Germany's foreign policy plans. They provide some clues as to how German political intentions were inferred. The Joint Planning Subcommittee (CAB 55) and Joint Intelligence Subcommittee (CAB 56) of the COS Committee circulated various intelligence reports to the cabinet. The Foreign Office's SIS reported on Hitler's political plans and intentions to use force, as did classified documents written by British military attachés in Berlin.[4] Taken together, these sources allow us to draw tentative conclusions about the British intelligence community's inference process on Germany's intentions.

Statements and Reasoning about Germany's Intentions

Benign Assessments (1934–35)

The COS Annual Review of 1933 asserted that Germany intended to "revis[e] ... the peace treaties" that ended World War I, based on reports circulated by the Foreign Office. Specifically, the COS envisioned three stages in the process by which Germany would seek to obtain this objective:

> The first stage in the policy which has been consistently pursued by Germany was the elimination of the most objectionable clauses of the peace treaties—reparations and military occupation. This stage has been completed. The second stage is rearmament and the recognition of the German demand for equality in armament is undoubtedly a step towards the completion of this stage. The first two stages are stepping stones to the third—the revision of frontiers, particularly in Eastern Europe, and including, to go by recent events, some kind of German control, direct or indirect, over Austria. It is even possible that these may lead to a final stage, an attempt to recover the Colonial Empire.[5]

The COS asserted that the immediate danger from Germany was to Central and Eastern Europe. This conclusion was justified by three arguments. First, consistent with the capabilities thesis and numerical preponderance hypothesis, the COS did not believe that Germany would launch an attack that would risk British involvement as long as the balance of military power was not in its favor. Second, consistent with the past actions hypothesis and capabilities thesis, the COS claimed that changes in France's defenses, in combination with lessons Germany had presumably learned from the First World War, should discourage a German attack on the West. Specifically:

The French . . . have rendered their eastern frontier immeasurably stronger than in 1914 and probably impregnable to land attack except by extensive and elaborate siege operations. It is inconceivable that the Germans with their bitter experiences of the last war would be so foolish as again to invade France and to seek a solution in a rapid knock-out blow.

Third, the COS invoked Hitler's public statements, arguing that "to attack France for a purely sentimental reason would be foolish. What Germany needs is an increase in territory in Europe. Such an increase can only be gained in the East." In sum, British intelligence believed that Germany would not risk escalating tensions to the point of war when it was not militarily ready to take the offensive. The working assumption during this period was that it would take Germany at least five more years of rearming before it could menace Britain. In 1934, the COS predicted that once fully rearmed, "Germany will, under the guise of moderation, continue her secret preparations during the period of respite, and until she feels strong enough to throw off the mask and to attain her ends in a war of offence in the East, combined, if necessary, with a defensive in the West."[6]

The next COS Annual Review, released a year and a half later in April 1935, focused on the military expansion of Germany. Germany's claim that it had already achieved parity with Britain in the air was a cause of much concern among British decision makers. The COS, however, reflected the opinion voiced by the air minister, who saw "no grounds whatsoever for anything in the nature of panic." Based on intelligence reports from the three military services, the COS drafted a Strategic Appreciation report, "Defense Plans for the Event of War against Germany," which concluded that the pace of German rearmament was moderate. It did not consider the German armed forces to be designed as a war machine for hegemonic purposes in the West. The COS instead envisioned scenarios in which Germany was the aggressor in a one-front war against the combination of Belgium, Britain, France, and possibly Holland. The COS did little to try to assess German intentions. Indeed, even the worst-case scenario—which included a German drive through the Low Countries followed by an air offensive against Britain—was "based more on common sense and the financial requirements of the British services, than on any analysis of German intentions."[7] The COS saw the likelihood of war through the prism of calculations of military capabilities, which at the time indicated Allied superiority over Germany. The 1935 COS report estimated that Germany could probably not defeat Britain militarily by 1939 due to the slow pace of German rearmament. The Annual Review concluded, therefore, that Germany was unlikely to risk war in 1939 (or earlier).[8]

Imagining War (1936–37)

British assessments of Germany's capabilities and its military intentions changed significantly in fall 1936. This change resulted primarily from the realization—

even overestimation—of the pace, scope, and offensive nature of Germany's military buildup. The evidence lends support to the capabilities thesis and selective attention theory's organizational expertise hypothesis. Throughout this period, the COS reasoned that Germany's decision about whether and when to engage in armed conflict with Britain would be based on its calculations of its military readiness.

In July 1936, the Joint Planning Subcommittee of the COS Committee prepared a strategic review of the world situation. According to this report, the COS believed that acute nationalist feelings in Central and Eastern Europe along with Germany's desire for economic independence were most relevant to the situation in Austria, Czechoslovakia, and Lithuania. The report reflected the dominant belief that Germany intended to revise the status quo, although it did not specify whether the country was committed to expansionism or whether instead its objectives beyond Austria were merely opportunistic in nature. Calculations of relative capabilities were perceived as the single most significant factor in determining the scope and timing of German expansion efforts. The report concluded that "while the spirit which at present actuates German policy continues, the danger that German ambition for expansion will cause war in Europe will endure. *As Germany's rearmament progresses and she becomes more ready for war, the danger of conflict increases*."[9]

These conclusions were reiterated in another report released by the COS a few months later.[10] It asserted that Germany's political intentions were revisionist, though with limited aims: "Germany's foreign policy aims at the inclusion in the Reich of all German peoples and the acquisition of new territory for her expanding population. It seeks to acquire new sources of foodstuffs and raw materials and an outlet for German manufactures, particularly in Eastern Europe and the former German colonies." This COS report argued that Germany had "renounced all intention of expansion westward." Still, it cautioned that this could change due to German fears about encirclement. The Franco-Soviet Pact of 1935 and possible French intervention in the event of German expansion in Central and Eastern Europe reinforced this fear. The report stated unequivocally that Hitler was prepared to use his growing military power to achieve his objectives: "Germany aims at achieving a dominant position in Europe based on her military strength." Detailing the significant expansion of Germany's military buildup, the report concluded that "Germany is doing everything possible to prepare the nation to withstand the strain of a prolonged war of national effort, should her attempt to gain an early favorable decision, at which she aims, fail."[11]

The second Strategic Appreciation report was released around the same time. Wark described this October 1936 report as "the closest thing to an essay in defeatism ever produced by the military authorities during this period."[12] It drew on a painful reevaluation of German military strength concluded by the three military services and warned of the possibility of a successful German aerial knockout blow against Britain as early as 1939. Despite an alarming increase in Germany's military capabilities the COS continued to claim that a war with Germany would not break out earlier than 1939, based on calculations about the future rate of Germany's military buildup. This was premised on the assumption that "Germany would not initiate a war unless her responsible statesmen believed that she would win." The COS presented the following scenario: "it should be assumed that our forces might have to be employed toward the end of 1939 against Germany in the state of war preparedness which she is likely to reach by that date. Our terms of reference also make it clear that we are to consider a war arising from German aggression." The COS was in no position to outline the political circumstances that could eventually lead to war. It did portray a worst-case scenario: "Germany's resources would enable her to carry out an air offensive against Great Britain accompanied, simultaneously, by a land offensive against France."[13] But the COS still assumed that Germany would plan for a quick victory.[14] Any prewar German advantage could be neutralized by an effective Allied naval blockade.[15]

The "intensive character" and "vast extent" of Germany's rearmament efforts, coupled with its reoccupation of the Rhineland, emerged in the COS revision of its "Review of Imperial Defence" from late 1936. The amended report, released in February 1937, basically repeated the conclusions from the previous year. Yet the COS expressed doubt that Germany could achieve the territorial expansion it sought in Europe through peaceful means.[16] A May 1937 report, which did not elaborate on Germany's foreign policy aims, contained an important section on the likelihood of war. It predicted that Germany would not be able to mobilize more divisions than France by 1939, but would have air superiority as early as 1937. Britain's naval superiority meant that London could apply economic pressure on Germany to dissuade it from embarking on war. With respect to industrial output for armament, the report claimed that Germany's industrial strength relative to its potential adversaries' would be greatest in 1937, but the COS concluded that Germany would not go to war in 1937 because it would not yet be ready to do so militarily.[17] This report, like previous ones, explicitly used indicators that are associated with the capabilities thesis to support its conclusion:

Germany is unlikely to plan to go to war in 1937 since at that time her military forces will be far from completely ready. If she were faced by a sudden emergency in which the possibility of going to war on her western frontier had seriously to be considered, her military position on land would be a factor tending strongly to dissuade, whereas her military position in the air and in relation to industry would be factors which might encourage her. Economically, however, she might seek a quick decision; and so long as she expects to meet the combined strength of France and Great Britain she must doubt whether her advantage in air power will be sufficient to promise a quick result. We may certainly be confident that unless assured of whole-hearted co-operation on the part of Italy, Germany would have no military justification for war.[18]

The 1937 memos of the British military attaché in Berlin similarly derived predictions about the German military's willingness to engage in war from calculations of the military balance, but pointed out that the German Nazi Party and German General Staff had different perspectives on the military balance. The attaché reported that Hitler placed "a very low estimate" on the present capacity of other European nations to mobilize against Germany, yet noted that the General Staff was far less optimistic.[19] At the time, the general consensus in Britain was that the General Staff was about "to regain the great power which it held before the war, and to assume a position of importance in the State vis-à-vis the Nazi Party." The War Office estimated that its "present tendency is to insist on sufficient time to establish the army and air force as a dominating factor before embarking upon any foreign adventures at the behest of individuals or of the Nazi Party."[20]

As 1937 came to an end, the COS released a report comparing the forces of the Allies with those of Germany and Italy. In estimating whether Germany would initiate war in early 1938, the report—written in November 1937—essentially repeated the conclusion that the COS had reached in its February 1937 report. The rationale that the COS provided was similar as well: the German General Staff's perception of the anticipated balance of capabilities would be the dominant factor in Germany's decision about whether and when to go to war. The COS report concluded, "The German General Staff are unlikely to consider that the strength of the German Army is sufficient to justify the prosecution of a land offensive before 1939–40. Further, they do not think that the Army will have attained its maximum efficiency until that date."[21]

The COS Estimates and Two Crises over Czechoslovakia (1938)

After the crisis over the Sudetenland in March, and again in September 1938, the COS prepared urgent updated assessments. Faced with the possibility of war with Germany, the COS's working assumption was that Hitler intended to revise the status quo within a limited scope. The SIS's reports indicated that German leaders did not intend to engage in war with either Czechoslovakia or Britain, nor did they seek to use the Sudeten crisis for ulterior ends. Nevertheless, both German moderates and extremists sought to make use of this crisis for their own purposes. They were willing, said the British reports, to "solve the issue by forcing a general crisis which might produce a general war" if negotiations failed.[22]

The COS report made it clear that Britain's military was in no position to act to save Czechoslovakia.[23] As cabinet discussions indicated, the COS's highly pessimistic reading of the European military balance in 1938 shaped the government's reaction to the Czechoslovakian crisis. In particular, as Paul Kennedy correctly points out, "the only consideration of whether it might be better to fight immediately or later . . . was couched (by General Ismay) overwhelmingly in terms of *air* strength."[24] The COS assessment that Britain could do little militarily to help Czechoslovakia was used strategically by the prime minister to counter those within the cabinet who wanted to stand firm. There is no evidence, however, that Chamberlain intentionally manipulated British intelligence to reach these conclusions.[25]

As for Germany's military intentions, COS reports concluded with great certainty that Germany planned to win a quick offensive war that included delivering an aerial knockout blow against Britain. Assessments about the timing of such a war were still difficult to gauge. This was partly due to changing estimates about when the German military would be at its highest state of readiness and would have the greatest advantage over the Allies. In April 1938, the COS estimated that as Germany aimed "to be able to mobilize on the outbreak of war the largest Army which the economy and man power of the nation are capable of sustaining," it would not be prepared for war before January 1942.[26] This estimate was based on Germany's steady rate of military growth. Then, in November 1938, the British military attaché in Berlin, Noel Mason-Macfarlane, predicted that Germany might go to war as early as fall 1939:

> The German army was more formidable and in a far better position to go to war last September [1938] than it is now. Similarly, it will again work up to a peak of efficiency in the autumn of 1939, but this will again be followed by another period when war would take it at a considerable disadvantage. . . . If we exclude the present winter, it is clear that the worst moment for war from the point of view of the German army will be the winter period 1939–40. Thereafter there will be no more abnormally unfavorable periods.[27]

A month later, Mason-Macfarlane argued that "from the technical point of view it is certain that the [German] army is unlikely to encourage any policy likely to involve it in hostilities before June at the earliest." He nonetheless cautioned that the German Army High Command was "extremely unlikely" to hold to this assessment in "opposition to an inspired führer, who has so far proved them wrong in every major situation where their opinions have clashed." Mason-Macfarlane was "nearly certain" that Hitler was contemplating taking military action in 1939. He "placed the odds on action in the East [specifically, against Czechoslovakia, Poland, and the Ukraine] as against action in the West at about 10 to 1."[28]

War Scares and a Lull (November 1938–February 1939)

During the three months after Germany signed the Munich Agreement, the Foreign Office's SIS continued to receive alarming intelligence from secret sources. Informants pointed to Hitler's disgruntled mood and warned of his intention to renege on his assurances at Munich.[29] The reports concluded that Hitler was "barely sane, consumed by an intense hatred of this country, and capable both of ordering an immediate aerial attack on any European country and of having his command instantly obeyed." The British government considered these sources highly credible because they had previously forecast Hitler's policy quite accurately during the Munich crisis.[30] In addition, Wark reports that sometime after Munich, cabinet members received signal intelligence, obtained from Security Service MI5 wiretaps in the German Embassy in London, which contained vivid "disobliging remarks about British statecraft and Chamberlain himself."[31]

The war scare of late 1938 evolved in two stages. First, in November and December, British intelligence expected German expansion moves toward the East. In January 1939, more alarmingly, intelligence pointed to an attack in the West.[32]

The Military Intelligence Directorate of the War Office largely agreed with these assessments. On January 17, British military intelligence reflected the growing understanding that Hitler was seeking world domination, but it was still convinced that Germany would only fight a short war if it had "the certainty of a quick success." This implied that Germany would target countries like Poland, Romania, or the Ukraine, which could provide Hitler with the economic resources he needed to solve his domestic economic crisis. Military intelligence was unable to assess whether Hitler would act if he risked "a dangerous provocation of the Western Powers."[33] On January 19, however, the SIS circulated a more troubling report indicating that the possibility of a German attack on the West should now be considered, and warning that a direct attack on Britain and France in the upcoming few weeks or months was a real possibility. The report noted that Hitler appeared to have embraced the methods of violent action in his foreign policy, was undoubtedly anti-British, and no longer felt bound by the Munich Agreement.[34]

Vansittart's intelligence reports, which drew on a wide variety of contacts, confirmed that Germany was preparing for an imminent war no later than spring 1939. Depicting Hitler as a decided extremist who could "not be fought successfully by gentlemanly weapons," these reports received much attention. They were circulated among members of the Foreign Office Committee, together with other SIS reports.[35] Still, during the month of February, other information from secret sources suggested that Hitler had abandoned the idea of precipitating an immediate crisis. Chamberlain therefore disregarded Vansittart's warning of an imminent German plan to occupy the rest of Czechoslovakia.[36]

Overall, British political intelligence reports painted a picture of long-term German intentions to dominate Europe by force. These reports relied mainly on clandestine agents and sources that the British perceived as credible, which vividly depicted Hitler's mood, state of mind, characteristics, behavior, and private conversations.[37] Perhaps the vividness of these reports, as opposed to those strategic assessments that often provided statistical data on force comparison, can explain why they achieved so much attention within the cabinet during that period. The set of indicators that these SIS reports relied on is not consistent with the capabilities thesis, organizational expertise hypothesis, or strategic military doctrine thesis. But the fact that this analysis was provided by one intelligence agency, the SIS, and was not part of the coordinated estimates puts it outside the scope of this study.

Surge of Optimism (February 1939)

By 1939, war seemed inevitable. The COS was finally optimistic about Britain's readiness for war with Germany. Nevertheless, as shown in chapter 2, British intelligence continued to believe that Germany's military arsenal was increasing dramatically, and a numerical reading of the balance of power indicated that the balance of forces had worsened for Britain: Germany would maintain military superiority in the immediate future. In early 1939, though, the intelligence services placed a greater emphasis on qualitative factors such as population attitudes, air defense, and latent economic power.[38] The COS reports pointed to Germany's poor morale and economic vulnerability, especially if there were a British blockade. The COS conveyed a more confident tone about Britain's own financial reserves, control of sea routes, aerial defenses, and public morale.[39] This is not to say that the British intelligence community abandoned its earlier quantitative practices. As Kennedy wrote, the 1939 Strategic Appreciation "still showed a strong tendency to count numbers rather than ask questions about the *range* of German bombers, or their *capacity* to find targets in cloudy conditions." The notion, he explained, that the German Luftwaffe's true mission was strategic bombing against Britain led to "anxious efforts of the Air intelligence directorate to get accurate figures of German production totals." This turned "much of the Air Staff's assessment in[to] 'bean counting,' which included preposterous and arcane calculations."[40] Trends in the numerical balance of power continued to guide British intelligence assessments of Germany's military intentions and the probability of an Allied victory.

Moreover, although more optimistic in tone, the 1939 strategic assessment did not lead to a more benign reading of Germany's political intentions. In fact, in its reports, the COS did not provide a meaningful reassessment of Hitler's political intentions and state of mind—an evaluation thought to be the Foreign Office's responsibility.[41] Other reports provide some clues about the COS's political assessments. In January 1939, the COS had already realized the gravity of the situation in Europe: when it reassessed the consequences of a transfer of colonies to Germany, it clearly viewed this proposal with disfavor. Given the growing sense that Germany's ambitions were unlimited, and the "force and determination with which Germany has carried through her programme in Europe," the COS insisted that no British or French colonies in Africa should be returned to Germany. "In light of our experience of German methods since 1936, there is more danger of her exploiting any territory she might be given in Africa for military purposes than our predecessors considered probable in 1936."[42] The COS conceded that this recommendation was inconsistent with its conclusions from 1936, which suggested that the COS had now become concerned with German aims beyond Central and Eastern Europe. Yet the documents do not offer a clear indication how much the COS had updated its views of Germany's political intentions prior to the invasion of Czechoslovakia.

Overall, however, the COS grew more confident about the potential of the Allies for success in a war against Germany. This was due to assessments of the domestic situation in Germany, strain of its rearmament program, dispersal of forces that a two-front war would require, and anticipated increase in Britain's capabilities.[43] The line of reasoning indicated by the capabilities thesis played a significant role in the COS assessments of when Germany would fight a war. For example, military attaché Mason-Macfarlane argued that the German Army's readiness would determine Germany's aggressiveness. As Germany was not yet militarily prepared to enter a major war with Britain, Mason-Macfarlane urged the latter to consider a preventive war. He reasoned that in the immediate aftermath of the invasion of Czechoslovakia, the German Army was still dispersed, "extremely unsound," and had yet to take advantage of Czechoslovakian weaponry. Mason-Macfarlane believed that Britain should establish an eastern front that would enable it to employ an effective economic blockade against Germany that could, he argued, "bring Germany quickly to heel." He warned that by waiting until fall 1939, Germany would be better able, militarily at least, to wage a successful war.[44] Though neither the COS nor Chamberlain's cabinet endorsed Mason-Macfarlane's call for a preventive war, his perception of the German Army's state of readiness was shared by members of the British intelligence community. It is difficult to judge whether and to what extent the COS changed its estimates about Germany's political intentions as a result of the German invasion of Czechoslovakia in March 1939.[45] The Foreign Office had by this time become the principal author of the political section in the COS Strategic Appreciation reports. As a result, these reports reflect the Foreign Office's views rather than those of the military intelligence services.

CONCLUSION

The structure of the British intelligence community during the interwar period, making the Foreign Office the principal provider of political intelligence, prevents me from reaching definite conclusions about COS's inferences concerning Hitler's long-term political intentions.[48] With this in mind, the available evidence indicates that throughout the 1930s (perhaps with the exception of the 1939 COS Strategic Appreciation report), the coordinated intelligence estimates by the COS carefully tracked quantitative trends in Germany's military arsenal, and repeatedly used this indicator to draw inferences about Germany's military intentions. As long as the intelligence community perceived Germany as militarily weaker than Britain, the buildup of German capabilities did not in itself signal aggressive intentions toward Britain, although it did indicate a desire on Germany's part to change the status quo elsewhere in Europe possibly by military means. After fall 1936, assessments of Germany's military intentions became more alarming. This change resulted primarily from the growing recognition that the intensity, scope, pace, and nature of the German buildup was aimed at achieving superiority, not just parity.

This practice is consistent with the predictions of the capabilities thesis and organizational expertise hypothesis of the selective attention thesis. Yet, as chapter 3 showed, British decision makers did not adopt a similar inference process. This separation is consistent with the predictions of the organizational expertise hypothesis alone. Intelligence documents provide only weak support for the strategic military doctrine and behavior theses. Some scholars allege that the intelligence community's pessimism and worst-case analysis of the German threat between 1936 and 1938 helped Chamberlain convince doubters of the necessity of appeasement. Others claim that the intelligence community's cautious optimism about Britain's ability to counter the German threat in early 1939 was also politicized, reflecting an "evolution in the minds of a department whose nation was committed to a new policy of resistance to German expansion."[46] The evidence indicates that the shift in the intelligence estimates from pessimism between 1936 and late 1938 to optimism in early 1939 reflected a highly selective reading of information that placed too much emphasis on numerical aspects pertaining to the balance of military as well as economic power. The available primary documents that I have consulted, however, did not reveal any process-tracing evidence that intelligence was systematically politicized.[47]

As for the role of military doctrine, the documents available link between Germany's military doctrine and British assessments of its intentions. The documents available for study did not discuss Germany's military doctrine in the context of assessing intentions. Hinsley, who conducted a comprehensive review of the British intelligence community's work during this period, reaches the same conclusion, noting that there was almost no discussion of how Germany was likely to employ its military power. This is clear in the series of Strategic Appreciations issued between February 1937 and February 1939. Only in the European Strategic Appreciation drawn up in February 1939 did the COS incorporate any intelligence bearing on the way in which Germany might use its armed forces. Even then, the report only referred to the air threat facing the United Kingdom.[49] The existing evidence thus lends little support to the strategic military doctrine thesis.

Finally, the evidence is inconclusive as to the predictions of the past and current actions hypotheses of the behavior thesis. The available documents do include some references to Germany's military actions and strategy during World

War I as well as Hitler's costly noncapabilities-based actions, but these are rare. They do not provide clear proof, for example, concerning whether Germany's annexation of Czechoslovakia shifted the British intelligence community's perceptions of German intentions to any degree. This is in part because, after the Munich crisis, British intelligence shifted its focus away from predictions about Germany's long-term aspirations. As its agents and spies reported on an imminent German attack, the intelligence community turned its attention toward the more immediate questions of Germany's wartime objectives and military readiness.

CHAPTER 5

The Carter Era and the Collapse of Détente, 1977–80

President Carter began his time in office with great optimism about the USSR and was committed to improving the US-Soviet relationship. By the end of his tenure, however, Carter's perceptions of the USSR had changed and his policies emphasized competition over cooperation. In his last year as president, Carter failed to meet with Soviet leaders, increased the defense budget, and withdrew the Strategic Arms Limitation Talks (SALT) II Treaty from Senate consideration. He articulated the Carter Doctrine, which identified the Persian Gulf as an area of vital national interest, and pledged the United States to use all means necessary to protect it from foreign encroachment. The détente had collapsed. What explains the dramatic changes in US perceptions of the Soviet Union?

THE SELECTIVE ATTENTION THESIS

Due to inherent differences between the two sets of perceivers, the selective attention thesis expects key decision makers in the Carter administration assessing intentions to attend to different indicators than the US intelligence community. Specifically, for reasons discussed in chapter 1, we should have observed Carter and his two main foreign policy advisers attending to information about vivid, subjectively credible behavior. By contrast, the US intelligence community should focus more on Soviet military capabilities.

The Vividness Hypothesis

At the heart of the vividness hypothesis is the notion that decision makers treat impressions of their counterparts derived from personal interactions or litmus tests as credible information of their intentions. President Carter had one private meeting with Leonid Brezhnev during the Vienna summit in June 1979. As we will see in chapter 6, Carter came out of this meeting with a positive impression of the Soviet premier, believing that the two had been able to establish a better level of trust and mutual understanding. According to the vividness hypothesis, this meeting should have influenced Carter's assessment of Soviet intentions. At the same time, the two leaders' single interaction occurred when the Soviet premier was visibly ill. According to Carter's report to Brzezinski, when Carter met alone with Brezhnev, the latter "seemed unable to cope with a direct and informal discussion. . . . Brezhnev would read his response to Carter's comments from the piece of paper" that his translator would hand to him.[1] Even under these circumstances, Carter was emotional during the meeting, later recalling, "Brezhnev kept his hand on my arm or shoulder to steady himself. This simple and apparently natural gesture bridged the gap between us more effectively than any official talks."[2] As a result, vivid information from personal interaction on Carter's assessment of intentions should have had a causal impact.

As for the impact of vividness on Vance's and Brzezinski's assessments, the predictions are less clear. Vance had frequent and repeated interactions with Soviet foreign minister Andrei Gromyko and Soviet ambassador Anatoly Dobrynin. In his memoirs, Vance describes these meetings in plain terms; some were more productive than others, but all took place in a "businesslike atmosphere."[3] Vance does not portray them as vivid or emotional, indicating that these meetings with these officials made neither a positive nor negative impression on him. The record also shows that he did not forge any special relationship with either of the two. As a result, the vividness hypothesis might not have a strong causal impact on Vance's inference process about Soviet intentions. Brzezinski's memoirs indicate that he too held frequent and prolonged meetings with Gromyko and Dobrynin—some of which included heated debates. But like Vance, none of Brzezinski's public or private writings refer to any personal insights that he gained from these meetings. We thus should not expect the vividness hypothesis to shed light on Brzezinski's assessments of Soviet intentions.

The Subjective Credibility Hypothesis

The subjective credibility hypothesis expects variation between Carter, Vance, and Brzezinski in how they perceived the credibility of Soviet behavioral indicators. To begin with, Brzezinski's image of the Soviet Union in early 1977 was more negative than those held by Carter or Vance. As I will show in chapter 6, the national security advisor "developed a very centrally hawkish image of the Soviet Union early on, which was reinforced later by his education . . . at Harvard as well as by domestic and international realities."[4] Brzezinski's hawkish orientation, however, does not necessarily imply that he saw the Soviet Union as an unlimited expansionist power. In fact, as I will note in the next chapter, his views of Soviet intentions were similar to Carter's in 1977: both described Soviet intentions as opportunistic. But Brzezinski was far more pessimistic and far less idealistic than Carter about the US-Soviet relationship when he assumed the post of national security advisor in 1977.

In contrast, Vance's image of the Soviet Union when he became secretary of state was relatively more benign. A comprehensive study of Vance's worldview depicts him as holding an "optimistic belief in further promoting détente with the Soviet Union by constraining competition and focusing on broadening areas of cooperation between the US and USSR, and an empathic image that understood and focused on the indigenous elements of conflict . . . , particularly within the developing world." This image of the Soviet Union as seriously seeking détente led Vance to reject the notion that the Soviet threat should dominate US foreign policy. His writings and speeches before and during his time as secretary of state further indicate that while he did not reject the policy of containment, he saw US-Soviet relations as involving elements of cooperation as well as competition. He was rather optimistic about the Soviets' ability and willingness to play a cooperative role.[5]

Studies of Carter's views of the Soviet Union when he assumed office place the president's stances closer to those of Vance than Brzezinski. Carter did not have a fully formed image of the Soviet Union, but his statements and policies on assuming office indicate a rather optimistic approach to the Soviet Union and building a cooperative global community. This orientation downplayed the threat posed by the Soviet Union.[6]

In light of the differences between the three decision makers on the eve of Carter's inauguration, the subjective credibility hypothesis would expect these decision makers to debate the informative value of various costly actions and rely on other types of costless information. It also predicts that Brzezinski, as compared to Carter and Vance, would have categorized more of the Soviets' costly hostile actions as informative. As a result, we should expect Brzezinski to proclaim that Soviet intentions were expansionist at an earlier point in time compared to either Carter or Vance.

The Organizational Expertise Hypothesis

The organizational expertise hypothesis posits that in inferring intentions, the coordinated estimates produced by the US intelligence community would have drawn on the indicators that received most prominence within the community at the time. I contend that, during the 1970s as well as the 1980s, Soviet military capabilities served as such an indicator. This conclusion is supported by the fact that the vast majority of the NIEs on the Soviet Union throughout the Cold War discussed at length different aspects of the Soviet military arsenal.[7] High-level officials who were in charge of the Soviet estimates during that time also confirm this conclusion. For example, Raymond Garthoff, a former Central Intelligence Agency (CIA) national intelligence officer on the Soviet Union as well as a prominent scholar of the Cold War and US intelligence community, remarked that "estimates of Soviet capabilities were the predominant focus of attention and received virtually all of the intelligence collection, analysis, and estimative effort."[8] Former Director of Central Intelligence (DCI) George Tenet similarly said:

> From the mid-1960s on to the Soviet collapse, we knew roughly how many combat aircraft or warheads the Soviets had, and where. But why did they need that many or that kind? What did they plan to do with them? To this day, Intelligence is always much better at counting heads than divining what is going on inside them. That is, we are very good at gauging the size and location of militaries and weaponry. But for obvious reasons, we can never be as good at figuring out what leaders will do with them.[9]

The organizational expertise hypothesis and capabilities thesis that I discuss below rely on different causal mechanisms. Nevertheless, the central observable distinction between them concerns whether decision makers and the intelligence community relied on the same indicators to assess intentions: the capabilities thesis expects both groups to attend to Soviet military capabilities, while the organizational expertise hypothesis makes different predictions specific to the intelligence community.

THE CAPABILITIES THESIS

Testing the capabilities thesis requires examining changes in Soviet nuclear strategic forces and their impact on the global military balance as a measure of what the Soviets thought they could achieve, and therefore potentially intended to achieve, in a direct conflict with the United States. One must also examine changes in the perceived Soviet forces in Europe and evaluate their impact on the military balance in the European theater. After all, an increase in these capabilities could have been perceived as an important indicator of Soviet intentions to change the status quo in Europe. Evidence from US intelligence reports, Department of Defense (DOD) reports along with and net assessments conducted by the National Security Council (NSC) staff in the Carter administration indicate that the USSR was believed to have undertaken a massive military buildup that had begun in the late 1960s and continued throughout the 1970s. Specifically, consensus existed among these actors on several issues concerning the military balance in the mid- to late 1970s. First, the USSR was building up its military capabilities such that the balance of power started to favor the USSR.[10] The United States was mostly concerned about the potential of the fourth-generation intercontinental ballistic missiles (ICBMs) that the Soviets were deploying.[11] The Soviets were believed to be ahead of the United States already in the number of delivery vehicles, enjoy a growing advantage in equivalent megatons (as a result of an increasing number of ICBMs with large throw weights), and hold an advantage in the silo hardness and accuracy of its ICBMs.[12] In 1979, the intelligence community reported that "substantial increases in our estimates of Soviet countersilo capabilities and MIRV [multiple independently targetable reentry vehicles] deployment over the next few years, combined with some slippages in US programs would lead the Soviet Union to achieve advantage sooner than had previously [been] anticipated and . . . this period [of Soviet advantage] would last longer." Further, the same estimate concluded that the Soviet ICBM force would "achieve the potential capability to destroy some four fifths of the US Minuteman silos in 1980–81, three to four years earlier than projected in last year's estimate."[13] The following year, the community reported that the numbers of Soviet counterforce capabilities were "increasing rapidly," and the Soviets were steadily improving the survivability and flexibility of their strategic forces.[14]

Second, trends in the balance of forces in Europe were also perceived as negative, especially in light of the growing realization that the Soviets had reached a position that could offset the West in both intercontinental and theater nuclear forces. Indeed, the Soviets were believed to have been expanding their already-large conventional ground and theater air forces from 1965–80, and have introduced modern systems, some of them equal or superior to those of the North Atlantic Treaty Organization (NATO).[15] In the nuclear realm, against the backdrop of strategic parity between the two superpowers, the new Soviet intermediate-range missile, the SS-20, produced a growing anxiety regarding the implications of Soviet continental strategic superiority.[16] Moreover, in 1978 the CIA concluded that improvements in Soviet tactical nuclear forces in Central Europe over the past several years had eroded much of NATO's long-standing nuclear advantage there. As a result, the basis of deterrence in Central Europe was believed to have shifted more to the conventional forces of both sides.[17]

Third, notwithstanding significant developments in the global balance of power, the consensus throughout this period was that the United States maintained "asymmetric equivalence" with the USSR. According to Presidential Review Memorandum 10 as well as a top-secret CNA conducted by the NSC staff in 1978, the United States held "significant advantages in economic, technology, diplomatic access and support, and political appeal." The trends in "the military component of national power," on the other hand, were judged "to favor the Soviet Union, except for a mixed trend in the NATO–Warsaw Pact military balance."[18] The CNA further concluded, however, that this strategic balance was likely to change adversely within a decade.[19] In terms of equivalent countermilitary potential, the basic trend as perceived in 1978 was increasingly unfavorable to the United States until 1987, when "it [would] level off at a very substantial Soviet advantage."[20] Finally, this 1978 report acknowledged that the inclusion of additional factors—such as readiness, mobilization, command ability, and doctrine of employment—would probably have made the strategic balance look worse for the United States.[21]

Decision makers were painfully aware of the trends in the correlation of forces. Brzezinski cautioned in a May 1979 NSC meeting that the strategic nuclear balance was deteriorating faster than he had expected in 1977, and would continue to do so into the early 1980s. The Soviets, he said, "have been outspending us in defense since the late 1960s, and military investment is important because it is cumulative."[22] He warned that in the 1980s, the United States would face "a strategic dip" and would "not meet the criteria established in PD-18: namely to maintain essential equivalence and a balance no worse than that existing in 1977." Vance agreed with Brzezinski's conclusions, and did not deny the basic proposition that trends were adverse, although he did question the notion that there might be a strategic dip in the 1980s. Secretary of Defense Harold Brown thought the assessment about the strategic forces balance was too pessimistic, but thought that by 1985, the Soviets would have greater strength than the United States in almost every military category, no matter what the United States did. Carter's own perceptions of the strategic balance are much harder to uncover, but Brzezinski does report that in the same NSC meeting, the president remarked that his advisers in "this group" (most likely the officials attending the meeting) had to an extent created the perception of Soviet superiority. Such perceptions, according to Carter, could exacerbate problems. He reminded the NSC that the United States had different military advantages over the Soviets; significantly, he cited the many allies that the United States had, while pointing out that USSR had alienated many nations and made many enemies.[23]

Summary of Predictions

US decision makers perceived the balance of military capabilities overall to be one of asymmetrical equivalence throughout the period, but were also alarmed that the balance was about to shift in favor of the USSR. According to the numerical preponderance hypothesis, the dramatic increase and modernization efforts in Soviet military capabilities, in spite of the attainment of strategic parity, should have led US decision makers during this period to view Soviet intentions as increasingly hostile. At the same time, from the prism of the offense-defense hypothesis under conditions of deterrence dominance, the Soviet increase in offensive capabilities should have made US observers perceive Soviet intentions as more hostile. The predictions that the two hypotheses offer with regard to the reasoning evidence are different, though. The numerical preponderance hypothesis expects decision makers to refer to the impact of trends in Soviet capabilities on the overall military balance between the superpowers when discussing Soviet intentions. The offense-defense hypothesis expects observers to focus the conversation on the offensive nature of the Soviet nuclear and conventional buildup when assessing Soviet intentions.

The Strategic Military Doctrine Thesis

Official Soviet military doctrine at the time was that of an offensive-defense one. That is, the sociopolitical aspect of Soviet military doctrine was described in Soviet writings as defensive and nonaggressive, reflecting Soviet state policy. During the period in question, however, the very definition of Soviet military doctrine did not incorporate the objective of war prevention. Nor was deterrence described as a constituent element of military doctrine. In contrast, the military-technical level of the Soviet doctrine—which then embraced the entire scope of military strategy, the operational arts, and tactics—continued to be unambiguously offensive. The operational plans of the Warsaw Treaty Organization (WTO) were based on the concept that if WTO forces came under NATO attack, they would resist and soon begin a counterattack that would involve the invasion (and occupation) of the aggressor's territory. The purported offensive-defense nature of the Soviet doctrine at the time led many in the United States to question whether the defensive sociopolitical aspect of the doctrine was merely propaganda, while its offensive technical-military aspect revealed the "real" orientation of the doctrine. The implications of the latter would be that once the WTO became convinced that the military balance was in its favor, it would launch an attack against Western Europe. Others claimed, in contrast, that "there is no necessary contradiction between a defensive *policy* and an offensive strategy for waging war if war should come," as this was exactly the doctrine adopted by the US Strategic Air Command from its inception.[24]

Although Soviet doctrine in Europe was recognized as offensive, the nature of Soviet nuclear doctrine was a major subject of debate within the US policy and intelligence communities. To some observers, the Soviets regarded warfighting and war-winning capabilities as providing the most credible deterrent as well as serving as a contingent resort if war should nonetheless come. Furthermore, according to this interpretation, the fact that the Soviets operationalized the requirements of mutual assured destruction differently from the way it was perceived in the United States created the impression that the Soviets were not focused primarily on deterrence.[25] Within the intelligence community, as we will see in chapter 7, this interpretation reflected the views held by the US State Department's INR. The more hawkish interpretation of Soviet military doctrine, endorsed by the DIA and military intelligence agencies, claimed that the Soviets believed in the fact of deterrence, but regarded it as "undesirable and transient."[26] Proponents of this interpretation argued that while the Soviets did expect immense losses in any nuclear exchange for all the combatants, they also assumed that Russia's superiority in offensive and defensive strategic forces would result in a Soviet victory should nuclear war nevertheless break out. Indeed, those believing that the USSR projected a war-fighting posture also emphasized that its leadership regarded victory in nuclear war as an objective to be consciously and diligently pursued.[27] Statements by decision makers in the

Carter administration reveal that the consensus during this period was that the Soviet leadership accepted nuclear deterrence.[28] Yet they differed on how Soviet leaders and military planners operationalized nuclear deterrence.[29]

Most Western analysts also fell into one of two schools of thought regarding the utility of nuclear weapons and Soviet ideas about victory in a nuclear war.[30] Within the intelligence community, the INR believed that Soviet writings were based on ideology rather than on objective, operational factors. Thus, the existence of military missions in Soviet doctrine was not proof of an operational concept of victory, given the lack of any identification of the requirement or character of victory. The opposite perspective, held by the DIA and military intelligence agencies, asserted that Soviet political and military leaders were in agreement on what would constitute victory in a nuclear war. Victory meant the survival of the Communist Party and its leadership, strategic and military neutralization of the United States, and seizure and occupation of Western Europe.

The prevailing stance held in the Carter administration was that the Soviets did not seek nuclear war, though they would be serious about fighting if one were to break out. Brzezinski claims that the NSC during this period nonetheless concluded that the Soviets "preferred and were eager to fight wars rather than to deter them." In his view, this Soviet posture was a method of enhancing deterrence, not an alternative to it. Brzezinski believed that despite their interventions in the third world, the Soviets were not seriously contemplating any unprovoked use of force against the United States or NATO. The Soviet High Command was also determined not to lose if there were a war.[31] Brown concluded that the Soviet civilian leadership did not believe that the USSR could fight and win a nuclear war. Top military officials, Brown argued, did not really expect the USSR to survive a nuclear war, but they still tried to improve Soviet chances for survival.[32] Fritz Ermarth, an NSC staff member, thought that Soviet doctrine was that "however awful, nuclear war must be survivable and some kind of meaningful victory attainable." He also claimed that the Soviet buildup in the 1970s transformed this "ideological imperative" into a more "plausible strategic potential" as the USSR "possibly" believed that it could win a central strategic war under specific operational conditions.[33]

By the late 1960s, Soviet military writings provided evidence that Soviet policy had changed to stress the acquisition of both launch-on-warning and assured second-strike capabilities in order to reduce the reliance on preemption.[34] The US intelligence community generally agreed that the Soviets would launch a preemptive intercontinental nuclear strike only if their leaders were to acquire what they considered "unequivocal evidence that a US strike was both imminent and unavoidable." Moreover, the community claimed that Soviet doctrine indicated a belief that the most likely way for intercontinental conflict to begin would be the escalation from a NATO–Warsaw Pact theater conflict with a NATO launch of nuclear strikes to avoid defeat in Europe. US decision makers, on the other hand, were divided in interpreting Soviet intentions over the issue of preemption. Both Brown and Secretary of Energy James Schlesinger saw Soviet preemption as a remote possibility. Relying on their interpretation of Soviet doctrine, they later suggested that, in Brown's words, "according to the Soviet military doctrine, the Soviets [would] preempt only if they [had been] convinced, based on their reading of American intentions, that the U.S. was going to launch a nuclear strike." Even then, it was uncertain whether the Soviet political leadership would decide to follow the military doctrine.[35] Other US officials in the Carter administration had perceived a greater likelihood of Soviet preemption.[36] But even Brzezinski "doubted that during a theater war, the USSR would strike preemptively at US strategic forces in the continental U.S."[37]

Summary of Predictions

Soviet nuclear doctrine from 1975 to 1980 was ambiguous, as demonstrated by the confusion that marked US debates over its form. Yet observers were clear about the offensive nature of the Soviet conventional doctrine in Europe. All else being equal, US observers should have erred on the side of caution, interpreting the Soviet doctrine as offensive or war fighting. Consequently, according to this thesis, they should perceive Soviet intentions as hostile. But because important differences existed among intelligence agencies and policy makers over how to read certain elements of Soviet military doctrine, we should see important divergence in what conclusions they reached about Soviet intentions. Thus, when we examine the perceptions of different intelligence agencies or individual decision makers, the strategic military doctrine thesis predicts that positions on perceptions of Soviet intentions at the time should have been highly correlated with the positions taken in the debate over the nature of Soviet doctrine. The thesis also expects assessments of intentions, regardless of their nature, to discuss or make reference to Soviet doctrinal writings and strategic thought during this period. Finally, based on this thesis, US decision makers should advocate policies that are consistent with their reading of Soviet military doctrine. We should see that those who perceived Soviet doctrine as explicitly one of war fighting should advocate even more hard-line policies aimed at balancing against the USSR.

The Behavior Thesis

Evidence from archival documents suggests that two particular sets of costly Soviet noncapabilities-based actions captured the attention of US observers during this time. The first was the signing in June 1979 of a binding arms control agreement, the SALT II Treaty, which assumed real reductions in strategic forces to 2,250 in all categories of delivery vehicles on both sides. From the perspective of the behavior thesis, the significance of this action is not in how it affected Soviet capabilities or the balance of power. Rather, it was important as a costly reassuring signal of intentions insofar as the Soviets proved willing to impose restraints on the future buildup of their strategic weapons. The second was Soviet interventions in crises around the world.[38] According to the International Crisis Behavior data set, the USSR intervened in twenty-six crises between 1975 and 1980.[39] The Soviets were involved in direct military activities in only two conflicts: Ethiopia, where the conflict reached a climax in 1978, and Afghanistan, where the crisis started in mid-March 1979, and after a full-scale Soviet invasion in December 1979, ended in February 1980.

US decision makers did not weigh all Soviet interventions equally; some were perceived as more significant than others. Declassified reports as well as diplomatic historians indicate that of the list of countries in which the Soviets intervened, particular US attention was paid to Afghanistan, Angola, Cambodia, Ethiopia, Laos, South Yemen, and Vietnam. Four of these seven interventions had occurred since January 1977.[40] Soviet actions in 1977 were not costly in any sense and did not cause any specific US concerns.[41] As for the Soviet intervention on the side of Somalia against Ethiopia in the 1978–79 Ogaden War, it is crucial to note that "until the end of 1977 the Western consensus was that the USSR posed no serious threat to the Red Sea area."[42] The United States, though, saw the major Soviet airlift and sealift operations in the last month of 1977 and early 1978 as a significant qualitative change in the type of Soviet activities as well as levels of involvement in the Horn of Africa.[43]

Indeed, starting in 1978 Soviet actions were increasing in quantity, and were contemporaneously judged to be undergoing a qualitative change in terms of both the means that the Soviets employed in these interventions and countries where they chose to intervene. The concerns were twofold: unlike the postindependence civil war in Angola (1975), in which the Soviets relied almost entirely on Cuban forces as their proxies, the Soviet presence in the Horn of Africa (1978) was more evident, although the Cubans were still believed to be carrying most of the burden. Later, the USSR's full-scale use of direct military force in Afghanistan transformed it into a "crisis actor" there. The second worry was that the observed pattern of Soviet actions in what became known as the "arc of crisis" from Africa to Southeast Asia might develop to encompass other regions and countries that were more important to US interests. The Soviet invasion of Afghanistan in 1979 significantly intensified this fear, especially in terms of its potential implications for US oil interests in Iran, Pakistan, Saudi Arabia, and elsewhere in the Middle East. Moreover, Soviet actions in Afghanistan were perceived as especially significant in that the pattern emerging from recent Soviet behavior represented, according to US officials at the time, the first direct use of force to restore a pro-Soviet regime other than in Warsaw Pact countries.[44]

Finally, US observers were alarmed in early 1979 by intelligence reports indicating that the Soviets had placed a "combat brigade" in Cuba. The issue of Soviet military activities in Cuba first surfaced in Brzezinski's May 7 report to Carter, in which he noted that the Soviets were expanding their military activities in Cuba, utilizing a pattern different from the one that had been established in the mid-1960s. Brzezinski was concerned that these activities "represent a sophisticated attempt by the Soviets to fulfill the letter of agreements on 'what is a [submarine] base' reached with [Henry] Kissinger while nonetheless developing an offensive military base in Cuba under the guise of joint basing and training arrangement."[45] On May 25, after further studying the issue, Brzezinski reported, "This Soviet activity comes very close but does not unambiguously violate earlier assurances and promises given since 1962."[46] In August, US intelligence confirmed that "there was an actual brigade in Cuba, with headquarters and regular organization and that in fact it is scheduled to hold firing exercises within a week."[47] The story was leaked to the press after key members of Congress were briefed on the issue, and the issue soon created a sense of a public crisis before the administration had completed its intelligence review or formulated a policy.[48] In the fall, the episode was defused when US decision makers realized that the brigade had been in Cuba continuously since 1962, and hence the Soviets did not violate the Kennedy-Khrushchev understandings regarding Soviet military presence in Cuba following the Cuban Missile Crisis.

Summary of Predictions

The current actions hypothesis posits that a country's costly actions under its current leadership provide important information about its intentions. During the second half of the 1970s, the USSR was involved in no fewer than twenty-six crises. In eleven of them, Soviet actions were limited to propaganda activities as well as political and economic assistance. In the majority of the cases, however, Soviet actions also included semi- or direct military involvement. This type of intervention became more frequent, extensive, and intense starting in 1978 with the intervention in the Horn of Africa. Moreover, the Soviet invasion of Afghanistan represented a qualitative shift in the USSR's behavior. If this proposition is correct, those quantitative and qualitative trends in Soviet actions should have had a significant impact on the way Soviet intentions were perceived by US decision makers and intelligence analysts during the period in question.

The past actions hypothesis, on the other hand, posits that current perceptions of intentions will be influenced by costly actions that had been taken by the USSR in the past—that is, prior to the tenure of either Carter or Brezhnev. This hypothesis, unfortunately, cannot in this case allow for specific predictions as to when and how perceptions of Soviet intentions should have changed at the time. After all, there was no one particular costly Soviet action before 1977 that appeared to be a focal point in discussions about the Soviets during the period in question. The thesis therefore can merely suggest that current statements about Soviet intentions are less likely to be correlated with and supported by assessments about costly Soviet past actions, and policies toward the USSR should be consistent with this reading of Soviet actions and intentions.

***

The next two chapters test the predictions of the various explanations. Chapter 6 looks at the statements and reasoning pattern that President Carter and his closest advisers—Brzezinski and Vance—used to describe Soviet intentions. Chapter 7 then shifts the focus to the US intelligence community's coordinated estimates and evaluates the importance of these various indicators of intentions in explaining how the coordinated NIEs assessed Soviet intentions during the same period.

CHAPTER 6

US Decision Makers' Perceptions of Soviet Intentions

THE COLLAPSE OF DÉTENTE

This chapter examines the beliefs of President Carter and his two main foreign policy advisers—Brzezinski and Vance. The reasons for focusing on the president's view are obvious: Carter had a hands-on leadership style and devised the structure of his administration so that it could provide him with a range of options. Brzezinski and Vance were the "most heavily involved individuals and closest advisors to the president in the area of foreign affairs."[1] Brzezinski represented Carter's bold side and a possibly imminent call to action, whereas Vance balanced those tendencies with a restrained and traditional approach.[2]

What indicators did Carter and his advisers use to assess Soviet intentions during this period? Using extensive evidence from US archives, this chapter compares the predictions of the selective attention and three competing theses outlined in the previous chapter with the assessments of Carter and his closest advisers about the USSR's intentions between 1977 and 1980.

My analysis relies most on newly declassified materials available at the Jimmy Carter Library and National Security Archive. Especially illuminating were Brzezinski's weekly reports to Carter. These are invaluable because they reveal the perceptions held by Brzezinski himself and reflect changes in his attitudes with great accuracy. Some reports also include Carter's handwritten comments in the margins, thus exposing to some extent the president's own opinions. Additionally, I rely on Brzezinski's comments during an interview I conducted with him.[3]

Other declassified sources include the protocols of meetings held by two formal bodies within the NSC system.[4] The Policy Review Committee was an ad hoc committee, usually chaired by Vance, whose responsibilities included formulating and implementing specific national security policy. The Special Coordination Committee, chaired by Brzezinski, addressed "specific cross-cutting issues requiring coordination in the development of options and the implementation of presidential decisions."[5] I also consulted memoirs, public statements, and interviews. In some instances these sources may be less reliable because of the problem of impressions management—that is, when decision makers use public statements strategically to, for instance, impress domestic audiences. I use them to supplement the archival documents when the public statements are consistent with what the primary documents of private correspondence reveal.

In the rest of this chapter, first, I examine statements made (mostly privately) by senior US decision makers about Soviet intentions. This strategy enables me to estimate these decision makers' baseline perceptions of Soviet intentions and identify when these perceptions changed. Then, I look at the reasoning US decision makers employed to justify their assessments of Soviet intentions. I also analyze the policies that individual decision makers advocated and those that the administration collectively adopted. These two measures allow me to see whether decision makers advocated policies that were congruent with their stated beliefs about intentions and evaluate the impact of beliefs about intentions on US foreign policy at the time.

STATED BELIEFS ABOUT SOVIET INTENTIONS

During the first year of the Carter administration, the key decision makers shared a rather optimistic view of Soviet intentions and the future of US-Soviet relations. Carter and Vance saw Soviet intentions to be cooperative in nature, and believed that the USSR could contribute to the administration's efforts to promote a global community. Brzezinski was more hawkish; his public statements and private correspondence with the president indicate that he was much more skeptical of Soviet intentions in 1977 than either Carter or Vance. But he too was still hopeful that the Soviets would remain relatively cooperative. Indeed, the conventional wisdom of Brzezinski being a "closet hawk" who perceived Soviet intentions as highly expansionist from the beginning is not supported by the available private documents.[6]

Carter's cooperative mood was reflected in his first letter to Soviet general secretary Brezhnev in which he stated that his goal was to "improve relations with the USSR on the basis of reciprocity, mutual respect and benefits."[7] Following a disappointing reaction from Brezhnev, Carter responded with a second letter that provided further details of initiatives for arms reduction along with a reassurance that the United States, and specifically Carter's human rights campaign, did not intend "to intervene in the internal affairs of the other nations" or "create problems with the USSR."[8] Despite these initial positive exchanges, the Soviets were quickly disillusioned with Carter's approach to SALT and human rights. They viewed his proposals for SALT as too aggressive, preferring that any agreement follow from the "basis that was agreed upon in Vladivostok" in 1974 when Gerald Ford and Brezhnev agreed to numerical parity in nuclear weapons.[9] Carter was deeply disappointed by the Soviets' response and even viewed it as "harsh."[10] But his perceptions of Soviet intentions remained unchanged.

Carter's early optimism about the future of détente was demonstrated in a series of public statements he delivered during the rest of 1977.[11] On numerous occasions he portrayed Soviet behavior as positive, noting, "The Soviets have been very cooperative up to this point, and we are pleased with their attitude."[12] Following a setback in SALT negotiations during summer 1977, he remained optimistic. "I don't agree that there are growing difficulties between ourselves and the Soviet Union. . . . I don't believe that the relations between us are deteriorating," Carter said in late June, adding, "I don't have any sense of fear or frustration or concern about our relationship with the Soviet Union. We have, I think, a good prospect of continuing our discussions, and I have every hope that these discussions will lead to success."[13] Although Carter was surprised that the Soviets were upset by his human rights campaign, he reassured them that he saw "no relationship between the human rights decision . . . and matters affecting our defense and our SALT negotiations."[14] The following month, Carter was asked outright whether he foresaw an end to détente. He downplayed his differences with the Soviets once again, and explained that disagreements stemmed from the fact that the two sides were attempting to address some controversial and important issues such as human rights for the first time.[15] Several times during the summer and fall he claimed to be encouraged by the relationship with the Soviets.[16] In October he stated, "I think we are approaching a settlement with the Soviets [on SALT], if they continue to act in as constructive a fashion as they have exhibited the last few weeks."[17] Overall, Carter concluded the year by observing that Soviet behavior in the Middle East (as well as on SALT II, terrorism, a comprehensive test ban, the Indian Ocean, and "many other items") left him with the impression that "our relations with them [the Soviets] are much better than they were shortly after I became President. . . . We've had a very constructive relationship with the USSR which I think is constantly improving."[18]

Brzezinski's weekly memorandums to Carter reveal that this more hawkish member of the administration viewed Soviet intentions as opportunistic, though not hostile or expansionist, throughout 1977. Brzezinski was more cautious in his optimism than Carter, indicating that "it is much too early to make confident predictions" about Soviet intentions. He was nevertheless able to reach some "preliminary conclusions" about the intentions of the Soviet leadership, pointing out that "Brezhnev has made a personal and public commitment to reestablishing the détente policy, based on an early SALT agreement." Brzezinski further noted that "the strategic-political weakness of the USSR in two critical areas—the Middle East and China—creates an added pressure to stabilize his [Brezhnev's] relations with the new American Administration."[19] A month later, following the Soviet rejection of two proposals put forth by the United States, Brzezinski became "rather skeptical about the prospects for progress." He felt that neither Carter nor Vance truly appreciated "the degree to which the Soviets were hostile to the SALT proposal and the extent to which they wished to put [the Carter administration] under pressure."[20]

Notwithstanding his frustration with Soviet actions regarding the SALT agreement, Brzezinski still expressed optimism during the rest of that year. For example, on June 3, 1977, Brzezinski raised the issue of SALT in his weekly report and asked Carter if he would like to "approach Brezhnev to visit the United States irrespective of the SALT outcome." The president noted "Yes" and underlined Brzezinski's sentence. Two weeks later, Brzezinski's weekly memo argued that there would be "an eventual turn in Soviet policy back toward something resembling détente." He contended that Brezhnev's policies were becoming more "certain and fixed" following the "crisis of expectations" that resulted from "President Ford's abandonment of détente." He also believed that Brezhnev "wished to end his career on a high point" and good relations with the United States—and particularly a SALT agreement—would secure his status as a "peace champion." Brzezinski remarked that "despite harsh words, the Soviets have in fact moved in the substantial position [on SALT], if only slightly." Thus, he concluded, the "consequences of a new round of competition [could not] be all that attractive to Brezhnev."[21] While these are not explicit statements about Soviet intentions, they still reveal that even Brzezinski viewed Soviet objectives as leaning toward cooperation, at least in the short term.[22]

As for Vance, the evidence suggests that he shared Carter's assessment that the Soviets were interested in détente and that he perceived their intentions as benign. One study, using a cognitive-psychodynamic perspective, argues that throughout his tenure, Vance possessed an optimistic détente image of the USSR; his image of the USSR as an adversary was "relatively fragile." According to this study, "Vance felt that the USSR shared an important interest with the US in avoiding military confrontation."[23] During his first two years in office, Vance did not elaborate on his views of Soviet political intentions per se but instead stated that "détente does exist today, and I believe and hope that it will continue to exist," and that the Soviets were bona fide negotiators in the SALT negotiations.[24]

Throughout 1978, SALT negotiations continued as third world conflicts grew in scope, intensity, and importance. Despite an increasing distrust of Soviet intentions, Carter did not dramatically change his beliefs about Soviet objectives during that year; instead, he remained quite hopeful about the future of the relationship between the superpowers. As Brzezinski put it, by the end of 1978, Carter "[had not made] any real determinations as to Soviet expansionism."[25] But the record also reveals that Carter's optimism became more cautious following Soviet involvement in the Horn of Africa. In the meantime, Brzezinski underwent a significant and rather-abrupt change in his perceptions of Soviet intentions during 1978. He was convinced that new Soviet initiatives and increased military involvement in Africa signified a grand design to expand. In contrast, Vance "did not believe Soviet actions in Africa were part of a grand Soviet plan, but rather attempts to exploit targets of opportunity."[26]

The conflict in the Horn of Africa provoked debate among the top foreign policy decision makers regarding their assessments of Soviet intentions. On January 13, 1978, Brzezinski reported to Carter that

> Soviet ambitions in third areas such as the Middle East and Africa continue unabated. The Soviets must be made to understand that there can be no watertight compartmentalization of our relationship so that what happens in one area is without effect on others. The danger nonetheless at this juncture is that they will push things to a point (in Ethiopia for example) that could come to damage the basis for cooperation in our overall relationship."[27]

Notwithstanding these concerns, Soviet actions up to that time had not led Brzezinski to conclude that they were necessarily motivated by a desire to expand. In that same report, he wrote, "Either by design or simply as a response to an apparent opportunity, the Soviets have stepped up their efforts to exploit African turbulence to their own advantage."[28] Brzezinski repeated these conclusions in another memo to Carter a week later: "Soviet leaders may be acting merely in response to an apparent opportunity, or the Soviet actions may be part of a wider strategic design. In either case, the Soviets probably calculate, as previously in Angola, they can later adopt a more conciliatory attitude and that the US will simply again adjust to the consolidation of Soviet presence in yet another African country."[29]

The task of gauging Soviet intentions continued to preoccupy Brzezinski in the following months. On February 17, 1978, he provided Carter with an explicit and rare account of his thoughts on Soviet intentions. Brzezinski presented a table in this report in which he categorized various Soviet actions as benign, neutral, and malignant (see table 2).[30] It reflects Brzezinski's uncertainty about how to read the Soviet leadership's intentions.

According to Brzezinski, the table "seems to indicate that the Soviet Union [was] prepared to be cooperative in those functional areas likely to cement a parity relationship with the United States," while simultaneously, the USSR was "unwilling to accommodate in ideological and political areas; in fact, it [was] quite prepared to exploit third world turbulence to maximize the difficulties and to promote its interests." Overall, Brzezinski described Soviet objectives as seeking "selective détente." Still, he believed that Soviet intentions could change in response to US actions and policies. He specifically indicated that the "proper US response should not be to undermine emerging cooperative relationships in the 'benign' category, but to increase the costs of Soviet behavior in the 'malignant' category."[31] In the following months the Ethiopians, backed by Cuban and Soviet forces, continued their successful drive to repel the Somali Army. By March, Brzezinski had formulated a coherent view of Soviet strategy. He maintained that Soviet intentions were not merely opportunistic, claiming,

Table 2 Brzezinski's Interpretation of Soviet Actions

Benign	Neutral	Malignant
SALT [Strategic Arms Limitation Treaty] (tough but serious)	Middle East (not helpful but not overtly destructive)	Neutron bomb (an intense propaganda campaign against the United States)
CTB [Comprehensive Test Ban] (clearly seeking accommodation)	Arms transfers (restrained; not actively cooperative and seeking to retain Soviet freedom of action)	Human rights (suppression at home and some success in toning down US criticism abroad)
Indian Ocean (seeking accommodation but rather one-sided in its proposals)		CSCE [Conference on Security and Cooperation in Europe] (uncooperative and obstructive)
Chemical warfare (positive and exploratory)		Southern Africa (uncooperative and encouraging extremism)
Radiological warfare (positive and exploratory)		African Horn (assertive intrusion with dangerous demonstration effects)
Nuclear proliferation (positive and cooperative)		

Source: NSC Weekly Report, no. 47, February 17, 1978.

"I do not believe that anyone serious can accept the argument that the Soviet Union is in Ethiopia for the sake of protecting Ethiopia's frontiers; it is there because it has a larger design in mind."[32] A month later, in another weekly report to Carter, Brzezinski summarized his interpretation of Soviet strategy:

1. Keep movement going forward on détente in the area of arms control relationships. This both restrains any US build-up, and generates a more passive US attitude on other issues;
2. Create the impression of a special US-Soviet relationship, which frightens both the Europeans and the Chinese;
3. To induce the Europeans increasingly into a self-Finlandized attitude, in part out of fear of the Soviet Union, and in part out of wishful thinking that a genuine détente really exists;
4. To prevent a rapid resolution of the Middle Eastern problem . . . in the hope of radicalizing the Arabs and of gaining greater leverage;
5. To exploit any opportunities in Africa, or elsewhere, to advance Soviet interests, either directly or indirectly;

6. To intimidate the US and its allies by massive propaganda campaigns, such as the one directed at the neutron bomb, and through general vilification of US motives, policies and society.[33]

Yet Brzezinski did not see the USSR's expansionist intentions as unlimited in scope. Reviewing Soviet behavior since World War II in a report to Carter in mid-May, Brzezinski explained that his "concern for the future [was] *not* that the USSR [would] emerge as the dominant world power, imposing a 'pax sovietica.'" Rather, he feared that "the destructive nature of Soviet efforts [would] increasingly make it impossible for us to give order and stability to global change and [could] thus prevent the appearance of a more cooperative and just international system."[34]

Vance did not share Brzezinski's interpretation of Soviet actions in Africa as indicators of Soviet expansionism but instead viewed them as attempts to exploit opportunities. While not dismissing Soviet actions as unimportant, Vance still felt that the Soviet leadership believed "their actions were within the bounds of acceptable competition."[35] The Soviets thought that Carter's "human rights efforts were aimed at overthrowing their system; they saw our behavior as unpredictable; and they were growing uncertain as to whether we still wanted a SALT Treaty."[36] Frustrated with some of Carter's policy decisions, Vance sought a formal review of US-Soviet relations on May 29, 1978. He explained in a memo to Carter that "many are asking whether this Administration has decided to make a sharp shift in its foreign policy priorities" and expressed his alarm about Brzezinski's growing influence over Carter's image of the USSR.[37]

Carter's moderate shift toward Brzezinski's views during 1978 was apparent in the president's public speeches.[38] During that period, Carter was visibly preoccupied with the ongoing SALT talks along with the conflicts between Israel and Egypt. He consequently attended only some NSC meetings on the Horn, and relied extensively on Brzezinski's crisp and short accounts of these meetings. Yet the record shows that Brzezinski's summaries did not always supply an accurate reading of these meetings. Betty Glad (she was a member of the NSC at the time too) explains that Brzezinski "provided closure on those items that he usually favored. . . . But he kept open other matters where he did not approve of the drift of the conversation." Carter favored Brzezinski's "bold, clear, and apparently broad perspective," and thus did not attend to some "key State Department memos [that] would have informed the president that not all conflicts in the Horn were Soviet-inspired, that the Cubans were not simply the proxies of the Soviet Union, and that religion could be a divisive rather than a uniting force in the region."[39]

Carter had not fully accepted Brzezinski's interpretation about Soviet intentions, though, and his statements throughout summer 1978 reflected a combination of Brzezinski's and Vance's images of the Soviet Union. In public statements, Carter expressed his concern, anger, and frustration with recent Soviet and Cuban behavior in Africa.[40] At the same time he reiterated his belief that the Soviets were "negotiating in good faith almost every day" on SALT II.[41] Carter's speech at the Naval Academy in Annapolis on June 7, 1978, illustrates the tension between two conflicting images of Soviet intentions. The speech itself was actually stitched together from two previous versions: one produced by Vance, emphasizing the complex nature of the US-Soviet relationship and need to lower political tensions on a reciprocal basis, and another, more confrontational version by Brzezinski. Overall, the speech was harsher in tone than Carter's previous statements, mirroring his growing frustration with Soviet behavior. Carter continued to see Soviet intentions as opportunistic, but now judged that Soviet leaders were willing to use military power to achieve their political goals. For example, in the Annapolis speech, Carter said that the USSR "apparently sees military power and military assistance as the best means of expanding their influence abroad." Specifically, they appeared "ready and willing to take advantage" of areas of instability, preferred to "use proxy forces to fight their battles" as "was obvious in Korea, Angola and Ethiopia," violated the 1975 Helsinki Accords with their "gross abuse of basic human rights," and "attempt[ed] to export a totalitarian and repressive form of government."[42] In summation, he warned that "the Soviet Union can choose either confrontation or cooperation. The United States is adequately prepared to meet either choice." Brzezinski was satisfied with this speech, but was not hopeful regarding future Soviet intentions: "They are not likely to desist entirely from what they have been doing—especially in Africa—but they might moderate some of their actions."[43]

Notwithstanding positive developments during fall 1978, by the end of that year the administration was clearly divided in its views of Soviet intentions, with Brzezinski and Vance in opposite camps.[44] Brzezinski's *NSC Weekly Report*, no. 65, discussing an informal meeting of a small group of specialists to assess Soviet objectives and the future of US-Soviet relations, underscored the division within the administration. The participants, he explained, presented "two distinct views":

> One view . . . was that "the Soviets have stomped all over the code of détente." They continue to pursue a selective détente. Their action reflects growing assertiveness in Soviet foreign policy generally. Brezhnev's diminished control permits the natural, historical, dominating impulse of the regime to assert itself with less restraint. (. . . it is the closest to my own).

> Another view (held mainly by Marshall Shulman) was that the record of Soviet action is much more mixed and has to be considered case-by-case The Soviets are acting on traditional lines and essentially reacting to US steps.[45]

The evidence is that Brzezinski changed his perceptions of Soviet intentions during 1978. He thought their intentions were not simply opportunistic but instead reflected a "larger, well-designed strategy." Still, he stopped short of describing the Soviet leadership as having unlimited expansionist goals and never expressed concern that the Soviets would contemplate a direct military attack against vital US interests. Vance, for his part, still tended to view Soviet actions as defensively motivated and reflecting opportunist intentions. By the end of 1978, Carter had become more skeptical about the true intentions of the Soviet leadership; he had come to believe that the Soviets were willing to use military force in support of their opportunistic intentions. At the same time, Carter did not reach a firm conclusion as to Soviet expansionism; he continued to view their intentions as largely opportunistic. For example, when asked in November, "What do you think the Soviets are up to? . . . [D]o you see them as primarily a defensive power . . . or do you see them as an aggressive power?" Carter replied,

> I think, first of all, they want peace and security for their own people, and they un-
> doubtedly exaggerate any apparent threat to themselves. . . . At the same time, as is
> the case with us, they would like to expand their influence among other people in the
> world, believing that their system of government, their philosophy, is best. . . . But I
> would say that those are their two basic motives, as is the case with us—security for
> themselves and to have their own influence felt in the rest of the world as much as
> possible.[46]

Between January and May 1979, Vance and Dobrynin met on a weekly basis in an attempt to finalize the SALT II agreement. Carter's public statements still emphasized the positive behavior that the Soviets were exhibiting in the SALT negotiations and his inclination not to link objections to Soviet behavior in Africa to those talks.[47] Nevertheless, Carter's closest advisers did not share his optimism about the possibility of obtaining an agreement with the Soviets. Unlike Brzezinski, Carter was optimistic about the Vienna summit set for June 15–18, 1979, and thought his personal meeting with Brezhnev would be significant. He was attuned to the advice of a former US ambassador, Averell Harriman, who told him that Brezhnev was committed to détente and avoiding war. Further, as Gaddis Smith notes and Carter's writings confirm, "Harriman's assessment appealed to Carter's own emotional belief that personal contact with Brezhnev would make a difference."[48] In his diary, Carter remarked, "It's impor-tant that I not embarrass Brezhnev and treat him as a friend, because quite often he's not well-informed on individual matters. He's human and emotional."[49]

The official records of the meetings in Vienna reveal that Carter was genu-inely concerned about Soviet involvement in third world conflicts, specifically in China, Cuba, Iran, Namibia, Rhodesia, and Zimbabwe.[50] He even issued a request to Brezhnev that Soviet interventionism in Africa should cease. Carter also appears to have come out of the meeting with a positive impression of Brezhnev despite the latter's obvious health issues. At the final signing cere-mony for SALT II, the two leaders embraced. In the words of Cold War historian Melvyn Leffler, "Carter sensed Brezhnev's warmth even while he felt the heat of his domestic critics."[51] The president believed he had established a good rapport with the Soviet premier. After Vienna, Carter wrote, "There is no doubt there were strong feelings of cooperation at the moment, and I was determined to pursue our search for peace and better understanding."[52] On June 18, he similarly noted in a public speech,

> Despite disagreements, our exchange in Vienna was useful, because it enabled us to clarify our positions directly to each other, face-to-face, and, thus, to reduce the chances of future miscalculations on both sides. . . . I would like to say to you that President Brezhnev and I developed a better sense of each other as leaders and as men.[53]

Yet the remainder of 1979 saw a significant deterioration of US-Soviet relations. On May 7, Brzezinski first reported to Carter that the Soviets were expanding their military activities in Cuba. Brzezinski was concerned that these activities "represent[ed] a sophisticated attempt by the Soviets to fulfill the letter of agreements on 'what is a [submarine] base' reached with Kissinger in October 1970, while nonetheless developing an offensive military base in Cuba under the guise of a joint basing and training arrangement."[54] On May 25, after further studying the issue, Brzezinski reported, "This Soviet activity comes very close but does not unambiguously violate earlier assurances and promises given since 1962."[55] In a weekly report in early July, he outlined for the president what he thought the Soviets' next steps would include:

> On rereading the Vienna protocols, I was struck by how intransigent Brezhnev was on regional issues. In spite of your forceful statement, the Soviets simply gave us no reason to believe that they will desist from using the Cubans as their proxies. . . . Accordingly, in the months ahead, I think we have every reason to believe that the Soviets will continue to transform Cuba into the strongest Caribbean and Central American military power, thereby further enhancing the revolutionary dynamism of a region close to us; that they will continue to supply and politically exploit the Cuban proxies in Africa; and that they will step up their pressure on Saudi Arabia (and we have evidence of South Yemen becoming a Soviet regional military warehouse).[56]

Three weeks later, Brzezinski reiterated his concern over what this Soviet brigade episode could indicate about Soviet intentions, claiming that the record of Cuban and Soviet interventions since 1977 suggested "the danger posed by Cuban troublemaking . . . is significant. Whether Cuba is acting as a Soviet surrogate, partner, or (in my mind least likely) simply dragging the USSR along, the results are clear: [Fidel] Castro's foreign activities have well served Soviet interests and created far reaching problems for us."[57] In September, several members of Congress leaked the reports of a Soviet brigade in Cuba to the press, creating a sense of a public crisis before the administration had completed its intelligence review or formulated a policy.[58]

While the Soviet brigade episode was a further confirmation of what Brzezinski already believed regarding Soviet intentions, Vance and Carter did not
agree with Brzezinski's interpretations. Vance saw the presence of a Soviet brigade in Cuba as potentially serious and believed it would have to be discussed
in bilateral relations between the two superpowers. But he also thought that
it was unlikely that the Soviets would agree to the brigade's withdrawal if it
became a public issue; the United States would not be on solid ground in claiming that the brigade violated the understandings on Soviet naval activities in
Cuba reached after the Cuban Missile Crisis, because these did not cover Soviet
ground forces. The brigade issue annoyed Vance due to its possible ramifications for SALT II negotiations, but it did not change his views about Soviet
intentions.[59] Carter similarly desired to defuse the crisis quickly and prevent
the political death of SALT II. While his skepticism about Soviet intentions
continued to grow during summer 1979, Carter still did not view the Soviet
leadership as expansionist. Overall, the president accepted Vance's suggestion
to treat the brigade episode as an "isolated incident" and not part of a larger
pattern in Soviet behavior that reflected expansionist motivations.[60] Thus, contrary to Brzezinski's advice, Carter decided to continue with the SALT ratification process; on October 1, 1979, he delivered a public broadcast explaining
that the Soviet brigade in Cuba posed no direct threat and there was "no reason
for a return to the Cold War."[61]

The Soviet invasion of Afghanistan in December 1979, however, induced a
turning point in Carter's beliefs about Soviet intentions. His statements, private and public, as well as actions and policies during and after the invasion
clearly indicate that his perception of Soviet intentions changed dramatically.
In a message to Brezhnev, sent via the hotline on December 28, Carter said,

> I want to ensure that you have fully weighed the ramifications of the Soviet actions
> in Afghanistan, which we regard as a clear threat to peace. You should understand
> that these actions could mark a fundamental and long-lasting turning point in our
> relations. . . . The Soviet military intervention in Afghanistan—a previously non-
> aligned country—obviously represents an unsettling, dangerous and new stage in
> your use of military force, which raises deep apprehension about the general trend
> of Soviet policy. . . . Neither superpower can arrogate to itself the right to displace or
> overturn a legally constituted government in another country by force of arms. Such
> a precedent is a dangerous one. . . . Unless you draw back from your present course
> of action, this will inevitably jeopardize the course of US-Soviet relations throughout
> the world.[62]

In a public interview, Carter said that "the action of the Soviets has made
a more dramatic change in my opinion of what the Soviets' ultimate goals are
than anything they've done in the previous time that I've been in office."[63] Further, he referred to the invasion as the "greatest threat to peace since the Second
World War," representing a "radical departure from the policy and actions of
the Soviet Union since the Second World War."[64]

But US decision makers did not interpret even that costly action as a credible signal of hostile and expansionist intentions. Brzezinski's report to the president, dated March 28, 1980, explains that although there was "genuinely solid unanimity" among members of the administration regarding the measures adopted in the invasion's aftermath, there were in fact two conflicting interpretations of the Soviet invasion of Afghanistan. Debate was "not merely an intellectual exercise"; it had significant policy implications.[65]

The first interpretation viewed the invasion as an "aberration" from usual Soviet behavior. Proponents of this stance, including Shulman and Vance, wrote Brzezinski, tended "to feel that the primary motive for the Soviet action was defensive, [and] that the Soviets do not have longer-term regional ambitions beyond Afghanistan." Moreover, while proponents of this view did not deny that the USSR occasionally acted aggressively, they saw Afghanistan "largely as an expedient reaction to opportunities rather than as a manifestation of a more sustained trend." Therefore, Brzezinski concluded, this group continued to "nurture hopes of a relatively early return to more normal East-West relations."[66]

The second interpretation regarded the invasion as "symptomatic" of Soviet behavior. Proponents of that perspective, chiefly NSC members, felt that the USSR was "currently in an assertive phase of its history, with the acquisition of military power giving its foreign policy both greater scope and more frequent temptations to use its power to advance policy goals." According to Brzezinski, this group thus concluded that

> Soviet behavior is still prudent, but it does involve a gradual shift from political encouragement of often geographically remote ideological sympathizers, to more direct support of them through the use of Cuban proxies in the mid-1970s, to even more direct projection of Soviet military power itself currently. In other words, Soviet behavior is symptomatic of a long-term historical drive, with military power supplanting Marxist ideology as its basic dynamic source.[67]

Brzezinski leaned toward the second school of thought and saw the invasion as clear confirmation of his existing views about the expansionist nature of Soviet intentions. The NSC perception was that Afghanistan signified a "qualitative turn in Soviet foreign policy" as it reflected "the first use by the Soviets of their armed forces in a combat situation outside the Soviet Bloc since the Second World War, and is therefore an extremely ominous precedent."[68] Brzezinski emphasized that the "Soviet occupation of Afghanistan is the first time since 1945 that the USSR used its military forces to expand its power."[69] Despite the perception of escalation, Brzezinski pointed out in another memo that "there are certain constants in Soviet foreign policy, and the drive toward the Persian Gulf is one of them."[70]

The private record indicates that in contrast to Brzezinski, Vance and his closest adviser on Soviet affairs, Shulman, both leaned toward interpreting the invasion of Afghanistan as an aberration from typical Soviet behavior. Senior decision makers in the State Department attributed defensive motivations to the Soviet leadership, claiming that the Soviet Union had gone into Afghanistan to avert an imminent, costly setback and secure its southern border. Vance and Shulman argued in private that the invasion was "probably not viewed by the Soviet leadership as a significant departure in the pattern of their behavior, nor as a significant departure from the prevailing international 'rules of the game.'" Believing that this was merely the latest manifestation of opportunistic behavior, they saw no reason to change their own assessments of Soviet intentions. Yet they did recognize that the invasion "mark[ed] a qualitative change in their behavior," especially because this "Soviet action crystallized U.S and world reaction to on-going trends in Soviet behavior." They also realized that Afghanistan put into "high relief the contradiction in Soviet policy between the efforts to pursue détente at the same time that it has been exacerbating local conflict situations" in Angola, Ethiopia, Indochina, Yemen, and elsewhere. The invasion of Afghanistan also "triggered US and world expressions of anxiety about Soviet intentions regarding the use of the military capabilities—strategic and conventional—which it has been building since the mid-1960s. It has been taken as an indication that the USSR is prepared to use this capability with less inhibition than was formerly the case."[71]

In their public statements, however, Vance and Shulman tried to downplay the relevance of analyzing Soviet motivations and intentions. Following the invasion, Vance was quoted as saying, "I don't think it does any good to try at this point, to psychoanalyze which of these [two interpretations of Soviet motivations] was the reason—or what combination of them. . . . [T]here must be a sharp and firm response."[72] Later, in a major speech on Afghanistan, Vance stated, "Not even the most penetrating analysis can determine with certainty Soviet interactions in the region—whether their motives in Afghanistan are limited or part of a larger strategy."[73] In fact, all Vance was willing to proclaim publicly was that the "Soviet Union clearly crossed a threshold in its action."[74] As late as December 10, 1981, asked how he perceived the Soviet Union's intentions in international politics, Vance's response indicated that he understood them as opportunistic:

> It's awfully difficult to say with any degree of certainty what the intentions of another country are. But, in general terms, I will try to outline for you what I believe to be the general thrust of Soviet foreign policy. First, the Soviets are determined to be roughly equal to the United States insofar as military power and the ability to project that power are concerned. This is particularly true in the case of nuclear weapons. . . . Insofar as non-military matters are concerned, the Soviet Union, in my judgment, will continue to press its view of the world, and by that I mean Marxism. In order to achieve this, *they will seek targets of opportunity wherever they may arise.*[75]

Yet when asked, "Do you believe the Soviet Union is pursuing a strategy to dominate the world?" he replied, "No, I believe they are realistic enough to recognize that they cannot dominate the world. I do believe, however, that they are going to take advantage of opportunities, wherever they may be found, which will advance their basic ideology or theology, whatever you want to call it."[76] When Shulman was asked whether Vance perceived the Soviets as being bent on world domination, he responded, "I think he [Vance] would put it differently; my impression is that he feels that the Soviet Union would take advantage of opportunities to expand its influence wherever it thought it could do so, safely, and then with acceptable cost."[77]

In sum, the preceding evidence shows us that despite initial disagreements in 1977, Carter began to share Brzezinski's suspicions that the Soviets were limited expansionists. Vance, by contrast, saw the Soviets as behaving opportunistically but without any fundamental change in their foreign policy.

REASONING ABOUT SOVIET INTENTIONS

President Carter's Reasoning

Carter was rarely explicit about the evidence he used to assess Soviet intentions. Nevertheless, the proof I did find, mainly from Carter's public statements, lends support to the behavior thesis. Since Carter might have been strategic in how he chose to portray his beliefs about Soviet intentions, we ought to regard this evidence with more caution. At the same time, declassified documents, Brzezinski's and Vance's memoirs, and Carter's own writings and statements after his tenure as president are consistent with the record of Carter's public statements during that period.

Carter's first litmus test of Soviet cooperative attitudes appears to have been related to SALT II negotiations. In 1977, Carter made numerous positive statements about the USSR in which he linked recent Soviet behavior to more general characteristics and attitudes. For instance, on March 24 he stated,

> The very fact that Mr. Brezhnev and his associates have welcomed Secretary Vance to the USSR and have helped us prepare a very comprehensive agenda is adequate proof that he has not broken off relationships in any way, and that he has hopes that the talks will be productive. . . . My belief is that he is acting in good faith.[78]

Referring to news of a visit by Dobrynin to the State Department a month later to discuss the SALT agreement, Carter noted, "It confirms my own unwavering opinion that the Soviets want a successful resolution of nuclear arms control, the same as we do."[79] In May, similarly, he commented that Soviet behavior so far indicated to him that the USSR did not want to "continue this armament race."[80] Carter's positive reading of the USSR's intentions on the basis of the SALT negotiations was reiterated in many of his public statements and interviews during the rest of 1977.[81] Carter explained that he was equally impressed with Soviet behavior on other issues, including the increasingly constructive Soviet role in the Middle East, its "more responsible position in deploring and working against terrorism," and its position on the Indian Ocean and a comprehensive test ban treaty.[82] Referring to these issues, Carter concluded that Soviet behavior was cooperative and positive, and he was thus optimistic about future bilateral relations.[83] Even when it came to Soviet involvement in regional conflicts, Carter chose to highlight the positive aspects of Soviet behavior in 1977.[84]

Carter's private writings from 1978 until the invasion of Afghanistan reveal that while the president was monitoring recent Soviet actions in Africa, he had yet to decide whether that behavior indicated opportunistic or expansionist intentions. For example, on February 9, 1979, Carter instructed Brown to emphasize certain issues in his meetings with Middle Eastern leaders. In a memo, Carter asked Brown to "make it clear that we see the region to be under serious threat," and "with or without a grand plan, determined Soviet efforts as evidenced in the Horn of Africa, the PDRY [People's Democratic Republic of Yemen], and Afghanistan, now abetted by turmoil in Iran, could lead to general disorder or the imposition of dominant Soviet influence, which the US and its friends cannot tolerate."[85]

The Soviet invasion of Afghanistan no doubt marked Carter's most radical shift in assessment.[86] The invasion represented a costly signal. Carter may have judged that the Soviets would be willing to undertake such a financially and militarily costly action only if they were truly an expansionist power. At the same time, Carter's reasoning does not seem to be based on such costly signaling logic per se. He instead seems to have adopted Brzezinski's interpretation, seeing the invasion as a departure from previous actions in that the Soviets had now placed their troops in a place that they had never been used before. Indeed, Brzezinski had been presenting Carter with this alternative interpretation of Soviet intentions since early 1978, arguing that the Soviets were becoming more assertive in their foreign policy. The invasion of Afghanistan did represent a qualitative shift in Soviet behavior and consequently validated Brzezinski's argument. On January 20, when Bill Monroe from the show *Meet the Press* asked Carter about his assessments of Soviet intentions, the president answered, "It is obvious that the Soviets' actual invasion of a previously nonaligned country, an independent, freedom-loving country, a deeply religious country, with their own massive troops is a radical departure from the policy or actions that the Soviets have pursued since the Second World War."[87] Later Carter reiterated this reasoning, adding that the invasion marked the first time the Soviets "have sent combat forces into an area that was not previously under their control, into a non-aligned and sovereign state," and this represented a "serious threat to world peace."[88]

Carter considered the change in the pattern of Soviet behavior pre- and post-Afghanistan as important evidence. In a telegram to West German chancellor Helmut Schmidt in February 1980, Carter wrote,

> To this point, I regret to say that we have seen no evidence that it is Moscow's intention [to withdraw its troops from Afghanistan,] and the continually growing USSR deployment in Afghanistan appears to us to suggest that the Soviet army went to this small and defenseless country to stay. In light of other Soviet activities in the region—especially in Ethiopia and Yemen—we would have to regard a prolonged Soviet occupation of Afghanistan as part of a calculated strategic thrust against the West's vital interests.[89]

If Brzezinski's insight were correct, the Soviets could be expected to continue to expand. In a State of the Union address on January 4, Carter called the invasion "an extremely serious threat to peace because of the threat of further Soviet expansion into neighboring counties."[90]

In addition to seeing the invasion of Afghanistan as a break from previous patterns of behavior, the interactions between affective and cognitive biases also help explain Carter's interpretation of Soviet behavior and his reaction. Emotions played a role in Carter's attribution of offensive intentions to this Soviet action. Carter's wife, Rosalynn Carter, commented that she had "never seen Jimmy more upset than he was the afternoon the Russian invasion was confirmed."[91] As Richard Ned Lebow and Janice Gross Stein point out, the egocentric bias may have led Carter to exaggerate the extent to which he was the target of Soviet actions and view the invasion as a personal affront.[92] In particular, the invasion contradicted the frank rapport and understanding that he felt he had achieved with Brezhnev during their meeting in June 1979 in Vienna. Indeed, during that summit meeting, Carter spoke of "continuing cooperation and honesty in our discussions," and on his return he had proudly reported to Congress, "President Brezhnev and I developed a better sense of each other as leaders and as men." Brezhnev's justification for the invasion— which asserted that the Soviet troops were sent in response to requests by the Afghan government—infuriated Carter, as he interpreted it as an "insult to his intelligence."[93] Finally, the Soviet invasion was also upsetting because it brought with it the realization that now neither he nor the US Senate would be able to seek Soviet cooperation over the SALT II Treaty. In a conversation with his chief of staff, Hamilton Jordan, following the invasion, Carter explained the sources for his frustration: "This is a deliberate aggression that calls into question détente and the way we have been doing business with the Soviets for the past decade. It raises grave questions about Soviet intentions and destroys any chance of getting the SALT Treaty through the Senate. And that makes the prospects for nuclear war even greater."[94] Carter wrote in his diary, "The Soviet invasion sent a clear indication that they were not to be trusted."[95] Thus, in a letter to Brezhnev in the immediate aftermath of the invasion, Carter communicated an explicit threat: "Unless you draw back from your current course of action, this will inevitably jeopardize the course of U.S.-Soviet relations throughout the world."[96]

Finally, the documents suggest that Carter did not use indicators of Soviet capabilities to support his assessments of Soviet intentions or justify the change in his assessments. After the invasion of Afghanistan, Carter noted that the Soviet military buildup had been going on for many years, but it was the departure in Soviet actions that changed how he perceived their intentions.[97]

Brzezinski's Reasoning

Brzezinski explicitly identified the indicators that shaped and reshaped his perceptions of Soviet intentions. It was not necessarily the costly actions that captured Brzezinski's attention. As early as his second weekly report to the president, Brzezinski explained that "certain preliminary conclusions" about the Soviets' objectives "seem to emerge from Soviet behavior and statements since the election, and more particularly, during the recent tensions over human rights." Even though Brzezinski was still uncertain about Soviet intentions, he pointed to current Soviet actions in several issue areas. The table he presented to Carter in February 1978 (see table 2) is illuminating not only because it reveals how Brzezinski analyzed Soviet intentions but also because of what it does not include.[98] We see no mention of capabilities, nor any reference to Soviet doctrine. The table shows that the behavioral signals Brzezinski attended to were not confined to Soviet interventionism but also extended to Soviet positions in arms control agreements, reactions to US diplomatic initiatives, and other noncostly or less costly actions. Brzezinski concluded that the Soviet Union was pursuing a strategy of selective détente, based on his classification of various Soviet actions as malignant, neutral, or benign.[99]

Soviet rearmament efforts in Ethiopia coupled with increased Soviet activities in sub-Saharan Africa induced a change in Brzezinski's views about Soviet intentions. He began to argue that Soviet actions demonstrated a predisposition to exploit local conflict for a larger purpose. In explaining his "grand design" thesis, Brzezinski started to refer to actions taken farther back in history and not only to recent Soviet behavior. In a memorandum to the president about Soviet motives, he wrote, "There are two possible interpretations":

> 1. Soviet leadership is divided. As a consequence, each bureaucracy does "its own thing." The diplomats and others are pursuing SALT negotiations; the secret police is cracking down on dissidents; and the military ideological section exploits any available opportunity to promote Soviet influence. I do not find this interpretation persuasive because a decision of this magnitude, involving such major possible consequences, is not likely to be undertaken simply on the basis of a condition-reflex.

2. The second interpretation is that the Soviet Union is pursuing deliberately a policy on which it embarked some fifteen years ago: to structure a relationship of stability with the United States in those areas that are congenial or convenient to the USSR, while pursuing assertively every opportunity for the promotion of Soviet influence. In promoting that influence, the Soviets are becoming bolder. There is thus a striking contrast between the Angolan operation—conducted entirely through proxies—and the Ethiopian affair—in which the proxies still carry the major burden but the Soviet presence is more self-evident.

What is even more striking is that the Soviets apparently have concluded that they can run such risks and get away with them.[100]

By the end of 1978, proponents of both contending views of Soviet intentions relied explicitly on recent Soviet behavior in Africa—namely, in Angola, the Horn of Africa, and Zaire—to draw inferences about Soviet intentions. The first group, representing the more hawkish officials in the administration, including Brzezinski, concluded that the Soviets were seeking selective détente because "their action reflects growing assertiveness in Soviet foreign policy." The second group, including Vance, representing less hawkish views, thought that the Soviets were "acting on traditional lines and essentially reacting to US steps," and emphasized that "the record of Soviet action is much more mixed and has to be considered case-by-case."[101]

The first significant debate over Soviet intentions during the second half of the Carter presidency revolved around the discovery of the Soviet brigade in Cuba.[102] Looking at the Soviets' past actions in Cuba, Brzezinski concluded that recent Soviet activities there represented another sophisticated attempt to execute their expansionist designs.[103] While Brzezinski could easily have mentioned the overall Soviet military buildup to reinforce his point, he chose instead to point out that Soviet intentions were most apparent in their "international behavior, particularly in relationship to the various trouble spots."[104] Again, Brzezinski turned to historical precedents, specifically the Berlin Wall analogy, to infer current Soviet intentions.

Less than two months after the furor over the Soviet brigade died down, in late December 1979, the Soviets invaded Afghanistan. Publicly, Brzezinski maintained that Soviet motives for the invasion could not be known.[105] Yet in private, Brzezinski argued that recent Soviet actions in Afghanistan represented a qualitative shift in the USSR's behavior and confirmed his beliefs about the expansionist nature of the Soviet Union. Therefore, he urged Carter to reconsider his evaluation of Soviet intentions. He noted that Afghanistan was the seventh state since 1975 in which Communist parties had come to power with Soviet military power and assistance.[106] The level and type of force employed by the Soviets pointed to an evolution in Soviet behavior, claimed Brzezinski, showing "a gradual shift from political encouragement of often geographically remote ideological sympathizers, to more direct support of them through the use of Cuban proxies in the mid-1970s, to even more direct projection of Soviet military power itself currently."[107]

In making his case, Brzezinski also referred to past actions—particularly Soviet behavior over the past forty years—to assert that "Soviet behavior is symptomatic of a long-term historical drive."[108] These were not necessarily costly actions but rather "some documentary evidence" of Soviet expansionist schemes in the Persian Gulf and Southwest Asian region that indicated the historical basis of Soviet intentions.[109] As Brzezinski explained,

> I am struck by the fact that the draft agreement between the Soviet Union and Nazi Germany, which was being negotiated secretly between Molotov and Ribbentrop in 1940, including the following passage: "the Soviet Union declares that its territorial aspirations center south of the national territory of the Soviet Union in the direction of the Indian Ocean." Moreover, the German Ambassador reported on November 25, 1940 that Molotov told him that the Soviet Union would associate itself with the Axis powers, "provided that the area south of Batum and Baku in the general direction of the Persian Gulf is recognized as the center of the aspirations of the Soviet Union."[110]

What is especially striking about Brzezinski's reasoning is how rarely he referred to capabilities and strategic military doctrine in the context of discussions about Soviet intentions. In fact, out of thousands of archival documents, I found few statements in which he or his colleagues mentioned Soviet capabilities or strategic military doctrine in debates about what Soviet objectives might be. As far as Soviet capabilities were concerned, Brzezinski remarked in one of his weekly reports to Carter that

> there is also a further point to be registered: Soviet defense programs are going beyond the needs of legitimate deterrence and are increasingly pointing towards the acquisition of something which might approximate a war-fighting capability. While we do not know why the Soviets are doing this (intentions?), we do know that their increased capabilities have consequences for our national security.[111]

This statement does not lend support to the capabilities thesis: although Brzezinski does sound concerned about recent trends in Soviet military buildup, he explicitly says that he cannot infer the Soviets' intentions from these indicators. The recent increase in Soviet capabilities had an effect on his overall assessment of threat, but not on the assessment of intentions.

Brzezinski also addressed capabilities in a discussion of Soviet civil defense programs. He presented Carter with an interagency report about these programs, saying that the report "reflects a general interagency consensus on key points, except for the State Department, which takes a more relaxed view of the Soviet program." According to Brzezinski, the conclusion of this classified report "about the meaning of the Soviet program to the Soviets tends to support the 'relaxed' view." Brzezinski, however, referred to this study not to make a point about Soviet intentions. Instead, his concern was with the impact that this report might have on SALT and domestic public opinion if leaked: "These findings, once they become known, will become grist for those alarmed about Soviet capabilities and intentions. Inevitably they will have an impact on the SALT debate in the country. Given the almost total lack of meaningful US civil defense programs, these findings will clearly generate demands that we 'do something' in this area."[112] Brzezinski was aware that *others* might interpret the Soviet military buildup of air defenses as an important indicator of Soviet intentions, but there is nothing in his memorandum to suggest that he himself was drawing such conclusions.

I located two references to Soviet declaratory doctrine that merit some consideration.[113] Both references indicate that Brzezinski monitored changes in Soviet military doctrine and capabilities, and viewed them as indicators of Soviet military objectives, though not necessarily of political intentions. In his second weekly report to Carter, Brzezinski talked about a recent speech by Brezhnev in Tula, concluding that the Soviets have "begun to say that their strategic intentions are indeed limited, and that they would in fact settle for 'parity,'" viewing it as "a sign that the case is being made in the Kremlin for tactical concessions to the Americans, lest the situation get out of hand, and the US embark on a major rearmament program." In short, he noted, "the indicators point to a Soviet desire to establish an accommodation with the new Administration and to nail this down as soon as possible.[114]

One year later, Brzezinski gave Carter a detailed report regarding a recent Soviet exercise in which, again, he used doctrine to infer Soviet military (not political) intentions. The report concludes that

> a recent Soviet Command Staff . . . exercise scenario shows continued Soviet movement away from a doctrine of early and massive initial nuclear use in Europe toward a doctrine more akin to "flexible response." The protracted length of the conventional conflict suggests a conventional-only option. Thus we appear to be seeing a more complex Soviet approach to both nuclear and conventional warfare, including a two front war, mixed nuclear and conventional phasing, intercontinental targeting, limited regional targeting and mobilization of the domestic front in conjunction with civil defense operations.[115]

Overall, Brzezinski's reasoning lends strong support for the selective attention thesis, adequate support for both hypotheses of the behavior thesis, and weak support for the capabilities and military doctrine theses.

Vance's Reasoning

Vance's reasoning clearly indicates that the secretary of state interpreted Soviet behavior differently from Brzezinski and Carter. While Vance, like Brzezinski and Carter, used Soviet noncapabilities-based actions in supporting his assessment, he did not see any of the costly Soviet actions during this period as credible indicators of expansionist intentions. He did not, as a result, update his beliefs about the nature and scope of Soviet goals. Accordingly, while the hawks focused on trends or patterns in Soviet behavior, Vance analyzed each Soviet action individually and perceived no pattern in Soviet behavior that marked a change in intentions.

Vance was clear in stating his belief that neither Soviet behavior in the Horn nor Soviet military actions in Cuba during the brigade affair were indicative of more hostile intentions. Still, recent Soviet actions worldwide heavily influenced Vance's public reasoning about Soviet intentions. This was especially true during the Soviet invasion of Afghanistan. While considering the invasion as threatening to US interests in the region, State Department officials, including Vance and his closest adviser, Shulman, continued to attribute opportunistic or even defensive intentions to the Soviets. They surely recognized that international audiences would draw different inferences. Indeed, in his public appearances as well as his memoirs, Vance conceded that the actions in Afghanistan represented a "sharp escalation" in resorting to direct military force to serve the Soviet Union's interests, however defined. He also looked at these actions as indicative of a significant change in Soviet national strategy, noting that the invasion represented "the first time since WWII" that the USSR had "used its own armed forces to impose its authority directly over a Third World county."[116] Like Brzezinski, Vance pointed to a trend in Soviet actions in his public speeches. This was evident in his last statement before the Senate Foreign Relations Committee prior to his April 1980 resignation: "The Soviet Union has shown a greater willingness to employ that [military] power directly, and through others. In that sense, Afghanistan is the manifestation of a larger problem, evident also in Ethiopia, South Yemen, Southeast Asia and elsewhere."[117] But in private, Vance saw Soviet actions in Afghanistan as aberrant relative to past behavior and therefore as not necessarily indicative of future intentions. Vance was among those who tended to feel that, in Brzezinski's words, "the primary motive for the Soviet actions was defensive, that the Soviets do not have long-term regional ambitions beyond Afghanistan."[118]

Vance makes only a few references to the Soviet military buildup in his public statements. It is unclear whether such references were presented as evidence to support his assessment of Soviet intentions or rather his overall threat assessment. An example of such ambiguity occurs in Vance's last appearance before Congress, where he declared, "Intentions cannot be known with certainty. Even if they could, intentions can change." Yet he believed that in assessing the threat, "our response must be based upon Soviet capabilities and Soviet behavior. To respond firmly to these realities now is not to be apocalyptic; it is simply to be prudent."[119] Even if this comment is interpreted as supporting the capabilities thesis, we should keep in mind how rarely Vance made such statements.[120]

US Policies concerning the USSR

This section tracks the consistency between decision-makers' statements about intentions and the policies they advocated and rejected, as well as examines the extent to which assessments of intentions by members of the Carter administration are reflected in the policies adopted by the administration as a whole. In what follows I argue that during the first year of Carter's presidency, most foreign policy decisions were largely cooperative and aimed at reassuring the USSR. In the following two years, however, the balance between the cooperative and competitive policies shifted. Carter began pursuing somewhat more competitive policies of internal and external balancing and deterrence alongside significant cooperative policies and reassuring gestures. Some of the changes in policies stemmed from Brzezinski's increased influence over Carter along with Carter's own growing criticism of Soviet behavior in the Horn of Africa. Other policies stemmed from strategic assessments pertaining to the future balance of power. Nevertheless, divergence of perceptions within the administration during 1978 and most of 1979 on the issue of Soviet intentions diminished the consistency between beliefs about Soviet intentions at the individual level and foreign policy behavior at the collective level. Throughout 1980, the administration's foreign policy behavior vis-à-vis the USSR shifted radically toward a confrontational posture. This critical shift produced decisions deemed necessary to punish, deter, and contain the USSR, and reflected Carter's own dramatic change in views about the nature of Soviet intentions. Internal debates within the administration reveal that the Soviet invasion of Afghanistan was the primary generator of the most significant policy shift. After Vance's resignation in April, the administration's foreign policy during the rest of 1980 reflected the image of Soviet intentions that Carter and Brzezinski now shared.[121]

We should be careful not to overstate the significance that changing perceptions had on the overall trajectory of the Carter administration's policies. Additional factors such as strategic considerations and domestic politics certainly played an important role in shaping particular policy initiatives.[122] Rather, I argue that the Carter administration's stance toward the Soviets was consistent, by and large, with the president's perceptions of Soviet intentions, and that the most significant turn in his administration's policies stemmed directly from changes in his views on Soviet intentions.

The First Two Years (1977–78)

The Carter administration's polices started out as cooperative in nature and reflected Carter's optimism about US relations with the Soviet Union. During 1977 this was apparent in a series of initiatives aimed at arms control, reductions in the defense budget, cancellations of defense programs, and a repeated refusal to link progress on SALT with revisionist Soviet actions in the third world or human rights. Moreover, Carter met several times with high-level Soviet officials and expressed his desire to meet with the Soviet premier. The Carter administration's decision to develop two types of cruise missiles as well as the neutron bomb, pursue an aggressive human rights campaign, and normalize relations with China also reflected the competitive aspect of US-Soviet relations. A close look at these policies, the debates that preceded them, and the reasoning provided to support them indicates that the vast majority of policies adopted in 1977 were designed to reassure the Soviets; that Carter rejected most of the harder-line policies Brzezinski advocated, preferring Vance's recommendations; and that the competitive policies Carter did pursue were influenced by domestic politics and were not primarily aimed at taking a harder line against the Soviets.

During 1977, even the more hawkish member of the administration, Brzezinski, supported a balanced approach toward the USSR. Brzezinski came to office believing that "the proper American response [to the Soviet Union] should not be a deliberate return to Cold War tensions, but a carefully calibrated policy of simultaneous competition and cooperation."[123] In response to Soviet actions in Africa, though, Brzezinski recommended in April 1977 that the United States should "press the Soviets to desist," and should "do so outside of Africa through diplomatic leverage, trade denial etc. but not through direct involvement in Africa per se."[124] A few months later Brzezinski noted that Soviet economic problems, the strengthening of Brezhnev, and the issue of political dissent in the USSR had led to a temporary cooling of US-Soviet relations.[125] By July, Brzezinski was explicitly pushing for an adjustment in US policies vis-à-vis the USSR, claiming that the United States should not appear to be responding to Soviet pressure nor accepting the Soviet position on SALT. Carter, on the other hand, responded that he saw "no need to change" the US attitude with regard to SALT and that the US public was "still with us."[126] Vance also advocated more cooperative, reassuring policies toward the USSR. In mid-1977, he wrote Carter a memorandum identifying a number of cooperative measures aimed at stabilizing US-Soviet relations. Brzezinski was nonetheless concerned that these "could be interpreted to imply that the cause of current strains is either the result of misconceptions or lack of US effort and that we need a series of steps to prove our seriousness or sincerity." He claimed that "if the Soviet leadership views the Administration's more assertive foreign policy as a sign of hostile intentions, then a number of good-will gestures will have little impact." But Carter approved most of Vance's measures and asked him to convey the list to Brezhnev as a signal of goodwill.[127]

As Soviet and Cuban involvement in Africa intensified during 1977, Brzezinski grew increasingly uncomfortable with Carter's cooperative policies, due in part to domestic political considerations. He feared that US policies regarding "Cuba, Vietnam, Korea, and SALT" as well as Carter's decision to cancel production of the B-1 stealth bomber would be perceived as "soft." He thus recommended that Carter "take, before too long, a decision of some sort either on security or foreign policy matters that has a distinctively 'tough' quality to it," and also "re-identify" himself "directly with the human rights issue even if it means some resentment abroad, notably from the Soviets."[128] Carter's human rights campaign, though it stemmed from his own moral sense, reflected a more competitive aspect in the administration's foreign policy. The record shows that Carter did not intend to incite tension with the USSR over the issue of human rights. In fact, he was surprised to learn that Soviet leaders regarded his human rights campaign as offensive and provocative. While supporting the renewed emphasis, Vance attempted to avoid singling out Soviet shortcomings or using the human rights campaign in a political offensive against the USSR.[129] During the latter part of 1977, Brzezinski repeatedly advocated using the human rights card to both project a tougher posture vis-à-vis the USSR and satisfy domestic audiences.[130]

There was a notable shift toward harder-line policies in 1978, reflecting Brzezinski's views of Soviet intentions and his increasing influence over Carter's views. In particular, Brzezinski continued to pressure Carter to take a tougher stance on the Soviets.[131] But Vance, who still viewed Soviet intentions as opportunistic, continued to advocate more cooperative policies. He thus opposed linking progress on SALT with Soviet actions in other areas and was reluctant to pursue military relations with China. What eventually contributed to the shift in US policies was Carter's own growing skepticism about Soviet intentions and consequently his increasing susceptibility to certain policies Brzezinski advocated with great persistence. The comments he left on Brzezinski's memos and actions he subsequently took reveal this process.

Brzezinski was also preoccupied with the possibility that the US public might wish to see Carter adopt a tougher position toward the Soviets. Accordingly, he suggested that Carter "tell the Soviets very frankly that their behavior in Africa is intolerable," and emphasize that "if Soviet/Cuban forces are introduced into the Southern Africa conflict, this will jeopardize détente as a whole, and we will react strongly." Judging from Carter's remarks in the margins of the document, he seemed to agree with Brzezinski's recommendations, instructing him, among other things, to prepare a draft letter of instructions to Vance saying that the United States "will not stand for a selective détente, in which the Soviet side arbitrarily defines the rules of the game," and that "decisions that will be made this summer on SALT *as well as on other issues* will affect our relationship for many years."[132] Carter did not indicate that he accepted Brzezinski's suggestions to "emphasize some other dimensions" in US-China relations in addition to technology. Nor did he agree to increase the defense budget. In July 1978, he also accepted Brzezinski's idea to pursue human rights issues despite Soviet sensitivities. He wrote "I agree" next to Brzezinski's statement that "I do not understand the argument that we must not link anything to SALT, but that we must also not do some things—on human rights, China, Africa, etc.—because the Soviets might link that to SALT."[133]

During summer 1978, aggressive Soviet activities in Africa as well as the Soviet decision to try two prominent dissidents caused another round of intense internal debate within the NSC and DOD, on the one side, and the State Department, on the other. This time the issue concerned technology transfer to the USSR and new trade initiatives toward the Soviets. Carter faced a serious dilemma on both issues: his senior advisers were sharply divided, with each side making cogent arguments, and he was being pressed, in effect, to make an explicit, inevitably highly visible choice between his secretary of defense and national security advisor, on the one hand, and secretaries of state and the treasury, on the other. On both issues, Carter took the advice of the former.[134] At the same time, the correspondence between Carter and Brzezinski indicates that Carter was highly reluctant to normalize relations with China or Vietnam as part of a balancing effort against the Soviets.[135] When Brzezinski raised this issue again in October, Carter again rejected the idea, noting, "Zbig, you have a tendency to exalt the PRC [People's Republic of China] issue."[136] Most of Brzezinski's recommendations regarding relations with China eventually prevailed, however. The completion of normalization was announced in December 1978, despite Vance's objections. Yet Carter rejected some of the more hawkish policies that Brzezinski began advocating during mid-1978. For example, Carter refused to pursue a strategy that included actions such as a "demonstration of force" meant to "establish credibility and determination and even to infuse fear." He also rejected the idea of manipulating the Soviets through deliberate lies and appeared to be angered by Brzezinski's idea of starting a proxy war with the Soviets.[137]

In September 1978, Carter was still optimistic, believing that pursuing cooperative strategies with the USSR might change the nature of the relationship as a whole. On receiving Brzezinski's analysis that "developments in Southern Africa or Afghanistan pose ample opportunities for renewed or even greater US-Soviet frictions," for instance, Carter responded in the margins, "I'm not sure about this, provided a summit meeting is held to conclude SALT II." Throughout the rest of 1978, Brzezinski urged Carter to reiterate the harder line he had taken in his Annapolis speech and abandon what Brzezinski called a "legal-contractual" foreign policy with the Soviets in favor of a more assertive foreign policy.[138]

Differing with Brzezinski, Vance insisted throughout 1978 that events in Africa were "local in nature" and did not indicate Soviet expansionism. As a result, he believed Carter should not link Soviet behavior in Africa to bilateral relations, especially the SALT negotiations. In a Special Coordination Committee meeting in March, he argued that if the administration were to pursue harder-line policies, it would "end up losing SALT and that will be the worst thing that could happen. If we do not get the SALT treaty in the President's first four years, that will be a blemish on his record forever."[139] Publicly, Vance insisted that the United States should not overreact to the events in Africa: "It will not be our policy to mirror Soviet and Cuban activities in Africa because such a course would not be effective in the long run and would only escalate military conflict with greater human suffering."[140] Vance believed that "a policy of confrontation was not a winning strategy: Congress and the American people would not support direct US military involvement."[141] In May, Vance asked Carter to review US-Soviet relations in light of Carter's toughening approach toward the Soviet Union. His memo to Carter summarized the evolution in Carter's foreign policy vis-à-vis the USSR:

> Increasingly, we are faced with two differing views of US-Soviet relations; although so far we have managed to combine the two in our public statements, it is becoming more difficult to do so. We have always recognized that the relationship between the US and the USSR has been a combination of cooperation and competition, with the competition not preventing either side from seeking agreements in our mutual benefit in such areas as SALT. Now however, we are coming to the point where there is a growing pressure on the part of some people to have us portray the competitive aspects of the relationship as taking clear precedence over the search for areas of cooperation.[142]

The Last Two Years: A Shift to a Harder Line (1979–80)

In 1979, Carter had not yet made any real determination about whether Soviet intentions were expansionist in nature and was therefore careful not to pursue policies that would negatively affect US-Soviet relations. The divergence of perspectives on Soviet intentions within the Carter administration was reflected in the ambivalent foreign policy adopted by the administration as a whole during that year. Following the invasion of Afghanistan at the end of 1979, however, a more substantial shift occurred in US foreign policy. The vast majority of policies adopted vis-à-vis the USSR were aggressive, aimed at punishing, balancing, and containing Soviet expansion. At the level of individual decision makers, we see strong congruence between the perceptions of Soviet intentions and the policies advocated or rejected. This finding should bolster our confidence that these decision makers' statements about Soviet intentions were not simply posturing.

The three major policy decisions facing Carter during 1979 concerned the development and deployment of the MX missile system, increases in the defense budget, and the ratification of SALT. These decisions were obviously linked, as the first two were needed to persuade domestic opponents to accept the third one. All senior members of the administration, with the notable exception of the president, believed that the United States would be at a strategic disadvantage if SALT II were not accompanied by new strategic deployment.[143] Indeed, throughout 1979, Brzezinski was worried that both domestic and international audiences perceived Carter's foreign policy toward the USSR as "indecisive, vacillating, and pursuing a policy of acquiescence."[144]

During the months leading up to the June 1979 Vienna summit, Brzezinski continued to press Carter to act more assertively vis-à-vis the USSR. On January 12, 1979, he wrote to Carter that while the war in Cambodia "has obvious indigenous roots, the Soviets clearly have provided a political umbrella for it, and maybe even more than that." Brzezinski perceived a pattern emerging from the recent behavior of the USSR that revealed something about the Soviets' ultimate objectives:

> A Cambodian invasion represents the third time that a country which has concluded a friendship and cooperation treaty with the Soviet Union has shortly thereafter engaged in a recourse to arms. . . . I am not suggesting that we go on a crusade against the Soviets over this issue. . . . However, the larger and longer term issue does involve the need for greater Soviet restraint in regard to regional conflicts, and the record is not reassuring. Precisely because we do not link SALT to other issues, we should similarly refrain from negative linkage: fearing to raise controversial issues because they would complicate SALT.[145]

Carter rejected Brzezinski's recommendations and wrote in the margin, "The Soviets *may* have trapped themselves by forcing a 3rd world up or down between them and China. Our present position is o.k. for now."[146]

The issue of linkage resurfaced in full force in late summer 1979, following the alarm over reports that there was a Soviet brigade in Cuba. Brzezinski advocated even more confrontational policies than he had previously, expressing the concern that the Soviet Union was increasingly the assertive party and the US side was more acquiescent. This was seen, Brzezinski wrote, "as especially true in terms of international behavior, particularly in relationship to the various trouble spots. For better or worse, we were passive in Iran; the Soviets are far from passive in Afghanistan. We pursued a diplomatically amiable policy in Africa; the Soviets relied on Cuban arms, not without some effect." He thus recommended "not a reckless policy of confrontation" but rather a "more assertive tone and a more assertive substance" to US foreign policy. Carter wrote "good" on the first page of the document, but did not offer his opinion regarding any of Brzezinski's suggestions.[147] Also, Brzezinski stressed that although he was not in favor of sending more troops to Guantánamo, he preferred to take "at least one" step that "genuinely hurts the Soviets" and maintain "for a few months a tough posture on the Soviets in our public pronouncements." (Carter wrote in the margins "o.k." referring to the latter suggestion.) Such moves included "more defense, more intelligence, some limited steps regarding China . . . , and a generally more tough line on Soviet adventurism and disregard for our interests."[148]

As for linking the brigade issue to SALT, Brzezinski suggested that the president will "not get SALT ratified if the public thinks we were timid on this [brigade] issue" and should adopt a tougher posture that would include: "1) more defense [budget]; 2) SALT ratification; 3) assertive competition."[149] Brzezinski further indicated that his interpretation of Soviet behavior was not "designed to suggest that we somehow adopt a reckless policy of confrontationalism, nor is it meant to hint that our policy has been one of appeasement." Rather, it was "meant to suggest that the US was becoming excessively acquiescent," and he believed that the president "ought to deliberately toughen both the tone and the substance of our foreign policy."[150] Carter rejected most of Brzezinski's policy suggestions and instead leaned more toward Vance's position, which favored treating the brigade affair as an isolated, if serious, problem.[151] As a result, Brzezinski considered resigning, telling Carter that "the way we handled this matter could be dangerous for the future because the Russians could miscalculate, and that is exactly what happened with [Nikita] Khrushchev and [John Fitzgerald] Kennedy." Carter appeared quite angry, wrote Brzezinski later, stating that he "had no intention of going to war over the Soviet brigade in Cuba."[152]

Discussions of a possible security relationship with China gained intensity in 1979. Following the June Vienna summit, Carter told Brown and Vance that he was willing to play the China card as a way "to counter [Soviet] moves (Third World Cuban activities, the buildup of an arsenal in South Yemen, reinforcement of Cuban military potential in Central America)."[153] Vance believed that Moscow was bound to perceive a proposed visit by the US secretary of defense to China while the furor over the brigade affair was at its height as a countermove.[154] Brown, backed by Brzezinski, disagreed.[155] On this issue, Carter rejected Vance's recommendations, and accepted the views of Brzezinski and Brown; the latter became the first US secretary of defense to visit the People's Republic of China, a year after normalization of US-China relations. Nevertheless, Carter declared in late 1979 that the relationship with China would "not include US arms sales at this time," and would "not be used to provoke a Sino-Soviet conflict or to manipulate Sino-Soviet tensions for tactical benefits."[156] These decisions were, however, reversed a few days later as a result of the Soviet invasion of Afghanistan.

The significant change in Carter's beliefs about Soviet intentions following the invasion of Afghanistan was matched by a dramatic change in his policies.[157] Within five days of the invasion, the administration had formulated a series of measures starting with the adoption of sanctions directed at punishing the USSR. Two of these sanctions—the grain embargo and boycott of the Moscow Summer Olympics—were met with much resistance from both domestic and international actors.[158] Second was the formulation of the Carter Doctrine, linking the security of the Southwest Asia–Persian Gulf region with that of the United States, along with a US effort to shape a regional security framework.

Third, improvements in US strategic forces were accelerated in terms of doctrine and defense budget.[159] These policy initiatives reflected important shifts in the administration's threat assessments and perceptions of Soviet intentions. An NSC report titled "Foreign Policy: Coherence and Sense of Direction" summarizes this point:

> The Soviet invasion of Afghanistan must focus our attention on a major new order of politico-economic-military threat to the non-communist world security—Soviet domination of Middle East oil. It is not Afghanistan *per se* which is strategically important but that aggressive Soviet behavior there, against the backdrop of constantly growing Soviet military power, betokens a grave and imminent threat to the entire world to which it must respond.[160]

The disagreements of the past three years subsided; there was consensus within the administration that a tough approach was required. The objective, said Carter, was to "make the Soviets pay for their unwarranted aggression without yielding to political pressures here at home."[161] Still, disagreements remained about what extent of punishment was appropriate and whether arms control negotiations should continue; these disagreements reflected the differences in interpretations about Soviet intentions. For example, believing that Soviet intentions were limited in scope and defensive in nature, Vance sought to continue to talk to the Soviets during the crisis.[162] Brzezinski, on the other hand, advocated more hard-line policies, most of which Carter now chose to accept.[163] On January 8, for instance, Brzezinski stated that "to counter Soviet aggressiveness, a long-term commitment is required. . . . US strategic modernization, increased defense spending, improvements in NATO, and the RDF [Rapid Deployment Force] are all steps which will in time work to deter the Soviets, if pursued diligently." The Soviets were likely to "embark on a peace offensive designed to separate us from our allies and to improve the Soviet image in the third world. We should anticipate this event and be prepared to counter efforts to deter us from our allies." In the margins, next to these lines, Carter wrote, "Let's do it to them."[164]

Carter and Brzezinski understood that they should have "no illusions about an early improvement" in US-Soviet relations, and that whatever the United States chose to do in the region, "*it will be costly*."[165] The most painful decision for the president was tabling SALT II. Linking Soviet actions with the treaty was not primarily intended to serve as a hostile signal to the Soviets; rather, it was understood that following the invasion, SALT ratification by the Senate had become impossible. Brzezinski warned Carter that "a Senate rejection of SALT will hurt TNF [Theater Nuclear Forces] in addition to hurting you." Accordingly he suggested, "If we conclude that SALT has to be delayed, placing the blame on Soviet aggression in Afghanistan will make it less of a political setback for us, while enabling us to insist with the Europeans that we all go ahead with TNF."[166]

The emerging strategy of containment involved three important elements.[167] First was the creation of a regional security framework to stop any further Soviet advance in the Southwest Asia–Persian Gulf area (i.e., the Carter Doctrine). There was also a renewed stress on building US military power across the board, including strategic forces and general-purpose land, air, and sea power as well as the Rapid Deployment Force.[168] Third was a more general diplomatic effort to balance against Soviet power, including using the China card.[169] The change in US perceptions of Soviet intentions stemming from its activities in Afghanistan was not the only factor to cause this significant shift in US posture, but it did generate a more forceful response to already-growing concerns about Soviet intentions.

CONCLUSION

Consistent with the expectations of the selective attention thesis, Carter and his advisers did not agree on the informative value of Soviet costly actions. Rather, they debated the importance of various indicators in inferring intentions and interpreted costly Soviet behavior markedly differently from one another. Specifically, decision makers' prior beliefs affected the credibility each of the three decision makers attached to various Soviet actions. For Brzezinski, the most hawkish of the three, the Soviet intervention in the Horn of Africa signified a qualitative change in Soviet behavior, since the Soviets were willing to devote more resources to changing the status quo in Ethiopia. He categorized that intervention as indicative of Soviet goals, leading him to see a shift from opportunism to expansionism in early 1978. For Carter, that intervention carried no such credibility. Thus, while becoming more concerned about Soviet actions, his assessment of its intentions did not change significantly. Yet following the invasion of Afghanistan in December 1979, Carter's image of the USSR transformed radically. The invasion, in Carter's view,was seen as informative not only because of the financial and military costs of that intervention but also because this action represented a radical change from past Soviet behavior as well as a rejection of his own personal request of Brezhnev during the Vienna summit to put an end to Soviet interventionism in Africa. The president thus experienced a strong emotional reaction of anger, betrayal, and disappointment toward the Soviet leadership. This emotional reaction might explain Carter's rejection of the more defensive interpretation of Soviet behavior that was promoted by Vance and Shulman. Indeed, a reading of Soviet actions in Afghanistan as defensive would have been more consistent with Carter's prior beliefs and would not have required him to abandon the SALT II agreement he had worked so hard to achieve. Finally, Vance did not see Soviet involvement in the Horn of Africa, its invasion of Afghanistan, or any other actions the Soviets undertook during this period as indicative of aggressive intentions. Vance disagreed with Carter's interpretation of the Soviet actions in Afghanistan, arguing that Afghanistan was in the Soviet sphere of influence, it did not necessarily have a profound strategic significance, and the invasion demonstrated at most a mix of defensive and opportunistic intentions. As a result, he regarded Soviet intentions as opportunistic at worst throughout the period, and saw no reason to update his assessments. This persistence in Vance's beliefs about intentions in the face of costly action highlights the subjective nature of credibility and hence is consistent with the expectations of the selective attention thesis more broadly.

The support for the alternative theses is mixed. To begin with, the evidence presented lends moderate support to the current actions hypothesis that is derived from the behavior thesis, as Carter and Brzezinski both used Soviet military interventions to infer political intentions. Yet the behavior thesis does not explain why, unlike Brzezinski, Carter and Vance did not infer hostile or expansionist motives from Soviet military involvement in the Horn of Africa; nor does it explain why the invasion of Afghanistan triggered such a dramatic change in Carter's beliefs about Soviet intentions but had no such effect on Vance. Then too, the behavior thesis fails to account for the differences between the decision makers' inference process—which largely relied on assessments of Soviet actions, albeit not necessarily costly ones—and the US intelligence community's inference process, which as we will see in the next chapter, largely relied on assessments of Soviet capabilities. The reasoning evidence further indicates that Carter and his advisers did not treat Soviet capabilities and military doctrine as key indicators of Soviet political intentions. Even Brzezinski, who held more hawkish views of Soviet intentions, rarely employed the Soviet military buildup to support his assessments, although clearly such evidence would have supported his case. When the issue of Soviet capabilities was raised, it was in the context of an overall assessment of the balance of power along with its effect on future US defense programs.

Finally, the historical record shows that notwithstanding the significant increase in Soviet military capabilities and recognition that Soviet military doctrine has clear offensive aspects, the Carter administration's foreign policy was cooperative in nature during most of the first two years. In fact, at the collective level, the evolution in the Carter administration's policies toward the USSR during 1979 and 1980 is generally consistent with the expectations of the current actions hypothesis of the behavior thesis, as the most significant shift in the administration's policy was triggered by the invasion of Afghanistan. Nevertheless, consistent with the selective attention thesis, we find that different decision makers changed their preferred policies at different times. Brzezinski's hawkish statements about the Soviet Union's intentions following its intervention in the Horn of Africa in 1978 and the episode of the Soviet brigade in Cuba in 1979 led him to pressure Carter to pursue more aggressive policies. Vance's assessments of Soviet intentions were reflected in the cooperative, reassuring policies he advocated. Even after the Soviet invasion of Afghanistan, Vance wished to moderate US reactions. The shift in the policies Carter chose to adopt and re-ject mirrors the patterns of change that took place in his perceived intentions, especially following the Soviet invasion of Afghanistan.

While the change in Carter's perceived intentions produced the most signifi-cant shift in the Carter administration's security policies, assessments of Soviet intentions were surely not the only consideration shaping specific defense ini-tiatives. Recent studies have convincingly shown that Carter's MX choice began before the Soviet invasion of Afghanistan, for example, and resulted from a "prudent (albeit late) change in the assessments of the Soviet Union's military power, of its power projection capabilities and potential possession of strategic geography relative to that of the United States."[170] Specifically, a more alarming picture of the future balance of power with the Soviet Union arose out of the administration's Nuclear Targeting Policy Review in 1978, the NSC's CNA of 1978, and the Pentagon's Consolidated Guidance of 1979.[171]

Other studies have pointed to the effect of domestic politics.[172] While it is beyond the scope of this book to analyze the different sources affecting Carter's policy choices, it is worth mentioning a few places where domestic political considerations were explicitly invoked to advocate a shift in policies toward the Soviets. For example, according to the documentary evidence, in 1979 Brzezin-ski believed that a tougher stance toward the Soviets was necessary for domestic political reasons. Brzezinski warned of an "increasing rebellion at home" due to Soviet involvement in the Horn of Africa if the United States were not tougher on the Soviets, contending that the ratification of SALT II was at risk.[173] Again, pushing for a more assertive response to the Soviet brigade affair, Brzezinski reasoned in a memo to Carter, "Every poll shows that the country wants you to be tougher. Unless you convey credibly the message that you will not let the Russians push us around (in addition to blasting Castro personally) you will lose SALT."[174] Thinking about Carter's standing within the Democratic Party, Brzezinski argued, "By toughening up our posture vis-à-vis the Soviets, you will either force [Senator Ted] Kennedy to back you, or to oppose you. . . . If he backs you, he is backing an assertive and tough President; if he opposes you, he can easily be stamped as a latter-day McGovernite."[175]

It thus seems that the Carter administration's overall stance toward the So-viet Union reflected and was largely shaped by Carter's perceptions of Soviet intentions, while strategic and domestic political considerations played impor-tant roles in determining the contours of specific defense policies.

CHAPTER 7

The US Intelligence Community's Assessments of Soviet Intentions

THE COLLAPSE OF DÉTENTE

This chapter examines NIEs produced on the Soviet Union between 1977 and 1980 to evaluate the degree to which history confirms the predictions of the selective attention's organizational expertise hypothesis, and also to test the three competing theses—the capabilities, strategic military doctrine, and behavior theses. I use the declassified NIEs on the Soviet Union.

The NIEs on the Soviet Union that I review in this chapter are a series of documents produced in coordination by US intelligence agencies, including the CIA, the DIA, the National Security Agency (NSA), the intelligence organization of the Department of State (the INR), the US Treasury, and representatives from the intelligence branches of the army, navy, air force and marine corps. Between 1953 and 1973 the Office of National Estimates (ONE) of the CIA was responsible for drafting the estimates of the USSR. In 1973, DCI William Colby fundamentally restructured the CIA's entire estimates organization. He abolished the ONE and replaced it with a group of national intelligence officers (NIOs), each responsible for specific geographic and functional areas. For example, one NIO had responsibility for the USSR, one for Soviet Strategic Programs, and another for Soviet General-Purpose Forces. Each NIO had a single deputy but no staff, depending instead on others in the intelligence community to provide analytic support. After 1979, the NIOs were members of a loose umbrella organization called the National Intelligence Council, but there was still no equivalent of the previous ONE staff to provide an expert peer review of estimates. Moreover, this organizational restructuring left the community with no body responsible for integrating overall coverage of Soviet intentions and capabilities.[1]

NIEs are the most authoritative product of the intelligence community. What makes them authoritative "is the fact that they have been vetted and approved by the heads of all agencies and issued in the name of the senior official of the Intelligence Community, that is, the DCI in his role, at that period, as the Head of the Intelligence Community. NIEs have gone to the top of the bureaucratic totem pole, and the heads of each agency have taken responsibility for the judgments and the tradecraft used to produce them."[2] The community regularly assessed Soviet intentions in the 11-4 and 11-8 series of NIEs, and supplemented these with occasional SNIEs. The 11-4 series explicitly assessed Soviet intentions, but did not appear on a regular basis, while the annual 11-3/8 series in part assessed overall Soviet intentions, yet mainly focused on Soviet intentions and capabilities for intercontinental warfare. In all NIEs, I analyze those sections that deal with the question of intentions.[3] Overall, these coordinated estimates constitute a discrete set of documents that reveal the judgments of a crucial set of actors whose job was to concentrate on assessing the intentions of US adversaries. Further, because these documents were prepared regularly and because agencies could record their dissents directly in the NIEs in cases of disagreement, I am able to trace changes in the assessments of intentions at the collective level as well as at the level of any particular intelligence agency.[4]

In addition to these NIEs, I conducted interviews with people who had been members of the intelligence community at the time, including Arnold Horelick (the NIO for the Soviet Union and Eastern Europe), Fritz Ermarth (the NIO on Soviet Strategic Programs), and William Odom (Brzezinski's military assistant).

The first section of this chapter provides a brief overview of the intelligence community's estimates of Soviet intentions earlier in the 1970s in order to establish a baseline for the assessments in the latter part of the 1970s. The second section shifts the focus to the intelligence community's views during Carter's presidency to test the predictions of the four theses against the statements and reasoning that the intelligence community offered in these NIEs.

BASELINE ASSESSMENTS

Questions about Soviet intentions preoccupied the intelligence community, especially from the moment the USSR acquired long-range offensive nuclear weapons. The continuous build up of Soviet capabilities throughout the second half of the 1960s and throughout the 1970s coupled with the prospect of a change in the global correlation of forces, opened a range of questions about the objectives underlying Soviet strategic force planning and their implications for future Soviet foreign policy. Knowing what the Soviets were planning was critical, given the apparent dualism in Soviet foreign policy: on the one hand, the Soviets had accepted détente and signed the SALT I agreement in 1972; on the other hand, they never ceased or slowed down the substantial modernization and general expansion of their armed forces that began after Khrushchev's fall from power in 1964. This ambiguity in their policies reinvigorated the US debate over Soviet political and military intentions, and figured prominently in the NIEs throughout this period.

NIE 11-3/8-74, drafted during the time that Colby was DCI, concluded that "while the Soviet leaders clearly agree on both the broad outlines of détente policy and the high value of strategic power, it is reasonable to suppose that they differ on priorities." The intelligence community could not estimate at that point whether the Soviets had firmly "settled on either acceptance of parity or a decision to seek clear-cut strategic superiority."[5] It decided that this "programmatic opportunism" probably stemmed from "attitudes of deep-seated fear as to the capabilities and intentions of the U.S. and other nations."[6]

These relatively benign conclusions about Soviet objectives in NIE 11-3/8-74 angered many on the President's Foreign Intelligence Advisory Board (PFIAB). The board's chair, Admiral George Anderson, sent a letter to President Ford advising a "competitive analysis of the intelligence on Soviet intentions and capabilities."[7] DCI Colby defended the conclusions reached in this NIE. In a letter to the president, he wrote, "NIE 11-3/8-74 was the product of a still-continuing evolutionary process. . . . While I would not contend that NIE 11-3/8-74 was a perfect document, I cannot agree with the PFIAB's contention that it errs by 'projecting a sense of complacency' or for that matter, in offering any judgments 'unsupported by the facts.'"[8]

In 1976, DCI George H. W. Bush eventually accepted Anderson's recommendation to appoint a team of outside experts headed by Dr. Richard Pipes—a group that came to be known as Team B—to review the Soviet strategic estimate prepared by the ONE (Team A).[9] Team B's mission was to concentrate on the most contentious aspects of the Soviet estimates, chief among them that of Soviet objectives.[10] The team released its findings on December 21, 1976, a month before the Carter administration began. In a letter to the estimate's recipients, Director Bush declared that the purpose of assembling panels of outside experts was to "determine whether those known for their more somber views of Soviet capabilities and objectives could present the evidence in a sufficiently convincing way to alter the analytical judgments which otherwise would have been presented."[11] Team B's estimates of Soviet intentions were significantly more alarming than suggested in previous NIEs. The Soviets' political intentions were described as including nothing less than the world triumph of "socialism" and world domination through the use of military force.[12] Team B asserted that the USSR was "preparing for a Third World War as if it were unavoidable." Overall the report was quite pessimistic about the speed at which the Soviets would become able to achieve their expansionist objectives, stating, "Within the ten year period of the National Estimate the Soviets may well expect to achieve a degree of military superiority which would permit a dramatically more aggressive pursuit of their hegemonial objectives, including direct military challenges to Western vital interests."[13]

Moreover, Team B accused the CIA of consistently underestimating the "intensity, scope, and implicit threat" posed by the USSR, because "the hard evidence on which the NIEs are based related primarily on the adversary's *capabilities* rather than his *intentions*, his weapons rather than his ideas, motives and aspirations."[14] Team B, in other words, pointed out that the CIA relied on so-called hard data that were collected by technical means and argued that it suffered from "mirror-imaging" (presuming that the people being studied think like the analysts themselves) while misinterpreting the large body of "soft data" concerning Soviet concepts.[15] Team B's own report claimed that its reasoning about Soviet intentions used indicators such as Soviet ideology, past actions, and Soviet doctrinal writings to explain the objectives of the Soviet leadership.[16] Yet a close reading of the report indicates that Team B, too, relied most substantially on information about Soviet capabilities to reach conclusions about the scope and nature of Soviet intentions in the next ten years.[17] Thus, the Team B report seems to have fallen into the same trap of estimating intentions from capabilities, despite an awareness of the problematic nature of such an inference process.

The CIA report that was issued around the same time, NIE 11-3/8-76 (which became known as the Team A report), described the Soviets as willing to use military force coercively in order to achieve their expansionist objectives and concluded that they were clearly seeking to achieve military superiority.[18] The Soviets also were seen as planning to win a nuclear war if it came. Unlike Team B, however, the intelligence community did not believe that the Soviets would seek direct military confrontation with the United States. It certainly did not share Team B's view that the Soviets were preparing for World War III. Moreover, it explicitly stated that its authors did "*not* believe [Team B's assertion] that the Soviet leaders presently count on a combination of actions by the USSR and lack of action by the US which would give them, in the next 10 years, a capability for intercontinental conflict so effective that the USSR could devastate the US while preventing the US from devastating the USSR."[19]

The intelligence community was divided, though. The sources of disagreement between the agencies stemmed primarily from differing readings of the Soviet Union's perception of its own military power and the balance of capabilities between the superpowers. The State Department's INR, while concurring with the NIE's estimated political intentions of the Soviet leadership, did not accept the view that the increase in Soviet military might was designed to achieve strategic superiority or a war-winning posture in the near future. The INR claimed that it was "unlikely" that the Soviets' perceptions of the correlation of forces "would substantially influence their behavior during periods of crises or otherwise."[20] The DIA, Energy Research and Development Administration, and military intelligence organizations presented more hawkish views, claiming that the Soviets did in fact see as "attainable" their objective of "achieving the capability to wage an intercontinental nuclear war, should such a war occur, and survive it with resources sufficient to dominate the postwar period." They also believed that this objective served as a "practical guideline for Soviet strategic force development even though the Soviets [had] not necessarily set a specific date for its achievement."[21] Air Force Intelligence, taking the most hawkish views on Soviet intentions (and the closest to that of the Team B report), alleged that while the present NIE was "much improved" over some of its predecessors, it nevertheless underestimated Soviet military intentions, adding that enough evidence existed to conclude that the "Soviets' negotiations at SALT and their détente, economic, and arms control diplomacy have thus been exploited by them for strategic advantage."[22]

To what degree were NIE 11-3/8-76 and subsequent NIEs changed to respond to Team B's criticism? Howard Stoertz, a retired CIA official who was the NIO for strategic programs from 1973 to 1980 as well as the leader of Team A, said that the specific effect of Team B or any other political intervention on a given year's NIE was subtle. Yet Stoertz conceded that some statements about Soviet intentions were changed to align more with those of Team B. These changes, for the most part, consisted of deleting statements not based on hard evidence; he told his analysts to make sure to include a brief description of the evidence beyond their major points and document their findings carefully.[23] Similarly, Admiral Stansfield Turner, who served President Carter as a DCI, noted that the Team B report changed the mentality, process, and politics of the CIA estimates, as it "caused intelligence analysts to lean over backward not to underestimate the USSR."[24] Garthoff said that the report gave a considerable "boost to the similarly minded Air Force Intelligence chiefs and to some extent to other military intelligence agencies on questions of Soviet objectives, and it made some CIA statements on that subject in the NIEs more cautious and equivocal. But it did not lead to a significant change."[25] Willard Matthias, an intelligence analyst, summarized the "Team A-B episode" as follows:

> I think one must recognize, as a result of the Team A-B exercise and the course events took after 1976, that the estimative process had lost its intellectual integrity. It was no longer rational research and analytic process, but a political-bureaucratic arena dominated by the military services and anti-Communist ideologists, collaborating under the aegis of the Committee on the Present Danger, in order to corrupt and harness the intelligence system.[26]

Former Secretary of Defense Robert Gates agrees, arguing that this episode reduced the CIA's morale, turning the agency into "just another Washington bureaucracy, and self-protection—conscious or not—would be its hallmark."[27]

Regardless of the Team B's influence on subsequent NIEs, this report appears to have had little effect on the decision makers of the incoming Carter administration. According to Matthias, Brzezinski and his deputy, David Aaron, were not much interested in intelligence estimates (Brzezinski described them as a "nuisance").[28] In an interview with this author, General Odom stated that the vast majority of the

NIEs, including the Team B report, did not matter much as far as the key decision makers in the Carter administration were concerned.[29] My interview with Brzezinski confirmed this claim; he stated that no one in the Carter administration, himself included, believed that the Soviets were planning for World War III.[30]

NIEs during the Carter Administration

How did the US intelligence community characterize Soviet intentions in the coordinated estimates during the Carter years? To what extent did their estimates converge with those held by decision makers in the Carter administration? What indicators of Soviet intentions did the community attend to when estimating Soviet intentions?[31]

Statements about Soviet Intentions

Carter's presidency began shortly after the completion of the parallel drafts of Team A and Team B. Because Carter rejected the experience in its entirety, the experiment in competitive analysis was never brought to its intended conclusion. A review of the subsequent available estimates reveals that during the first two years of the Carter administration, the intelligence community described Soviet political intentions as expansionist with regard to certain geographic regions and opportunistic with regard to others. Soviet behavior was expected to become more assertive in the future due to the USSR's increased military capabilities. Yet the intelligence community as a whole argued that while exploiting détente, the Soviet Union would not act aggressively enough to risk its relations with the United States. On the issue of military intentions, the intelligence community continued to see the Soviets as having a high propensity to use military force to achieve their political objectives. It believed that their objectives in war included the seizing of territory in Central Europe and possibly Western Europe as well. It declared that the Soviets were clearly seeking military superiority over the United States and NATO.

The first NIE on Soviet intentions during the Carter administration, titled "Soviet Strategic Objectives," concluded that the Soviets' intentions were "far reaching" as well as "reinforced by both defensive and offensive expansionist impulses" that did not "aim at long-term equilibrium between the two powers" but instead sought for the USSR a "continual enhancement of its own power and influence."[32] Furthermore, the Soviets were perceived as inclined to see their military power "as a key instrument which [could] be used to attain strategic objectives without war."[33] It was believed that the USSR did not aim at nuclear war.[34] But the community could not agree on the following questions. First, did the Soviets seek to achieve strategic superiority over the United States, or should their efforts be viewed as "more pragmatic," aimed at achieving advantages where they could? How did the Soviet leadership perceive the feasibility of attaining superiority? And third, did the USSR have realistic expectations of achieving war-winning capabilities, and if so, in what time frame?

The INR presented a more benign interpretation in the NIE than did the intelligence community as a whole, claiming that the Soviet leadership had more defensive and "pragmatic" objectives (namely, countering the growing power of the United States), and that it did not regard nuclear war-winning capabilities as attainable.[35] Accordingly, while the INR expected Soviet foreign policy to be "more assertive" in the future, it nonetheless estimated that Moscow did not expect at this point "a series of advances that, by the mid-1980s, [would] cumulate in a finally decisive shift in the struggle."[36] The military intelligence agencies, in contrast, claimed that the Soviets were preparing to "win a nuclear war should it occur and to survive as a viable national entity," that the Soviets viewed the objective of achieving a "decisive strategic superiority" and "overall dominance in the world" as "practical and attainable in a programmed fashion," and that "they expect to move closer to that goal over the next ten years."[37] As we will see in the next section, these two different readings of intentions stemmed largely from differences in the reading of current and projected Soviet military capabilities as well as the Soviet confidence level about its own military power.

The next two NIEs, 11-3/8-77 and 11-3/8-78, did not contain estimates of Soviet objectives, and on this point both referred readers to NIE 11-4-78.[38] Titled "Soviet Goals and Expectations in the Global Power Arena," NIE 11-4-78 is especially relevant because, like NIE 11-4-77 just discussed, it deals explicitly with the question of Soviet intentions. Also, perhaps more important, this estimate was formulated in the midst of the crisis in the Horn of Africa, when the Soviets were believed to have stepped up their military involvement. Gates describes it as follows:

> The secret assessment (now declassified) . . . signaled a perceptible shift in the intelligence community's thinking about the USSR—a shift toward a more somber assessment of the main thrust of Soviet military policy and of likely Soviet behavior, especially in the Third World. It was not an alarmist estimate, but it was sobering, a cold shower. And it hit the administration just at a time when Brzezinski and others were deeply concerned about Soviet aggressiveness around the world.[39]

In the preface to that NIE, DCI Turner explained that while the estimate took into account the views and criticisms of the various agencies of the National Foreign Intelligence Board (the body responsible for approving NIEs before they are delivered to policy makers) "to a much higher degree than is customary for major intelligence estimates, it bears the stamp of a unified integrated view."[40] When assessing Soviet political intentions, the NIE repeated some of its statements from previous years, and predicted that the Soviets would continue to press global and regional issues of security in which "the weight of their military power can be brought to bear to political advantage."[41] It portrayed the Soviets as treating détente as a way to "control costs and risks" while allowing them to "exploit fresh opportunities for gain." The NIE concluded, however, that when it came to those geographic areas perceived by the Soviets as linked to vital US interests, the Soviets were more likely to act rationally, and weigh the costs and risks of disrupting détente.[42] It observed that "on the whole, such a prognosis, while projecting some increase in the assertiveness of the Soviet Union's external behavior, represents a fairly natural evolution of the USSR's foreign policy."[43]

Indeed, the intelligence community's conviction that the Soviets would not pursue policies that might risk US-Soviet détente led it, according to CIA deputy director Richard Kerr, to fail to see the possibility that the Soviets would launch a major military invasion into Afghanistan a year later.[44] Soviet foreign policy in the 1980s was also expected to include "a purposeful, cautious exploration of the political implications of the USSR's increased military strength." In practice, this meant that Soviet policy would "continue to be competitive and assertive in most areas of engagement with the West," and that the Soviet leadership would "probably continue to assert the right to experiment with unsettled political military conditions" to increase Soviet influence.[45] The use of military force on these occasions was perceived as probable.

The INR, the only agency dissenting, claimed that the estimate had overemphasized the "Soviets' perceptions of their own military power," and had undervalued the challenges presented by "political and economic considerations" that had been discussed in NIE 11-4-77. Moreover, the INR thought that the Soviets had a "less positive view" of the military balance in Europe, and that this would lead them to be "less confident in the superiority of the Warsaw Pact's forces over those of NATO than the net judgments of this Estimate suggest."[46]

During the second half of the Carter administration, the intelligence community produced three estimates that dealt implicitly with the question of Soviet objectives.[47] In January 1979, against the background of Soviet interventions in Angola and Ethiopia, the US intelligence community viewed the third world as a likely arena for Soviet expansion. NIE 11-10-79 described Soviet political objectives as aimed at "creating and exploiting opportunities in distant areas."[48] In terms of their military intentions, the Soviets were believed to be determined to utilize "wherever possible their comparative advantage in military instruments of influence" and as most likely to "regard military means . . . as the most feasible way of bringing about the changes they seek in the political structure of the Third World."[49] Yet the community continued to maintain that the Soviets were sensitive to calculations of risks in applying military force in the third world and explicitly stated that the Soviets were "unlikely to invade a Third World country."[50] Nevertheless, the January 1979 estimate concluded that increased Soviet confidence in its own military capabilities would allow it to accept measured risks of escalation.

NIE 11-3/8-79 was released in March 1980, only three months after the invasion of Afghanistan, and was the first estimate to be prepared following the failure of the Senate to ratify SALT II. This NIE had to take into consideration that the Soviets would be uninterested in arms control negotiations and would instead resume an unrestrained expansion of their strategic forces. The estimate is striking for the fact that it describes moderate and limited Soviet objectives. This estimate, written in large part by DCI Turner himself, claimed that the important aims underlying the Soviet programs were to "strengthen USSR's deterrent, to support its foreign policy, and to foster strategic stability through Soviet advantage."[51] More specifically, the estimate judged that Soviet intentions, although opportunistic, were cautious: "[The Soviets] probably do not see the present situation of approximate strategic parity as providing them with the latitude to safely confront the United States directly in areas where they perceive US vital interests to be involved."[52]

This estimate overall portrayed the USSR as still enjoying an improved strategic position, but as becoming highly concerned by adverse trends in the correlation of forces that would come into effect from the mid- to late 1980s. This concern was due largely to recent US and NATO initiatives to modernize and deploy new weapons systems, especially Pershing IIs and ground-launched cruise missiles. The estimate concluded by noting that the intelligence community did "not expect immediate, irreversible responses by the USSR to US deferral of the SALT Treaty," and expressed the belief that the Soviets would "wish, at least initially, to avoid visible changes in strategic programs that could seriously jeopardize the chances of eventual US ratification." Absent from this estimate was the usual terminology to describe Soviet intentions that had been characteristic of NIEs in the immediately preceding years. This estimate, for instance, did not go so far as to state unequivocally that the USSR sought world domination and strategic superiority. In a way, this NIE appears to reflect the views stated previously by the INR. Indeed, its relatively benign description of Soviet objectives led the DIA and each of the military intelligence agencies to "disassociate themselves from the volume and its characterization as a Summary of the Estimate," as they believed the summary was "not representative of the intelligence analyses developed in the Estimate."[53] Their own conclusions about Soviet intentions attributed more revisionist aims including an "attempt to secure *maximum* political advantages from its military arsenal in anticipation of US force modernization programs."[54]

The 1980 NIE was made in the midst of a US election-year debate over Soviet strength and objectives as well as charges of US military weakness. Against this background, it is hardly surprising that the controversy over Soviet strategic objectives once again came to the fore.[55] To prevent a repetition of the military's disassociation from NIE 11-3/8-79, in the following year, NIE 11-3/8-80, published in December 1980, contained two separate sets of "key judgments." It opened with those judgments of DCI Turner, who "did not hold major disagreement with the key judgments coordinated by the Intelligence Community agencies" but did believe the coordinated estimate failed to address the interests of senior policy makers adequately. Turner stated clearly that the Soviets were fully aware of the devastating consequences of fighting a nuclear war. Soviet leaders were depicted as "generally pleased" with their achievement of "'parity' or perhaps 'superiority' with the United States," but also as concerned that trends in the strategic balance might shift against them later in the 1980s. Thus, Turner judged with a high degree of confidence that they would encourage the US ratification of SALT II or some other form of nuclear arms limitation.[56] Turner estimated that the Soviet leadership could be expected to continue to assess US resolve and act accordingly, but

> their sense of strategic parity or superiority may well, however, make them judge the risks to be less than they were in the past. In short, the "window of opportunity" in the early-to-middle 1980s with respect to the strategic equation will make the Soviets more willing to be adventuresome but not so much as to "go for broke" in exploiting every opportunity that represents itself in the Third World. Their perception of the strategic balance is unlikely to induce them to take action in Europe or against the United States.[57]

As for immediate objectives, the CIA, INR, and NSA agreed with the DCI's assessment that the USSR's perception of its strategic position provided a "more favorable backdrop than before to the conduct of an assertive foreign policy and to the projection of Soviet power abroad." The Soviet leadership was viewed as likely to risk escalation only in those regions "where the USSR or its allies would have the advantage in conventional forces," which would "enhance Soviet confidence that the risk of direct US military response would be low."[58] A divergent view, held by the DIA and military intelligence agencies, argued that the Soviet leadership was now confident that the strategic military balance had shifted in the Kremlin's favor and the aggressiveness of its foreign policy would continue to increase as the Soviet advantage grew. This growth would lead the Soviets to "create and exploit foreign policy opportunities for expansion," not just to exploit existing opportunities, and "accelerate" their assertiveness.[59]

In sum, the NIEs produced by the intelligence community during 1977 appear to portray Soviet intentions in a less alarming light than NIEs from the previous year, and certainly less worrisome than the conclusions reached by Team B. The following year, 1978, saw a change toward more hawkish assessments of Soviet intentions, as expressed in NIE 11/4-78. These changes are consistent with the predictions of both the capabilities and behavior theses, especially the shift toward more hostile assessment in 1978 following Soviet adventures in the Horn of Africa. We should be cautious, though, about drawing definitive conclusions from the congruence test performed above. A variety of factors not examined here could have contributed to the fluctuations in the intelligence community's statements about Soviet intentions. For example, the principal drafter of NIE

11-4-78, Horelick, explains that in retrospect, the conclusions reached regarding Soviet intentions were overstated, as the purpose of this NIE was to alert the decision makers that the previous NIE 11-4 on Soviet objectives did not correctly reflect Soviet ambitions and expectations. Similarly, the evolution in the statements expressed in the NIEs about Soviet intentions during the last two years of Carter's presidency do not perfectly match the expectations of any of the three competing theses. NIE 11-3/8-79 (released in March 1980) reached less hawkish views about Soviet intentions (and was similar in tone to NIE 11-4-77), yet this NIE was the one from which all the military intelligence agencies and DIA dissented. The coordinated key judgments of NIE 11-3/8-80 appear to present somewhat more hawkish views than the ones present in NIE 11-3/8-79. Nonetheless, every participating organization except for the CIA dissented. These fluctuations in perceived intentions do not appear consistent with the predictions of any of the three competing theses per se.

The congruence test is thus only useful to a limited extent. I consequently turn now to tracing the reasoning that the intelligence community used to reach its conclusions about Soviet intentions in order to shed more light on the inference process the community used to evaluate Soviet intentions as well as the kinds of indicators that drove its assessments.

Reasoning about Soviet Intentions

The NIEs discussed above were often explicit in their reasoning about the estimates of Soviet intentions and source of the disagreements among the agencies. Throughout this period, the different agencies that contributed to the NIEs all indicated that they based their conclusions primarily on changes in material indicators of Soviet capabilities and the effects of these changes on the perceived correlation of forces. Moreover, while reaching varying conclusions about Soviet intentions, all the agencies referred to Soviet capabilities to support their inferences. In the rest of this section I provide supporting evidence and explain the effect of this logic—that "intentions follow from capabilities"—on the conclusions the community reached.

The centrality of current and projected trends in the Soviet military buildup is evident from the first NIE that dealt with Soviet intentions during the Carter administration. In fact, the two contending interpretations of Soviet intentions outlined in NIE 11–4-77 both explicitly relied on this logic. The more hawkish interpretation highlighted the steady growth in Soviet strategic forces and resulting shift in the global correlation of forces as proof of a more assertive Soviet policy in the future.[60] The alternative, less hawkish view also focused on similar indicators of capabilities, asserting that "it too perceives an increased Soviet confidence, stemming much more from the achievement of parity in strategic forces than from other, non-military trends."[61] Still, this less hawkish analysis attributed to the Soviets "*not* a programmatic design to achieve advantages where they can" but rather "a more patient approach to continuing tough competition together with a dedication to high and steady levels of effort in the elements of power."[62]

Disagreements over the scope and purpose of this buildup prevented the community from presenting unanimous assessments of Soviet intentions in subsequent NIEs. Nevertheless, the basic thread running through almost all coordinated estimates on the USSR was that the growing Soviet military strength and USSR's perceptions of the correlation of forces were good indicators of their future intentions, as these indicators had affected prior Soviet conduct. NIE 11-4-78, for instance, estimated that the "more assertive Soviet international behavior" observed in the latter half of the 1970s in Angola, Ethiopia, and Afghanistan (even before the Soviet military intervention) was "likely to persist as long as the USSR perceives that Western strength is declining" even as its own strength is steadily increasing.[63]

Overall, in trying to estimate the likely impact on Soviet policy of the forthcoming leadership succession (Brezhnev was known to be in ill health), the NIE turned to estimates of capabilities, concluding, "If the new leaders believe the 'correlation of forces' to be favorable, especially if they are less impressed than Brezhnev with US military might and more impressed with their own, they might employ military power even more assertively in pursuit of their global ambitions."[64] The INR's dissent from NIE 11-4-78 similarly revolved around the question of "how much" and "in what way" the USSR's perception of its own military strength was likely to affect its military intentions in Europe. Thus, even though it reached conclusions that differed from other agencies, the INR continued to refer to Soviet capabilities:

> The Soviets have a less positive, even more ambivalent view of the military balance in Europe and would be less confident of the superiority of the Warsaw Pact's forces over those of NATO than the net judgments of the Estimate suggest. . . . [The] INR believes that Soviet programs to improve tactical aviation, upgrade armored forces, and enhance tactical nuclear capabilities are intended to remedy what Moscow evidently regards as weakness rather than maintain or enlarge existing advantages. If so, Soviet motives would appear to be more compelling than the text suggests, and Moscow's efforts may be more intense.[65]

The predominance of inferences about military intentions from capabilities is also clearly visible in the intelligence assessments regarding Soviet objectives in Europe. The intelligence community as a whole believed it was highly unlikely that the Soviets would launch an attack against any NATO member. This analysis relied on the assumption that "the Soviets take a conservative view of NATO capabilities and understand that a stiff NATO defense might prevent a quick Pact victory."[66] At the same time it was judged that "a significant weakening of NATO's military potential would encourage the Soviets to think that they could exercise more influence in Western Europe and might tempt Moscow into using pressure tactics."[67]

During the following two years, 1979 and 1980, the community was more visibly split over how to characterize Soviet intentions. While the two significant NIEs on this issue drafted by Turner portrayed a more benign interpretation of Soviet political objectives and the likelihood of the USSR using military force, indicators of capabilities also drove dissenting views. For example, the dissenting perspective of the DIA and military agencies in NIE 11-3/8-79 reasoned, "As they [the Soviets] see this superiority increase during the next three to five years, they will probably attempt to secure maximum political advantage from their military arsenal in anticipation of [the future] U.S. force modernization program."[68] The competing stance claimed that Soviet perceptions of the global correlation of forces were "providing them with the latitude to safely confront the US" or its vital interests, while the more favorable local correlation of forces in places where the Soviets did enjoy the "advantage of proximity" or "a preponderance of conventional forces" made these areas more prone to aggressive Soviet behavior.[69] By 1980, NIE 11-3/8-80 (also drafted by Turner) repeated the claim that "the Soviet leadership is now confident that the strategic military balance is shifting in the Kremlin's favor," and stated, "The aggressiveness of its foreign policy will continue to increase as the Soviet advantage grows."[70] The Kremlin was thus perceived as "likely to accelerate pursuit of its global ambitions, weighing the local 'correlation of forces' in those regions where it wishes to increase its influence or gain control."[71]

One reason for the differences between the conclusions that Turner and the CIA reached about Soviet intentions and those reached by the military intelligence agencies may stem from the different metrics used to determine the correlation of forces between the two superpowers. Unlike previous NIEs, 11-3/8-79 and 11-3/8-80 included explicit net assessments in addition to the traditional static description of Soviet forces and capabilities. The task of preparing net assessments, traditionally assigned to the Pentagon's Office of Net Assessment, involved judgments of not only Soviet force performance but also the interactions of Soviet forces with US and other Western forces. In the 1979 NIE, in addition, Turner decided to introduce the use of what he termed "quasi-dynamic indicators" intended to reflect what the forces of both sides could actually accomplish.[72] According to Garthoff, the imminent massive US buildup meant that the effect of Turner's approach was to diminish the significance of growing Soviet military capabilities, and hence to lower the confidence levels that intelligence analysts believed the Soviet military derived from those capabilities. Given the implications of net assessment on estimates of Soviet capabilities, it is unsurprising that this estimate reached less hawkish conclusions about the adversary's intentions. The DIA and all the military intelligence chiefs strongly objected to this new approach, alleging that this metric, which placed a premium on "quantitative information," "drives and distorts the Estimate's judgments."[73] Further, the DIA challenged the CIA's estimate, arguing that it "produces misleading results with respect to trends in military balance, sheds little light on the question of deterrence or escalation control, and comprises an unrealistic net assessment." The disagreements over what techniques to use when measuring capabilities produced a disagreement over Soviet objectives: the DIA and military intelligence agencies concluded that the CIA had underestimated the adversary's confidence in its strategic advantage, and consequently the degree to which future Soviet policies were likely to be more aggressive than they had previously been.[74]

The community was split during this period as what to make of Soviet civil defense efforts. In NIE 11-3/8-79, for example, the CIA judged that the "present and projected civil defense programs would not embolden the Soviet leaders to take actions during a crisis that would involve deliberately accepting a high risk of nuclear war." The DIA and military intelligence agencies objected, claiming that the "continuing Soviet investment of major resources in the civil defense program clearly demonstrates the confidence the Soviet leaders have in its value. . . . [This program]—through its potential for influencing political perceptions, providing leverage for coercion during a crisis, affecting nuclear exchange outcomes, and contributing to postwar recovery—impacts on both the reality of the strategic balance and on perceptions of the balance in the USSR and elsewhere." And these perceptions, noted the preceding paragraphs of the estimate, determine how aggressive the Soviets will be in their foreign policy behavior.[75]

Bureaucratic interests often tainted the interpretations of Soviet capabilities and intentions. Whatever the parochial motives of analysts from different agencies, the key point is that despite their disagreement about Soviet intentions, all based their estimates of intentions on Soviet capabilities. This logic was clear, explicit, and powerful, ultimately overriding other potential indicators of Soviet intentions. As such, it is consistent with the predictions of the capabilities thesis as well as those of the organizational expertise hypothesis of the selective attention thesis. The offense-defense hypothesis of the capabilities thesis also receives support.

Although perceptions of Soviet intentions were most heavily influenced by perceptions of Soviet capabilities, it is also apparent that the community was attempting to draw at least some inferences about Soviet intentions from Soviet doctrinal and strategic writings. I contend that this practice had the effect of impeding the intelligence community from reaching unified and meaningful conclusions regarding Soviet intentions. As a result, the community had to admit that the practice of inferring Soviet objectives from its military doctrine was problematic. The community could not agree on three related questions: To what extent did the Soviet war-fighting doctrine determine the USSR's strategic policy and force developments?[76] Did the Soviet doctrine indicate that the Soviets "see as an achievable objective a strategic relationship in which they escape the constraints of mutual deterrence?"[77] Was Soviet doctrine a good predictor of future behavior and an inclination to use military force?[78]

These disagreements are apparent in NIE 11-4-77. The military intelligence agencies saw the answer to all these questions as a decisive "yes."[79] An alternative view, reflecting mainly the INR's perspective, claimed that the Soviet leaders did "not regard the achievement of decisive strategic superiority as a feasible objective," and did "not count on gains that would be substantial enough to give them confidence about their ability to survive and win an all-out nuclear war." The CIA, taking a middle ground, estimated that the Soviets believed that success in war, even nuclear war, was attainable; the CIA analysts based this assessment on what the "Soviets explicitly stated" in "their military doctrine." Yet the NIE concluded that while these documents represented the Soviets' objectives if war were to start, the USSR did not aim for war. The NIE noted that the operational side of Soviet doctrine maintained that deterrence would best be achieved through war-fighting capabilities. The NIE's conclusion was, accordingly, that the Soviets had "never accepted the concept of mutual assured destruction," although they had come "to recognize mutual deterrence as the present reality that [would] be very difficult to change."[80] After presenting the alternative views, the NIE conceded that Soviet doctrine was an imperfect signal of Soviet intentions: "It is difficult, *and perhaps not fruitful*, to try to separate offensive and defensive element and purposes in the Soviet approach to military power, as Soviet military doctrine looks at them in an integral fashion."[81]

This debate over Soviet doctrine was not repeated in the next two NIEs, which reflected the CIA's position.[82] NIE 11-4-78 discussed at length the plausibility of the Soviet use of nuclear weapons under different scenarios. Referring primarily to Soviet doctrinal writings in classified military theoretical journals and military exercises, this NIE concluded that there was "no evidence or reasonable set of inferences that support the notion of their deciding to launch a surprise strategic attack."[83] It nonetheless determined that an "escalation of superpower military conflict [if begun was] highly likely."[84] Moreover, while notable contradictions in Soviet strategic thinking were said to lead to ambiguous conclusions regarding Soviet nuclear crisis management, it was "likely" that Soviet decision makers "would behave with the greatest of caution in handling and threatening the use of their strategic weapons" to achieve political objectives.[85]

The reliance on Soviet military doctrine as evidence for present and future intentions remained controversial in subsequent NIEs to such an extent that the intelligence community could not produce a uniform assessment of Soviet intentions. For example, in explaining why they did not share the relatively benign conclusions in NIE 11-3/8-79, the DIA and all the military intelligence agencies accused DCI Turner of overly "concentrat[ing] on quantitative information at the expense of intelligence concerning Soviet doctrine, policy, capabilities, future programs and possible initiatives.[86] The various agencies continued to debate the intentions signaled by Soviet military doctrine in NIE 11-3/8-80, leading the drafter to express skepticism about the utility of looking at the adversary's doctrine to evaluate its intentions: "Intelligence judgments made on the basis of these sources are necessarily tentative, because we [the intelligence community] seldom obtain direct evidence on what the political military leadership [thinks or] on the extent to which pragmatic considerations would override the tenets of military doctrine."[87] This echoed the argument voiced by the INR in this NIE—that is, "in assessing the Soviet threat, more weight must be put to a realistic assessment of Soviet capabilities than to its doctrine."[88]

Finally, the NIEs during the Carter years rarely referred to past or current costly Soviet noncapabilities-based actions as potential indicators of future Soviet intentions. Even when Soviet behavior was mentioned, Soviet capabilities were the driving force behind any prediction about how the Soviet foreign policy would look in the future. This is somewhat surprising given that Soviet actions in the third world or even past Soviet interventions could have served as potentially powerful evidence of hostile intentions that the military intelligence services could have used to bolster their reasoning. In addition, the discourse that emerges in these NIEs appears to be markedly different from the discussions on Soviet intentions that were taking place in the White House at the same time (discussed in the preceding chapter).

Some estimates during this period do lend some support to the behavior thesis. For instance, current Soviet actions are mentioned in NIE 11-4-78 in the context of assessing Soviet intentions toward détente and the SALT negotiations. It asserted that in principle, these processes "oblige[d] Soviet leaders to calibrate their own competitive behavior against the risks of disrupting détente in areas where US interests are perceived to be deeply engaged." The estimate then points to Soviet actions in Africa and the "growing military aid efforts" as indicating scant Soviet concern with disrupting détente.[89] Similar examples are found in NIE 11-10-79, which attempted to assess Soviet capabilities and intentions to exert influence in distant areas. Indeed, this was one of the few intelligence estimates that looked closely at patterns in Soviet behavior. But the estimate's bottom line was that the most recent expansionist Soviet behavior in the third world stemmed primarily from the USSR's increased confidence in its military power along with perceptions of the global and regional correlation of forces, and it predicted that these trends would dictate Soviet behavior in the future.[90] Here, the community concluded that the Soviets intended to continue to expand their military activity in the third world, but were not likely to invade a third world country. Two months later, the Soviet Union invaded Afghanistan.

CONCLUSION

An effort to understand the adversary's political intentions did not play a significant role in the NIEs' judgments of the threat posed by the USSR. Most NIEs produced in that period were dedicated to estimating current and projected Soviet strategic forces as well as military intentions. Some NIEs entirely avoided the task of estimating Soviet political intentions, while others offered no more than one or two paragraphs on the subject. In nearly all the NIEs where Soviet objectives were evaluated, though, some intelligence agencies dissented from the NIE's judgments. Some agencies portrayed a more pragmatic USSR, whose ambitions were to take advantage of existing opportunities using military force as long as the benefits involved were higher than the risks; others saw a more confident power that was more inclined to use its military arsenal to pursue an expansionist agenda. Moreover, many estimates of Soviet objectives during the 1970s were shaped by political and bureaucratic interests. This is not surprising. After all, any conclusions about Soviet objectives had fundamental implications for public policy.[91]

Consistently throughout this period, the single most important indicator that the US intelligence community used to infer future Soviet intentions was the material capabilities of the USSR. That is, the Soviet military buildup, perceived strategic balance, and type of weapons that the Soviets were amassing heavily influenced the explanations that all the intelligence agencies provided to support their estimates of Soviet intentions. The predictions of the capabilities thesis—including the numerical preponderance and offense-defense hypotheses derived from it—are thus confirmed. At the same time, the emphasis on military capabilities that guided the intelligence analysis in the collective reports is also consistent with the organizational expertise hypothesis that is derived from the selective attention hypothesis. Indeed, the vast majority of the available NIEs on the Soviet Union pertained to Soviet military capabilities, and even the sections in the NIEs dealing with the issues of Soviet intentions pointed repeatedly to these types of indicators, which reflected the community's expertise and shared knowledge during this period.

Soviet capabilities did not always lead to worst-case predictions about Soviet intentions. Instead, the relationship between capabilities and intentions was more nuanced, and at times verged on tautology. Continuous and persistent increases in Soviet capabilities triggered the interest in understanding the USSR's intentions. In many cases the community implicitly assumed the Soviets intended to maximize their capabilities (that is, the development, production, and deployment of weapons). In turn, most of the inferences about future Soviet political intentions rested on these assessments of current and future trends of Soviet capabilities.[92] Interagency debates about Soviet intentions stemmed from (and reflected) disagreements about Soviet power, or more precisely, how the Soviets perceived their own military strength and the evolving correlation of forces. Nevertheless, while all the intelligence agencies agreed that trends in Soviet capabilities should have brought the Soviets more confidence in what they could (and would want to) achieve, the different agencies disagreed over whether the Soviets had come to believe that the correlation of forces between the two superpowers had in fact significantly changed to their advantage. According to one view, the Soviets now thought that this was the case, and consequently their future objectives were bound to be more revisionist. The alternative perspective held that the Soviets remained unsure that they had reached strategic superiority, and therefore were considered unlikely to behave in ways that would be radically different.

As for the relevance of other potential indicators, the collective estimates show that Soviet military doctrine was inconsistent, at best, as an indicator of Soviet intentions. This might have been due to the fact that most source materials on Soviet doctrine at the time were unreliable or inadequate, or because Soviet doctrine was ambiguous. It is unsurprising, then, that different intelligence agencies were able to find what they expected (or wanted) to find to support their particular evaluations of Soviet intentions. Some intelligence agencies, such as the INR, concentrated on Soviet political intentions and saw Soviet sociopolitical doctrine as evidence that the USSR wanted to avoid war. The military intelligence agencies focused on the question of how the Soviets would approach war if it came, and thus pointed to the offensive aspects of the Soviet operational doctrine that called for war-fighting capabilities in support of their claim that the Soviets were preparing to fight World War III. In large part, the opposing groups in this debate reached different conclusions about the intentions of the USSR because they addressed different kinds of intentions and looked at different aspects of Soviet doctrine. Neither side, however, stated this explicitly in the NIEs.[93]

Consistent with the predictions of the selective attention thesis, the US intelligence community and Carter administration attended to different indicators of intentions. As such, in stark contrast to the way senior decision makers in the Carter administration assessed the USSR's intentions, the intelligence community made few, if any, references to past and current Soviet actions to support its inferences about Soviet political intentions. Even if this type of evidence was more prominent in the reports each agency produced individually or the oral presentations of intelligence officers, this line of reasoning did not play a significant role in the collective discourse expressed in the NIEs. Further, the NIEs, by their nature, did not convey vivid information about intentions to the president. As this book argues, however, decision makers tend to rely on vivid information, especially their own personal impressions and insights, to infer intentions. This might explain why members of the Carter administration tended not to regard these NIEs as providing real insight into the minds of Soviet decision makers.

This practice of inferring intentions from capabilities rendered US political intelligence rather unperceptive and not particularly useful. To be sure, the focus on Soviet military capabilities in the coordinated estimates as well as in the president's daily briefs, according to Brzezinski, made these products "excellent on the level of factology." Indeed, Brzezinski adds, they were "informative" and "comprehensive in providing us a very detailed, essentially accurate picture of Soviet strategic development, deployments, weapons characteristics, arms control negotiating postures, and so forth." Yet Brzezinski emphasizes that these intelligence products were also "weak on the level of 'politology,'" and "the President, and people around him, needed 'politological' assessments and insights." In that respect, the intelligence estimates on the Soviet Union "did not provide much help to the President . . . in determining what the Soviets, in general, were trying to do . . . for example, in the Persian Gulf/African area, in South Africa, in the Ethiopian Horn, subsequently in Afghanistan, and in 1980 in Poland." Brzezinski speculates that this might have been the case because it "is very difficult for an institution which has to concentrate on being reliable, whose data has to be verifiable, to provide such broad insights, and yet that is what policymakers need."[94]

The US intelligence community was painfully aware of this criticism, as Brzezinski was not the first to raise concerns about the political analysis in the NIEs. Brzezinski's weekly reports also reveal that Carter himself was highly dissatisfied with the quality of the political intelligence he received. In May 1979, Brzezinski explained to Carter that in response to the president's request from November 1978, there had been interagency efforts to "determine the factors contributing to [the] unsatisfactory performance [of political intelligence]," and as a result, several comprehensive steps had been taken to improve both the collection and analysis of political intelligence. "All U.S. diplomatic posts have been directed to reorder collection priorities to ensure better reporting on internal political dynamics," for example, "and, to this end, recognize the important role of clandestine collection and the need to develop additional clandestine assets."[95] CIA analysts viewed the problem as stemming from the intelligence community's inability to supply the kind of vivid information about intentions that decision makers tended to use to form judgments. As Turner said,

> Sometimes they [decision makers] have better information than you do. I mean, whenever I briefed President Carter, I always had to keep in the back of my mind that "he met with Brezhnev last week." I'd never met with Brezhnev, so if he interpreted what Brezhnev was going to do tomorrow differently than we interpreted what

Brezhnev might do tomorrow, I had to give him credit that maybe he understood Brezhnev better than we.[96]

⁂

As we will see in the next three chapters, a decade later the intelligence community continued to use a similar inference process to gauge the Soviet Union's intentions under the leadership of Gorbachev. Once again, this practice left the consumers of intelligence unsatisfied with the quality of the political analysis.

CHAPTER 8

Indicators of Soviet Intentions and the End of the Cold War, 1985–88

With the collapse of détente, Soviet-US relations entered a period of flux that would last through the 1980s. Reagan came into office in 1981 after a presidential campaign that expressed alarm over a "window of vulnerability" that endangered US national security. Such a concern motivated his administration's thinking for several years until its refutation by the Scowcroft Commission's "sobering" report in 1983. Even so, an emerging pillar of Reagan's national security strategy—the Strategic Defense Initiative (SDI)—aimed at supplying the United States with a ballistic missile defense shield. Critics alleged that this initiative would undermine the stability of mutual assured destruction and spark a new arms race with the Soviet Union.

Reagan's second term in office evinced important differences. The coming to power of a reform-minded Soviet leader in Gorbachev in 1985 led to crucial changes to the Soviet Union's domestic political institutions (e.g., perestroika and glasnost) and its relationship with the United States. Whereas a hawkish foreign policy characterized the first half of Reagan's presidency, the second half featured a variety of arms control proposals such as the Intermediate-Range Nuclear Forces (INF) Treaty and Strategic Arms Reduction Treaty (START I). Both leaders participated in major summit meetings intended to defuse the Cold War. Gorbachev even implemented unilateral cuts to Soviet conventional forces. These changes had unanticipated consequences, including the collapse of the Soviet Union and end of the Cold War. The shifts in Reagan's foreign policy suggest a change in US perceptions of Soviet intentions. Indeed, observers often assert that costly signals of reassurance by the Soviet Union helped end the Cold War.[1] What was the substance of these changes in perceptions of intentions, and more important, what occasioned them?

I am less concerned with determining the relative significance of the various factors that contributed to the end of the Cold War. Instead, this chapter and the next two focus more specifically on how, when, and to what extent US perceptions of Soviet intentions changed between 1985 and 1988. Addressing this perception shift helps us understand the broader changes that eventually led to the Cold War's conclusion.

This chapter measures and derives predictions for the selective attention thesis as well as the three competing theses: the capabilities, military-doctrine, and behavior theses. These predictions are subjected to empirical testing in the two subsequent chapters. Chapter 9 assesses the relative impact of these indicators on the perceptions held by President Reagan, Secretary of State Shultz, and to a lesser degree, Secretary of Defense Weinberger. Chapter 10 traces the evolution in perceived intentions from the vantage point of the US intelligence community.

THE SELECTIVE ATTENTION THESIS

According to the selective attention thesis, we should observe differences between the inference process of members of the Reagan administration and that of the US intelligence community. US decision makers should have selectively given greater attention to indicators that were vivid in nature and greater credence to such indicators for inferring Soviet intentions. The US intelligence community, on the other hand, should have relied more on indicators that reflected its organizational expertise—namely, the monitoring of military capabilities.

The Vividness Hypothesis

The vividness hypothesis leads us to expect that personal interactions between US decision makers and their Soviet counterparts as well as Soviet responses to litmus tests would serve as salient sources of information. The repeated and positive interactions between Reagan and Shultz and their Soviet counterparts, Gorbachev and Eduard Shevardnadze, respectively, should have led them to view Soviet intentions as more benign over time.

Reagan and Gorbachev interacted during four summit meetings—in Geneva (November 1985), Reykjavik (October 1986), Washington, DC (December 1987), and Moscow (May 1988). During these summits, they held long private meetings. Reagan had a positive impression of the Soviet leader. The 1986 Reykjavik summit was the only meeting that did not achieve its intended results from Reagan's perspective, leaving Reagan angry and frustrated. (Gorbachev conditioned his concessions on a US pledge not to implement strategic defenses for the next ten years, but Reagan was unwilling to accept such a linkage). On a personal level, however, Reagan came out of this summit with positive impressions of Gorbachev, and saw the latter's proffered concessions on strategic arms as unprecedented and significant. Indeed, Reagan viewed this summit as an enormous breakthrough that eventually facilitated agreement on the INF Treaty. During private meetings and in public after the Reykjavik summit, Reagan outlined a series of actions that the Soviet leader could take to signal his benign intentions, including the withdrawal of Soviet forces from Afghanistan, tearing down the Berlin Wall, and the release of Soviet dissidents.[2]

Shultz spent hundreds of hours with Soviet minister of foreign affairs Shevardnadze. The two gradually developed mutual trust, to a point where Shultz felt that he could be confident of Shevardnadze's private assurances on a variety of issues. In his public statements, Shultz communicated a litmus test to the Soviets similar to Reagan's, calling for a change in Soviet human rights policies and withdrawal from Afghanistan. Weinberger did not have much interaction with the Soviet leadership. According to Shultz, Weinberger always resisted the idea of bringing Soviet and US defense ministers and top military officers together.[3]

The vividness hypothesis predicts that Reagan and Shultz would pay attention to information gleaned from personal meetings with Gorbachev and Shevardnadze as well as Soviet actions such as the withdrawal of Soviet forces from Afghanistan, bringing down the Berlin Wall, and the release of Soviet dissidents. Furthermore, it predicts Reagan and Shultz would refer to their impressions in explaining the change in their perceptions of Soviet intentions.

The Subjective Credibility Hypothesis

The subjective credibility hypothesis expects variations among these decision makers as to what Soviet actions they categorized as informative. Those decision makers who held more hawkish views of the Soviet Union prior to 1985 should have been less inclined to see Gorbachev's costly actions of reassurance as credible indicators of benign intentions. They should have been slower to change their perceptions of Soviet intentions than were decision makers with less hawkish views.

All three primary foreign policy decision makers came into office sharing somewhat-hawkish views of the Soviet Union, but they exhibited some important differences in outlook. Of the three decision makers, Weinberger held the most hawkish views of the USSR. In his comprehensive study on perceptions of the Soviet Union during the Reagan administration, Keith Shimko notes, "Weinberger's views of the Soviet Union were about as hard-line as one could get; it is difficult to imagine a collection of beliefs that would be less conducive to negotiation, compromise, and diplomatic solutions."[4] Weinberger saw Soviet intentions prior to 1985 as expansionist in nature and unlimited in scope. Shultz's image of the Soviet Union was less uncompromising; prior to 1985 he had never depicted Soviet intentions in terms of a desire for global domination. According to Shimko, Shultz's image of the USSR was not as fully developed as Weinberger's, as he had less experience dealing with strategic issues pertaining to relations with the Soviet Union. The basic outlines of Reagan's views as he came into office were closer to those of Weinberger than Shultz. During his first term as president, Reagan repeatedly described the Soviet Union as an ideologically motivated power bent on global hegemony. Shimko writes, though, that Reagan exhibited a rather-superficial attachment to his ideas about the Soviet Union that was not necessarily accompanied by knowledge, comprehension, and understanding.[5] The extent to which Reagan's beliefs about the USSR formed a fully integrated or coherent image is not entirely clear.

All else being equal, the subjective credibility hypothesis suggests that Weinberger should have been slower to alter his beliefs about Soviet intentions than Reagan or Shultz. Weinberger and Reagan should have been more reluctant than Shultz to acknowledge Soviet reassuring actions as costly or informative. Still, if these decision makers did not attribute any credibility to reassuring Soviet actions—even if such actions would be considered as costly by outside observers—the subjective credibility hypothesis would expect no change in their beliefs about Soviet intentions.

The Organizational Expertise Hypothesis

The organizational expertise hypothesis examines how the common practices and shared knowledge of the US intelligence community affected its assessments of Soviet intentions. Without access to intelligence training manuals from the 1980s, and without behind-the-scenes insight on the coordination process that preceded the writing of the NIEs, it is hard to judge what the organizational expertise at the collective level truly was. It is also difficult to judge the degree to which shared practices shaped the conclusions reached in the NIEs. In analyses of the Soviet Union throughout the Cold War, however, the military threat posed by the Soviet Union clearly received priority over all other issues. Within that context, the intelligence community considered Soviet military capabilities as the most important target of collection and analysis as well as the most convenient. The majority of the NIEs on the Soviet Union during the 1980s were devoted to estimating different aspects of the Soviet military arsenal.[6]

As a result, the organizational expertise hypothesis suggests that in determining Soviet intentions, the NIEs would have relied predominantly on assessments of Soviet military capabilities. The observable implications from this hypothesis are identical to those of the capabilities thesis in all but one respect. Although the capabilities thesis expects both decision makers and the intelligence community to infer intentions from capabilities, the organizational expertise expects only the intelligence community to have relied heavily on such indicators.[7]

THE CAPABILITIES THESIS

Despite the positive developments in arms control in the second half of the 1980s, members of the Reagan administration, defense establishment, and US intelligence community believed that the Soviet modernization of strategic forces was extensive, and was centered on increasing survivability, operational flexibility, and advantage in prompt, hard-target kill capability.

The annual report on *Soviet Military Power*, published by the DOD, along with numerous intelligence estimates noted rapid modernization and increased sophistication in the Soviet ICBM arsenal between 1980 and 1988.[8] Soviet missiles with greater accuracy and survivability were reportedly replacing older models. DOD analysts estimated that due to the sustained growth of the Soviet Strategic Rocket Forces, the Soviets would field a completely new generation of mobile and increasingly accurate missiles by the mid-1990s that would pose a "heightened threat" to US strategic forces.[9] As in the late 1970s, of greatest concern were the SS-18 heavy ICBMs that the Soviets modernized during the 1980s, which the United States believed capable of destroying most US ICBM silos. The modernized SS-17s and SS-19s were capable of flexible targeting. Accordingly, observers believed that these missiles would enable the USSR to adjust to the reduction in the US threat created by the INF's call for the withdrawal of all Soviet and US intermediate-range nuclear missiles from Europe (the "zero option").[10] The intelligence community believed that Soviet efforts at modernizing their ICBM systems were not abating in the late 1980s.[11] As late as December 1988, the US intelligence community warned that "without START constraints, if the Soviets were to modernize their forces in a manner that generally follows past efforts, in the next 10 years intercontinental nuclear weapons would probably grow from the current level of about 10,000 to between 12,000 and 15,000."[12]

The Soviets were also thought to have been improving their long-range strategic bomber force to close the gap with the United States during the second half of the 1980s.[13] The Soviets were said to be strengthening Moscow missile defenses, and equipping them with a new generation of radars and interceptor missiles.[14] In addition to active defenses, the Soviets appeared to be pursuing an extensive program of passive defense measures, including civil defense, mobility, and hardening, with the aim of limiting the effects of nuclear strikes on Soviet territory. Intelligence reports concluded that the "Soviets continue to invest as heavily in active and passive strategic defenses as they do in offensive forces, and their capabilities will improve in all areas."[15] This was seen as a destabilizing effort to limit the effectiveness of the US nuclear deterrent.

Estimates of Soviet defense spending, however, painted a more complicated picture. According to CIA estimates, Soviet spending on defense between 1985 and 1988 climbed sharply, but then dropped abruptly between 1988 and 1990, reflecting changes in allocation to different resource categories and military missions. Between 1985 and 1988, the CIA judged that Soviet defense spending grew not only because of aircraft and missile purchases but also because of a significant increase in the costs of maintaining growing stocks of weapons and equipment. Between 1988 and 1990, the CIA concluded, spending in nearly all resource categories had dropped dramatically. The CIA also tracked trends in spending on specific military missions to analyze changes in Soviet priorities. Between 1985 and 1987, spending on strategic offense was seen to increase slightly, while spending on strategic defense showed rapid growth. There was some acceleration in spending on ground forces and nonstrategic navy as well. Reports on the following three years (1988–90) showed a reversal of these trends: spending on strategic offense went down substantially, as did spending on strategic defense and tactical air; spending on ground forces plummeted as Gorbachev took steps to cut Soviet military personnel levels.[16]

Prior to the 1987 INF Treaty, Soviet nonstrategic nuclear forces had been seen as extremely threatening. The Soviets had begun a vigorous effort in 1977 to modernize and expand their intermediate-range nuclear forces, deploying highly mobile SS-20 missiles (each equipped with three MIRVs), nearly doubling their number between 1980 and 1987. The INF Treaty, which came into effect in 1988, called for both superpowers to eliminate all ground-launched nuclear force missiles (including cruise missiles) in the five hundred to fifty-five hundred kilometer range, including the SS-20, over a three-year period. Yet the INF did not cover short-range nuclear missiles with a range of less than five hundred kilometers, dual-capable aircraft, or artillery pieces. Consequently, although the INF reduced the threat from Soviet medium-range ballistic missiles along with short- and intermediate-range nuclear forces, the USSR was still expected to "be able to satisfy their critical tactical, theater and intercontinental targeting requirements as effectively as with their current arsenal due to their ongoing modernization of their strategic forces."[17] In other words, according to the intelligence community, the INF Treaty did not diminish the Soviet's ability to wage nuclear war.[18] In December 1988, the intelligence community still argued that "in terms of what the Soviets spend, what they procure, how their strategic forces are deployed, how they plan, and how they exercise, the basic elements of Soviet defense policy and practice appear thus far not to have been changed by Gorbachev's reform campaign."[19]

The extent to which the Soviet buildup of the mid-1980s was seen as an indicator of malign intentions also hinges on the perceived military balance. Throughout the second half of the 1980s, despite some notable deficiencies, the strategic balance was essentially one of stable parity.[20] Prior to 1985, Secretary of Defense Weinberger and Assistant Secretary of Defense for Global Strategic Affairs Richard Perle had viewed Soviet military capabilities as superior to those of the United States in all categories. After 1985, though, neither described the military balance in these terms, nor did they make any references to Soviet superiority.[21] Instead, Weinberger and Perle repeatedly characterized the strategic balance as adequate to deter Soviet nuclear aggression against the United States and its allies.[22] The conventional balance of military power in Europe was also relevant to the assessment. The United States believed that the Warsaw Pact had a strong advantage over NATO in almost all categories of forces, especially since the pace of Warsaw Pact weapons production had outstripped

NATO's efforts during the 1980s.[23] In December 1988, Gorbachev announced that Soviet forces would be reduced by five hundred thousand troops by 1991. He also noted that Soviet forces in the Atlantic-to-the-Urals area would be cut by ten thousand tanks, eighty-five hundred artillery pieces, and eight hundred combat aircraft, and that six Soviet tank divisions would withdraw from Eastern Europe.[24] Soviet and East European divisions were to be reorganized with a sharply reduced number of tanks.[25]

In the early 1980s, Reagan, Shultz, and Weinberger all apparently shared the intelligence community's assessments that as the Soviets increased and modernized their military power, the strategic balance was still one of asymmetrical equivalence. Even Shultz, the more dovish member of the second Reagan administration, said in public in April 1988 that the Soviet nuclear buildup "showed no signs of abating, even after the achievement of strategic parity."[26] Shultz also acknowledged the Soviet Union's numerical superiority in conventional forces and "great advantage" in throw weight, but believed that the overall strategic balance had been more or less restored by 1985.[27] In contrast, Reagan stated in 1985 that the Soviet military arsenal outnumbered that of the United States "by a great number," and a year later he described the Soviet military buildup as a "relentless effort to gain military superiority over the United States."[28] Reagan did not discuss the strategic balance at all in his public speeches in 1987 or 1988.[29] Weinberger's January 1987 report to Congress stated,

> The Soviets have built, and are continuing to build, an enormous military capability at great cost to their society . . . far more than any other nation on earth; *far more than could possibly be needed for self-defense.* They maintain elaborate plans and preparations for large-scale Soviet invasion far beyond their borders. They modernize constantly and never complete deployment of one system without beginning at once the development of a follow-on next generation system.[30]

On the basis of these indicators, it would appear that the Cold War was in full force. Yet these changes in Soviet military capability took place against the backdrop of a Cold War that was in fact ending, thereby suggesting that some government officials held inaccurate perceptions of Soviet weaknesses. How do we expect these observations to affect assessments of intentions?

Summary of Predictions

Soviet conventional military programs, nuclear programs, and defense spending were seen as increasing between 1985 and 1987. US observers viewed the military balance as asymmetrically equivalent, Soviet military build up of counterforce capabilities as offensive, and increase in Soviet capabilities as beyond the requirements of security. The USSR's commitment to eliminate intermediate-range nuclear forces under the INF Treaty came into effect in 1988 and constrained the Soviet's ability to change the European status quo in its favor. Nevertheless, the United States continued to worry about the comprehensive build up and modernization of Soviet counterforce capabilities and defensive systems beyond what it perceived to be required for Soviet self-defense. Both the numerical preponderance and offense-defense hypotheses would lead us to expect that US decision makers and the US intelligence community would perceive Soviet intentions as hostile until 1988. Then, after the elimination of intermediate-range nuclear forces as well as the substantial decrease in Soviet conventional forces and defense spending, US perceptions of Soviet hostility should have moderated. We should see both sets of observers refer to qualitative and quantitative trends in Soviet military capabilities to justify their assessments.

THE STRATEGIC MILITARY DOCTRINE THESIS

One of the most dramatic changes in Soviet military thinking during the second half of the 1980s involved the reformulation of Soviet military doctrine. In 1986, Soviet officials made numerous announcements that to promote security in Europe, "the military concepts and doctrine of the military alliances must be based on defensive principles," and called for "the reduction of military potentials to the limits necessary for defense."[31] By mid-1987, Soviet military doctrine had been publicly redefined. Among its declared principles were that the prevention of war is the most fundamental objective of Soviet military doctrine, no war can be considered the continuation of politics, security is mutual, the primary means of enhancing security are political and not military-technical, not only the political means of security but also the military-technical means should be defensive in character, and Soviet armed forces should be developed according to the principle of "reasonable sufficiency." The challenge was bringing the military-technical aspect of the doctrine in line with the new declared emphasis on defense and defensive missions. During this time, debates about the meaning of a defensive Soviet strategic and military doctrine became intense within both the USSR and United States.[32]

These revolutionary changes in Soviet declaratory military doctrine caught the attention of Western students of the USSR and international security. At the same time, both classified and public studies raised doubts about the credibility as well as durability of the Soviet Union's declaratory "defensive-defense" doctrine and Gorbachev's ability to institutionalize these new conceptual elements. The DOD, CIA, and military intelligence agencies did not acknowledge any meaningful change in Soviet doctrine prior to mid-1988.[33] Skepticism among analysts regarding the credibility and sustainability of a Soviet defensive-defense posture persisted until 1989. It was only in 1989 that US perceptions of Soviet doctrine significantly altered.

In 1985, the US intelligence community reported that Soviet military planning and doctrine were designed to decisively defeat opposing conventional

and nuclear forces through offensive operations and occupy the enemy's territory, while avoiding the initiation of nuclear use in a theater conflict unless
the Soviets perceived that NATO was about to do so.[34] The NIE released in July
1987 acknowledged the "potential impact of Gorbachev's declaratory policy,"
which took an "apparently more benign approach to issues of nuclear war"
than had been "typically characterized in previous years in this Estimate."[35] The
intelligence community, though, did not expect any significant reduction in
the priority that the Soviets gave to nuclear forces, nor any serious revision of
Soviet operational priorities and practices.[36] Soviet strategy was still described
in this estimate as bellicose, and the view of Soviet ultimate objectives in a war
against NATO remained essentially unchanged from those presented in previous estimates.[37]

In mid-1988, intelligence assessments regarding the nature and orientation
of Soviet doctrine began to change somewhat.[38] In June 1988, a CIA assessment acknowledged that Soviet discourse over the size and composition of its
forces "goes beyond mere propaganda and involves fundamental issues that
have potentially important ramifications for Soviet security policy and military
forces over the longer term."[39] The assessment recognized that two important
and related areas in Soviet military policy had changed since Gorbachev came
to power. First, although both Khrushchev and Brezhnev had used the term
reasonable sufficiency, it had not previously been embraced by the military, or
formalized in party or military doctrine. Under Gorbachev, however, Soviet
civilian and military officials both considered it to have critical policy ramifications, although the assessment cautioned that the meaning and practical
implications of this concept were still unsettled. Second, the report recognized
the significance of the new declaratory Soviet defensive-defense posture, yet it
viewed the primary objective of the public discourse in the USSR on defensive-
defense as propaganda, meant to influence Western and especially European
opinions. It also averred that most Soviet military writings remained skeptical
about how exactly defensive military forces would differ from offensive ones.
Notwithstanding the changes in Soviet declaratory doctrine and Gorbachev's
success in getting the Soviet defense establishment to acknowledge that nuclear
sufficiency could be reached with lower levels of forces, the report asserted that
imminent significant changes in force or strategy were unlikely.

NIE 11-14-89, which tracked trends in Warsaw Pact theater forces and
doctrine, recognized Gorbachev's policy-making achievements for the first
time in early 1989.[40] Despite uncertainty about the durability of these initiatives, the NIE concluded that the concepts of reasonable sufficiency and
defensive-defense would become "lasting features of Soviet national security
policy, helping ensure continued party control over defense policy and defense
spending."[41] Still, the NIE indicated that the intelligence community had not yet
detected significant changes in the military-technical dimension of Soviet military doctrine that would clearly demonstrate a change in nuclear war-fighting

doctrine.[42] Recent decisions to reduce and restructure Soviet theater forces, it said, indicated that the peacetime readiness posture of the Warsaw Pact forces facing NATO would underscore the ability to mobilize and deploy large reinforcements before hostilities, rather than the ability to sustain forward forces to initiate a quick, unreinforced attack, suggesting that the capability for such an attack was no longer a priority. Furthermore, it noted that after the completion of force reductions by 1991, the Soviets would no longer be capable of major offensive operations against NATO.[43]

Neither Reagan nor Shultz appears to have detailed his views about Soviet military doctrine on the record. It does appear that Shultz believed that the Soviets had an offensive doctrine that was "designed for preemption." He stated in 1987 that "Soviet military doctrine stresses war fighting and survival in a nuclear environment [and] the importance of numerical superiority." Shultz did not think that the Soviets genuinely believed that nuclear war could be fought and won.[44] Reagan saw Soviet military doctrine as offensive in nature, aimed at "striking first and disarming the adversary."[45] He thought that the Soviets were seeking to gain superiority because they believed that nuclear war was both possible and winnable. Unlike Weinberger, who maintained that the Soviets were willing to incur the destruction of a nuclear war, Reagan believed that the Soviets wished to avoid a nuclear confrontation if they could achieve their objectives by other means.[46]

Shortly before first meeting with Gorbachev at the Geneva summit in late 1985, Reagan expressed his thoughts on Soviet military thinking in private. Reagan wrote, "Our recent PFIAB study makes it plain the Soviets are planning a war. They would like to win without it and their chances of doing that depend on being so prepared we could be faced with a surrender or die ultimatum."[47] According to the US ambassador to the Soviet Union at the time, Jack F. Matlock Jr., Reagan was not actually counseled by the President's Foreign Intelligence Advisory Board that the Soviets were contemplating war but rather that if war came, they planned to fight and win a nuclear war. On rereading these lines, Reagan altered his statement to read: "They would like to win by being so much better prepared we could be faced with a surrender or die ultimatum."[48] Yet the evidentiary record is still unclear about whether and to what extent Reagan or Shultz took into account the evolution in Soviet military thinking. It is uncertain how these impressions influenced their perceptions of the nature of Soviet military doctrine.

Summary of Predictions

The DOD and intelligence community started to give more credence to changes in Soviet declaratory doctrine in 1988, but through 1989 remained skeptical of the significance and durability of declared changes to Soviet operational doctrine. In 1989, however, US defense and intelligence analysts began to see

Soviet operational doctrine in Europe as a defensive doctrine guided by the concept of reasonable sufficiency. They still believed that the military-technical aspects of Soviet nuclear doctrine reflected an offensive war-fighting strategy. The strategic military doctrine thesis predicts that an offensive Soviet doctrine should have led observers to perceive Soviet intentions as hostile (given beliefs about the dominance of defense or deterrence brought about by the nuclear revolution) and point to Soviet doctrine as an indicator of Soviet intentions. But with the shift in Soviet declaratory doctrine announced in late 1988 and growing confidence by 1989 that Soviet military doctrine in Europe was indeed becoming defensive, the thesis expects that Reagan and his advisers as well as the US intelligence community would begin to perceive Soviet intentions as less hostile, and would explicitly link their assessments of Soviet intentions to changes in Soviet doctrine.

THE BEHAVIORAL THESIS

There is a general consensus in the literature that costly Soviet reassuring actions were the central factor that contributed to ending the Cold War. Costly reassuring actions by the Soviet Union included arms control and arms reductions, changes in nature of Soviet involvement in the third world (such as the withdrawal from Afghanistan), and reforms of Soviet domestic institutions. US decision makers did not give equal weight to all behavioral signals. Actions taken by the Soviets that might be considered intrinsically costly or represented Soviet commitment to changing US-Soviet relations indicate that Gorbachev's concessions were substantial and irreversible only from 1987 onward. The behavior thesis would suggest that from 1985 to 1986, Soviet intentions would still be perceived as hostile, but that this perception should have changed after 1987 with Soviet costly reassuring actions.

Gorbachev assumed power in March 1985. Shortly afterward, high-level US and Soviet officials resumed their dialogue on arms control. In April, Gorbachev announced a six-month moratorium on SS-20 intermediate-range ballistic missile deployment, which would become permanent if the United States joined.[49] In July, he announced a moratorium on all nuclear weapons testing. The United States did not see either of Gorbachev's two unilateral arms control initiatives as indicating a significant change in Soviet policies but rather regarded them as gestures, merely cheap talk. US decision makers were quick to characterize the moratorium on the further deployment of SS-20 missiles as actually serving Soviet interests. The USSR, after all, had completed its deployment while NATO was still in the early stages of its own deployment. Moreover, the fact that Gorbachev had not discussed his proposal with the US president before making a public announcement raised suspicions about his true motivations.[50] As for the moratorium on testing, US government officials and intelligence agencies suspected that Soviet scientists had recently completed a series of tests, and thus did not need to conduct additional testing in the coming months. US officials worried that the United States could not detect low-yield underground tests without instruments near the testing site.[51]

Gorbachev also made a particularly important speech at an April 1985 meeting of the Central Committee. The April plenum included a decision to reactivate a wide range of arms control and disarmament issues, another decision to make Soviet military doctrine defensive based on the criteria of reasonable sufficiency, recognition of the need to disengage Soviet military forces from Afghanistan, and an announcement that a new, revised party program would be presented in the forthcoming Communist Party Congress, the first to be convened in a quarter century. The next year started with another Soviet arms control initiative calling for the complete abolition of nuclear weapons by the year 2000. Most US government agencies considered this proposal, again, as nothing more than "smoke and mirrors," and advised the president to flatly reject it.[52] In October 1986, Reagan and Gorbachev held their second summit meeting in Reykjavik. Gorbachev offered dramatic concessions in the negotiations on strategic and intermediate-range ballistic missiles, but the summit broke down over deep disagreements about the US SDI.[53] Reagan was not ready to give up the SDI, and the two leaders departed Reykjavik without reaching any clear agreement about which arms control issues remained open to discussion.[54]

Moscow's agreement to accept the US "zero-zero" proposal on the INF during 1987 was the first significant Soviet reassuring action. Some critics argued that the INF Treaty would not benefit NATO, because the West's nuclear missiles were necessary to provide a "ladder of deterrence" to counter the large Soviet advantage in conventional forces, which were not part of the agreement. If that were the case, the INF Treaty was as costly to the United States as it was to the USSR.[55] Nevertheless, this action represented a genuine departure from previous Soviet proposals: Gorbachev was willing to destroy many more missiles than the United States.[56] He exhibited an unprecedented readiness to accept extensive and intrusive on-site verification and monitoring arrangements. By the criteria of the behavior signals thesis, this was a costly signal.

Soviet behavior during 1988 offered additional costly reassurances to the United States. First, in February 1988, Gorbachev announced that the USSR would withdraw its troops from Afghanistan. Following the April signing of the Geneva Accords, which sought to settle the Soviet war in Afghanistan, the Soviets began the process of disengagement according to the agreed timetable. That year, the USSR also started to pursue multilateral negotiations on several other regional conflicts, including Angola, Ethiopia, and Nicaragua.[57] These steps were seen as a genuine shift in Soviet thinking on security issues and policy toward pro-Soviet authoritarian regimes in the third world, which had been a central issue of the Cold War since the mid-1970s.[58] Shultz later labeled the withdrawal from Afghanistan a "tremendous triumph" and signal of the death of the Brezhnev doctrine, which had justified Soviet intervention in support of socialist regimes around the world.[59]

Second, Gorbachev took decisive action to restructure the domestic political system in the USSR—a move appreciated by US observers. Gorbachev and the Soviet political leadership had made significant initiatives prior to 1988, especially the introduction of competitive elections for party posts within the Communist Party of the Soviet Union.[60] But it was only after mid-1988 that Gorbachev's actions aimed at fundamental institutional and ideological change.[61] The Nineteenth Party Conference, in June 1988, initiated comprehensive institutional and ideological reforms that paved the way for political liberalization in the USSR. These included the establishment of competitive elections with secret ballots, term limits for elected officials, separation of powers with an independent judiciary, and provisions for freedom of speech, assembly, conscience, and the press.[62] The conference delegates adopted all the proposed resolutions, including one that set a timetable for the implementation of these reforms.[63] Many senior US decision makers immediately grasped the extent of the reforms and their potential significance.[64] Matlock, then the US ambassador to the Soviet Union, believed that these unprecedented steps, if implemented, would put the USSR on an irreversible course toward a European-style social democracy. Then, in December 1988, Gorbachev surprised Western audiences with his announcement of a unilateral troop reduction in Eastern Europe.

Summary of Predictions

The behavior thesis posits that we will find evidence that assessments of intentions are linked to the adversary's costly noncapabilities-based actions. The historical record suggests that from 1985 to 1988, Gorbachev repeatedly reassured Western observers by initiating and pursuing, at times unilaterally, actions that represented a significant break from previous Soviet patterns of behavior. Some of these actions were in the realm of foreign policy; others pertained to domestic ideological changes within the USSR. Beginning in 1987, the totality of Gorbachev's actions were judged by most US observers as significant and reassuring, even though the relative importance of any single initiative was debated by the Reagan administration and intelligence community. Soviet willingness to accept asymmetrical reductions in the INF in 1987, withdrawal of the Soviet troops in Afghanistan, and the other reassuring costly actions that Gorbachev undertook throughout 1988 should, according to the current actions hypothesis, have led US decision makers and the intelligence community to reevaluate their assessments of Soviet intentions.

In contrast, the past actions hypothesis posits that perceptions of intentions would be most influenced by costly actions undertaken by the USSR prior to the tenure of either Gorbachev or Reagan. The Soviet invasion of Afghanistan was the single most frequently mentioned representation of past Soviet behavior in public discourse during this period. Thus, according to the past actions hypothesis of the behavior thesis, observers should have continued to perceive Soviet intentions during the second Reagan administration as hostile, based on Soviet military interventions in the latter part of the 1970s.

CHAPTER 9

US Decision Makers' Perceptions of Soviet Intentions

THE END OF THE COLD WAR

During his first term in office, Reagan believed that Soviet intentions posed an existential threat to the United States. He referred to the USSR as an "evil empire." Reagan's views, however, changed dramatically during his second administration (1985–88). Following the Moscow summit of May 1988, Reagan asserted that his speech five years earlier was no longer relevant and his comment about an evil empire belonged to "another time, another era."[1] When asked if he could declare the Cold War over, the president responded, "I think right now, of course."[2]

This chapter addresses how Reagan and his top advisers—especially Shultz and Weinberger—assessed Soviet intentions during the second Reagan administration. The chapter first weighs the empirical validity of the selective attention thesis and competing three theses by looking at the statements, reasoning, and policies of US decision makers. Reagan's level of involvement in foreign policy making is a topic of considerable debate among scholars. Some argue that Reagan was a "passive president" who lacked control over his administration.[3] Others contend that Reagan was just marginally involved in foreign policy making details during his tenure: though responsible for the broad outlines of US policy, he tended to let his senior advisers establish specific foreign policy objectives and strategies.[4] If so, Reagan would have had little to do with the change in the administration's approach toward Moscow, as high-level officials such as Shultz brought about the more conciliatory policy.[5] A third group of scholars claim that although Reagan generally "was not as interested in foreign affairs as he was in domestic issues," he nevertheless took an active interest in certain foreign policy issues that were important to him, such as the SDI, Iran-Contra affair, and US-Soviet relations.[6]

While the extent to which Reagan relied on his advisers is still a contentious issue among scholars, the official most involved in US policy making on the USSR was undoubtedly Shultz. A significant source of evidence is the available documents drafted by Shultz that pertained to the USSR. The views of Weinberger are also crucial, especially related to the arms control negotiations with the Soviets. Weinberger was quite vocal in expressing skepticism about Soviet intentions throughout this period and even after Reagan's presidency. Tracing the sources of stability in Weinberger's views and the reasoning evidence he used to justify them is pertinent to this study.

The task at hand is challenging because a significant number of the relevant documents are still classified. Yet the declassified material already available is noteworthy in terms of both quality and quantity. It includes primary sources from the Reagan Presidential Library, National Security Archive, and State Department. In addition to archival US government documents, all relevant public statements made by Reagan, Shultz, and Weinberger from 1985 to 1988 for which printed transcripts could be obtained were examined, as were available transcripts of congressional testimony, interviews, and personal memoirs and diaries. Relevant statements delivered by these officials along with prepared testimony where there is a reasonable expectation that these officials read the statement and approved it are also considered. In addition, I draw on personal interviews I conducted with Shultz and Matlock, the principal Soviet expert on the NSC staff who was later the US ambassador to Moscow from 1987 to 1991.

DECISION MAKERS' STATED BELIEFS ABOUT SOVIET INTENTIONS

Reagan's first detailed report about Gorbachev came from Shultz, who had met the new Soviet general secretary at Konstantin Chernenko's funeral in 1984. Shultz recalls that he was impressed with Gorbachev's "quality of thought," "intensity," and "intellectual energy."[7] British prime minister Margaret Thatcher had privately informed Reagan in December 1984 that Gorbachev was an "unusual Russian," "charming," and "open to discussion and debate."[8] Still, in his memoir Reagan admits, "I can't claim that I believed from the start that Mikhail Gorbachev was going to be a different sort of Soviet leader." He had noted at the time that "Gorbachev will be as tough as any of their leaders. If he wasn't a confirmed ideologue, he would have never been chosen by the Politburo."[9] Notwithstanding the positive tone of initial correspondence between Reagan and Gorbachev, US-Soviet relations soon experienced a new crisis due to the shooting death of a member of the US Military Liaison Mission in Germany (Major Arthur Nicholson) by a Soviet sentry, the Soviet presence in Afghanistan, domestic Soviet human rights violations, differences over the SDI, and arms control proposals. Relations further worsened after Reagan's public announcement in June 1985 that the Soviet violation of SALT II had undercut the integrity as well as viability of arms control as an instrument to assist stability and security.[10]

Despite early disagreements between Weinberger and Shultz over the SDI and implementation of the Antiballistic Missile (ABM) Treaty, Reagan, Shultz, and Weinberger held similar views regarding the Soviet motivations for its

1985 proposal for a 50 percent reduction in offensive strategic weapons. They all claimed that this offer stemmed from Soviet preoccupation with the SDI. While Shultz saw the Soviet proposal as "a breakthrough of principle," Reagan was not impressed; he claimed in his memoir that he had made the same proposal in 1983. Reagan treated the Soviet proposal as mainly "propaganda."[11] Weinberger was even blunter, implying that the United States should consider breaking the ABM Treaty.[12]

At the time no one actually believed that the USSR had benign intentions. Indeed, both Shultz and Reagan continued to describe the USSR's aims publicly in terms of expansion of power and influence through military means. Shultz, too, thought that the Soviets were willing to use their military force to change the status quo, directly or indirectly. He further maintained that the Brezhnev Doctrine, which expressed the USSR's intent to preserve its influence in the Soviet bloc, demonstrated revisionist objectives along with the Soviet's unwillingness to sustain deterrence and prevent war.[13] Never during the first (or second) Reagan administration, though, did Shultz describe Soviet intentions as inexorably expansionist. As Shimko observes, "There was no mention of a Soviet quest for world 'domination,' 'revolution,' 'hegemony,' or a 'world-wide communist state.' There was nothing in Shultz's writings about the Soviet Union desiring the elimination of the United States, the destruction of democracy and capitalism, or the ultimate triumph of communism."[14]

In contrast to Shultz, Reagan repeatedly referred to the USSR as an expansionist power seeking nothing less than "world domination."[15] Neither had reason to believe in 1985 that Gorbachev was about to change the USSR's policies and forgo what they perceived as traditionally hostile objectives. "I can't see," Reagan said in 1985, that "there would be a great change of direction. It would only come about if that was the desire of that same Politburo."[16] Shortly before the two superpowers' first summit meeting in Geneva in November 1985, Reagan's public statements did change to a certain degree; he blamed the tension between them on "misunderstandings" as well as the Soviets' failure to draw correct inferences about US intentions and policies. He further emphasized the need to "reduce the suspicion and mistrust that have led us to acquire mountains of strategic weapons," and acknowledged that "nuclear weapons" rather than an evil adversary "pose the greatest threat in human history to the survival of the human race."[17]

The strongest clues about Reagan's perceptions of the Soviet leader and his intentions at the time are found in Reagan's private thoughts. The president dictated his personal opinions to Matlock shortly before leaving for the Geneva summit. Reagan stated, "I believe Gorbachev is a highly intelligent leader totally dedicated to traditional Soviet goals." The president speculated that in the short run, Gorbachev would not "want to undertake any new adventures," but his ultimate goal was "weaning our European friends away from us" by "making us look like a threat to peace." Reagan privately judged that Gorbachev's

motivation in pursuing arms control was to "reduce the burden of defense spending that is stagnating the Soviet economy," especially the costs of competing with
the United States on the SDI. He thought Gorbachev was no different from
former Soviet general secretaries. In Reagan's view, Gorbachev was "dependent
on the Soviet Communist hierarchy," and therefore aimed "to prove to them his
strength and dedication to Soviet traditional goals."[18] Similarly, Shultz appears
to have believed strongly at the time that the new Soviet leadership was "skilled
and determined to protect the legacy they inherited from Brezhnev, Yuri Andropov and Chernenko." Perceived continuity in the Soviet posture meant that
US policy makers saw no reason to hope that the Soviets would give up their
traditional revisionist objectives.[19]

The Geneva Summit (November 1985)

Robert McFarlane, Reagan's national security advisor, anticipated that through
Reagan's personal interactions with Gorbachev in Geneva, the president
"should be able to get a feel for Gorbachev's intentions." He suggested that Reagan should be "looking for indications as to whether Gorbachev is willing to
adjust Soviet policies on concrete issues sufficiently to permit a lowering in
overall tension."[20] Reagan did exactly that.

After spending over an hour in private conversation, the two leaders
emerged smiling. Reagan confessed that he and Gorbachev "hit it off well." In
his memoir, Reagan remarked, "As we shook hands for the first time, I had to
admit . . . there was something likable about Gorbachev. There was warmth in
his face and his style, not the coldness bordering on hatred I'd seen in most senior Soviet officials." In the afternoon, Reagan commented to Gorbachev, "We
get along pretty well talking alone," and the two chatted by the fire for another
hour; "both were obviously in a good mood," according to Shultz.[21] Their private meeting also produced concrete results: the leaders agreed to reciprocal
visits for two follow-on summit meetings, which Shultz asserted was one of
the main objectives of the Geneva summit. The rapport between the two leaders was obvious to everyone in the room. Reagan later explained that he was
impressed by Gorbachev's sense of humor, noting that he "could tell jokes about
himself and even about his country, and I grew to like him more."[22] He was also
impressed by Gorbachev's style of arguing, saying that "we fought it out and
maybe knew that we were going to fight it out again, but when the meeting was
over we were normal." Reagan continued, "He was not stalking out of there and
[saying] 'down with the lousy Americans' or anything."[23] Nevertheless, during
one of his meetings with the Soviet delegation, Reagan stated several times that
"the United States also sees an expansionist Soviet Union," and recalled "that
the Soviet government had talked about a one world communist state and had
been inspiring revolutions around the world." Reagan observed that the USSR
had satellite states in Afghanistan, Angola, Cuba, Ethiopia, and Yemen, all of

which gave a "basis for American concern and mistrust."[24] Yet Reagan concluded his conversations with Gorbachev on a positive note. He stated that if the two countries learned to trust one another, "then those mountains of weapons will disappear quickly as we will be confident that they are not needed."[25]

The summit may not have produced substantive achievements, but it did foster greater optimism regarding the US-Soviet relationship.[26] Further, Reagan mentioned that it had occurred to him following their conversation that "not once during our private sessions at the plenary meeting did he [Gorbachev] express support for the old Marxist-Leninist goal of a one-world Communist state or the Brezhnev Doctrine of Soviet expansionism," adding that "he was the first Soviet leader I know of who hadn't done so."[27] These positive feelings were reflected in the handwritten draft of a letter Reagan sent to Gorbachev immediately following their meeting. In it Reagan wrote that as a result of the frank conversations, "I came away from the meeting with a better understanding of your attitudes. I hope you also understand mine better." Reagan further indicated that he thought Gorbachev was determined to "take steps to see that our nations manage their relations in a peaceful fashion." Reagan wrote that although the "United States does not believe that the Soviet Union is the cause of all the world's ills," the USSR "had exploited and worsened local tensions and conflicts by militarizing them." The president concluded the letter on a positive note, reiterating how pleased he was about their private meeting and suggesting that the two leaders "set a goal—privately, just between the two of us—to find a practical way to solve" remaining issues on the agenda by their next summit meeting.[28]

In public, Reagan reported that as much as he enjoyed his conversations with the Soviet leader, he still had little reason for optimism. He stated in late November: "Suffice it to say that the United States cannot afford illusions about the nature of the USSR. . . . This implies enduring competition."[29]

Hope and Disappointment (1986)

The year 1986 was one of alternating hope and disappointment. During the first half of 1986, Gorbachev was reluctant to accept Reagan's invitation for a second summit. He avoided discussing Reagan's concrete arms proposals that might have formed the basis for agreement at the next summit. On January 15, 1986, Gorbachev publicly announced a proposal to abolish nuclear weapons by the year 2000. Many in the White House and most US government agencies perceived the proposal as an indicator that Gorbachev "had nothing more than propaganda in mind." Reagan, however, was actually in favor of the total elimination of nuclear weapons. While he was concerned about some aspects of the Soviet proposal, he claimed that it was "the first time a Soviet leader had suggested a certain date." Gorbachev's proposal fitted Reagan's dream of putting the world on the road to abolish nuclear weapons. Matlock explains it had an "important psychological effect on the president."[30] But Reagan still treated this move by the Soviets as "a publicity stunt," noting in his diary, "At the very least it is a h—l [sic] of a propaganda move. We'd be hard put to explain how we could turn it down."[31] He wrote to Gorbachev,

> Recent actions by your government are most discouraging. What are we to make of your sharply increased support of a local dictator [Libya's Mu'ammar Gadhafi] who has declared a war of terrorism against much of the rest of the world, and against the United States in particular? How can one take Soviet declaration of opposition to terrorism seriously when confronted with such actions? And, more importantly, are we to conclude that the Soviet Union is so reckless in seeking to extend its influence in the world that it will place its prestige . . . at the mercy of a mentally unbalanced local despot?[32]

In the following months, Soviet behavior in the third world would continue to reinforce Reagan's pessimistic reading of Soviet intentions. In another handwritten draft of a letter to Gorbachev, Reagan wrote "candidly" that debates within the administration over Gorbachev's intentions and US policies toward the USSR "began to fall into a predictable pattern."[33] That is, Soviet-US relations appeared to be entering a new phase marked by stability. Shultz was optimistic that "contrary to the Defense Department and the CIA line," the Soviets are "not an omnipotent, omnipresent power gaining ground and threatening to wipe out the world." Weinberger, on the other hand, continued to believe that the USSR was an unrelenting expansionist power and saw Gorbachev's proposals as mere propaganda. Similarly, Shultz noted that CIA intelligence analyses, presented at NSC meetings, concluded that although Gorbachev's rhetoric had changed, Soviet actions had not. The rest of the officials present in these routine meetings, Shultz explained, "would try to stimulate the president's fear that any US diplomatic engagement with Moscow would jeopardize the future of SDI."[34]

During this period, Reagan still asserted that Soviet intentions were expansionist, although he had begun to view Gorbachev's policies as signaling a change in attitude. Reagan was therefore cautious not to offend Gorbachev in his public statements. In June, for example, Reagan was asked why in an earlier speech he had likened Gorbachev to Castro, Yasser Arafat, and Gadhafi. Reagan replied, "It was a bad choice of words, because I didn't mean to do that. As I've said, he is the first Russian leader, to my knowledge, that has ever voiced the idea of reducing and even eliminating nuclear weapons. So, I must have goofed someplace, because, believe me, I don't put them in the same category."[35] Later in the summer Reagan again expressed his thoughts about the Soviet leader and his motivation, reiterating that he found Gorbachev "completely different than others that I had dealt with." Still, Reagan believed Gorbachev's proposals and initiatives, innovative as they were, stemmed primarily from domestic economic difficulties, and by and large were designed to make the Soviet system stronger. In an interview on July 25, 1986, Reagan said of Gorbachev,

> I think that he, of course, has been raised in all of his entire life in that system. I think he's dedicated to the system, believes in their system. But I think also that he is a modern man in contrast to some that we have dealt with there in times past. He realizes that there are great economic problems. . . . He believes that, for the sake of their economy, that it might be in their own interest and practical for them to join in reducing these great stores of arms and ending an arms race, which is so costly to them that it has been the principal cause of their economic problem.[36]

Then, in September 1986, Gorbachev agreed to meet Reagan in Reykjavik the following month. In a paper prepared for this meeting, the NSC warned that

> Gorbachev's long-term goals are clear enough: to unravel the Western consensus behind tougher policies toward the Soviet Union, to stabilize US-Soviet relations in a way that gives him greater latitude in his domestic policies, and over time to regain a more favorable position in the global balance of power. Arms control negotiations play a central role in this strategy.[37]

At Reykjavik, Gorbachev's generous proposals on strategic and intermediate-range missiles, space, defense, and nuclear testing "astonished" Reagan.[38] The president wrote in his memoir that "George [Shultz] and I couldn't believe what was happening. We were getting amazing agreements. As the day went on I felt something momentous was occurring."[39] Gorbachev was, according to Shultz, "laying gifts at our feet" as he made "concessions after concessions." Differences over the SDI and ABM Treaty broke up the summit talks, though. As Reagan recalls in his memoir (and as is supported from the transcripts of the meeting), when Gorbachev stated that his concessions all hinged on the US giving up the SDI, Reagan "could not believe it," and was "very disappointed" and "very angry" with the Soviet leader.[40] Reagan took it as a personal insult that Gorbachev mistrusted his commitment to share the Star Wars technology. Yet despite Reagan's disappointment, correspondence between the two leaders following the summit shows that Reykjavik marked, in Matlock's words, an important "psychological turning point." Although no agreement on strategic defense was reached, Reagan had a strong positive impression of Gorbachev that was rooted in the latter's apparently sincere desire to eliminate nuclear weapons and engage in serious constructive dialogue across a full spectrum of issues.[41] On returning to Washington, DC, Reagan informally reported to his adviser, "Maggie [Thatcher] was right. We can do business with this man [Gorbachev]."[42] Publicly, however, neither Reagan nor Shultz changed their rhetoric about the nature of Soviet intentions. In speeches on October 4 and 13, 1986, Reagan remarked that he "had no illusions about the Soviets or their ultimate intentions."[43]

Initial Process of Reassessment (1987)

In the first half of 1987, perceptions of Soviet intentions had yet to change. The White House's "National Security Strategy" of January 1987 explicitly stated that "Moscow seeks to alter the existing international system and establish Soviet global hegemony. These long-range Soviet objectives constitute the overall conceptual framework of Soviet foreign and defense policy."[44] According to Garthoff, "The discussion of the Soviet threat and of Soviet policy aims [in this report] could have been written in the 1950s at the nadir of relations."[45] In public, Reagan stated that the administration's intention to continue negotiations with the USSR was "not based on false hopes or wishful thinking" but rather "on a candid assessment of Soviet actions and long-term understanding of their intentions." He cautioned that on issues pertaining to regional conflicts, the Soviets continued to exhibit a policy of "global expansionism."[46]

Reagan noted in May that he was hopeful Gorbachev was serious about "taking a different tack and really means to set a different course than had been set before."[47] In June, Reagan reiterated that Gorbachev was the first Soviet leader to advocate the elimination of nuclear weapons and that he found him to be "a personable gentleman." But Reagan was clear that he did not entirely trust the Soviet leader, frequently citing the Russian proverb "trust but verify" as the best way to characterize his relations with Gorbachev.[48] During this time, Reagan also urged Gorbachev to "prove to the world that his glasnost campaign is more than words" by making "tangible changes" in Soviet policies.[49]

The road to the third summit, held in December 1987 in Washington, DC, was not a smooth one, although some positive signs were registered along the way. In September 1987, Shultz received private assurances from his Russian counterpart, Shevardnadze, that the Soviets would withdraw from Afghanistan within a year. During the following months, Shultz also reported on important changes in Soviet policies on human rights and dissidents. In mid-September, Shevardnadze came to Washington for discussions. Reagan later described the visit as "a turning point," noting in his diary, "They were good meetings, free of the hostility we used to see even if we were disagreeing on some things."[50]

Meanwhile, Gorbachev expressed his willingness to delink agreement on the SDI from achieving reductions in nuclear weapons and accepted US proposals for alteration of the INF Treaty due to be signed at the Washington summit. This was a big achievement for Reagan, who saw it as a reassuring sign that Gorbachev could be trusted. Reagan pointed to other developments within the USSR that caught his attention:

> We are seeing more and more evidence that Gorbachev was serious about introducing major economic and political reforms in the Soviet Union. There would be the first free elections in the Soviet Union; there was official encouragement to entrepreneurs to establish businesses in the Soviet Union; and, on the seventieth anniversary of the Russian Revolution, Gorbachev made a blistering attack on Stalin, opening a way for a new freedom to examine the Soviet past and its mistakes.[51]

Reagan mentioned these domestic actions in interviews and public speeches during this period, but he continued to list additional steps Gorbachev could take to signal a shift in policy and "show that the new thinking in the Kremlin is supported by action as well as words." In September, Reagan stated, "I believe that the Soviet Union has not abandoned its stated objective of promoting its Communist ideology throughout the world. I also think that the Soviets have built up a massive military force that far exceeds their requirements for defense. Continuing Soviet aggression in Afghanistan cannot be forgotten."[52] On October 28, 1987, Reagan publicly declared that he still believed that the USSR was an expansionist power: "It is in regional conflicts where Soviet performance has been most disturbing. Anyone searching for evidence that the Soviets remain expansionist, indeed imperialist, need look no farther than Nicaragua or Afghanistan."[53]

Shultz's assessments of Soviet objectives were more optimistic than Reagan's. In November 1987, the secretary of state found himself in fundamental disagreement with some in the administration and CIA over the meaning of Gorbachev's actions. DCI William Webster forwarded an analysis by Gates (then deputy DCI) to Reagan and other key US officials.[54] Gates asserted that Gorbachev was seeking "a breathing space with the West" that would allow the USSR to revive internally and gather strength for another era of confrontation with the United States. He pointed out that "Gorbachev has not cut military research and development and has poured in more weapons to regional conflicts." Shultz, however, rejected these assessments. He claimed that whatever the Soviet ultimate goals might be, Gorbachev was taking real steps that would make the USSR less of a threat to the United States.[55] Matlock, who witnessed these debates, later explained that both Gates and Shultz could find evidence to support their conclusions, because Gorbachev "was still trying to do contradictory things." Gates focused on the continuities in Soviet policies, said Matlock, while Shultz was "alert to the unmistakable signs of change and to the potential this would have for the future." In my interview with Matlock, he questioned whether intelligence assessments affected the perceptions of key decision makers in the Reagan administration. Reagan, like Shultz, "would base his judgment on his interactions with Gorbachev and Shevardnadze."[56] In the end, Matlock added, "Gorbachev's behavior in Washington would loom larger in their minds than any number of intelligence briefings."[57]

The Washington Summit (December 1987)

The positive interactions between Reagan and Gorbachev during the Washington summit marked an important step. The president interpreted Gorbachev's political intentions in a manner consistent with the vividness hypothesis. According to Matlock, "Reagan's meetings with Gorbachev in Washington were notably more harmonious than they had been in either Geneva or Reykjavik."[58] Lou Cannon observes that "in signing the INF treaty, Reagan and Gorbachev demonstrated a comfortable familiarity with each other that was the by-product of their meetings in Geneva and Reykjavik."[59] And Leffler writes that "good feelings infused the concluding sessions of the Washington summit. The warmth that Reagan and Gorbachev felt for one another grew as they took pride in their mutual achievement."[60] At the time, Reagan wrote in his diary, "I think the whole thing was the best summit we've ever had with the Soviet Union."[61]

During the months following the Washington summit, relations between the USSR and United States improved rapidly. As Matlock notes, "From late 1987 . . . we began to register significant results in all parts of the US-Soviet agenda. The speed of change was dizzying for those of us who had worked for decades on what had for long seemed the intractable problems of dealing with the USSR."[62] Shifts in Reagan's assessments of Soviet intentions following the summit were evident from his public statements in December 1987. Explaining his sense of optimism, Reagan frequently referred to the special rapport he had established with Gorbachev. Asked whether he still believed the USSR was an evil empire, Reagan was defensive. His reply was quite different from previous statements, reflecting his changing assessments of Soviet intentions under Gorbachev:

> With regard to the evil empire I meant it when I said it, because under previous leaders they have made it evident that they were based—or that their program was based on expansionism, on going forward toward the Marxist philosophy of the one-world Communist state. All of those things were true. . . . And it was true that there was a philosophy then, under the previous leaders, that there was no immorality in anything that furthered the cause of socialism, therefore permitting themselves to violate trust, to lie, and so forth. [Now, however,] there seems to be an entirely different relationship.[63]

Reagan was reassured that the military intentions of the USSR were changing as well. He increasingly came to believe that the Soviets, like the United States, did not think that a nuclear war could be won. In an interview from December 11, 1987, Reagan said, "To hear this man [Gorbachev] now, without any urging from me, express his wish that we could totally eliminate nuclear weapons because of the threat they represent—and he quoted back to me a line that I used as long ago as 1982 in speaking to some foreign parliaments . . . and that is: A nuclear war cannot be won and must never be fought."[64]

Others in the administration were not as impressed by changes in the USSR and saw no reason for optimism. Weinberger (who resigned as secretary of defense in October 1987 because of his wife's ill health) contended that Gorbachev's policies represented nothing more than a well-crafted public relations campaign. He believed Gorbachev pursued domestic reforms only to maintain the viability of the Soviet regime.[65]

Reevaluating Soviet Intentions (1988)

The process of reevaluating Soviet intentions continued throughout 1988, following additional costly and reassuring Soviet actions as well as another positive personal exchange between Reagan and Gorbachev at the Moscow summit in May. The documents reveal that while some understood Gorbachev no longer adhered to traditional Soviet objectives of expansionism and world domination, many doubted whether these observed changes reflected a deep-seated shift in the nature of the Soviet regime. For example, in an address before the World Affairs Council of Washington on December 4, 1987, Shultz said that the "winds of change blowing from Moscow may prove as revolutionary as Mr. Gorbachev has declared," referring to Gorbachev's statements that acknowledged the need to change the Soviet system. Yet Shultz was skeptical about the "ultimate impact" of these changes.[66] He questioned the durability and depth of change in the USSR, and whether they would affect the adversarial nature of US-Soviet relations. In a public statement in February, Shultz said:

> I find it difficult to believe that our relations with the Soviet Union will ever be "normal" in the sense that we have normal relations with most countries. . . . We are vastly different in the ways we view the role of the individual in our societies and in the ways we relate to other countries. The relationship between us will always be unique. It seems unlikely that the U.S.-Soviet relationship will ever lose what always has been and is today a strongly wary and at times adversarial element.

> Nor do I think that the accumulation of individual agreements or cooperative arrangements will, by itself, result in a quantum leap to a qualitatively different kind of relationship. The differences between us and the suspicions they generate are too deep. Experience has proved that agreements alone cannot bridge such a divide.

At the same time, Shultz pointed to significant changes, saying, "The case can be made that we are near a threshold of a sustainable US-Soviet relationship. On the US side, there is, for the first time in many years, a strong consensus on how we should deal with the Soviet Union. On the Soviet side, there may be—for the first time ever and as a result of necessity—a willingness to reexamine Soviet security and other interests in ways that are closer to international norms."[67]

Like Shultz, in early 1988 Reagan was balanced in his characterization of the USSR and its intentions. He noted the recent changes in Soviet behavior. For instance, while attending the NATO summit in March 1988, Reagan commented on the "encouraging signs of change in the policies of the Soviet Union," but said he would look "beyond pronouncements for tangible and lasting policy changes."[68] In a speech a month later, Reagan said that US-Soviet relations had taken "a dramatic turn into a period of realistic engagement." He indicated that the Soviet withdrawal from Afghanistan was an unprecedented achievement, which he attributed to "pressure from the West." Reagan discussed the issue of human rights at length, acknowledging signs of change in the USSR. "But if there is change, it's because the costs of aggression and the real moral difference between our systems were brought home to it."[69] Matlock observes that much of the emphasis on human rights in Reagan's public speeches prior to the Moscow summit stemmed from domestic political reasons, reflecting his desire to signal to conservatives at home that "he was not forgetting the condition of human rights in the Soviet Union in order to obtain a favorable vote on the [INF] treaty."[70]

When Shultz explained to Reagan that Gorbachev had been genuinely offended by such comments, Reagan became more careful about his rhetoric. According to Matlock, "He continued to call attention to problems in the relationship that needed to be solved, but did so only after he had noted progress already achieved." Furthermore, Reagan began to stress that Gorbachev was indeed a different kind of Soviet leader, who was truly interested in cooperation abroad and reform at home.[71] Asked in Moscow whether, at the beginning of his presidency, he could have imagined traveling to Moscow for a summit, Reagan replied,

Probably not, because very frankly, I have to say I think there is a difference between this General Secretary and other leaders of your country that I had met within the past. I don't think they had any dreams of perestroika. And yet, I felt that we had to exist in the world together. Our systems are different, we're going to be competitive in a number of ways, and that'll continue, but we can be competitive without being hostile to the point of conflict with each other. And I think this is what we're aiming at. And no, I could not have foreseen your present leader.

When asked what sources he had consulted to support his past assertions that Soviet goals were expansionist, Reagan answered,

I also know—and this didn't require reading [Vladimir Ilyich] Lenin—that every leader, every General Secretary but the present one had, in appearances before the Soviet Congress, reiterated their allegiance to that Marxian theory that the goal was a one-world Communist state. This man has not said that. So, I wasn't making anything up; these were the things we were told. For example, here in our government, we knew that Lenin had expressed a part of the plan that involved Latin America and so forth. And the one line that sounded very ominous to us was when he said that the last bastion of capitalism, the United States, would not have to be taken; it would fall into their outstretched hand like overripe fruit.[72]

While in Moscow, Reagan also made it clear that he believed that Gorbachev was responding to the US litmus test: "Many of the reforms that [Gorbachev] is undertaking are aimed at the things that we have always criticized in the Soviet Union. And if there is a way to be helpful in that, and certainly to at least acknowledge our approval of what he is doing, that we should do that."[73] In the same interview, Reagan also admitted for the first time that his relations with

Gorbachev had evolved. When asked whether he considered Gorbachev a "real friend," Reagan responded,

> Well, I can't help but say yes to that because the difference that I've found between him and other previous leaders that I have met with is that, yes, we can debate, and we disagree, and it is true he's made it apparent that he believes much of the Communist propaganda that he's grown up hearing about our country that—the big corporations and whether they dictate to government or not and things of that kind. I try to disabuse him of those beliefs. But there is never a sense of personal animus when the arguments are over, and I'm reasonably optimistic, although at the same time I'm realistic. The only Russian I know is a little Russian proverb. And I've used it so many times on him that he's going to hit me over the head one day if I use it again. And that is, *Dovorey no provorey*—trust but verify.[74]

In an interview with the Soviet magazine *Ogonyok*, Reagan was asked whether he had reconsidered his comment from a few years back, in which he characterized the USSR as an evil empire. Reagan replied that while he had noticed some progress on certain issues, such as the Soviet withdrawal from Afghanistan and more open discussion on human rights, he still believed that more could be done on issues of freedom of religion, movement, and free speech.[75] Although Reagan did not yet disavow his characterization of the Soviet Union as an evil empire, he would do so a month later.

The Moscow Summit and Its Aftermath (May–December 1988)

Reagan would describe the fourth summit between the two leaders in May 1988 as the most memorable one. Shortly before the meeting, two developments altered perceptions held by Reagan and some of his advisers. First, in April the Soviets began to withdraw their troops from Afghanistan—an act that symbolized to some in the administration that the expansionist Brezhnev Doctrine was dead. In his memoir, Shultz explained that the dominant perception in the administration was that "if the Soviets left Afghanistan, the Brezhnev Doctrine would be breached, and the principle of 'never letting go' would be violated."[76] Reagan treated this move as a "historic triumph" that opened up the possibility of resolving additional regional conflicts involving the Soviets.[77] Yet some US officials still believed that the withdrawal from Afghanistan represented just another phase in Gorbachev's propaganda campaign and stemmed from the Soviets' desire to cut their losses. Weinberger, who had retired as secretary of defense by then, claimed in his memoirs that neither agreement on the INF nor the withdrawal from Afghanistan meant the Soviet Union was no longer an expansionist power. That withdrawal, he said, "is simply an admission that they would not win, and indeed have lost, their goal of trying to pacify the Mujaheddin with their own troops, so that their 'puppet government' would be safe."[78]

Second, Gorbachev proposed comprehensive reforms at the Nineteenth Communist Party Conference, held shortly after the Moscow summit, calling for elections, term limits, separation of powers, and freedom of speech, assembly, conscience, and the press. Gorbachev's proposals signaled to many in the US administration that he intended to change the USSR radically and make it difficult for any future Soviet leaders to reverse the reforms. These proposals, Matlock writes, "provided evidence that Gorbachev was finally prepared to cross the Rubicon and discard the Marxist ideology that had defined and justified the Communist Party dictatorship in the Soviet Union." Briefing the president a few days before Reagan departed for Moscow, Matlock explained the significance of these proposals, saying, "If Gorbachev means what he says—and he must mean it or he wouldn't present it to a Communist Party Conference—the Soviet Union will never be the same."[79]

The Moscow summit was a success. The two leaders held two private meetings at which Reagan pushed Gorbachev on the issue of freedom of religion, suggesting that if the Soviet leader were to change Soviet policies on this matter, Reagan "felt very strongly that he [Gorbachev] would be a hero, and that much of the feeling against his country would disappear like water in hot sun." Reagan reassured Gorbachev that he would never say in public that he had given Gorbachev advice on this issue.[80] Reagan later summarized the meeting in his memoir as follows:

> Gorbachev listened and seemed to take in my opinions; from his expression I knew that he didn't like some of things I was saying, but he didn't try to say anything harsh in rebuttal. Whether my words had any impact or not I don't know, but after that the Soviet government began allowing more churches and synagogues to reopen and, of course, in time, the wall came tumbling down.[81]

Still in Moscow following the summit meetings, when asked whether he could declare the Cold War over, Reagan replied, "I think right now, of course."[82] Similarly, Shultz announced, after the opening of the UN General Assembly in September, that "the world had changed." He added, "Margaret Thatcher had it right . . . [when] she said flatly 'We're not in a Cold War now.'" He later wrote that "despite this new reality, many in the United States seemed unable or unwilling to grasp this seminal fact. But to me, it was all over but the shouting."[83] In sharp contrast to Reagan and Shultz, however, Weinberger did not view these reassuring costly actions by the Soviet Union as credible. "Not only did Gorbachev give up all of the Soviet 'non-negotiable' demands [in the INF Treaty], but he gave us precisely the kind of treaty that the president had sought for seven years. That act of course does not mean—any more than does the Soviet withdrawal from Afghanistan—that the USSR has given up its long-term aggressive designs."[84]

REASONING ABOUT SOVIET INTENTIONS

The reasoning evidence I present below provides strong support for the selective attention thesis and moderate support for the behavior thesis.

Reagan's Reasoning

A close reading of Reagan's reasoning pattern lends support to the past actions and current actions hypotheses of the behavior thesis as well as the vividness hypothesis of the selective attention thesis. In gauging intentions, Reagan attended to certain Soviet noncapabilities-based actions. His views about Soviet intentions were influenced to a large degree by his positive personal impressions of Gorbachev and the latter's responsiveness to Reagan's litmus tests.

During 1985 and 1986, Reagan repeatedly referred to past Soviet foreign actions to support his conclusion that Soviet intentions were expansionist. He relied in particular on examples of Soviet interventions in the third world during the 1970s. In November 1985, Reagan stated, "We believe, and I think with some evidence, that their [Soviet] policy had been expansionist; that's evidenced by Afghanistan, Ethiopia, South Yemen, and Angola."[85] In a message to Congress in 1986, Reagan emphasized the link between costly Soviet actions and their intentions, noting that Soviet interventionism since the 1970s "make[s] up the disturbing pattern of Soviet conduct in the past fifteen years.... That the Soviet leadership persists in such policies despite the growing burden they impose only testifies to the strength of Soviet commitment."[86] Reagan believed that the invasion of Afghanistan was particular proof of Soviet aggressive intentions. In August 1985, he noted that the United States had "good reason to believe—to think—that they [Soviets] do have hostile intent—their expansionism worldwide, their invasion of Afghanistan and so forth."[87] Responding to a letter from Gorbachev in April 1985, Reagan asked rhetorically how he could accept Gorbachev's declaration of peaceful competition, given the history of "Soviet military actions in Afghanistan or of your country's policy of arms to minority elements in other countries which are attempting to impose their will on a nation by force."[88] Later, at the 1985 Geneva summit, Reagan told the Soviet premier that the United States "sees an expansionist Soviet Union" and then pointed out that the USSR has "a satellite in Cuba just 90 miles off our shore.... Now we see Afghanistan, Ethiopia, Angola and Yemen—with for example, 35,000 Cubans in Angola."[89] Reagan continued to reason that Soviet involvement in regional conflicts constituted the greatest source of US mistrust, pointing out in 1986 "how difficult it is for the United States to accept Soviet assurances of peaceful intent" with Soviet troops present in Afghanistan, Angola, Cambodia, Ethiopia, Nicaragua, and Vietnam.[90]

If past Soviet actions indicated hostile intentions, then Reagan reasoned that a tangible change in behavior was needed to demonstrate benign intentions. In October 1985, for instance, he stated, "If they [the Soviets] really want to live in a peaceful world and be friends and associate with the rest of the world, then, we need more than words. And the deeds could be the stopping of their attempt—either themselves or through proxies and through subversion—to force their system on other countries throughout the world. And that could be one of the greatest proofs there is."[91] He viewed Gorbachev's statements on arms control with skepticism. Reagan believed that Soviet proposals for nuclear test moratoriums and a chemical-weapons-free zone in Europe were merely anti-Western propaganda. The deployments of significant numbers of Soviet or Soviet-backed troops in third world conflicts reinforced his skepticism.[92]

Reagan's assessments of Soviet intention did not change in 1986, but he repeatedly mentioned his strong positive impressions of Gorbachev during their meetings at the Geneva summit. For example, referring to the release of human rights activist Natan Sharansky, Reagan remarked, "I don't have any way to determine what their motives are in doing this. I only know that since the Geneva meeting there have been not only this but others released, more so than in a great many years."[93] In March 1986, Reagan said of Gorbachev's arms control proposals that "this is the first time I can recall any Soviet leader actually being willing to eliminate weapons they already have."[94] Reagan repeated similar words following Gorbachev's proposals in July 1986: "To my knowledge, [Gorbachev is] the first Russian leader who has actually proposed reducing the number of weapons and who has also voiced the opinion that our goal should be the total elimination of nuclear weapons. . . . So, obviously there's more reason for optimism."[95]

Reagan's line of reasoning did not change significantly during 1987. In spring and summer 1987, Reagan challenged Gorbachev to move beyond a "campaign of words" and exhibit instead "tangible changes" in Soviet actions. Reagan maintained, for one, it would be premature to describe glasnost as signifying a dramatic change in Soviet behavior. "Good sense . . . dictates that we look for tangible change in behavior—for actions, not words—in deciding what is real or illusionary" in reports on reform in the USSR.[96] But unlike previous years, Reagan outlined concrete actions Gorbachev could take, both domestically and internationally, to signal benign intentions. These constituted Reagan's litmus test. He urged Gorbachev to change Soviet policies on human rights, exhibit glasnost in Soviet military affairs, tear down the Berlin Wall, withdraw Soviet forces from the third world (especially Afghanistan), and renounce the Brezhnev Doctrine.[97] On these two last points, Reagan reasoned in late October 1987 that "it is in regional conflicts where Soviet performance has been most disturbing. Anyone searching for evidence that the Soviets remain expansionist, indeed imperialist, need look no farther than Nicaragua or Afghanistan."[98]

Though he recognized that Gorbachev's intentions and objectives were perhaps different, Reagan's beliefs about the nature of the Soviet Union itself continued unchanged until the end of 1987. On December 3, 1987, he said, "I haven't changed from the time when I made a speech about an evil empire."[100]

By 1988, however, Reagan no longer referred to the USSR as an expansionist power. He explained his changing perceptions by referring primarily to recent Soviet recent behavior, which appeared to match what Reagan had requested of Gorbachev to demonstrate benign intentions. The documents along with my interviews with Shultz and Matlock offer strong evidence that the more time Reagan spent with Gorbachev, the more he trusted the Soviet leader. Gorbachev's behavior during and following these meetings constituted the most important proof in Reagan's eyes that the Soviet Union under his leadership was much less threatening. This supports the current actions hypothesis of the behavior thesis and vividness hypothesis of the selective attention thesis.

In early 1988, Reagan's rhetoric was still not conciliatory. According to Matlock, the president sought to placate conservative domestic opponents of INF ratification. So when Reagan acknowledged that that there was "evidence of some change in the Soviet Union," he would add that relations with the West would not improve "while Soviet troops still occupy Afghanistan."[101] Reagan was still unconvinced that the policy of glasnost was a durable one. He cautioned, "Swings between glasnost and the gulag are not new or even peculiar to the Soviet regime. In history they recurred again and again as the throne passed from czar to czar, and even within the reign of a single czar. We cannot afford to mortgage our security to the assessed motives of particular individuals or to the novel approaches of a new leadership, even if we wish them well." By March, though, Reagan conceded that improvements in Soviet behavior on issues pertaining to human rights and Afghanistan made him more optimistic about progress in relations between the two superpowers.[102] Reagan continued to challenge Gorbachev to remove the Berlin Wall, while simultaneously "applauding the changes that have taken place [in Soviet human rights policies] and encouraging the Soviets to go further." Reagan believed, even as late as May 1988, that Soviet behavior could be reversed in the future. He cautioned that only an institutionalization of the changes would lead him to think that Soviet intentions had in fact become benign.[103]

At the same time, Reagan's strong impressions of Gorbachev dominated in his reasoning about Soviet intentions. On multiple occasions Reagan referred to Gorbachev as a friend who was "very sincere about the progressive ideas that he is introducing there and the changes that he thinks should be made."[104] Reagan came to respect and admire the Soviet premier:

> It's clear that there was a chemistry between Gorbachev and me that produced something very close to a friendship. He was a tough, hard bargainer. . . . I liked Gorbachev even though he was a dedicated Communist. . . . He was different from the Communists who had preceded him to the top of the Kremlin hierarchy. . . . He was the first not to push Soviet expansionism, the first to agree to destroy nuclear weap-

ons, the first to suggest a free market and to support open elections and freedom of expression.[105]

Gorbachev's most important actions, Reagan held, were those that responded to his own requests. For example, Reagan notes that by late 1987, "there were tentative indications that 'quiet diplomacy' was working with Gorbachev: Although neither he nor I discussed it publicly, some of the people whose names were on the lists I'd given him, of people who we knew wanted to leave the Soviet Union, began receiving exit permits."[106] During a National Security Planning Group meeting in September 1987, Reagan noted, "I have a friend who tells me that in the Soviet Union the right-wingers are starting to call Gorbachev 'Mr. Yes' because he agrees with everything that I propose."[107]

On June 1, 1988, Reagan declared that the Cold War was over. He attributed the change in his perceptions of Soviet intentions to Gorbachev: "I think that a great deal of it is due to the General Secretary, who I have found different than previous Soviet leaders have been; but that also as we have pursued this, we have found them willing to enter into negotiations with us. And I think that enough progress has been made that we can look with optimism on future negotiations." In a follow-up question, Reagan insisted that a change in his perceptions was not because he had had an opportunity to learn more about the Soviet Union over the years. Rather, he claimed, "A large part of it is Mr. Gorbachev as a leader. And I think there have been changes here as they have sought to make—well, I read 'Perestroika,' and I found much in it that I could agree with."[108] In an interview in October, Reagan summarized his views about the nature, meaning, and potential success of Gorbachev's reforms:

> I believe that one of the things that explains what he's trying to do is that he had hurdled over Stalin—and I have reason to believe and know that he has no respect or regard for Stalin whatsoever—but he's gone back to some of the teachings of Lenin. Now, Lenin, admittedly, was the starting Communist force. But at the same time, remember some of the things that he advocated, that he publicly said to the people of Russia: You may find yourselves working beside Capitalists, but don't be concerned. You'll learn from them. Well, now, you didn't hear anything like that from Stalin or any of the people that have followed him. But this man [Gorbachev] seems to have some ideas of that in mind. I hope that he can continue and will continue on this path.[109]

On December 7, Reagan was asked whether Gorbachev's recent announcement of a unilateral reduction in conventional capabilities was merely an attempt to drive a wedge between the United States and its European allies. Reagan responded, "I think that he is sincerely dealing with the problems that he has in his own country." When asked whether Gorbachev had achieved "a propaganda advantage with his major proposal," Reagan dismissed the question as "not serious."[110]

Reagan's personality—specifically his openness to contradictory information, belief in his power of persuasion, and emotional intelligence—allowed him to rely heavily on his personal impressions of Gorbachev.[111] These traits also affected the extent to which he believed Gorbachev acted in response to Reagan's own requests. As Barbara Farnham's study of Reagan's foreign policy notes, for Reagan, "personal experience counted for everything."[112] Reagan himself noted during the Moscow summit that "systems may be brutish, bureaucrats may fail. But men can sometimes transcend all that, transcend even the forces of history that seem destined to keep them apart."[113] Indeed, many of Reagan's confidants have pointed to his tendency to reduce issues to personalities. As George Breslauer and Richard Ned Lebow explain, "If he liked and trusted someone, he was more prone to give credence to the policies they espoused."[114] Matlock similarly notes that Reagan had a "conviction" that "human beings could change by communication."[115]

The significance Reagan assigned to personality and personal diplomacy, combined with his confidence in his ability to persuade and judge others, made him more likely to change his views based on what he saw as salient indicators of intentions. Reagan's impressions of Gorbachev were central to inducing change in his perceptions of Soviet intentions. Other members of his administration noticed this. Matlock thus commented that "once he [Reagan] and Shultz started meeting with Gorbachev they relied on their personal impressions and personal instincts."[116] "This should not come as a surprise," Matlock added. "If [a] person reaches a top political system in a country they know how decisions are made even in a foreign country." In other words, high-level decision makers all follow a similar process. In the case of Reagan and Gorbachev, that led to a special relationship. National Security Advisor Frank Carlucci observed that "the personal bonds that began to develop between the president and Gorbachev, between George [Shultz] and Shevardnadze," led to "the gradual building of trust."[117] Shultz said, "One reason they respected each other was that they both could see that the other guy was saying what he thought. Maybe you did not agree with him and maybe you did. But there it was. It wasn't maneuvering and manipulating and trying to make some obscure point. It was right there. It was real. What you saw was what you got."[118]

In a counterfactual analysis on the end of the Cold War, Breslauer and Lebow argued that the personal rapport as well as special chemistry between the two leaders helped reshape the leaders' preferences, commitments, and expectations of reciprocity. They maintain that this explains why the Cold War ended when it did. Specifically, they claim that the trusting relationship at the leadership level played a significant role in encouraging Gorbachev to keep offering so many costly unilateral concessions. "Confronted with a different general secretary, who had neither Gorbachev's personality nor his commitment to reduce the nuclear threat, Reagan might have remained an anti-Soviet ideologue."[119]

As for the validity of the alternative theses, Reagan saw a connection between Soviet capabilities, actions, and intentions. He repeatedly contended that Soviet expansionist conduct occurred at a time when the United States had lost its supe-riority over the USSR in strategic nuclear weapons. "In Europe," Reagan asserted,

> the effect of this loss was not quickly perceptible, but seen globally, Soviet conduct changed markedly and dangerously. First in Angola in 1975, then when the West failed to respond, in Ethiopia, in South Yemen, in Kampuchea, and ultimately in Af-ghanistan, the Soviet Union began courting more risks and expanding its influence through the direct and indirect application of military power. Today [1985] we see similar Soviet efforts to profit and stimulate regional conflicts in Central America.[120]

In May 1985, Reagan claimed that "there had been theories that Soviet bel-ligerence would wane as their relative strength to the United States increased. Those theories went by the wayside in the late 1970s as Soviet advisers and mil-itary equipment, along with thousands of Cuban surrogate troops, poured into Africa."[121] Reagan did not believe that intentions follow from capabilities, as So-viet intentions were historically aggressive both when the USSR was militarily weaker and when it was stronger than the United States. Soviet behavior, not its military buildup, was to Reagan the most convincing evidence of Soviet aggres-sive intentions.[122] In fact, one of Reagan's favorite quotations, which he and his advisers reiterated many times in public and private meetings with Gorbachev and other foreign leaders, was that "nations do not mistrust each other because they are armed; they are armed because they mistrust each other." This quota-tion implies that Reagan thought that capabilities are reflected in intentions, not vice versa. Reagan similarly acknowledged that the adversary's capabilities alone were insufficient and perhaps even misleading as indicators of intentions. They were products of how each side perceived the other's intentions. Accord-ingly, in October 1985, he stated that it was important to remember that "arms, whether nuclear or conventional, do not come to exist for no reason. They exist because nations have very real differences among themselves and suspicions about each other's intentions."[123] Simply put, capabilities might reflect inten-tions, but Reagan nevertheless felt that capabilities cannot be used to infer cur-rent or future intentions. After all, capabilities can at once imply hostile intent or insecurity. The noisiness of this signal made it too unreliable as an indicator for intentions.

Finally, Soviet ideology along with changes in it also played a role in altering Reagan's perceptions of Soviet intentions during this period.[124] Reagan viewed Marxist-Leninist ideology as the root cause of Soviet expansionist behavior, and motivation and legitimation for Soviet foreign policy. In 1986 he stated, "Marxist-Leninist regimes tend to wage wars readily against their neighbors as they routinely do against their own people."[125] Even after the 1986 Reykjavik summit, Reagan blamed mistrust between the two superpowers on the "Soviet Union's record of seeking to impose its ideology and rule on others."[126] Never-theless, it is nearly impossible to disentangle changes in Soviet ideology from those in Soviet domestic institutions during this period. The two occurred si-multaneously. US decision makers' references to Soviet ideology almost always included references to the observable implications of these ideological changes on Soviet domestic institutions. Mark Haas's study on the role that ideology and perceptions played in shifting Reagan's beliefs about Soviet intentions, reaches similar conclusions: "Gorbachev needed to propose major democratic institutional changes before most U.S. leaders believed his commitment to liberalism was genuine. Greater tolerance and respect for basic human rights were insufficient."[127]

Shultz's Reasoning

Shultz was less explicit than Reagan in his reasoning about Soviet intentions. However, available documents indicate that he shared Reagan's views of Soviet intentions. Initially, Shultz concentrated on past Soviet behavior in the Third World as evidence that the Soviet Union was an expansionist power. In a meeting with Gorbachev, Shultz explained, "There is much skepticism in the United States about the Soviet Union because of your past actions. Jimmy Carter . . . certainly learned a lesson when the Soviet Union invaded Afghanistan. The shooting of the Korean air liner [in 1983] is another episode."[128] Shultz's early pessimism correlated with his perception of Soviet capabilities and the recent Soviet military buildup. However, like Reagan, Shultz explained that his assessments were based on observing the Soviet Union's behavior and its use of its capabilities in crisis situations, rather from the military buildup itself. In April 1986, Shultz said, "This concentration of [Soviet] military forces is of considerable concern given the demonstrated willingness of the Soviet Union and its proxies—in Afghanistan, Cambodia, and Korea—to use their military power for their political ends."[129] Even more than Reagan, Shultz connected Soviet behavior with Soviet capabilities and the balance of power. Yet his reasoning stopped short of claiming that capabilities cause aggressive behavior, or that they are a good predictor of a country's future intentions:

> I think that for you to say that there is no importance to a dramatic difference in force balance is to ignore the history of the late 1970s when the Soviets were no longer strategically inferior. It altered their behavior, and they began to move through surrogates—through Angola, Ethiopia, South Yemen, Afghanistan, Indochina, Nicaragua. In short, there is a correlation between the power imbalance and [the] behavior of people. Now to say that would translate tomorrow, or the next day, to a coercion of the United States itself, is a long leap, but one shouldn't dismiss it.[130]

Shultz's reasoning for his reassessment of Soviet intentions in 1987 and 1988 is consistent with the current actions hypothesis of the behavior thesis as well as the vividness hypothesis of the selective attention thesis. Following the announcement of withdrawal from Afghanistan, Shultz claimed he felt "that a profound, historic shift was underway; the Soviet Union was willingly or unwillingly, consciously or not, turning a corner; they were *not* just resting for round two of the Cold War."[131] The abandonment of the expansionist Brezhnev Doctrine was, according to Shultz, "a development of immense importance—and a dramatic moment."[132] In his debates with the intelligence community over its assessment of Gorbachev's objectives, Shultz referred to the withdrawal from Afghanistan and other regional hot spots as noteworthy indications of change.[133]

Shultz presented changes in Soviet human rights policies as the most revealing indicator of changes in Soviet intentions. In my interview with him, Shultz asserted that the most significant marker of change was the relationship between the state and its society, especially on issues like human rights.[134] He noted how impressed he was in 1986 that Gorbachev was willing to treat human rights as a legitimate subject for discussion: "The Soviet agreement that human rights belonged on the agenda was astonishing."[135] In 1987, Shultz reported to Reagan that "the signs of change were unmistakable." In their private discussions, he highlighted to Shevardnadze these aspects as revealing information about Soviet intentions. Shultz told Shevardnadze that "an important change has occurred. And the increased liberty we are seeing in the granting of visas for travel to the United States, this increased ability for Soviet citizens to come and go, is an encouraging part of the pattern that seems to be developing and that we welcome."[136] In public he declared, "The most telling indicator will be the Soviet human rights situation," because

> the world is looking for results that bear out the rhetoric—not only for the sake of the individuals and the families involved but because human rights as practiced at home are related to international security. For a government that does not respect the rights it has guaranteed to its own people will not respect its international obligations and the general norms of the world community.[137]

Shultz found Shevardnadze to be "responsive" to his personal requests and suggestions.[138] He was touched by Shevardnadze's willingness to look at the list of people who Shultz believed should be allowed to emigrate.[139] Shultz was impressed that as he sought to convince Shevardnadze of the importance of human rights in an information age, "Shevardnadze paid close attention. He did not interrupt. When I finished, he thanked me and said that his note takers had recorded what I had said."[140] Shultz wondered whether the change in Soviet policies on human rights was due in part to his own urging and insights. When Shevardnadze explained to him that the Soviet Union was taking actions to open its society because the Soviets believed it to be in their own interest, Shultz "harked back to my having made that very argument to him the previous April," and asked himself, "Was my line of argument having some impact?"[141] In my interview with the secretary of state, he explained that one could not help but realize that if someone gives you their word, and then things happen as promised, one learns to trust that person's word. Indeed, his numerous personal interactions with Shevardnadze produced a sense of trust over time that made Shevardnadze's assurances to withdraw from Afghanistan "different" from previous statements. Shultz commented, "I had enough confidence by this time in my relationship with Shevardnadze that I knew he would not deliberately mislead me."[142] Vividness in the form of personal impressions was central to inducing change in Shultz's assessments. Shultz, however, was much less explicit than Reagan when it came to using these impressions in his public statements.

Weinberger's Reasoning

Weinberger was unequivocal in stating his belief that despite changes in Soviet actions and military capabilities, the USSR still harbored unlimited expansionist intentions. In his public appearances before Congress, Weinberger rarely talked about the sources of Soviet political intentions per se. Rather, he referred to the overall threat that the USSR posed. In Weinberger's appearances, he was seeking authorization for increases in the defense budget or to develop new weapon systems; he had an incentive to exaggerate the Soviet threat. As a result, the reasoning Weinberger provides in these instances appears eclectic. Weinberger's inference process and reasoning are entirely inconsistent with the current actions hypothesis of the behavior thesis. Still, the question remains: Why didn't Weinberger change his beliefs about Soviet intentions in the face of repeated Soviet costly actions of reassurance? One interpretation points to the principle of cognitive consistency, which prevented Weinberger from giving credence to information that contradicted his beliefs about the Soviet Union. Weinberger held well-established hawkish views of the Soviet Union and its intentions. According to the subjective credibility hypothesis, these stances should have led him to discount most of Gorbachev's costly actions of reassurance as either meaningless or attempts to portray a deceptively benign image. Another explanation would suggest the absence of vivid information in Weinberger's case. Unlike Reagan or Shultz, Weinberger interacted little with Gorbachev, Shevardnadze, and the Soviet defense minister, Sergei Sokolov, so he was not exposed to the same type of vivid personal information.

Weinberger's later statements in the aftermath of the Cold War reveal that he saw Gorbachev's commitment to Communism as the most critical indicator of Soviet intentions. Even as late as 2002, in Weinberger's view, "Gorbachev to this day is a committed Communist and still believes that what is necessary is to strengthen communism. But [Boris] Yeltsin was not. Yeltsin had the courage to oppose it, and that's how the Cold War ended." Later in that interview, Weinberger noted that although Reagan was impressed by Gorbachev, he himself "didn't, frankly, ever trust Gorbachev or believe that he was fully committed [to abandoning Communism]. . . . I guess the first sign [that Yeltsin was 'genuinely an anti-Communist'] was when the border guards stopped shooting people who were trying to leave."[143] These statements may only reflect Weinberger's post hoc rationalization for why and how the Cold War ended. But Weinberger's repeated references to Yeltsin's commitment to anti-Communist ideology are telling.

Consistent with the vividness hypothesis, Weinberger's lack of updating might be attributable to him not having any personal interaction with Soviet leaders. Shultz and Reagan had extensive personal interactions with Soviet leaders, and changed their beliefs accordingly. Even though the observable implications that follow from the vividness hypothesis are similar to those of other hypotheses—for example, that Weinberger's failure to update his beliefs about Soviet intentions stemmed from his deeply ingrained beliefs of Soviet aggression or strong bureaucratic interests as the head of the DOD—my argument here is that the actions that scholars would consider to be especially costly actions of reassurance were regarded by Weinberger as irrelevant to his assessment of Soviet intentions.

US POLICIES CONCERNING THE USSR

This section has two goals. The first is tracking which decision makers advocated aggressive or conciliatory policies, and when they did so. The second goal is to determine whether a correlation exists between the assessments of Soviet intentions made by key individuals in the Reagan administration and the foreign policies they advocated in private. Those decision makers who held more benign interpretations of Soviet intentions, such as Shultz, often advocated more conciliatory policies and more negotiations. Meanwhile, those who held hostile views of Soviet intentions (e.g., Weinberger) advocated more hardline policies and saw little benefit in negotiating with the Soviets. This finding should bolster confidence in the statements on Soviet intentions traced in the first section of this chapter.

Reformulating Soviet Policy (1983)

I first return to the period when, according to key members of the administration, a new or modified policy toward the Soviet Union was devised. During its first two and a half years, the Reagan administration had pursued a highly confrontational policy toward the USSR.[144] The new policy of 1983–84 did not signify a dramatic shift but rather a limited change. It reflected an interest in normalizing relations with the Soviets through a comprehensive dialogue. The objectives of this new policy were to "reduce the use and threat to use force in international disputes"; "lower high levels of armaments by equitable and verifiable agreements"; "establish a minimal level of trust to facilitate the first two objectives" by examining the Soviets' compliance with past agreements and their human rights performance; and pursue "specific confidence-building measures" along with "bilateral ties when mutually beneficial."[145]

The approach adopted by Reagan, Shultz, McFarlane, and Matlock was based on principles of "realism," "strength," and "dialogue" (sometimes referred to as RS&D). Realism acknowledged that competition with the USSR would persist, and the US and Soviet systems would never converge. Strength meant that the United States needed military and economic power, alliance cohesion, and political will to deal with the Soviet Union effectively: only a powerful United States would make the Soviets willing to negotiate. The final principle, dialogue, implied a US willingness to negotiate differences as well as seek concrete and productive ways to reduce tensions between the two superpowers.[146] The decisions to renew dialogue with Chernenko, who had recently succeeded Andropov as general secretary, and resume arms control negotiations with the USSR were highly controversial within the Reagan administration. Weinberger and William Casey (Reagan's former campaign manager who became his first DCI during 1981–87) questioned whether such policies were in the US interest. Reagan, though, sided with Shultz.[147] Alongside attempts to engage the Soviets on arms control, Reagan and his advisers continued through 1984 to emphasize the need to contain the Soviets, bolster US defense efforts, and support "freedom fighters" in such places as Afghanistan and Nicaragua.

Reagan explicitly and repeatedly stated that the Soviet Union was an expansionist power with a "relentless drive to conquer more and more lands" in Asia and Central America.[148] His perception of these Soviet intentions played a large role in shaping the new policy toward the Soviets. Chernenko, in Reagan's eyes, "was cut from the same cloth as Brezhnev and Andropov—a tough old-line Communist addicted to Lenin's secular religion of expansionism and world domination, so one thing hadn't changed regarding US-Soviet relations." But Reagan did later acknowledge that throughout 1984, his "attitudes about the Soviets were changing a little." In his memoir, he links his decision to engage the Soviets more with what he had learned in late 1983 from the Soviet reaction to a major NATO exercise (discussed in chapter 10). He wrote,

> The more experience I had with the Soviet leaders and other heads of state who knew them, the more I began to realize that many Soviet officials feared us not only as adversaries but as potential aggressors who might hurl nuclear weapons at them in a first strike; because of this, and perhaps [out] of a sense of insecurity and paranoia with roots reaching back to the invasions of Russia by Napoleon and Hitler, they had aimed a huge arsenal of nuclear weapons at us. Well, if that was the case, I was even more anxious to get a top Soviet leader in a room alone and try to convince him we had no designs on the Soviet Union and Russians had nothing to fear from us.[149]

During an NSC meeting just before his first summit meeting in Geneva, Reagan pointed out that "Soviet historical fear of invasions and suspicions of foreigners" had reached "extreme proportions in some cases."[150] This line of reasoning nevertheless does not indicate that Reagan believed Soviet future *intentions* were benign (or that they would not want to induce a change to the status quo in the future). Instead, he was starting to think that perhaps their *motivation* for building their military power stemmed at least partly from insecurity.

In addition to Reagan's changes in perceptions about Soviet motivation, several other trends could have affected the shift in the administration's policy from mid-1983 to early 1984. Changes in personnel within the administration around that time may have lessened the ideological component of the policy in favor of a more realistic view of the relationship between the two superpowers.[151] In addition, historian Beth Fischer argues, the downing of KAL flight 007 by the Soviets, the television movie *The Day After*, a Pentagon briefing on the effects of nuclear war, and the Soviets' alarm over NATO military exercises in Europe served as a "turning point experience" for Reagan, as they "made the issue of nuclear annihilation especially salient."[152] Domestic political calculations might have played a role as well. The year 1984 marked the opening of the presidential election campaign; Reagan may have been seeking to cultivate the image of a man of peace. Finally, the US military buildup in the preceding years had halted the perceived decline in US military capability; the administration believed it was now able to negotiate with the Soviets from a position of strength.[153] Intelligence sources reported signs of growing strains in the Soviet economy; Reagan hoped that economic troubles would prevent the USSR from engaging in another round of arms races with the United States.[154]

While there is supporting evidence for each of the explanations above, the only finding relevant for the analysis here is that openness to negotiations with the USSR in early 1984 was not the result of changing perceptions of Soviet intentions as such: Reagan continued to state publicly and privately that he thought the Soviet Union was determined to continue to expand, and was not deterred from using military means to achieve its objectives.

More of the Same (1985–86)

During 1985 and 1986, the Reagan administration did not revise its policy toward the USSR. US decision makers repeatedly referred to RS&D principles when they described the US stance toward the USSR. The practical meaning of the principle of realism and continuing adherence to the Reagan Doctrine in the third world can be regarded as hard-line policies aimed at deterring as well as containing Soviet expansionism.[155] At the same time, Reagan and Shultz also promoted the principle of dialogue. They actively sought ways to engage the Soviets on a variety of issues.

Throughout 1985, the administration placed emphasis on gaining domestic support for increases in the military budget (especially the MX missile and SDI), debating the unratified SALT II agreement, and assisting anti-Communist insurgencies. During 1985 and 1986, none of the key foreign policy officials in the Reagan administration deviated from the view that Soviet political intentions were expansionist. The debates within the administration did not reflect differences about perceptions of Soviet intentions. Rather, they reflected differences about the role that negotiations and cooperation could play in inducing a significant turn in the relations between the two superpowers. Weinberger, for instance, sought to link Soviet actions and the US willingness to negotiate on arms control. After US Army military intelligence officer Nicholson was shot and killed by a Soviet sentry in March 1985, Weinberger and other hard-liners in the administration pressed Reagan not to meet with Gorbachev, and to halt the negotiation process. Weinberger was convinced, Matlock said, "that there was no potential benefit in negotiating anything with the Soviet leaders and that most negotiations were dangerous traps."[156] Reagan, however, sided with Shultz and McFarlane, and expressed a commitment to establishing dialogue with the Soviets. Nonetheless, as Shultz points out, "the struggle [among Reagan's advisers] over setting the president's course was never-ending."[157]

At the same time, Reagan pressed for the development of the SDI even though it was clear to all that the Soviets felt threatened by it. While everyone in the administration supported Reagan's SDI, some, including Shultz, recognized that it could have a negative impact on the INF negotiations. Weinberger, Perle, and others urged Reagan not to compromise on the SDI or commit himself to the more restrictive reading of the ABM Treaty. In the end, as Garthoff points out, "Reagan decided on a compromise solution that deferred but did not defuse the issue. Shultz was authorized to state that the administration would continue to limit testing and development of [the] SDI according to the traditional 'restrictive interpretation' of the [ABM] treaty," but Reagan himself made no public commitment to continue to abide by the traditional interpretation of the ABM Treaty.[158]

Following the 1985 Geneva summit, Reagan resumed dialogue with the Soviets on arms control issues and expressed his interest in meeting with Gorbachev again. Further steps were taken to establish US-Soviet cooperation on issues pertaining to regional conflicts, chemical weapons, and educational, scientific, and cultural exchanges. But Reagan also reaffirmed his commitment to containing and cutting back Soviet influence around the world by US support for what he saw as freedom fighters. The second Reagan administration reemphasized that the principle of realism meant a renewed application of the Reagan Doctrine—a strategy of assisting anti-Communist resistance movements in an effort to roll back Communism in the third world—in Afghanistan, Angola, Cambodia, Nicaragua, and elsewhere.[159] Reagan chose to side with Weinberger and other hard-liners in his administration on the issue of SALT II, declaring in June 1985 that the United States would no longer consider the treaty binding.[160] During the following few months, tensions within the administration increased over the issue of the SDI and negotiations with the Soviets. Some in the State Department, including Shultz, wanted Reagan to hint to the Soviets that the United States might be willing to give up the SDI in exchange for greater Soviet concessions on offensive weapons. Reagan reported Weinberger's argument that "if the Soviets heard about this split in the administration and decided I was wavering on the SDI, it would send the wrong signal to Moscow and weaken our bargaining positions." Reagan's views, he said in his diary and memoir, were similar to those of Weinberger.[161]

Toward Increased Cooperation (1987–88)

During the last two years of Reagan's second administration, US policies toward the Soviet Union, and specifically the administration's arms control proposals, reflected a more accommodating stance.[162] Some of Reagan's National Security Decision Directives (NSDDs) continued to assert the strategic threat posed by the Soviet Union. Nevertheless, there was a clear change in the administration's overall policy orientation toward the Soviet Union that reflected Reagan and Shultz's changing perceptions of Soviet intentions. That change was reflected, for example, in the increased patterns of cooperation between the two superpowers, efforts to arrange summit meetings, an eagerness to reach agreements on arms control and regional conflicts, and changes in the language used in most NSDDs to describe the nature of the relationship with the Soviet Union.

The debates surrounding arms control in general and the INF Treaty in particular reveal that the content of individual decision makers' beliefs about Soviet intentions were correlated with their policy positions. All the key US decision makers advocated asymmetrical reductions in which the Soviets would cut greater numbers of weapons than the United States, although the character and extent of these cuts were fiercely debated. Weinberger and Perle, advocating a delay in the resumption of negotiations as long as possible, were unwilling to accept anything but the zero option, whereby all intermediate-range nuclear missiles on either side would be withdrawn from Europe.[163] Shultz, in contrast, "wanted to engage in deeper discussions with Gorbachev and Shevardnadze about the shape of the future."[164] Even amid allegations of Soviet espionage in the US Embassy in Moscow, Shultz insisted that Reagan should allow him to continue the negotiations on the INF. Shultz believed that demanding a zero outcome could "kill the whole deal and, ironically, could jeopardize our best chance to achieve the zero outcome we all wanted."[165] Reagan, who now favored communication with the Soviets, encouraged Shultz to travel to Moscow to get the negotiations back on track. The INF was signed during the Washington summit. Reagan and his advisers viewed the achievements of the INF Treaty and summit as signs that their policy toward the USSR was beginning to pay off. They saw no reason to fix or change it. In a secret NSDD issued on November 10, 1987, Reagan wrote,

> The signing of the INF treaty represents a triumph and vindication for the policy that this Administration has followed toward the Soviet Union from the start. It demonstrates that realism, strength, and unity with our allies are the prerequisites for

effective negotiations with Moscow. . . . We must also bear in mind that the nature of the Soviet regime, while it may be changing slowly, sets limits to what we can achieve with Moscow by negotiation and diplomacy.[166]

Reagan still had a strong hard-line component to his policies. He cautioned members of his administration not to "foster false illusions about the state of US-Soviet relations." The president emphasized that a cooperative stance toward the Soviets and the conduct of members of the US delegation during the Washington summit "must in no way complicate our efforts to maintain a strong defense budget and key programs like [the] SDI; they must help us maintain support for the Contras, Mujahidin, UNITA [in Angola], and the democratic resistance in Cambodia; and they must reinforce Alliance unity."[167] Shimko found that Reagan's specific positions in arms control negotiations, such as the INF and START, did not change significantly after 1983.[168]

Yet given the changing perceptions of Soviet intentions, especially following the 1987 Washington summit, greater stress was placed on institutionalizing patterns of cooperation with the USSR. For example, in March of the same year, US secretary of defense Carlucci and Soviet minister of defense Dmitry Yazov began planning for meetings between the defense ministers and military chiefs of staff from the two superpowers. In June, Reagan issued a secret NSDD in which he commissioned the establishment of an Interagency Group as well as Senior Interagency Group on US-Soviet Defense and Military Relations.[169] Although the emphasis on cooperation with the Soviets was not intended to signal a fundamental change in the administration's foreign policy, it did play a more significant role in the administration's agenda.[170] Progress during the 1988 Moscow summit allowed for the later signing of several other bilateral accords that symbolized the growing pattern of cooperation between the two superpowers.[171] In December, agreements were reached on other regional issues that included elections in Namibia, South African withdrawal from Namibia and Angola, and Cuban military withdrawal from Angola. Following the summit, Reagan's policy declarations reflected a more benign stance toward the USSR. Reagan declared that the Cold War was over as far as he was concerned, and his public speeches following the summit highlighted the RS&D elements of dialogue and cooperation with the Soviets, rather than the two other principles of realism and strength.

In sum, decision makers' perceptions of Soviet intentions correlated with their policy preferences. Weinberger's extremely hawkish views of the Soviet Union shaped his adamant policy positions on arms control with the Soviets, and unwillingness to compromise or show flexibility in negotiations. Shultz's more moderate beliefs about Soviet intentions led him to encourage the president to negotiate with the Soviets and pursue more accommodating policies on several issue areas. As for Reagan, his reading of Soviet intentions is less revealing of his policy preferences on arms control. Shimko attributes this in part to

Reagan's lack of substantive knowledge of issues like arms control and poorly developed image of the Soviet Union more generally.[172]

As for the evolution in the collective policies, the evidence reveals that unlike the abrupt reversal in the Carter administration's USSR policy after the Soviet invasion of Afghanistan, the transformation of the Reagan administration's policy was incremental and subtler. None of the theses can account for the precise contours of the Reagan administration's foreign policy. A closer look at the reasoning and justification of US decision makers indicates that assessments of Soviet intentions did not play a role in the 1983–84 shift in policy. During this period decision makers saw the USSR as an expansionist power with a leadership dedicated to world domination. Reagan's willingness to send more reassuring signals to the Soviets starting in 1984, scholars have argued, might have stemmed from a variety of factors including his growing uncertainty about the motivation for Soviet expansionist behavior, based on suggestions that perhaps the Soviets were "so defense minded, so paranoid about being attacked." Changing assessments of Soviet intentions played a more significant part in the gradual shift in policy that took place from 1987 onward. That is, as Reagan and Shultz began to view Soviet intentions as more benign and oriented toward the status quo, the administration increasingly adopted a conciliatory policy toward the USSR.[173]

Conclusion

Evidence from both public and private documents reveals how Reagan and Shultz gradually reevaluated their perceptions of Gorbachev's intentions during the second half of 1987. A more dramatic change in spring 1988 led them to conclude that an important qualitative shift had taken place in relations between the superpowers and that the Soviet leadership's intentions should no longer be described as expansionist.

This case study presents an easy test case for the behavior thesis. The evidence demonstrates adequate support for the two hypotheses of the behavior thesis. There is plenty of proof that during 1985 and 1986, Reagan and Shultz focused mainly on past Soviet actions, especially interventions in the third world during the 1970s, and treated these episodes as significant evidence that Soviet expansionist intentions remained unchanged. During 1987 and 1988, they began to turn their focus toward more recent Soviet reassuring behavior under Gorbachev. But the behavior thesis fails to account adequately for crucial pieces of evidence. The selective attention thesis provides a stronger explanation for the patterns we observe.

Decision makers, first of all, did not agree on the informative value of Gorbachev's costly actions of reassurance. Most notably, throughout this period Weinberger believed that Gorbachev was a traditional Soviet leader whose long-term intentions were to further the USSR's power and influence. He regarded none of Gorbachev's costly actions of reassurance as credible indicators of his intentions. As a result, his views of the expansionist nature of Soviet intentions remained static. Weinberger's inference process fails to support the costly signaling argument and underscores the subjective nature of credibility.

Second, the behavior thesis fails to capture the impact of vivid actions on how Reagan and Shultz inferred Soviet intentions. While both senior individuals acknowledged costly Soviet efforts at reassurance, their beliefs changed most drastically following close, positive, and repeated interactions with their Soviet counterparts. Reagan and Shultz relied greatly on these impressions in assessing the sincerity of Soviet reassurance efforts. In other words, rather than referring to Soviet actions in general, these decision makers pointed specifically to their personal impressions of Gorbachev and Shevardnadze as evidence of changing Soviet intentions. Reagan's positive impressions of Gorbachev were gained largely from private interactions in four summit meetings. The president repeatedly emphasized that his growing sense of Gorbachev's sincerity and trustworthiness allowed him to change his beliefs about the nature of the competition between the United States and USSR. Reagan's perceptions were only later reinforced by the signals conveyed through costly Soviet actions.

The vividness hypothesis of the selective attention thesis also describes how these decision makers interpreted Gorbachev's responsiveness to their particular and at times private requests. Beginning in 1987, Reagan and Shultz stated explicitly, and at times publicly, what concrete actions they expected Gorbachev to take in order to signal a change in Soviet political intentions. In this employment of litmus tests, they did not demand that Gorbachev reduce the Soviet Union's military capabilities or change its military doctrine. Instead, Reagan and Shultz insisted on domestic and international shifts in Soviet behavior. These included some costly actions, such as a withdrawal of Soviet troops from Afghanistan and the institutionalization of greater transparency in Soviet security policy. Other changes were more symbolic in nature, including the release of Jewish dissidents. Once Gorbachev appeared to be complying with his demands, Reagan was significantly more willing to acknowledge that a genuine change in the USSR was taking place, perhaps because he believed that he was personally responsible for the positive change in Soviet behavior.

The capabilities and military doctrine theses find weak support in this case. Soviet military capabilities and doctrine were important indicators of the Soviet threat. But they can explain neither the direction nor timing of change in the perceptions of Soviet political intentions. Despite the INF and conventional force reductions, other features of Soviet military policy—as indicated in chapter 8—would have led decision makers to view Soviet intentions as hostile. Further, in explaining why a change occurred in their perceptions of Soviet intentions, these decision makers only rarely and indirectly referred to the indicators associated with these two theses.

Finally, with regard to the influence of perceived intentions on US foreign policy during this period, there is a close correlation between decision makers' stated beliefs about Soviet intentions and the policies they advocated. These results should bolster confidence in the sincerity of these decision makers' statements about intentions. Perceptions of Soviet intentions, on the other hand, did not play an exclusive role in determining the policies that the Reagan administration adopted toward the Soviet Union from 1985 to 1988. As the last section of this chapter shows, these policies were influenced by a variety of factors in addition to changing perceptions of Gorbachev's intentions.

Taken together, the evolution in the statements of Reagan and his advisers about Soviet intentions, reasoning they used to support their assessments, and policies they advocated and rejected offer strong support for the vividness and subjective credibility hypotheses of the selective attention thesis. The evidentiary support for the three competing theses is mixed. The current actions hypothesis of the behavior thesis receives only modest support even though this episode constitutes an easy test case of this thesis.[174] The predictions of the capabilities thesis and strategic military doctrine thesis are not supported.

CHAPTER 10

The US Intelligence Community's Assessments of Soviet Intentions

THE END OF THE COLD WAR

During the first half of the 1980s, the dominant US view was that the USSR was an expansionist power, unlikely to use military force against the United States or its allies, but inclined to use military force in other regions. The hawkish perspective on the USSR held by key officials within the Reagan administration and Casey certainly played a critical role in the view of Soviet intentions as especially hostile. The alarming estimates of the early 1980s were in part prompted by Soviet interventionism in the third world during the late 1970s and the continuing Soviet military buildup. They may also have been a reaction to criticism in the late 1970s that the intelligence community, especially the CIA, had been too soft in judging Soviet objectives.[1] Existing divisions within the intelligence community on the issue of Soviet intentions and motives were further accentuated during Gorbachev's tenure. During this period, "the highest priority tasks for US intelligence estimation were Gorbachev's political intentions, and his political capabilities, vis-à-vis the Soviet Union as well as toward the West."[2] While more effort was devoted to tracking Soviet capabilities than Soviet political intentions, the community during this period was explicitly tasked with estimating Gorbachev's foreign policy intentions.

By the early 1990s, after the Soviet Union collapsed, the intelligence community (especially the CIA) was criticized for having incorrectly assessed its political, military, and economic strength during the 1980s. Senator Daniel Patrick Moynihan, for example, said, "the CIA failed in its single, overriding defining mission, which was to chart the course of Soviet affairs."[3] Many studies discuss the extent to which the CIA failed to predict the USSR's collapse, but this chapter focuses on a narrower set of questions: What were the intelligence assessments of intentions during the last years of the Cold War, and what impact did alterations in Soviet capabilities, doctrine, and behavior have on these assessments?[4] The primary purpose of the analysis is not to judge the accuracy of the intelligence assessments retrospectively but instead to gain a better understanding of the community's inference process as reflected in the coordinated estimates (namely, the integrated NIEs), and evaluate whether and why the intelligence community concentrated on the same indicators as decision makers in assessing Soviet intentions.

BASELINE ASSESSMENTS

During his first administration Reagan and Casey both held clearly defined conceptions of the USSR and its objectives. Other Soviet hawks were also well represented in the CIA leadership. As a result, the debate within the CIA over Soviet objectives would be "subsumed by a new analytic paradigm that understood the strategic arms race in context with 'the main threat,' which was defined by Casey as 'the Soviet ability and will to project its power worldwide through subversion and insurgency.' "[5] This characterization of the Soviet threat worried Shultz, who distrusted all intelligence documents, suspecting that Casey had biased their contents. In his memoir Shultz explains,

> He [Casey] had very strong policy positions, which were reflected in his intelligence briefings. He claimed he was objective. But his views were so strong and so ideological that they inevitably colored his selection and assessment of materials. I could not rely on what he said, nor could I accept without question the objectivity of the "intelligence" that he put out, especially in policy-sensitive areas.[6]

According to Gates, Casey insisted that the NIEs on the USSR should become "more aggressive and more timely"; his strong convictions about the nature of the Soviet threat led him to pressure the intelligence community to "do more on the subjects that he considered important to his war against the Soviets."[7]

The NIEs during the first half of the 1980s presented hostile interpretations of Soviet intentions. In 1981, Casey disseminated a Memorandum for Holders of NIE 11-4-78 that depicted a USSR that based its confidence and expansionist objectives on how its leaders perceived trends in the correlation of forces. The report asserted that Soviet expansionism was "likely to persist as long as the USSR perceives that Western strength is declining and as it further explores the utility of its increased military power as a means of realizing its global ambitions." It judged that in light of changes in the strategic balance and continued expansion of general-purpose forces, the Soviets "are now more prepared and may be more willing to accept the risks of confrontation in a serious crisis, particularly in an area where they have military or geopolitical advantage."[8] The position of the INR, among others, ran counter to this interpretation. It perceived Soviet intentions as opportunistic, and posited that a closer look at past Soviet actions actually exposed a weak correlation between

Soviet relative capabilities and their expansionist behavior. "Moscow has pursued opportunities and advantages during periods of relative military weakness as well as during periods of enhanced strength. . . . The factors, moreover, that have influenced Soviet actions in these regions have been more their view of the [local] situation and opportunities and of the potential US responses to Soviet initiatives than the precise state of development of Soviet military programs."[9] The intelligence community never concluded that the Soviets were seeking a direct military confrontation with the United States, but the assumption was that the Soviets were ready and willing to expand their power and influence around the world using military force. These actions could raise the risk of US-Soviet confrontation.

The intelligence community's reasoning during Reagan's first term supported the capabilities thesis and organizational expertise hypothesis. Perceptions of Soviet capabilities dominated the discussion of Soviet intentions in the NIEs, while Soviet doctrine and past actions were less central. Unlike intelligence analyses in the mid- to late 1970s, analyses in the 1980s considered the implications of US strategic force improvements on Soviet threat perceptions along with military and political objectives. SNIE 11-4/2-81, for example, recognized that the modernization of US strategic forces increased the Soviet Union's uncertainty about its ability to carry out its missions during the intercontinental phase of a nuclear war. This SNIE predicted that the Soviets would "seek to slow these trends through a combination of threats, inducements, and arms control negotiations, while trying to maximize prospects for a continuation of the trends favorable to them."[10] Soviet military capabilities and the evolving military balance were also central to estimating Soviet political intentions: the "most significant manifestation" of Soviet antagonism, noted NIE 11-4-82, was "growing Soviet military power and capabilities which form the cutting edge of Moscow's persistent efforts to expand its global presence and influence at the expense of the United States and the West."[11] At the same time, this 1981 NIE depicted the USSR as constrained by a variety of economic, international, and domestic factors. It portrayed Soviet foreign policy as more cautious in areas of crucial importance to the United States, while the third world offered "relatively low-risk opportunities for Soviet exploitation of regional instabilities."[12] With respect to the ongoing START and INF negotiations, the intelligence community concluded that Soviet intentions included protecting the Soviets' own military capabilities and programs, while constraining the further development and deployment of US forces.[13]

The 1983 "Soviet War Scare"

The issue of Soviet insecurity was raised again in several NIEs during 1983 and 1984.[14] Shortly after NATO's November 1983 command post exercise "Able Archer," US intelligence reports indicated that the Soviets had pursued large-scale military exercises, had engaged in "anomalous behavior with respect to troop rotation and withdrawn military support for harvest activities, had demonstrably deployed weapon systems in response to NATO's INF deployment, and had heightened internal vigilance and security activities."[15] These activities, which were part of what is now known as the war scare episode, raised serious concerns within the US intelligence community, which had to decide to what degree these actions reflected "abnormal fear of conflict with the US, a belligerent intent that might risk conflict, or some other underlying Soviet purpose."[16]

Ermarth, then the CIA's NIO for the Soviet Union, drafted a special NIE.[17] In it, he concluded that Soviet claims of a war scare were essentially part of a propaganda campaign aimed at discrediting US policies. Their contentions therefore did not reflect "authentic leadership fear" of an "imminent" conflict with the United States.[18] The SNIE did acknowledge that recent Soviet behavior reflected "increased Soviet perceptions of a threat from [recent changes in] US foreign and defense policy."[19] In other words, it warned, a Western arms buildup could "in the future increase [Soviet] willingness to consider actions—even at some heightened risk—that recapture the initiative and neutralize the military challenge by the United States."[20] SNIE 11-9-84, published in August 1984, reiterated these conclusions.[21] It judged any fundamental moderation in Soviet military and international aims "highly unlikely," and asserted that the Soviets were not about to shift to a policy of genuine and far-reaching accommodation toward the United States. Soviet leaders were "likely to remain attached to expanding their military and international power." They were said to be willing to use détente as a way of limiting the costs and risks of pursuing these objectives, so long as détente did not entail forswearing the expansion of their power.[22] In retrospect, as Gates writes in his memoirs, the intelligence community "did not really grasp just how much the Soviets felt increasingly threatened by the United States and by the course of events."[23]

NIEs DURING THE SECOND REAGAN ADMINISTRATION

During the second Reagan administration, the NIEs continued to assess Soviet intentions primarily through perceived changes in the correlation of forces.

The NIEs relied heavily on Soviet military capabilities—trends in Soviet military buildup, modernization efforts, and presumed Soviet perceptions of the correlation of forces—to assess Soviet intentions and wartime objectives. They also considered, to a lesser extent, Soviet economic capabilities. The community's overestimation of Soviet military capabilities and its underestimation of the degree of Soviet economic problems made its assessment excessively pessimistic. In contrast to the line of reasoning used by US decision makers, the NIEs did not treat Soviet actions (apart from those relating to capabilities) or vivid indicators as important signals of long-term political intentions. The NIEs mostly considered Gorbachev's actions of reassurance, even costly ones, as mere propaganda intended to put the United States on the defensive.

Statements about Soviet Intentions

In 1985 and 1986, the intelligence community produced several NIEs and SNIEs on the USSR. The estimates explored a range of issues, from Soviet capabilities and arms control objectives to economic and domestic stresses on the Soviet system. Of particular interest are those NIEs that included information on the intentions of the USSR and its leader. The first such NIE was released in March 1985, the same month that Gorbachev became the Communist Party of the Soviet Union's general secretary. Titled "Soviet Strategic and Political Objectives in Arms Control in 1985," this special NIE judged that the Soviet arms control agenda was driven by the Soviet Union's traditional strategic calculations. The USSR's plans aimed to protect and strengthen Soviet strategic capabilities, constrain US and NATO force modernization (especially the SDI that Reagan had announced two years before), and drive a wedge between European NATO nations and the United States. The intelligence community projected that the Soviets would conduct a major propaganda campaign that would seek to pressure the administration and influence the US Congress.[24] The text of the SNIE unambiguously shows that in 1985, the intelligence community did not believe that the new Soviet leadership might be seriously interested in ending the arms race. In many respects, this SNIE echoed the main conclusions reached in the NIEs from previous years.

The community recognized in 1985 that economic difficulties would affect the speed with which the Soviet Union could modernize its strategic force. Yet it maintained that the Soviets would neither forgo important strategic programs nor make substantial concessions in arms control in order to relieve economic pressures.[25] NIE 11-18-85, titled "Domestic Stresses on the Soviet System," represented the first time that the intelligence community analyzed the potential impacts of internal problems on Gorbachev's foreign and strategic policy.[26] The NIE judged that despite the worsening of Soviet domestic maladies, the USSR was still "a very stable country"; it predicted that neither societal nor economic problems would pose a challenge to the Soviet political or economic system for the "next five years and for the foreseeable future." The implications were that Gorbachev's reform efforts would be conservative, system-preserving measures, similar to those initiated by his predecessor as general secretary, Andropov.

By the end of 1985, the intelligence community still perceived Gorbachev as giving "every indication of endorsing well-established Soviet goals for expanded power and influence." Since Gorbachev was thought to be constrained by domestic and technological problems, though, the intelligence community expected him to pursue Soviet interests through a policy of détente and accommodation. The intelligence community believed that he would employ tactical accommodation techniques in order to gain a "breathing space" for economic progress, domestic relief, and military modernization. The US intelligence community anticipated that this opportunistic posture of détente would be accompanied by aggressive Soviet behavior in the third world and efforts to divide US alliances. But these conclusions were not universally accepted. The DIA registered exception to the CIA's view in two footnotes, asserting that Gorbachev's primary goal was still the "advancement of his foreign and strategic goals."[27]

This sense of skepticism about Gorbachev's intentions continued throughout 1986. The tone was vividly reflected in an SNIE titled "Gorbachev's Policy toward the United States, 1986–1988," published in September 1986. The intelligence community again judged that Gorbachev's motivation for pursuing détente with the United States was neither defensive nor reassuring but rather deceptive. According to this estimate, Gorbachev's strategy was intended "not to suspend the competition" but instead to persuade the United States to reduce its challenges and decrease its defense efforts; over the long term, it was meant to "preserve and advance the USSR's international influence and its relative military power." Moreover, the Soviet motive for reducing its offensive nuclear weapons (through, for example, the INF) was attributed to "reasons that include cost avoidance, increasing interest in enhancing the quality of Soviet nonnuclear forces, and a desire to undermine the credibility of US nuclear strategies," specifically the SDI.[28] As a result, the estimate declared, "Neither the domestic situation nor the foreign policy outlook of the regime obliges Gorbachev to compromise substantially on central arms control nor security issues in dispute with the United States." Should the United States not give up the SDI, it added, Gorbachev would become more uncompromising over the next thirty months. He would wait out Reagan and deal with his successor, rather than come to the table and risk legitimizing Reagan's Soviet policies.[29] This estimate also emphasized continuity in the Soviet approach to the third world: "Gorbachev sees himself able to defend Soviet interests in the Third World, particularly with regard to embattled Marxist-Leninist client states. He expects a more active Soviet foreign policy overall to open up new opportunities in the Third World and among US Allies."[30]

The intelligence community continued to attribute traditional motivations and hostile intentions to Gorbachev during 1987 and 1988, in spite of Gorbachev's reassuring actions. This undercuts the current actions hypothesis of the behavior thesis. The theme of continuity in the intelligence assessments is evident in NIE 11-18-87, published a month before the Reagan-Gorbachev summit meeting in Washington, DC. This NIE continued to assert that "Gorbachev adheres to traditional objectives: first and foremost enhancing the security of the Soviet homeland; expanding Soviet influence worldwide; and advancing Communism at the expense of capitalism around the globe." Yet implementing these goals would force Gorbachev to introduce "potentially profound changes in Soviet strategy and tactics," and "make significant changes in the system, not just tinker at the margins."[31] As for Gorbachev's "ultimate goal[s]," the NIE listed the same issues as in previous estimates. It repeated that Gorbachev was pursuing a clever plan to advance Communism not through the use of blunt force but instead via a deceptive posture of accommodation with the West.[32] The NIE gave no hint that Gorbachev had already established and announced new military objectives, doctrines, and requirements. It described Soviet defense policy as "committed to improving Soviet military capabilities and maintaining a global presence." The intelligence community predicted in this estimate that even if Gorbachev were successful in rejuvenating the system or introducing systemic reforms in the USSR, the Soviet Union's "superpower ambitions, military power, and ideological predilections" dictated that it would "remain the West's principal adversary."[33]

Notwithstanding these pessimistic assessments, the community recognized that the current state of flux within the USSR could produce a variety of different outcomes. The most likely scenario was a "rejuvenation of the existing system," under which "traditional approaches to West-East issues would remain intact."[34] The Soviets would "continue to rely on military power as their primary means of influence" and employ "traditional instruments of control in Eastern Europe."[35] But even under the most revolutionary scenario, if the USSR were to undergo a "systemic reform," the NIE predicted that Soviet intentions would continue as more of the same. Soviet leaders still "would not end the competition, risk the relative gains they have made over the past 20 years, accept an inferior military position, or draw back from the pursuit of a global superpower status."[36]

The director of the NSA, Odom, advanced a dissenting footnote to the NIE, asserting that Gorbachev was actually seeking to revitalize the Communist Party and the NIE overstated the significance of Gorbachev's reforms. Odom argued that regardless of the outcome of Gorbachev's reforms, Soviet foreign policy would present an increasing challenge to US interests both in the third world as well as the advanced industrial states of Europe and East Asia.[37] Gates (now acting DCI) shared these views, believing that Gorbachev sought to "strengthen the USSR at home, to further [his] own personal power, and to permit the further consolidation and expansion of Soviet power abroad." Despite changes in Soviet rhetoric and diplomacy, Gates contended, it was "still hard to detect fundamental changes, currently or in prospect, in the way the Soviets govern at home or their principal objectives abroad." He predicted continuity in the monopoly of the Communist Party. Primary Soviet plans would include "the further increase in Soviet military power and political influence."[38]

Thus, even as Reagan and Shultz were declaring the Cold War finished, the intelligence community continued to depict Gorbachev's foreign policy as traditional.[39] In an SNIE published in December 1988, the community asserted that the Soviet stance on arms control issues (including Soviet positions on the INF and START) was designed primarily to "constrain US and NATO force modernization." The 1988 SNIE portrayed the Soviets as unlikely to offer any proposals that would result in "strategic forces that the Soviets would perceive as less capable of waging a nuclear war."[40] This estimate also characterized Gorbachev's announcement of unilateral cuts in conventional forces as primarily designed to "secure maximum political impact in the West without unduly disrupting Soviet military capabilities."[41] On the eve of Gorbachev's December 1988 announcement of a unilateral cut in Soviet conventional capabilities, as NIO Bob Blackwell noted, "the community could not imagine that Gorbachev would actually make such a bold declaration."[42] This was the case, explained Douglas MacEachin, then director of the CIA's Office of Soviet Analysis (SOVA), because the intelligence community had "never really looked at the Soviet Union as a political entity in which there were factors building which could lead to the kind of—at least the initiation of political transformation that we seem to see." As MacEachin said, the political environment in the United States at the time saw the Soviet Union as a powerful enemy, and this factor constrained what the intelligence community could and would publish on the USSR. Had an analysis suggesting that the Soviet Union was not bent on world domination "existed inside the government," MacEachin observed,

> we never would have been able to publish it anyway, quite frankly. And had we done so, people would have been calling for my head. And I wouldn't have published it. In all honesty, had we said a week ago that Gorbachev might come to the UN and offer a unilateral cut of 500,000 in the military, we would have been told we were crazy. We had a difficult enough time getting air space for the prospect of some unilateral cuts of 50 to 60,000.[43]

The intelligence community did not significantly change its evaluation of Soviet political and military intentions despite the cues coming from Gorbachev's Soviet Union in 1987–88. The NIEs, unlike Reagan and Shultz, did not perceive a genuine shift in Soviet intentions during this period.

Reasoning about Soviet Intentions

The NIEs during Reagan's second administration draw primarily on indicators associated with the capabilities thesis, which also reflected the organizational expertise of the intelligence community as the selective attention thesis predicts. Soviet military doctrine served as a secondary (but not clear) indicator of Soviet military intentions and wartime objectives. Still, it was not seen as an indicator of political intentions. The intelligence community made few references to Soviet past or current actions to support its estimations of Soviet political intentions.

THE "BREATHING SPACE" THESIS

The NIEs produced between 1985 and 1988 show that the community relied on a simple thesis based on the logic that "intentions are reflected in capabilities." This is similar to the predictions of the capabilities thesis. Soviet intentions were also viewed through the prism of military calculations. That is consistent with the organizational expertise hypothesis of the selective attention thesis.[44] Specifically, the intelligence community repeatedly interpreted Gorbachev's policy as aimed at "achieving strategic advantage" and "prevent[ing] any erosion of the military gains the USSR has made over the past decade." Analysts argued that the Soviets recognized that the proposed SDI, coupled with the prospective NATO deployment of major new offensive systems, could undercut Soviet advantages. Viewed through this lens, Gorbachev's initiatives looked like "tactics" aimed at keeping the United States from forging ahead.[45] According to the intelligence community, Gorbachev's attempts to present a benign posture were deceptive and did not reflect a genuine interest in improving relations with the West.

This line of thinking was explicit. As NIE 11-3/8-85 stated, "Moscow has long believed that arms control must first and foremost protect the capabilities of Soviet military forces relative to their opponents. The Soviets seek to limit US force modernization through both the arms control process and any resulting agreements."[46] SNIE 11-9-86 flagged Soviet concerns about the SDI as the primary motive behind Gorbachev's pursuit of a détente-like policy toward the West. The intelligence community believed that the Soviets feared that the SDI could "produce a military and technological revolution" that would "undermine the war fighting strategies of Soviet nuclear forces" as well as give the United States enough confidence to launch a nuclear first strike.[47]

Soviet economic problems also affected the conclusions the community reached about Soviet foreign policy. US intelligence did not know whether or to what degree domestic economics would affect Soviet military capabilities. During the first half of 1985, the intelligence community did not think that economic imperatives would compel the Soviets to discontinue their military buildup or make serious concessions during the next phase of arms control negotiations.[48] By late 1985, however, it appeared that economic problems posed a threat to the USSR. This increased Gorbachev's desire to project a benign foreign policy and exhibit benign national security behavior in the short run. After all, "tactical accommodation with the United States" would allow Gorbachev to gain "the advantage of economic interaction with the West, facilitating both relief from domestic economic constraints and continued military modernization. At the same time, the Soviets would continue to pursue greater influence in the third world and efforts to divide US alliances."[49]

During 1985 and 1986, intelligence officers disagreed over the potential impact of domestic economic problems on Gorbachev's foreign policy. The DIA and air force intelligence were reluctant to attribute anything but traditional Soviet goals to the USSR.[50] The DIA contended that even if Soviet efforts to revitalize the economy were to fail, this would not impede the USSR from preserving and expanding its military capabilities. Economic considerations were thought to play only a secondary role in motivating Soviet pursuit of détente. The primary goal behind the Soviet Union's posture, according to the DIA, continued to be "long-held strategic objectives, such as splitting the Western alliances, isolating the United States from its allies, and constraining US defense efforts."[51]

Gates also doubted the sincerity of Gorbachev's initiatives, because the USSR was still "going forward with Soviet strategic programs and deployments in R&D."[52] He saw no reason at the time to prepare policy makers for the consequences of change in the USSR.[53] The CIA's working assumption was that despite serious economic problems since the mid-1970s, Soviet objectives remained unchanged. NIE 11-3/8-86 observed that

> the Soviets have continued to procure large quantities of new strategic weapons. Strategic forces, more than any other single element of power, are the foundation of Soviet superpower status. While the Soviets are attempting a major restructuring of their industrial production capability, we do not believe that economic considerations alone would lead them to abandon major strategic weapon programs, to forsake force modernization goals, or to make substantial concessions in arms control.

"The evidence shows clearly," this NIE continued, that "Soviet leaders are preparing their military forces for the possibility that they will actually have to fight a nuclear war." The authors of NIE 11-3/8-86 did recognize that there was no "specific evidence" to indicate how the Soviet Union assessed its prospects for prevailing in a nuclear war.[54]

During this time, the NIEs' overestimation of the projected Soviet strategic weapons systems prompted increasing concern by the CIA's SOVA. SOVA argued that the NIEs' inflated estimates "would imply that Moscow has no intentions of [even] attempting to carry out" the industrial modernization program Soviet leaders recently announced in public because even the "low forces" projected in the estimates would require an average annual growth rate of 11 percent; MacEachin said that such a growth rate had occurred only once before, over the five-year period from 1966 to 1970, when Brezhnev had built up the military after he ousted Khrushchev. The hawks in the CIA Directorate of Intelligence, though, refused to record this dissent in the coordinated estimates. According to MacEachin, high-level officials in the CIA including Gates "believed that Gorbachev's plan was not real, but rather a gambit to buy 'breathing space.'" SOVA, on the other hand, "was coming to the conclusion that 'breathing space' was not an achievable end because attaining Gorbachev's objectives would instead require the kind of systemic reforms that could change the threatening nature of the USSR." Indeed, by 1986 the CIA recognized a problem in how it had been deriving forecasts of Soviet forces under conditions of uncertainty. Even the "low" force projections in the 1982 NIE 11-3/8 reports had, it now appeared, been inflated.[55] Yet MacEachin's proposal to insert a CIA DI footnote into NIE 11-3/8-86 explaining the source of the overestimation was immediately dismissed by Gates and Odom.[56]

In 1987 and 1988, the intelligence community noted a trade-off between Gorbachev's goals of revitalizing the economy and the traditional Soviet emphasis on the military. The community nonetheless ultimately judged that the Soviets would neither significantly reduce the importance of nuclear forces nor seriously revise their operational priorities and practices by the mid-1990s. This analysis was based on the "large sunk cost in production for new strategic weapons and the fact that such production facilities cannot readily be converted to civilian uses." The community believed that a move toward civilian production would be too costly, financially and politically, for Gorbachev. As a result, intelligence agencies did not expect any meaningful reductions in Soviet projected capabilities. US views of the Soviet Union's perceptions of the correlation of forces, its "genuine concern about NATO's military prowess," and its concern about the particular types of weapons NATO had been developing, especially the "advanced technology mononuclear weapons," suggested that Gorbachev's posture of accommodation was a short-term deception intended to gain an advantage over the United States in the long run, and as such, his declared intentions were not genuinely reassuring.[57]

The intelligence community inferred Soviet propensity to use force primarily through an assessment of the relative military balance between the two superpowers. In 1987, for example, the community believed that the Soviets lacked "high confidence in the capability of their strategic offensive and defensive forces to accomplish all of their wartime missions." It consequently predicted that the USSR would not launch a "bolt-from-the-blue" strategic attack, or provoke "a direct clash with the United States and its allies that could potentially escalate to global nuclear war."[58] But based on the intelligence community's careful tracking of Soviet development of offensive and defensive weapons, it concluded that the Soviets were preparing their forces for the possibility of waging and winning a nuclear war. Thus their approach to nuclear war was thought to remain unchanged. "The Soviets continue to be committed to acquiring capabilities that could be important in achieving the best possible outcome in any future war."[59]

In sum, the NIEs during this period largely described Gorbachev as a leader alarmed by US strategic advances and facing important domestic issues. The intelligence community's official position declared that Gorbachev was pursuing a deceptive posture of détente in order to ease the burden of arms competition and be able to devote resources to economic revival. Soviet intentions were not seen as genuinely cooperative. The apparent continuation of the Soviet Union's efforts to augment and modernize its offensive as well as defensive arsenal, the modest increases in its defense spending, and its arms control initiatives all led the community to predict that once the correlation of forces was in Soviet favor, the USSR would return to its expansionist plans. This line of reasoning is consistent with the capabilities thesis and selective attention's organizational expertise hypothesis.[60]

THE ROLE OF SOVIET DOCTRINE

Notwithstanding the community's reluctance to acknowledge changes in Soviet military thinking and doctrine, the NIEs during this period did discuss Soviet military doctrine.[61] Soviet military doctrine was used not to draw inferences about Soviet political intentions but rather the Soviet inclination to use force. Even then, some agencies did not believe that doctrine offered much insight. Significant disagreements existed about how Soviet military doctrine might explain Soviet behavior. Indeed, as noted earlier, the CIA had observed significant changes in Soviet doctrine, but these views were not reflected in the NIEs. This lack of discussion might have stemmed from the hawkish atmosphere within the intelligence community. Any talk of Soviet military doctrine as an indicator of intentions was, according to Garthoff, stuck in a "sterile standoff of 'alternative views' or a brief statement in the text balanced by a dissent, neither going beyond general assertions."[62] The NIEs in general rejected the idea that Soviet doctrine was becoming more defensive. The theme of apparent continuity in Soviet military policy and doctrine is captured in NIE 11-3/8-88: "The evidence presented in this Estimate indicates . . . that in terms of what the Soviets spend, what they procure, how their strategic elements are deployed, how they plan, and how they exercise, the basic elements in Soviet defense policy and practice thus far have not been changed by Gorbachev's reform efforts."[63]

Doctrine constituted a "noisy" signal for the US intelligence community because there were also signs that the Soviets were continuing to improve their strategic military arsenal. Nevertheless, there were some attempts to understand the implications of a change in the Soviet discourse on military issues. The CIA at one point suggested it was possible that "the evolution of Soviet doctrine on the nature of future general war" had in fact led the Soviets to "consider reduced nuclear arsenals on both sides as militarily tolerable and perhaps even attractive for Soviet military strategy."[64] Several intelligence agencies and members of the National Foreign Intelligence Board did not believe that Soviet doctrine was an informative indicator. Continued modernization of the Soviet nuclear forces left National Foreign Intelligence Board agencies "skeptical about the impact of evolving Soviet military doctrine upon attitudes toward nuclear force reductions." They doubted that any "possible shifts in Soviet military doctrine would greatly influence Soviet willingness to reduce nuclear forces in the next few years."[65] The DIA advanced another interpretation, claiming that it was "the new threats and opportunities posed by technically advanced conventional weapons" that had led the Soviets to consider changing their military doctrine and force requirements.[66] In this view, Soviet intentions in advocating reductions in offensive strategic nuclear forces stemmed from the emergence of improvements in nonnuclear military technologies versus from Soviet doctrine. This line of reasoning is consistent with the logic of the offense-defense hypothesis that is part of the capabilities thesis.

Intelligence agencies also mentioned Soviet military doctrine when estimating military intentions, but this application was quickly dismissed. For example, Soviet doctrine indicated that the Soviets were unlikely to initiate a nuclear attack in a theater conflict unless they perceived that NATO was about to attack. The intelligence community saw the doctrine as offering insufficient guidance on whether the "Soviets would seize the initiative and strike, as would be consistent with the general military doctrine, or be more cautious in the hope of averting large-scale war on the Soviet homeland."[67] Similarly, the intelligence community believed that the Soviets' strategic war-fighting doctrine would not predispose them to exercise restraint if they saw a high risk of global nuclear war. In NIE 11-3/8-86, the community concluded that it could not judge how the Soviets would weigh the trade-offs between the risks and benefits involved in nuclear preemption.[68]

Even during 1988, the intelligence community dedicated lengthy discussions to Soviet military doctrine and strategic thought in an attempt to envision whether as well as how the Soviets would utilize their military forces.[69] Because "many key doctrinal issues are far from settled among the Soviets themselves," the intelligence community believed that "it was only prudent to adopt a wait-and-see attitude toward the prospects for longer term change in the Soviets' fundamental approach to war."[70] It further noted that "the Soviets' recent positions on strategic arms control could not be taken as an indicator of whether or not they are implementing fundamental change in their approach to nuclear war."[71] The community relied instead on current and projected Soviet capabilities as evidence. It decided that the Soviets were not "making fundamental changes in their approach to actually fighting a nuclear war" but instead trying to "cope with NATO's improving capabilities." The intelligence community judged that the Soviets were "probably pessimistic" about the implications of ongoing US strategic modernization programs, and "did not have high confidence in the capability of their strategic offensive and defensive forces to accomplish their war time missions." It was these perceptions of the future correlation of forces as opposed to new Soviet doctrinal thinking that led the intelligence community to the view that the Soviets would probably refrain from "deliberately risking a direct clash with the United States or its NATO allies."[72] Such reasoning supports the predictions of the capabilities thesis, but not the strategic military doctrine thesis.

The evidence, in short, shows that elements of the strategic military doctrine thesis served as imperfect and contentious indicators for the intelligence community. Overall, the intelligence agencies inferred future Soviet military intentions and wartime objectives while mostly ignoring Soviet political intentions. The US intelligence community preferred to rely on observable indicators associated with Soviet military capabilities, as both the capabilities thesis and organizational expertise hypothesis predict. Hence, "only after the unilateral Soviet initiative of force reduction and retraction from Eastern Europe," Garthoff explains, "did the ice crack and begin to move."[73]

ADDITIONAL FACTORS SHAPING ASSESSMENTS OF SOVIET INTENTIONS

On several occasions during 1985 and 1986, the intelligence community discussed Gorbachev's public rhetoric and recent behavior. Repeated Soviet calls for US ratification of both the Threshold Test Ban Treaty and Peaceful Nuclear Explosives Treaty, resumption of US-Soviet negotiations toward a comprehensive test ban treaty, and a chemical weapons ban were mentioned, but these were not considered revealing indicators of Soviet political intentions. Analysts saw Gorbachev's actions as either part of a "broad political and propaganda campaign," or tactics aimed at building public and allied pressure on the United States to make concessions.[74]

In 1987 and 1988, the intelligence community was concerned about the extent to which Gorbachev was likely to achieve his foreign policy goals. Discussions included frequent references to both Soviet behavior and the rhetoric of other senior Soviet leaders. For example, when explaining why Gorbachev was expected to introduce "potentially profound changes in Soviet strategy and tactics in the international arena" in the short run, the intelligence community referred to a speech made by Shevardnadze at a conference of foreign ministry officials in May 1987.[75] Assessing Soviet confidence in waging war, the NIE reasoned,

> On the one hand, the asymmetric reductions and acceptance of intrusive on-site inspections entailed by the INF Treaty and apparent Soviet willingness to accept deep strategic force reductions in START do reflect a marked change in political attitude on security issues under Gorbachev. On the other hand, the Soviets' stance on arms control thus far allows them to continue to pursue certain combat advantages, while seeking to constrain U.S. and NATO force modernization . . . and at the same time seeking to protect the key capabilities of their own forces. Further, the Soviets see the INF Treaty and a potential START agreement as helping to establish a more predictable environment in which to plan strategic force modernization. Overall we do not see Moscow's recent arms control positions resulting in strategic forces that the Soviets would perceive as less capable of waging a nuclear war.[76]

The intelligence community inferred Gorbachev's future strategy on arms control from his recent and past actions: "Already evident in his approach to [the] INF and START, we think it likely that this new flexibility will eventually promote initiatives that could offer a significant reduction in the size and composition of Warsaw Pact conventional forces facing NATO in return for compensating military or political gains for the USSR." Although none of these are references to costly action, this line of reasoning is implicitly consistent with the current actions hypothesis of the behavior thesis. The intelligence community relied on this type of evidence not to understand Gorbachev's long-term political intentions or underlying motivation but rather to predict what tactical steps he might take next.[77]

Finally, changes in Gorbachev's third world policies did not affect intelligence perceptions of intentions. Any alterations were either missed or dismissed. The intelligence community provided "no warning of the Soviet withdrawal from Afghanistan, Cam Ranh Bay in Vietnam, or the littoral states of Africa."[78] Only after Gorbachev's announcement on February 8, 1988, that the USSR would begin its withdrawal in May did the CIA write an estimate reporting that Gorbachev was serious about pulling out of Afghanistan.[79] Blackwell explained that the delay in predicting the Soviet withdrawal from Afghanistan was motivated not by caution to prevent disclosure of CIA covert operations but simply a lack of knowledge of any supporting evidence.[80] Gates conceded that the CIA did not believe that the Soviets could or would take all their forces out of Afghanistan. Even after Shevardnadze stated to Shultz that the Soviets had made a decision to withdraw in 1988, Gates was sure that Gorbachev's signals constituted "political deception."[81]

CONCLUSION

Reviewing the NIEs on the Soviet Union, Garthoff concludes that "the greatest shortcoming of the NIEs on Soviet military power from 1987 to 1991 was the failure to give even cautious recognition to the radical changes already underway in Soviet outlook, doctrine, policy and strategy."[82] Throughout Reagan's second administration, the NIEs continued to describe Soviet intentions as hostile. Their reasoning shows that these conclusions were based on indicators associated with Soviet military capabilities. To be more precise, most agencies believed that the Soviet motivation for the short-term pursuit of a benign posture vis-à-vis the West reflected Gorbachev's need for breathing room to execute domestic economic reforms. The intelligence community anticipated that more profound changes would take place in Soviet strategy and tactics, but maintained that none of these changes would produce significant discontinuity in traditional Soviet goals and intentions.

The elimination of Soviet intermediate-range missiles from Europe did not have much effect on the intelligence community's assessments of Soviet intentions. Neither did the Soviet withdrawal from Afghanistan nor Gorbachev's initial announcement of forthcoming unilateral cuts in conventional forces. Indeed, the intelligence community discounted these moves because they saw them as part of a policy of political and economic retrenchment intended to preserve long-term Soviet hegemony, which accordingly, did not signify a new and benign Soviet security posture. Further, by the end of 1988, the intelligence community had not yet seen a de facto change in Soviet conventional weapons. As long as the Soviet nuclear arsenal was intact and modernization of its strategic forces continued, the US intelligence community did not see a need to change its interpretation of Soviet intentions. The evidence thus lends strong support for the capabilities thesis as well as the selective attention theory's organizational expertise hypothesis.

Intelligence organizations relied on Soviet strategic military doctrine to infer Soviet military intentions and wartime objectives, but not political intentions. The community continued to debate the significance of the evolution in Soviet doctrine along with its potential impact on Soviet force posture and military objectives. Due to continued Soviet modernization and development of what the intelligence community perceived as war-fighting capabilities, the community concluded that no far-reaching changes were taking place by the end of 1988.[83]

The empirical record does not match the predictions of the current actions hypothesis of the behavior thesis. The intelligence community remained highly suspicious of Soviet intentions. It dismissed Soviet actions and statements as noise intended to deceive the United States and its allies into thinking that the USSR was interested in cooperation. The intelligence community did not prioritize those costly actions of reassurance undertaken by Gorbachev that were not based on capabilities. One explanation for this is that leading intelligence figures understood the task of assessing Gorbachev's motivations and intentions as subject to inescapable uncertainty. According to McEachin, "Soviet intentions . . . were impossible to know." He added that "nothing is more subject to social-political atmospherics than one's perception of intentions."[84] This issue, said Gates, engendered skepticism from decision makers: "The apparent lack of CIA access to Soviet Politburo discussions . . . leads policymakers to question whether anything the agency says about Soviet intentions or politics has value, regardless of its other source of intelligence."[85]

This skepticism had implications for how decision makers received the intelligence community's assessments. Moderates within the Reagan administration were increasingly bothered by the NIEs' pessimistic conclusions about Gorbachev's intentions and particularly the breathing space notion. Shultz described himself as having become a "very dissatisfied customer" of the intelligence reports on the USSR. He recalled having told Gates and Carlucci in 1987 that he did not have "any confidence in the intelligence community," especially its assessments of Gorbachev:

> When Gorbachev first appeared at the helm, the CIA said he was "just talk," just another Soviet attempt to deceive us. As that line became increasingly untenable, the CIA changed its tune: Gorbachev was serious about change, but the Soviet Union

had a powerfully entrenched and largely successful system that was incapable of being changed, so Gorbachev would fail in his attempt to change it. When it became evident that the Soviet Union was, in fact, changing, the CIA line was that the changes wouldn't really make a difference.[86]

Whatever the accuracy of intelligence assessments, the documents, memoirs, and interviews I conducted with policy makers and intelligence analysts who were active at the time suggest that the NIEs' estimates about Soviet intentions did not alter the perceptions held by Reagan, Shultz, or Weinberger. According to Matlock, Reagan did not spend much time reading the NIEs, and even those he did read left little impression on him.[87] Paul Pillar, a former CIA official, asserts that Reagan's "incuriosity about fact and details and the jaundiced view of the bureaucracy meant almost no opportunity for the intelligence community . . . to influence the president's thinking, except occasionally in supplying some piece of information that buttressed his existing beliefs." Even data on Soviet military capabilities—which according to Pillar, "made Reagan's head swim"—had no impact on the president's assessments. Pillar argues that Reagan and his advisers, apart from Shultz, "brushed aside as irrelevant any careful analysis of Soviet intentions, just as Carter and Brzezinski had brushed aside the question of the Soviets' reason for intervening in Afghanistan."[88]

This disconnection between the intelligence community and decision makers stemmed in large part from the importance the latter placed on personal insights and judgments. In Shultz's view, even when the intelligence community attempted to take a closer look at Gorbachev's personality and outlook, it did not use information from people who had spent many hours conversing with him. Most intelligence analysts working on the Soviet Union were bright people, Matlock said, but typically had no direct personal experience with the Soviet Union, or with Soviet or Russian decision makers. This stood in stark contrast to Reagan, Shultz, and of course Matlock himself. Matlock observed that in lieu of relying on intelligence estimates, Reagan and Shultz trusted their own "personal impressions" and insights. "They are very experienced people and experienced politicians and it meant much more to them what they were experiencing."[89] The lack of vividness might also explain why Reagan and Shultz did not pay more attention to the NIEs on the Soviet Union.

CHAPTER 11

Summary and Implications

This chapter summarizes the book's theoretical argument and findings, discusses the book's implications for international relations theory, offers an agenda for further research, and ends with a look at the study's relevance for contemporary policy issues.

WHAT INDICATORS OF INTENTIONS MATTER, AND FOR WHOM

This book has systematically tested four theses about perceived intentions. The selective attention thesis that I develop draws on insights from psychology and organizational theory, and is pitted against three alternative theses. For each of the three historical episodes analyzed, the book subjected thousands of primary documents to three types of tests: a covariance test examining the fit between thesis predictions and changes in perceived intentions; a reasoning test that considered the evidence observers cite to support their assessments; and a policy consistency test exploring the fit between a decision maker's statements about intentions and the policies they advocate as well as the evolution in the administration's collective policies over time. Although the three competing theses are agnostic about whether the perceiver is an individual or organization, the empirical chapters look separately at the inference process of a state's key civilian decision makers and intelligence organizations. This division is necessary because the selective attention thesis argues that these two sets of perceivers will use different filters when assessing the adversary's intentions.

The capabilities, strategic military doctrine, and behavior theses fail to account fully for the empirical patterns we observe. The selective attention approach this book develops is more successful. The cases demonstrate that when gauging intentions, decision makers do not pay equal attention to all costly signals made by their adversaries. Nor do they restrict their focus exclusively to costly actions. Rather, they rely on their personal impressions and are influenced by indicators that are consistent with their own theories about how the world operates as well as their preexisting stance toward an adversary. Intelligence organizations tasked with assessing an adversary's intentions, in contrast, pay selective attention to those indicators that match their bureaucratic expertise. Organizational dynamics shape how bureaucracies read and understand signals. Consequently, bureaucrats' interpretations of the adversary's intentions diverge from those of decision makers who are not immersed in the same organization.

Although the capabilities thesis can describe the practice of intelligence organizations in all three cases, it does a poor job of explaining how civilian decision makers read and interpret intentions. Between 1934 and 1936, for example, British intelligence saw the German military buildup as moderate in pace and largely defensive in nature. As a result, the British intelligence community did not conclude that Germany harbored hostile intentions. As Germany was perceived to enjoy military superiority and continued its military expansion, though, British intelligence began to infer more aggressive intentions. Throughout the interwar period, British intelligence used calculations of military capabilities to determine when Germany was likely to engage in war. Germany's buildup, together with other indicators, led British decision makers to ask hard questions about Germany's intentions, but they rarely relied on the scope or nature of Germany's military buildup per se as a primary indicator of its political intentions.

The Cold War episodes reveal a similar pattern. During the 1970s, the US intelligence community was alarmed by the Soviets' buildup and modernization efforts in the domain of nuclear weapons. Different intelligence agencies debated how much and in what way this military buildup would affect Soviet determination to change the status quo in different regions. But they all relied on material indicators to infer Soviet foreign policy and military intentions. At the same time, however, members of the Carter administration focused on other, nonmilitary-based indicators of Soviet intentions. Even those within the administration who held more hawkish views, such as Brzezinski, rarely used the Soviet buildup as evidence of aggressive intentions and a desire to abandon détente.

Reagan's second administration, which lasted from 1985 through 1988, saw an important change in Reagan's attitude toward the Soviet Union. The US intelligence community nonetheless retained its belief that Gorbachev continued an adherence to traditional Soviet goals, seeing evidence in sustained modernization and increases in the Soviet nuclear arsenal. In stark contrast to the significant shifts in Reagan and Shultz's perceptions, the US intelligence community emphasized continuity in Soviet long-term political intentions during this period.

In brief, this study does not refute the capabilities thesis. The adversary's military capabilities—both in terms of quantity and orientation—played a central role in intelligence estimates; armament efforts also had crucial "framing effects" because they forced decision makers to raise questions about the adversary's long-term objectives. Still, in none of the three episodes were these indicators regarded by the state's civilian leadership as primary evidence in the assessment of the adversary's long-term intentions.

The behavior thesis performs better than the capabilities thesis in explaining how decision makers gauge intentions. Indeed, for some British and US decision makers, current costly actions such as the German invasion of Czechoslovakia and observed shifts in Soviet behavior induced a change in beliefs about the adversary's intentions. The empirical analysis, on the other hand, provides many examples that contradict the causal mechanisms and underlying logic of the behavior thesis. Significantly, decision makers rarely agreed on what constituted a truly credible signal even when the signals were costly. For example, British decision makers debated the meaning of Germany's remilitarization of the Rhineland even though it involved an unprecedented use of military force outside the Reich and thus constituted a clear violation of the Treaty of Versailles. Members of the Carter administration disagreed on the significance of Soviet military involvement in the Horn of Africa, and some (such as Vance and Shulman) did not view even the Soviet invasion of Afghanistan as a diagnostic indicator of Soviet expansionist intentions, despite its considerable scale and cost. Even at the end of the Cold War—a relatively easy test of the behavior thesis—we find officials such as Weinberger who did not regard Gorbachev's costly actions as informative signals of reassurance. In fact, neither the hawkish Weinberger nor the more dovish Vance updated their beliefs during their time in office in spite of facing signals that would otherwise be categorized as costly.

The prediction of the behavior thesis that decision makers will discount the informational value of costless communication and indicators does not withstand empirical scrutiny. Leaders as different as Chamberlain and Reagan repeatedly as well as explicitly drew on their personal insights about the sincerity of the adversary's leaders. Chamberlain and other British decision makers repeatedly referred to Hitler's verbal assurances, writings, and other types of costless actions along with cheap talk to infer his future policy goals. The behavior thesis also does not explain why intelligence organizations ignored or dismissed those costly noncapabilities-based actions that civilian decision makers used—a practice especially pronounced in the collective NIEs during the 1980s. These findings appear to challenge the empirical validity of the behavior thesis, but they do not negate the costly signaling logic, as there is some evidence that certain costly behavioral signals were seen as informative in some decision makers' eyes. Yet these findings do highlight the need for scholars who use the costly signaling mechanism to be clearer and more transparent about the scope and operationalization of this term in empirical cases. I return to this point in the next section.

The strategic military doctrine thesis receives weaker support compared to the capabilities and behavior theses. Put differently, the adversary's military doctrine was not seen as the primary indicator from which its intentions were inferred. British decision makers and intelligence organizations rarely discussed Germany's military doctrine in their deliberations about its political intentions. In fact, historians have noted that one of the major faults of British intelligence during this period was its failure to pay attention to how Germany might employ its military power. The US intelligence community's NIEs during the 1970s focused significant attention on Soviet doctrine at the time, but could not reach any meaningful conclusions about Soviet political intentions. Intelligence agencies drew different inferences about what the doctrine actually stated along with its implications for understanding Soviet military intentions and wartime objectives. In other words, it was a noisy signal. Neither the US intelligence community nor members of the Carter administration viewed Soviet strategic doctrine as indicative of Soviet *political* intentions. The change in Soviet military thinking under Gorbachev was an equally problematic signal. The NIEs were reluctant to acknowledge that any significant changes were taking place, especially as long as Soviet strategic weapons remained intact.

The evidence, finally, lends strong support to the selective attention thesis. Theoretically, this thesis attempts to capture the interaction between information, on the one hand, and individual perceptual and organizational filters, on the other. The vividness hypothesis concerns the importance of personal interactions and litmus tests in how decision makers assess intentions. The evidence in support of this hypothesis is overwhelming in the interwar case. British decision makers, although holding different beliefs about Germany's intentions, repeatedly and explicitly relied on their personal insights to derive conclusions about the extent to which Hitler intended to change the status quo in Central and Eastern Europe and beyond. This method of inference is extremely risky, but Chamberlain, Eden, Halifax, and Henderson relied on it to derive their own conclusions, and used these impressions to convince other cabinet members of their perspectives.

Reagan's personal impressions gleaned from private meetings with Gorbachev also played a critical role in transforming his assessments of Soviet intentions. Indeed, on nearly every occasion that Reagan talked optimistically about future relations between the two superpowers, he mentioned how impressed he was by Gorbachev and the chemistry they had shared. In the late 1970s, that form of vivid information was present, but to a lesser extent, when Carter met with an ailing Brezhnev. That meeting did not produce a major change in Carter's perceptions, but the president came away believing that they had established trust and understanding about Soviet behavior in the third world. Consequently, Carter viewed the Soviet invasion of Afghanistan as a personal betrayal.

At times vividness and costly signaling jointly produced a radical change in decision makers' beliefs. Both Carter and Reagan underwent dramatic shifts in their beliefs about Soviet intentions during their time in office. Vivid information from personal meetings provided context for understanding Gorbachev's costly signals, thereby allowing for Reagan's gradual transformation. Similarly, the Soviet invasion of Afghanistan was costly, but it was also salient and exerted an emotional toll on Carter because of his belief that Brezhnev had betrayed him personally. This combination induced a drastic change in the president's perceptions of Soviet intentions. One can debate what to make of Chamberlain's change in beliefs, yet here too we note that expectations, vividness, and certain costly actions were responsible for the nuanced changes in his beliefs during the 1930s.

The predictions of the selective attention's second hypothesis, the subjective credibility hypothesis, receive strong support in all three cases. At the heart of this hypothesis lies the idea that "credibility depends on how observers assess evidence and on what evidence they decide to assess."[1] Decision makers' own explicit or implicit theories or beliefs about how the world operates along with their expectations significantly affect both the selection and interpretation of signals. Decision makers in the British Cabinet, Carter administration, and second Reagan administration debated what to make of different indicators of intentions. To a large degree, the reading of signals was influenced by what each expected to see. Those decision makers with relatively hawkish views, like Vansittart or Brzezinski, were quicker to read early actions by the adversary as proof of its malign intentions. Some clung to their original beliefs and interpreted all incoming information through the prism of these beliefs. Thus, Weinberger did not revise his beliefs about the expansionist nature of Soviet intentions even when faced with costly reassuring actions. Vance likewise interpreted Soviet actions in the Horn and Afghanistan through the prism of his existing belief that the Soviets were merely opportunistic. Weinberger and Vance perhaps reflect extreme cases of the perseverance of belief in the face of disconfirming evidence. Taken together, the vividness and subjective credibility hypotheses provide a powerful explanation for the inference process of decision makers.

The selective attention's third hypothesis pertains to the filters that intelligence organizations use in estimating intentions. Organizational theory has long recognized that the missions and practices of bureaucracies strongly shape which information they will regard as informative. Thus, notwithstanding individual variation among decision makers, collective intelligence assessments in the United States and Britain notably used military indicators over other types in their analysis of intentions. During the interwar period, British intelligence was focused on counting elements of Germany's military arsenal, and derived its conclusions about Germany's intentions in large part by referring to these military indicators. The NIEs on the Soviet Union carefully tracked changes in Soviet military inventories and future capabilities. The analysts did not always recognize the circular logic they were using: that in estimating capabilities, they used certain assumptions about Soviet intentions (in most cases, that the intention was to maximize Soviet capabilities), and then employed the resulting estimates of Soviet capabilities to infer future political intentions. By contrast, decision makers were more inclined to rely on their own experiences, expectations, and needs. These divergent uses of information had adverse implications for the relationship between decision makers and intelligence organizations, leading the former to criticize and ignore intelligence input, or create alternative sources of information.[2]

This study has also shown that decision makers' policy positions reflected their assessments about intentions, thereby building greater confidence in the authenticity of those judgments. Significant changes in the perceptions of the key decision maker in each episode—Chamberlain, Carter, and Reagan—corresponded to a significant change in policies. This should lead us to reject the null hypothesis that perceived intentions do not influence states' policies. Additional factors, however, appear to have shaped particular policy initiatives that we cannot explain by reference to perceived intentions alone.

Finally, the foregoing analysis revises our understanding of these historical cases in several respects. To begin with, as much as the Soviet invasion of Afghanistan was critical for pushing Carter toward adopting a more pessimistic view of Soviet intentions, it is important to note that his reassessment was already under way. The significance of the Soviet invasion of Afghanistan was not that it was a costly signal per se but that Carter understood it as a personal betrayal by Brezhnev. In fact, that Vance differed in his understanding of the invasion demonstrates that readings of costly signals can be highly subjective. Another insight drawn from the two Cold War studies is that both Carter and Reagan did not heed the intelligence community's assessments. Carter expressed dissatisfaction with the political intelligence he was receiving. Like Carter, Reagan paid more attention to information that was vivid and emotional. The case study on the interwar period shows how Chamberlain as well as other decision makers also relied on their personal insights to assess intentions. Interestingly, the trigger for the change of British policies cannot be understood by considering Germany's invasion of Czechoslovakia as a strong and unambiguous signal of Germany's intentions.

A counterintuitive finding concerns the similarity that characterizes the inferential processes used by the three decision makers. Indeed, no two major democratically elected, twentieth-century decision makers appear as different from each as Chamberlain and Reagan. The former is associated with the failures of appeasement and missed opportunities for properly confronting Nazi Germany. By contrast, Reagan's first presidency was so hawkish that it risked escalating tensions with the Soviet Union into open armed conflict. Yet a common underlying logic guides the assessments of these two leaders. Further, as much as it may be difficult to explain how decision makers can correctly divine intentions, it appears they think that they can gauge intentions correctly. Reagan might have been right, and Chamberlain was certainly wrong, but these cases suggest that a leader facing another leader who is manipulative and even charismatic, like Hitler, is more likely to err in their inferences. Regardless of the accuracy of their assessments, they engage in diplomacy and draw inferences about the behavior of their adversaries in a way that departs from major claims found in the international relations scholarship. Accordingly, this similarity between Chamberlain and Reagan (and Carter) suggests that personal interactions are another source of information that should be studied.

IMPLICATIONS FOR INTERNATIONAL RELATIONS THEORY

This study's empirical findings offer mixed support for realism.[3] Decision makers in the cases studied certainly did not behave as Mearsheimer's theory of offensive realism claims they should. They did not assume the worst about the adversary's intentions and did not exclusively focus on military indicators per se. The inference process of decision makers was more consistent with that predicted by defensive realists (and the insights from offense-defense theory that follow from it) in several ways. First, defensive realists believe that states can effectively signal their intentions, thereby either reducing or exacerbating the security dilemma. The evidence is consistent with this general proposition. What the realist logic misses is that neither quantitative nor qualitative (offense-defense) changes in the adversary's military capabilities are typically viewed by decision makers as informative indicators of the adversary's political intentions. Second, consistent with Stephen Walt's balance of threat theory, beliefs about the adversary's intentions have an important effect on the policies that states adopt at the collective level.[4] This study thus complements Walt's theory in that it shows how leaders derive predictions about aggressive intentions, and explores the relationship between perceived intentions and policy initiatives at the individual and collective levels. Third, offense-defense variables and trends in the adversary's armament efforts were central to US intelligence organizations' analysis. Defensive realism therefore characterizes the inference process of intelligence organizations.[5]

Offense-defense theory receives much less support when operationalized in terms of military doctrines rather than military hardware. This study has demonstrated that decision makers and intelligence organizations find it hard to extrapolate another state's political intentions from its military doctrine, even though it can be viewed as an adequate indicator of the adversary's wartime objectives.[6] It might be the case that the relevant factor to consider is not whether the other's doctrine is defensive or offensive but rather whether the adversary and perceiver share similar perspectives about how to use military power. Indeed, a recent study has shown that adversaries' doctrinal differences can cause misperceptions as well as the failure of attempts at coercion or deterrence.[7] Nevertheless, in its current form, offense-defense theory as applied to the study of doctrines reveals that the latter constitutes a noisy and highly problematic signal of intentions.

The logic of the costly signaling approach, as explained above, also deserves more scrutiny. The findings indicate that certain types of costly actions receive more attention than others. While decision makers' inference processes diverge significantly from those predicted by the costly signaling literature, this study should not be seen as disproving the costly signaling concept. It instead reveals certain shortcomings and ambiguities in how to translate the concept of a costly signal from its origins in the field of economics into a testable proposition in international politics.[8] International relations scholars have been somewhat ambiguous about how we should operationalize a costly signal; that is, how financially (or politically) costly must an action be in order to be deemed significant. Moreover, the rationalist literature is not always clear about what inferences observers are even expected to draw from a costly action: What, for instance, should a withdrawal from a foreign military intervention signal to observers? Others could equally see this action as a sign of weakness or a costly reassuring signal of intentions. These two possible inferences may create different perceptions about the adversary's long-term intentions, and as such, shape the policies that observers will adopt toward them. As Jervis similarly points out, high defense spending might be taken as a costly signal of one's willingness to devote financial resources to military buildup—an action that would only be implemented by "tough" types. And yet throughout the Cold War, the "Soviets claimed that the periodic increases in the US defense budget reflected the power of arms manufacturers or the needs of the economy, in which case they would not have been taken [by the Soviets] as indications that the US was willing to sacrifice blood in a limited war or run high risks during a crisis."[9] In other words, although some categories of actions can be consistent with one interpretation of types, others are ambiguous.

This study's findings, then, are more in line with recent game theoretical scholarship that has pointed to the informative value of costless communication—cheap talk—under particular conditions. Theoretically, this book has focused on vividness as a form of cheap though apparently informative data; the empirical evidence, however—especially from the 1930s and late 1980s—also underscores the informative value of verbal assurances and threats that are communicated behind closed doors. This finding suggests that even nonpublic, financially cheap signals may be seen as trustworthy indicators of intentions.[10] More work should be done to explore other mechanisms, besides vividness, that make private diplomacy a credible channel of communication of assurances and threats.[11]

Another question is what role the bureaucratic affiliations of civilian decision makers play in their assessments of intentions. It is certainly tempting to reduce individual decision makers' perceptions to their bureaucratic role and interests. After all, it is intuitively appealing that secretaries of defense might be more likely than secretaries of state to see the adversary's intentions as hostile. Empirically, such an explanation might account for Vance's and Weinberger's beliefs, and perhaps even reveal why they did not revise their beliefs about Soviet intentions in the face of contradictory costly actions.[12] Viewed through the lens of bureaucratic politics, Vance and Weinberger presumably understood the implications of certain assessments of Soviet intentions for the budgets of their departments. Nevertheless, the historical record does not consistently support the perspective that "where you stand depends on where you sit." Bureaucratic interests, for example, did not correlate with views in the British case. If anything, the Foreign Office was more alarmist in its views of Germany's intentions even compared to the COS. Further work is needed to investigate the influence of bureaucratic roles on the perceptions of the individuals who run these bureaucracies.

This study also shows that the process of gauging intentions is influenced by an actor's prior theories and expectations, which in turn guide the selection of information and process of updating. In most cases, a decision maker's learning process diverges from that described in a rational Bayesian formula. The principle of belief perseverance or cognitive consistency led most decision makers in the three cases to interpret their adversary's behavior initially as consistent with their preexisting beliefs. Accordingly, they revised their beliefs slowly over time in response to repeated moves that were inconsistent with these beliefs and especially salient in nature; for some decision makers (Carter, for instance), this updating process was particularly drastic. Nonetheless, some decision makers failed to revise their beliefs even in the face of contradictory evidence. The variation among decision makers in the fashion and extent to which they changed their beliefs requires a more careful investigation. The key questions are: Who changes? Under what conditions? And what forms does change take? Attempting to answer these questions, scholars have pointed to several factors such as a decision maker's complexity of belief structure, style of thinking, open-mindedness to contradictory evidence, and so on. These factors fall beyond the scope of this study. But applying these factors to international politics, even when primary documents are available, is not always straightforward. For example, one might ask whether Carter was more open than Vance to contradictory evidence—specifically, the possibility that the Soviets were seeking to exploit détente—and thus capable of "learning" about Soviet intentions during his tenure. But it could also be the case that Carter was less committed than Vance to the idea of détente and SALT, and therefore found it easier than Vance did to change his views.[13]

This study challenges certain theoretical approaches to signaling and perceptions while complementing others. There is, though, a cautionary note that deserves mention. Although the evidence presented here draws on a substantial quantity of primary documents, and is at times augmented by personal interviews and leaders' records of public statements, the conclusions I reach here should not be considered definitive. Portions of the historical record that might be relevant have not yet been declassified. It is likely that such records would be consistent with the documentary evidence already available. Still, there is always a possibility that they will not. Second, the book has examined three case studies. We should be careful not to make overgeneralizations about these conclusions until they have been replicated using data from additional cases.

Extending the Research

The findings highlighted in this book point to several avenues for promising research. For one, because this study largely focuses on which indicators decision makers and intelligence organizations used to infer intentions, it has been silent on who perceived intentions correctly. To explore this question, future projects must determine how decision makers of the adversarial state understand their own intentions. At least two steps are needed to make this determination. The first involves establishing the baseline of the adversary's intentions. The second step tracks the evolution, if any, of these intentions, as it is possible that an adversary's decision makers might update their intentions upon receiving new information about the capabilities or resolve of the observer state (that is, actions taken by the observer's country induce a change in the adversary's intentions). These details are necessary to establish a yardstick against which to measure whether decision makers or intelligence organizations have inferred intentions correctly.

Second, this book's case studies explore how democratic states infer the intentions of adversaries, but it is possible that nondemocratic states perceive intentions differently. Several hypotheses are worth testing. It could be, say, that autocratic leaders believe that their state's political survival is closely related to their personal survival. Because they do not want to be caught off-guard by rivals, they are more likely to consider worst-case scenarios when judging the intentions of their adversaries; this may lead them to behave in accordance with the predictions of offensive realism. Alternatively, autocratic leaders might exhibit a greater confidence in their own personal diplomatic abilities because they were able to maneuver into high political office in closed political systems. Thus, they might display stronger attribution biases, greater reliance on personal insights, and be more prone to other psychological pathologies than their democratically elected counterparts. A stronger correspondence between the intelligence organizations and decision makers also might exist in nondemocratic settings when some governmental institutions lack independence from executive interference. Indeed, intelligence organizations might be more likely to offer assessments that appeal to and reinforce decision makers' biases.

Another possible avenue of research involves examining how states infer their adversaries' intentions when their leaders do not interact with each other.

In the absence of informal diplomacy, summit meetings, or conferences, how do leaders gauge intentions? Cases of such adversarial relations exist. As of June 2013, for instance, members of the Israeli and Iranian governments do not appear ever to have had face time that might have conveyed important information regarding each other's intentions. What alternative indicators do such decision makers adopt in such situations?

Finally, the selective attention framework looks at the influence of organizational roles and affiliations on the indicators that decision makers and intelligence organizations use to infer intentions. But it is unclear how individuals revise their methods of discerning intentions when they move between bureaucracies. For example, are individuals such as Gates—who after having been trained in the intelligence service, then move to a decision-making role—more likely to refer to capabilities in assessing an adversary's intentions? This research question spotlights another area of inquiry: To what extent do educational or career backgrounds affect an individual's proclivity to attend to certain indicators? Do those individuals with a background in the military perceive intentions differently from those with entirely civilian backgrounds? International relations scholarship has shown a renewed interest in individual-level variables in explaining foreign policy outcomes, but no study yet exists on how such variables shape assessments of intentions.

Implications for Policy

This study has several practical policy implications. The good news for decision makers is that the signaling of long-term intentions is possible. The bad news is that there does not seem to be a "magic signal" that would consistently lead all observers to draw similar inferences. That said, this analysis has shown that personal diplomacy is one effective tool in influencing other leaders' perceptions. Trust in positive personal impressions can allow leaders to move beyond previous patterns of hostility, and in doing so, open up possibilities for future cooperation. Yet as the case of Chamberlain and Hitler demonstrate, this basis of cooperation might be extremely risky: leaders might be highly capable of deceiving others in personal interactions. Furthermore, in meeting with foreign leaders, decision makers should be conscious of the fact that the former will draw inferences not just from what they say but also from *how* they convey their message. Personal meetings might sometimes lead to negative impressions. Perhaps the most well-known case is the interaction between then new president Kennedy and Soviet premier Khrushchev at the Vienna summit. There exists evidence suggesting that Kennedy's performance during that summit left Khrushchev believing Kennedy was young, inexperienced, and unprepared to make tough decisions when facing a determined adversary. Some have claimed that these impressions led Khrushchev to think that Kennedy would not risk a war over Berlin and gave him confidence to challenge Kennedy by placing missiles in Cuba a few years later.[14] The lesson to be drawn from the Vienna summit is that leaders must be cautious in using personal diplomacy. It is true that politicians who rise to key positions may have experience measuring the trustworthiness of their domestic opponents, but the tendency to rely on personal impressions to gauge the intentions of foreign leaders when the stakes are high may be a less than ideal practice. The interaction between Chamberlain and Hitler on the eve of the crisis over the Sudetenland should be a reminder to leaders that caution is essential in using personal impressions to infer intentions.

Second, leaders may read this study as suggesting that building up their military or deploying offensive weapons is not likely to induce a change in other leaders' perceptions of their political intentions. Prudent decision makers should not take this to mean that their own armament policies do not have implications. Rather, this analysis has shown that trends in the adversary's military arsenal have an important framing effect and have played a crucial role in shaping intelligence assessments. This study also seems to indicate that military actions have more impact on others' perceptions of a state's intentions than military buildup itself. In the context of contemporary events, this may lead us to speculate that the US decisions to invade Afghanistan and Iraq may have been more alarming to others than steady US efforts to improve its "counterforce" capabilities or maintain its military superiority.

Third, leaders should realize that although personal diplomacy and reassuring actions might help persuade a foreign leader of one's benign intentions, this is by no means guaranteed even when costly reassuring actions are taken. Instead, policy makers should attempt to uncover what theories a foreign leader uses to understand how the world works. Do foreign leaders' statements, for example, reveal that they place a premium on nuclear deterrence? Do they believe in the cooperative role of international institutions? Do they divide the world according to regime type? What litmus tests of a state's intentions has a foreign leader communicated in private or public? What elements do they emphasize in them? Uncovering the theories that foreign leaders hold may allow policy makers to be wiser about the types of reassuring actions they should send, and focus on those that will resonate with the foreign leader's theories rather their own.

Fourth, this study may help in evaluating the US leadership's assessments of China's long-term political intentions during the last decade. A definite answer will have to wait until the archival documents from this period are declassified, as the currently available documentary evidence is too slim to allow for any meaningful discussion. Nevertheless, this study predicts that US decision makers would have begun asking questions about China's foreign policy objectives around the time that they recognized Beijing was building up its military capabilities. But this research might also suggest that in private conversations about

China's intentions, US decision makers will vary in which aspects of China's behavior they emphasize, and will draw different inferences about its intentions that are consistent with their own theories and expectations. It is fair to assume, however, that China's costly international and domestic behavior—such as its participation in binding international organizations, behavior vis-à-vis its regional neighbors, and treatment of dissidents—will have been used by some decision makers to support their conclusions about China's political intentions, more so than discussion of China's military doctrine or its military buildup. At the same time, it is expected that the NIEs concerning China's intentions will have focused heavily on different aspects of China's military capabilities, and will view these as the primary indicators of its likely long-term foreign policy behavior. Yet if the historical cases offer any insight about future practices, these NIEs are likely to be playing a rather limited role in the conclusions that US decision makers have been reaching about China's political intentions.

Lastly, regardless of whether it is the civilian decision makers or intelligence assessments that get the question of intentions "right," this study suggests that decision makers tend to reach conclusions about the adversary's foreign policy objectives independent of intelligence estimates, based instead on their own knowledge, personal insights, and intuition. This phenomenon is not unique to the United States. At the same time, decision makers have repeatedly complained about "the ponderousness, obviousness, and mushiness of typical [National Intelligence] estimates, and consider reading them a waste of time."[15] On issues of high politics, such as estimating the adversary's intentions, decision makers might be especially prone to ignore the NIEs that contradict their own attitudes, impressions, and policies. Personal intelligence briefings or intelligence reports that contain anecdotes or vivid information may catch the attention of decision makers more than the often-dull NIEs. There are powerful domestic political pressures at times for the selective use or manipulation of intelligence.[16]

Recent policy reports containing interviews with decision makers and members of Congress show that the latest wave of reforms of the intelligence community has done little to improve policy makers' opinion of it. A Brookings report from 2009 observes that "many NIEs are regarded by officials who work with the issues as an elaborate restatement of Washington conventional wisdom." Further, according to interviews with former senior policy makers, "the finished NIE itself frequently is too late, too long, and too detailed for high-level policymakers."[17] Most would concur that the "NIEs can be very useful for technical consumers, such as actual war planners and war fighters who read [the] NIEs that focus on particular military developments and capabilities of an adversary. But for high-level civilian policymakers, the NIE process often falls short of playing the role for which it was designed."[18] Policy makers and scholars have proposed various ways to reform the NIEs. Some have asserted that the NIEs should resemble Supreme Court decisions, presenting contending arguments distinctly, along with the evidence for and against each argument. "The only useful purpose served by NIEs was to produce an intra-IC process to pull together views on a topic—the system would be better if the effort stopped there and did not then lead to issuance of an actual NIE."[19] Others maintain that "a more public role for [the] NIEs in debates on national security policy issues could obscure their inherent limitations and distort the discussion of the policy issues."[20] Analysts and scholars alike, though, must realize that decision makers' inclination to rely on their own judgments to infer political intentions is pervasive and universal, and getting inside the adversary's mind is perhaps one of the most difficult tasks of intelligence organizations. Consequently, it is hard to imagine that decision makers will become more attuned to the coordinated intelligence assessments on these issues. Understanding the inference process of one another may at the same time allow intelligence organizations and leaders to better understand why the other may be reaching different conclusions about the adversary's intentions, and thus be better positioned to probe the basic assumptions on the basis of which these inferences are made. As the United States is facing increasingly complex relationships with countries such as China, Iran, North Korea, and Russia, it is imperative that both intelligence organizations and decision makers be transparent and precise about the analytic assumptions they are making as well as the indicators they are using to gauge the intentions of these countries.

Appendix: Summary of Hypotheses

PREDICTIONS FROM THE SELECTIVE ATTENTION THESIS

1. The Vividness Hypothesis: Information about the adversary's intentions that is vivid, salient, and personalized is more readily available psychologically to decision makers, and thus they will give it more attention than abstract or statistical information even when the latter may have greater evidentiary value.

    1.1. All else being equal, personalized information that is positive should lead observers toward a more benign assessment of the adversary's intentions, whereas personalized information that is negative should lead observers toward a more hostile assessment of the adversary's intentions.

2. The Subjective Credibility Hypothesis: Assessments of intentions are guided by information that is perceived by the observer as credible. Decision makers' evaluation of what information is credible will be affected by subjective measurements of credibility that are consistent with each decision maker's theories and expectations.

    2.1. Decision makers who initially hold more hawkish views of the adversary's intentions will be less likely (and those with dovish views will be more likely) to categorize reassuring behavioral actions as credible signals of benign intentions. Decision makers who initially hold more hawkish views of the adversary's intentions will be more likely (and those with dovish views will be less likely) to categorize hostile behavioral actions as credibly signaling malign intentions.

    2.2. Hawks will change their perceptions of intentions more quickly compared to those with more dovish views (and doves will changes their perceptions more slowly compared with hawks) when faced with hostile actions, and doves will change their perceptions more quickly compared with hawks when faced with reassuring actions.

3. **The Organizational Expertise Hypothesis:** Organizational goals and the standard operating procedures designed to realize them affect the kind of information that is most available, and hence most attended to, by an organization's members. The primary organizational mission of intelligence communities will tend to make information about the adversary's military capabilities especially salient. Expertise about the adversary's capabilities developed over time will thus be used to infer the adversary's political and military intentions.

3.1. Intelligence organizations will discount information that is outside their realm of expertise. Given the tendency of intelligence organizations to collect and analyze data on patterns in the adversary's military arsenal, their assessments of the adversary's intentions is likely to be significantly shaped by both the adversary's military capabilities and changes in such capabilities over time.

3.2. The assessments of decision makers and intelligence communities of the adversary's intentions are likely to converge (diverge) when the perceptions of the adversary's military capabilities or changes in such capabilities match (do not match) the decision-maker's subjectivity assessments of its diplomatic behavior.

PREDICTIONS FROM THE THREE COMPETING THESES

1. **The Capabilities Thesis:** Observers will infer intentions based on calculations of the adversary's military capabilities

1.1. The numerical preponderance hypothesis suggests that if the adversary already enjoys military superiority over the observer, then observers will perceive an increase in the adversary's military capabilities as clear evidence of hostile intentions. If the observer detects a decrease in the adversary's capabilities, they will view it as a reassuring signal, leading them to infer that the adversary's intentions are less hostile.

1.2. The offense-defense hypothesis suggests that under conditions of defense or deterrence dominance, observers will view a perceived increase in the adversary's offensive capabilities as an indicator of hostile intentions. A perceived decrease in such capabilities under similar conditions will be considered a reassuring signal of benign intentions. Under conditions of offense dominance, a perceived increase in the adversary's defensive capabilities will be associated with perceptions of benign intentions.

2. **The Military Doctrine Thesis:** Observers will infer intentions on the basis of the perceived orientation of the adversary's military doctrine.

2.1. The military doctrine hypothesis suggests that observers will view an adversary's offensive and war-fighting nuclear doctrines as evidence of hostile intentions. Perceived defensive and deterrence-based doctrines will be seen as reassuring signals of benign intentions.

3. The Behavior Thesis: The behavior thesis suggests that observers will infer intentions on the basis of costly behavioral actions by the adversary. Foreign military interventions and territorial conquests, withdrawals from arms control agreements and international institutions, and in cases where the observer is a democracy, the dismantling of domestic democratic institutions will be seen as evidence of hostile intentions. Observers will view an adversary's withdrawal from foreign military interventions, entry into binding international institutions and arms control agreements, or adoption of democratic practices and institutions as reassuring signals of benign intentions.

3.1. The current actions hypothesis suggests that observers will infer intentions from the costly actions of the adversary under its current leadership.

3.2. The past actions hypothesis suggests that observers will infer intentions from the costly actions that an adversary has taken under a different leadership.

Notes

INTRODUCTION

1. Kenneth Lieberthal and Wang Jisi, "Addressing U.S.-China Strategic Distrust" (Washington, DC: Brookings Institution, 2012), vi. This report finds that "a large portion of the two countries' national security and defense establishments, as well as their intelligence communities, work on the premise that the U.S.-China relationship is unfriendly" (ibid., 35).

2. Gary Locke, "China Is a Country of Great Contrasts," National Public Radio, January 18, 2012, http://www.npr.org/2012/01/18/145384412/ambassador-locke-shares-his-impressions-of-china (accessed May 16, 2012).

3. US Department of Defense, *Quadrennial Defense Review Report*, February 2010, 31.

4. Mark Jeffrey A. Bader, *Obama and China's Rise: An Insider's Account of America's Asia Strategy* (Washington, DC: Brookings Press, 2012). For instance, Chinese observers were quick to claim that President Barack Obama's recent visit to the East Asian summit in November 2012 was intended to "contain a fast-growing China and to maintain . . . ebbing [US] dominance in the region." Quoted in "Some Cast Obama's Trip as Effort to Contain China's Influence," *USA Today*, November 20, 2011, http://www.usatoday.com/news/world/story/2011-11-21/China-US-relations-Obama/51321096/1 (accessed May 16, 2012).

5. For a good study that seeks to answer a similar question, see David M. Edelstein, "Choosing Friends and Enemies: Perceptions of Intentions in International Politics" (PhD diss., University of Chicago, 2000). On fallacies in intelligence assessments of intentions during the Cold War, see Raymond L. Garthoff, "On Estimating and Imputing Intentions," *International Security* 2, no. 3 (1978): 23–24; and in the post-Cold-War era, see Robert Mandel "On Estimating Post-Cold War Enemy Intentions," *Intelligence and National Security* 24, no. 2 (2009): 194–215.

6. For more on the psychological literature on vividness, see Craig A. Anderson, "Abstract and Concrete Data in the Perseverance of Social Theories: When Weak Data Lead to Unshakeable Beliefs," *Journal of Experimental Social Psychology* 19, no. 2 (1983): 93–108; Eugene Borgida and Richard E. Nisbett, "The Differential Impact of Abstract vs. Concrete Information on Decisions," *Journal of Applied Social Psychology* 7, no. 3 (1977): 258–71; Chaim D. Kaufmann, "Out of the Lab and into the Archives: A Method for Testing Psychological Explanations of Political Decision Making," *International Studies Quarterly* 38, no. 4 (1994): 557–86; Amos Tversky and Daniel

Kahneman, "Availability: A Heuristic for Judging Frequency and Probability," *Cognitive Psychology* 5, no. 2 (1973): 207–32; Richard E. Nisbett and Lee Ross, *Human Inference: Strategies and Shortcomings of Social Judgment* (Englewood Cliffs, NJ: Prentice Hall, 1980); Robert Jervis, "Understanding Beliefs," *Political Psychology* 27, no. 5 (October 2006): 641–63.

7. Robert Jervis, *The Logic of Images in International Relations* (New York: Columbia University Press, 1989).

8. Richard E. Nisbett and Lee Ross, *Human Inference: Strategies and Shortcomings of Social Judgment* (Englewood Cliffs, NJ: Prentice Hall, 1980), 167–88; Susan T. Fiske and Shelley E. Taylor, *Social Cognition* (Reading, MA: Addison-Wesley, 1984), 270–73.

9. Robert Jervis, *Perception and Misperception in International Politics* (Princeton, NJ: Princeton University Press, 1976), 117; Ole Holsti, *Crisis, Escalation, War* (Montreal: McGill-Queen's University Press, 1972). See Ole Holsti, "The Belief System and National Images: A Case Study," *Journal of Conflict Resolution* 6, no. 3 (1962): 244–52. At times, decision makers will regard ambiguous evidence not only as consistent with preexisting beliefs but also as confirming them. Robert Jervis, "Understanding Beliefs," *Political Psychology* 27, no. 5 (2006): 641–63.

10. I thank Robert Jervis for pointing this out to me. See Jervis, "Understanding Beliefs," 650.

11. Jervis, *Perception and Misperception in International Politics*, 181–87; Nisbett and Ross, *Human Inference*, 188–91; Fiske and Taylor, *Social Cognition*, 278–79. Studies on belief change have also shown that timely belief change depend on a decision maker's open-mindedness to contradictory information along with the position of these beliefs in the individual belief system. Arie W. Kruglanski, "Motivated Closing of the Mind: 'Seizing' and 'Freezing,'" *Psychology Review* 103, no. 2 (1996): 263–83; Philip E. Tetlock, "The Impact of Accountability on Judgment and Choice: Toward a Social Contingency," in *Advances in Experimental Social Psychology*, ed. Mark P. Zanna (New York: Academic Press, 1992).

12. For analyses of how organizations influence information processes, see, for example, Philip E. Tetlock, *Expert Political Judgment: How Good Is It? How Can We Know?* (Princeton, NJ: Princeton University Press, 2005); Martha S. Feldman and James G. March, "Information in Organizations as Signal and Symbol," *Administrative Science Quarterly* 26, no. 2 (1981): 171–86; Yaacov Y. I. Vertzberger, *The World in Their Minds: Information Processing, Cognition, and Perception in Foreign Policy Decisionmaking* (Stanford, CA: Stanford University Press, 1990); Isaiah Berlin, *The Hedgehog and the Fox: An Essay on Tolstoy's View of History* (London: Weidenfeld and Nicolson, 1953).

13. Charles L. Glaser, *Rational Theory of International Politics: The Logic of Competition and Cooperation* (Princeton, NJ: Princeton University Press, 2010).

14. Signaling in this book refers to any aspects of a state's behavior that might influence the other side; it does not necessarily imply a deliberate intent to influence the observers' perceptions of a state's intentions.

15. James D. Fearon, "Signaling Foreign Policy Interests: Tying Hands versus Sinking Costs," *Journal of Conflict Resolution* 41, no. 1 (1997): 68–90; Andrew H. Kydd, *Trust and Mistrust in International Relations* (Princeton, NJ: Princeton University Press, 2005).

16. Robert F. Trager, "Diplomatic Calculus in Anarchy: How Communication Matters," *American Political Science Review* 104, no. 2 (2010): 347–68. Thus, the audience costs are in fact costless. See Anne E. Sartori, *Deterrence by Diplomacy* (Princeton, NJ:

Princeton University Press, 2005), 58. Furthermore, costliness and publicness are not necessary conditions for actions to be informative. Sartori accordingly argues that private diplomatic communications are credible if the sending states wish to uphold a bargaining reputation. Bluffing risks compromising those reputations. For a similar assertion, see Alexandra Guisiner and Alastair Smith, "Honest Threats: The Interaction of Reputation and Political Institutions in International Crises," *Journal of Conflict Resolution* 46, no. 2 (2002): 175–200. Trager shows that even costless communication mechanisms have important influences on conflict processes.

17. According to models found in the economics literature, the credibility of cheap talk increases as the interests of the sender and receiver become more aligned. See Vincent P. Crawford and Joel Sobel, "Strategic Information Transmission," *Econometrica* 50, no. 6 (1982): 1431–51; Joseph Farrell and Robert Gibbons, "Cheap Talk Can Matter in Bargaining," *Journal of Economic Theory* 48 (June 1989): 221–37. For a less technical discussion, see Joseph Farrell and Matthew Rabin, "Cheap Talk," *Journal of Economic Perspectives* 10, no. 3 (1996): 103–18. See also Trager, "Diplomatic Calculus in Anarchy." For the reasoning why cheap talk does not matter, see Thomas C. Schelling, *The Strategy of Conflict* (Cambridge, MA: Harvard University Press, 1980). Fearon is more cautious, but his work in "Signaling Foreign Policy Interests" strongly implies that only costly actions are informative.

18. There is no one or unified rationalist perspective on signaling. Rather, multiple game-theoretical models exist, and each comes with its own set of conditions and parameters. They do not always adopt the unitary actor assumption.

19. See David Skidmore, *Reversing Course: Carter's Foreign Policy, Domestic Politics, and the Failure to Reform* (Nashville: Vanderbilt University Press, 1996); Mark L. Haas, "The United States and the End of the Cold War: Reactions to Shifts in Soviet Power, Policies, or Domestic Politics?" *International Organization* 61, no. 1 (2007): 147–79; Dale C. Copeland, "Trade Expectations and the Outbreak of Peace: Détente 1970–74 and the End of the Cold War 1985–91," *Security Studies* 9, no. 1–2 (1999): 15–58.

20. Norrin M. Ripsman and Jack S. Levy, "Wishful Thinking or Buying Time? The Logic of British Appeasement in the 1930s," *International Security* 33, no. 2 (2008): 148–81.

21. John J. Mearsheimer, *The Tragedy of Great Power Politics* (New York: W. W. Norton and Company, 2001).

22. Stephen M. Walt, *The Origins of Alliances* (Ithaca, NY: Cornell University Press, 1987); David M. Edelstein, "Managing Uncertainty: Beliefs about Intentions and the Rise of Great Powers," *Security Studies* 12, no. 1 (2002): 1–40.

23. Robert Jervis, "Cooperation under the Security Dilemma," *World Politics* 30, no. 2 (1978): 167–214.

24. Stephen Van Evera, "Offense, Defense, and the Causes of War," *International Security* 22, no. 4 (1998): 5–43; Charles L. Glaser, *Analyzing Strategic Nuclear Policy* (Princeton, NJ: Princeton University Press, 1991); Charles L. Glaser and Chaim D. Kaufmann, "What Is the Offense-Defense Balance and Can We Measure it?" *International Security* 22, no. 4 (1998): 44–82.

25. Schelling, *The Strategy of Conflict*; Jervis, *The Logic of Images in International Relations*; James D. Fearon, "Threats to Use Force: Costly Signals and Bargaining in International Crises" (PhD diss., University of California at Berkeley, 1992).

26. Charles L. Glaser, "The Security Dilemma Revisited," *World Politics* 50, no. 1 (1997): 171–201; Glaser, *Rational Theory of International Politics*; Andrew H. Kydd, "Sheep in

Sheep's Clothing: Why Security Seekers Do Not Fight Each Other," *Security Studies* 7, no. 1 (1997): 114–55.

27. For arguments that stress the role of institutions in signaling intentions, see Robert O. Keohane, *After Hegemony: Cooperation and Discord in the World Political Economy* (Princeton, NJ: Princeton University Press, 1984); G. John Ikenberry, *After Victory: Institutions, Strategic Restraint, and the Rebuilding of Order after Major Wars* (Princeton, NJ: Princeton University Press, 2001); Seth Weinberger, "Institutional Signaling and the Origins of the Cold War," *Security Studies* 12, no. 4 (2003): 80–115; Songying Fang, "The Informational Role of International Institutions and Domestic Politics," *American Journal of Political Science* 52, no. 2 (2008): 304–21; Terence L. Chapman, "International Security Institutions, Domestic Politics, and Institutional Legitimacy," *Journal of Conflict Resolution* 51, no. 1 (2007): 134–66.

28. Barbara Farnham, *Roosevelt and the Munich Crisis: A Study of Political Decision-Making* (Princeton, NJ: Princeton University Press, 1997); Deborah Welch Larson, *Origins of Containment: A Psychological Explanation* (Princeton, NJ: Princeton University Press, 1985); Robert Jervis, Richard Ned Lebow, and Janice Gross Stein, *Psychology and Deterrence* (Baltimore: Johns Hopkins University Press, 1989); Chaim D. Kaufmann, "Out of the Lab and into the Archives: A Method for Testing Psychological Explanations of Political Decision Making," *International Studies Quarterly* 38, no. 4 (1994): 557–86.

29. Jonathan Mercer, "Rationality and Psychology in International Politics," *International Organization* 59, no. 1 (2005): 88. See also Janice Gross Stein, "Building Politics into Psychology: The Misperception of Threat," *Political Psychology* 9, no. 2 (1988): 245–71; Jack S. Levy, "Political Psychology and Foreign Policy," in *Oxford Handbook of Political Psychology*, ed. David O. Sears, Leonie Huddy, and Robert Jervis (New York: Oxford University Press, 2003), 253–84.

30. Indeed, central in most rationalist accounts is the idea of the credibility of signals. They have examined the conditions under which (and extent to which) benign states can credibly communicate their intentions to and achieve cooperation with other states with benign intentions. These approaches have therefore modeled both the sending and perceiving states as unitary actors that use costly signals to reveal and update, respectively, information about intentions. The psychological approaches, though, focused less on what *should* allow states to determine others' intentions and more on actors' deviation from rationality due to psychological pathologies of misperception.

31. Robert Jervis, "Signaling and Perception: Drawing Inferences and Projecting Images," in *Political Psychology*, ed. Kristen Monroe (Mahwah, NJ: Lawrence Erlbaum Associates, 2002).

32. Janice Gross Stein and Raymond Tanter, *Rational Decision-Making: Israel's Security Choices, 1967* (Columbus: Ohio State University Press, 1980), 263.

33. Jervis, "Signaling and Perception," 297.

34. Much of the literature on intelligence organizations focuses on either intelligence failures or the politicization of intelligence. For recent examples, see Joshua Rovner, *Fixing the Facts: National Security and the Politics of Intelligence* (Ithaca, NY: Cornell University Press, 2011); Robert Jervis, *Why Intelligence Fails: Lessons from the Iranian Revolution and the Iraq War* (Ithaca, NY: Cornell University Press, 2010).

35. Glaser, *Rational Theory of International Politics*, 23, 29, 30.

36. Jervis, "Signaling and Perception," 293–314.

37. See, for example, Trager, "Diplomatic Calculus in Anarchy"; Sartori, *Deterrence by Diplomacy*; Alexandra Guisinger and Alastair Smith, "Honest Threats: The Interaction of Reputation and Political Institutions in International Crises," *Journal of Conflict Resolution* 46, no. 2 (April 2002): 175–200; Jervis, *Logic of Images*; Shuhei Kurizaki, "Efficient Secrecy: Public versus Private Threats in Crisis Diplomacy," *American Political Science Review* 101, no. 3 (2007): 543–58; Andrew H. Kydd, "Which Side Are You On? Bias, Credibility, and Mediation," *American Journal of Political Science* 47, no. 4 (2003): 597–611; Kristopher W. Ramsay, "Politics at the Water's Edge," *Journal of Conflict Resolution* 48, no. 4 (2004): 459–86; Schelling, *The Strategy of Conflict*. For an analysis of the efficacy of costless diplomatic signals, see James D. Fearon, "Rationalist Explanations for War," *International Organization* 49, no. 3 (summer 1995): 379–414.

Chapter 1: Theories of Intentions and the Problem of Attention

1. This distinction between short- and long-term assessments is important because during crises and wars, observers are likely to focus on questions that are distinct from those that normally inform their assessments of an adversary's intentions. I define intentions as the actions the adversary is expected to take under given circumstances. This definition captures most accurately what policy makers are trying to predict. Robert Jervis, *Perception and Misperception in International Politics* (Princeton, NJ: Princeton University Press, 1976), 48. It is crucial to differentiate the term intention from motive or motivation. Glaser, for example, categorizes states according to their motives. His typology includes greedy and security states. Greedy states are essentially expansionist states whose motive for expansion stems from nonsecurity reasons. Security states, by contrast, are those that are willing to run risks if they feel insecure, but are unwilling to run risks for nonsecurity reasons. See Charles L. Glaser, "Political Consequences of Military Strategy: Expanding and Refining the Spiral and Deterrence Models," *World Politics* 44, no. 4 (1992): 501–2; Charles L. Glaser, *Rational Theory of International Politics: The Logic of Competition and Cooperation* (Princeton, NJ: Princeton University Press, 2010), 38–39.

2. In other words, I do not consider what a state believes its adversary intends to do during an unfolding crisis or war, if these assessments do not influence observers' readings of that adversary's intentions in the longer run. This division parallels the intelligence community's concepts of "current" and "long-term intelligence." In this study, I am interested in basically any assessments produced by civilian decision makers or the intelligence community that are strategic-political in nature with a time horizon longer than a week or two into the future. See Mark M. Lowenthal, *Intelligence: From Secrets to Policy* (Washington, DC: CQ Press, 2009), 61–63, 115–16.

3. This typology is a composite of those found in Keith L. Shimko, *Images and Arms Control: Perceptions of the Soviet Union in the Reagan Administration* (Ann Arbor: University of Michigan Press, 1991), 15–17; Richard W. Cottam, *Foreign Policy Motivation: A General Theory and a Case Study* (Pittsburgh: University of Pittsburgh Press, 1977); Hans J. Morgenthau and Kenneth W. Thompson, *Politics among Nations: The Struggle for Power and Peace*, 6th ed. (New York: McGraw-Hill, 1985); Ole R. Holsti, "The 'Operational Code' as an Approach to the Analysis of Belief Systems," in *Final*

Report to the National Science Foundation, Grant SOC 75–14368 (Durham, NC: Duke University Press, 1977); Glenn H. Snyder and Paul Diesing, *Conflict among Nations: Bargaining, Decision Making, and System Structure in International Crises* (Princeton, NJ: Princeton University Press, 1977).

4. See, for example, Douglas Seay, "What Are the Soviets' Objectives in Their Foreign, Military, and Arms Control Policies?" in *Nuclear Arguments: Understanding the Strategic Nuclear Arms and Arms Control Debates*, ed. Lynn Eden and Steven E. Miller (Ithaca, NY: Cornell University Press, 1989), 47–108; Jervis, *Perception and Misperception*.

5. An adversary can be seen as opportunistic with regard to certain issues or territories, and expansionist regarding others. Later in this book I examine how observers reach these conclusions, and whether and why their perceptions change over time.

6. Holsti, "The 'Operational Code' as an Approach to the Analysis of Belief Systems," 95.

7. In addition to these ideal-type categories of political and military intentions, I also assess whether the intentions of the adversary are perceived as becoming more hostile or more benign.

8. Unmotivated or cognitive biases result from an individual's theoretical preconceptions along with the simplifying strategies or heuristics that they use to make sense of a complex, ambiguous world. Unmotivated biases lead people to see what they expect to see. Motivated biases, by contrast, lead people to see what they want to see. See Irving L. Janis and Leon Mann, *Decision Making: A Psychological Analysis of Conflict, Choice, and Commitment* (New York: Free Press, 1977); Robert Jervis, "Perceiving and Coping with Threat," in *Psychology and Deterrence*, ed. Robert Jervis, Richard Ned Lebow, and Janice Gross Stein (Baltimore: Johns Hopkins University Press, 1985); Janice Gross Stein, "Building Politics into Psychology: The Misperception of Threat," in *Political Psychology: Classic and Contemporary Readings*, ed. Neil Jeffrey Kressel (New York: Paragon, 1993); Jack Levy, "Political Psychology and Foreign Policy," in *Oxford Handbook of Political Psychology*, ed. David O. Sears, Leonie Huddy, and Robert Jervis (New York: Oxford University Press, 2003), 267–68. See also Daniel Kahneman, Paul Slovic, and Amos Tversky, eds., *Judgment under Uncertainty: Heuristics and Biases* (New York: Cambridge University Press, 1982).

9. Richard E. Nisbett and Lee Ross, *Human Inference: Strategies and Shortcomings of Social Judgment* (Englewood Cliffs, NJ: Prentice Hall, 1980), 62. See also Craig A. Anderson, "Abstract and Concrete Data in the Perseverance of Social Theories: When Weak Data Lead to Unshakeable Beliefs," *Journal of Experimental Social Psychology* 19, no. 2 (1983): 93–108; Eugene Borgida and Richard E. Nisbett, "The Differential Impact of Abstract vs. Concrete Information on Decisions," *Journal of Applied Social Psychology* 7, no. 3 (1977): 258–71; Chaim D. Kaufmann, "Out of the Lab and into the Archives: A Method for Testing Psychological Explanations of Political Decision Making," *International Studies Quarterly* 38, no. 4 (December 1994): 557–86; Amos Tversky and Daniel Kahneman, "Availability: A Heuristic for Judging Frequency and Probability," *Cognitive Psychology* 5, no. 2 (1973): 207–32.

10. See, for example, Jonathan Mercer, "Emotional Beliefs," *International Organization* 64 (2010): 1–31; Rose McDermott, "The Feeling of Rationality: The Meaning of Neuroscientific Advances for Political Science," *Perspectives on Politics* 2, no. 4 (2004): 691–706.

11. Kaufmann, "Out of the Lab and into the Archives"; Nisbett and Ross, *Human Inference*, 59–61, 123–27.

12. Borgida and Nisbett, "The Differential Impact of Abstract vs. Concrete Information," 269.

13. Kaufmann, "Out of the Lab and into the Archives," 563.

14. See, for example, Tversky and Kahneman, "Availability"; Borgida and Nisbett, "The Differential Impact of Abstract vs. Concrete Information"; Anderson, "Abstract and Concrete Data"; Rose McDermott, *Political Psychology in International Relations* (Ann Arbor: University of Michigan Press, 2004), 64.

15. Antonio R. Damasio, *The Feeling of What Happens: Body and Emotion in the Making of Consciousness* (New York: Mariner Books, 2000).

16. Even if this inference process is rational, we can still observe decision makers using such insights in a way that is not effective. In other words, such an inference process may be rational but not optimal. At the same time, there might be circumstances where a reliance on vivid information would be inconsistent with rationality.

17. Quoted in "Press Conference by President Bush and Russian Federation President Putin, Brdo Pri Kranju, Slovenia" (Washington, DC: White House, Office of the Press Secretary, June 16, 2001).

18. Alexander J. Groth, "On the Intelligence Aspects of Personal Diplomacy," *Orbis* 7 (1964): 833–48.

19. Quoted in Daniel Yergin, *Shattered Peace: The Origins of the Cold War and the National Security State* (Boston: Houghton Mifflin, 1977), 65.

20. Robert Jervis, *The Logic of Images in International Relations* (New York: Columbia University Press, 1989), 32–33.

21. Robert H. Frank, *Passions within Reason: The Strategic Role of the Emotions* (New York: W. W. Norton and Company, 1988), 96–145.

22. Jervis, *The Logic of Images in International Relations*, 32–33.

23. Groth, "On the Intelligence Aspects of Personal Diplomacy."

24. Maria Ida Gobbini, Aaron C. Koralek, Ronald E. Bryan, Kimberly J. Montgomery, and James V. Haxby, "Two Takes on the Social Brain: A Comparison of Theory of Mind Tasks," *Journal of Cognitive Neuroscience* 19, no. 11 (2007): 1803–14; Brooks King-Casas, Damon Tomlin, Cedric Anen, Colin F. Camerer, Steven R. Quartz, and P. Read Montague, "Getting to Know You: Reputation and Trust in a Two-Person Economic Exchange," *Science* 307, no. 5718 (2005): 78–83; Daniela Schiller, Jonathan B. Freeman, Jason P. Mitchell, James S. Uleman, and Elizabeth A. Phelps, "A Neural Mechanism of First Impressions," *Nature Neuroscience* 12, no. 4 (2009): 508–14; Tania Singer, Stefan J. Kiebel, Joel S. Winston, Raymond J. Dolan, and Chris D. Frith, "Brain Responses to the Acquired Moral Status of Faces," *Neuron* 41, no. 4 (2004): 653–62; Predrag Petrovic, Raffael Kalisch, Mathias Pessiglione, Tania Singer, and Raymond J. Dolan, "Learning Affective Values for Faces Is Expressed in Amygdala and Fusiform Gyrus," *Social Cognitive and Affective Neuroscience* 3, no. 2 (2008): 109–18.

25. McDermott, *Political Psychology in International Relations*, 173–76.

26. Furthermore, those leaders who possess less capacity for mastering cognitive and integrative complexity may be more prone to rely on such personal forms of impression formation. Rose McDermott, Jonathan Cowden, and Stephen Rosen, "The Role of Hostile Communications in a Simulated Crisis Game," *Peace and Conflict: Journal of Peace Psychology* 14, no. 2 (2008): 165.

27. Susan T. Fiske and Shelley E. Taylor, *Social Cognition* (Reading, MA: Addison-Wesley, 1984); Michael Ross and Fiore Sicoly, "Egocentric Biases in Availability and

Attribution," *Journal of Personality and Social Psychology* 37, no. 3 (1979): 322–36; Jervis, *Perception and Misperception*, 343–55; Janice Gross Stein, "Building Politics into Psychology: The Misperception of Threat," *Political Psychology* 9, no. 2 (1988): 245–71.

28. See Melvyn P. Leffler, *A Preponderance of Power: National Security, the Truman Administration, and the Cold War* (Stanford, CA: Stanford University Press, 1992), 34; David M. Edelstein, "Choosing Friends and Enemies: Perceptions of Intentions in International Politics" (PhD diss., University of Chicago, 2000).

29. See Dale T. Miller and Michael Ross, "Self-Serving Biases in the Attribution of Causality: Fact or Fiction?" *Psychological Bulletin* 82, no. 2 (1975): 213–25; Miron Zuckerman and Robert W. Mann, "The Other Way Around: Effects of Causal Attributions on Estimates of Consensus, Distinctiveness, and Consistency," *Journal of Experimental Social Psychology* 15, no. 6 (1979): 582–97; Jeffrey A. Knight and Robin R. Vallacher, "Interpersonal Engagement in Social Perception: The Consequences of Getting into the Action," *Journal of Personality and Social Psychology* 40, no. 6 (1981): 990–99.

30. Robert Jervis, "Signaling and Perception: Drawing Inferences and Projecting Images," in *Political Psychology*, ed. Kristen Monroe (Mahwah, NJ: Lawrence Erlbaum Associates, 2002), 31.

31. The strength of the effect of vivid information also depends on the structure of an individual's belief systems. Core beliefs—basic assumptions that help organize and simplify the decision maker's world—are protected more strongly than peripheral or instrumental beliefs, and will therefore be slower to change. This study does not probe this aspect of belief systems, however, and instead assumes that for all involved decision makers, beliefs about the nature of the adversary constitute a core belief that would be hard to change in the face of contradictory evidence.

32. See Deborah Welch Larson, *Origins of Containment: A Psychological Explanation* (Princeton, NJ: Princeton University Press, 1985), 39; Kaufmann, "Out of the Lab and into the Archives," 563.

33. McDermott, Cowden, and Rosen, "The Role of Hostile Communications," 156.

34. In his seminal study on signaling, Jervis argued that only signals that are perceived as impossible for the adversary to manipulate—which he terms indexes—are likely to be seen as credible by the perceiver. Jervis, *The Logic of Images in International Relations*, 32–33. More recently, rationalist scholars in international relations have found that costly actions can reveal credible information about intentions, and all actors can be expected to update their assessments in response to new facts. See, for example, James D. Fearon, "Threats to Use Force: Costly Signals and Bargaining in International Crises" (PhD diss., University of California at Berkeley, 1992); Charles L. Glaser, "Realists as Optimists: Cooperation as Self-Help," *International Security* 19, no. 3 (1994–95): 50–90; Andrew H. Kydd, "Trust, Reassurance, and Cooperation," *International Organization* 54, no. 2 (2000): 325–27; James D. Morrow, "The Strategic Setting of Choices: Signaling, Commitment, and Negotiation in International Politics," in *Strategic Choice and International Relations*, ed. David A. Lake and Robert Powell (Princeton, NJ: Princeton University Press, 1999), 88; Jeffrey S. Banks, *Signaling Games in Political Science* (New York: Harwood Academic, 1991), 23. An adversary's actions can also be seen as costly because they provide insurance against a policy reversal; in this sense, they tie the hands of the adversary. James D. Fearon, "Signaling Foreign Policy Interests: Tying Hands versus Sinking Costs," *Journal of Conflict Resolution* 41, no.

1 (1997): 68–90; Deborah Welch Larson, *Anatomy of Mistrust: U.S.-Soviet Relations during the Cold War* (Ithaca, NY: Cornell University Press, 1997), 27. Related to the notion of costly signaling is the idea of proportionality bias. Generally, leaders expect their adversary to expend efforts proportionate to the ends it seeks. They make inferences about the intentions of others from the costs and consequences of the actions that those others initiate, because they assume that an adversary will expend efforts proportionate to the ends it seeks. Consequently, when an adversary is believed to have incurred high costs, observers will infer that important objectives were at stake for the leadership. Gross Stein, "Building Politics into Psychology," 254–55; Richard Ned Lebow and Janice Gross Stein, *We All Lost the Cold War* (Princeton, NJ: Princeton University Press, 1994), 329.

35. Jervis, *The Logic of Images in International Relations*, 32–33; Mercer, "Emotional Beliefs."

36. Philip E. Tetlock, "Social Psychology and World Politics," in *Handbook of Social Psychology*, ed. Daniel T. Gilbert, Susan T. Fiske, and Gardner Lindzey, 4th ed. (New York: McGraw-Hill, 1998). For more on belief change, see Nisbett and Ross, *Human Inference*. On cognitive consistency, see Jervis, *Perception and Misperception*, chapter 7; Yaacov Y. I. Vertzberger, *The World in Their Minds: Information Processing, Cognition, and Perception in Foreign Policy Decisionmaking* (Stanford, CA: Stanford University Press, 1990), 113–27; Deborah W. Larson, *Anatomy of Mistrust* (Ithaca, NY: Cornell University Press, 1994), 32–34. On images, see Martha Cottam and Dorcas E. McCoy, "Image Change and Problem Representation after the Cold War," in *Problem Representation in Foreign Policy Decision Making*, ed. Donald A. Sylvan and James F. Voss (Cambridge: Cambridge University Press, 1998), 117–18, 123. On attitude change, see Jervis, *Perception and Misperception*; Jon A. Krosnick, "Attitude Importance and Attitude Change," *Journal of Experimental and Social Psychology* 24, no. 3 (1998): 240–55.

37. Ole R. Holsti, "Cognitive Dynamics and Images of the Enemy," in *Enemies in Politics*, ed. Richard Fagan (Chicago: Rand McNally), 25–96; Jervis, *Perceptions and Misperceptions*.

38. For useful debates on the role of "common prior beliefs" in bargaining models, see Alastair Smith and Allan Stam, "Bargaining and the Nature of War," *Journal of Conflict Resolution* 10, no. 6 (2004): 783–813; Mark Fey and Kristopher Ramsay, "The Common Priors Assumption: A Comment on 'Bargaining and the Nature of War,'" *Journal of Conflict Resolution* 50, no. 4 (2006): 607–13.

39. The subjective credibility hypothesis cannot indicate a priori when exactly observers will change their assessments about intentions. The hypothesis can only predict the possibility of change in perceived intentions relative to other observers on the basis of their varying initial beliefs about the adversary's intentions.

40. In explaining this logic, Jervis points to President George W. Bush's clear inclination toward second-image beliefs. Bush's statements reflect a belief in a clear division between democracies and tyrannies—a division that he believes strongly shapes their intentions; this belief is also reflected in his policies toward them. P. Schouten, "Theory Talk #12: Robert Jervis on Nuclear Weapons, Explaining the Non-Realist Politics of the Bush Administration and U.S. Military Presence in Europe," *Theory Talks* (2008), http://www.theory-talks.org/2008/07/theory-talk-12.html (accessed August 19, 2013).

41. See Jervis, *Perception and Misperception*; Alan Gerber and Donald P. Green, "Rational Learning and Partisan Attitudes," *American Journal of Political Science* 42, no. 3

(1998): 794–818; Charles S. Taber and Milton Lodge, "Motivated Skepticism in the Evaluation of Political Beliefs," *American Journal of Political Science* 50, no. 3 (2006): 755–69.

42. Some rationalists may object by pointing out that Bayesian adjustment can be so "glacial as to be unnoticeable, if the amount of evidentiary significance was very small compared to prior data." Yet "this is implausible for high-stakes decisions made under conditions of uncertainty . . . where current information is likely to be of considerable value." Kaufmann, "Out of the Lab and into the Archives," 565.

43. Finally, this hypothesis does not exclude the possibility that indicators based on changes in the adversary's military capabilities or doctrine could function as credible signals of intentions. Rather, it posits that credibility appears to be more easily associated with noncapabilities-based indicators. This may be the case because, as described above, noncapabilities-based behavior tends to be more vivid and is therefore more likely to influence decision makers. Additionally, decision makers may lack the nuanced expertise required to interpret and draw inferences from complex abstract information about the adversary's military capabilities and doctrine. Since they are comparatively disadvantaged in interpreting capabilities, decision makers are likely to leave that to their intelligence agencies and focus on other criteria to assess intentions. This distinction is not generalizable to all decision makers, since there is variation in decision makers' military experience and education. Some decision makers have no military background; others have extensive military experience, such as President Dwight D. Eisenhower, who served as a US Army general.

44. This is not to claim that individual intelligence analysts will not give extra weight to information that is vivid, as individual decision makers do. In general, however, we should not expect intelligence analysts to make much use of information that is vivid because, as Richards Heuer puts it, "Intelligence analysts generally work with second-hand information. The information that analysts receive is mediated by the written words of others rather than perceived directly with their own eyes and ears. Partly because of limitations imposed by their open CIA employment, many intelligence analysts have spent less time in the country they are analyzing and had fewer contacts with nationals of that country than their academic and other government colleagues. Occasions when an analyst does visit the country whose affairs he or she is analyzing, or speaks directly with a national from that country, are memorable experiences. Such experiences are often a source of new insights." Richards J. Heuer, *Psychology of Intelligence Analysis* (Washington, DC: Center for the Study of Intelligence Publications, 1999), 117.

45. On the difference between organizations and small groups, see Vertzberger, *The World in Their Minds*, 192–93.

46. Martha S. Feldman and James G. March, "Information in Organizations as Signal and Symbol," *Administrative Science Quarterly* 26, no. 2 (1981): 172–75.

47. Lowenthal, *Intelligence*, 234–35.

48. Analysts have noted these trends in international businesses. See, for example, William G. Egelhoff, "Information-Processing Theory and the Multinational Enterprise," *Journal of International Business Studies* 22, no. 3 (1991): 344.

49. Isaiah Berlin, *The Hedgehog and the Fox: An Essay on Tolstoy's View of History* (London: Weidenfeld and Nicolson, 1953).

50. Philip E. Tetlock, *Expert Political Judgment: How Good Is It? How Can We Know?* (Princeton, NJ: Princeton University Press, 2005), 20–21.

51. Ibid., 118.

52. Note that I do not examine the individuals who head the intelligence organizations to test this thesis. Instead, I use collective assessments (e.g., the NIE) to evaluate competing hypotheses.

53. On the neglect and politicization of intelligence, see Joshua Rovner, *Fixing the Facts* (Ithaca, NY: Cornell University Press, 2011); Robert Jervis, *Why Intelligence Fails: Lessons from the Iranian Revolution and the Iraq War* (Ithaca, NY: Cornell University Press, 2010); Richard K. Betts, *Enemies of Intelligence: Knowledge and Power in American National Security* (New York: Columbia University Press, 2009).

54. Stephen D. Krasner, "Are Bureaucracies Important? (or Allison Wonderland)," *Foreign Policy* 7 (1972): 159–79.

55. The record of the adversary's public statements is not analyzed here as a category of indicators. This is because the rationalist literature on the security dilemma, and signaling more broadly, has not highlighted such information as a particularly informative signal of intentions outside crisis situations. My decision to exclude public statements from the analysis does not bias the results, given that in the empirical chapters I track whether observers referred to such statements in their assessments of the adversity's intentions.

56. An important body of literature called *constructivism* has also contributed to the scholarship on interstate communication, but is not explicitly addressed in this book. In his seminal work, Alexander Wendt argues that an ideational structure formed of shared ideas, norms, and values constitutes states' interests and identities. Alexander Wendt, *Social Theory of International Politics* (Cambridge: Cambridge University Press, 1999). Still, he downplays the importance of uncertainty as a powerful influence on interstate relations, and offers little guidance on how states can determine genuine signals from deceptive gestures in their assessments of each other's interests and identities. It is also not entirely clear in Wendt's theory which actions should lead states to draw revised assessments of each other's intentions. One possible variable pertains to changes announced in domestic ideology and domestic institutions. In the presence of a greater convergence in ideology and domestic institutions, the adversary and perceiver should reach more positive assessments of each other's intentions. Yet the prediction of this hypothesis is indistinguishable from aspects of the behavior thesis, described above, that claims that costly actions in domestic or international politics relay credible information about a state's intentions. Consequently, in this book I do not directly or explicitly explore the role of changes in a state's ideology and domestic practices per se. See also Dale C. Copeland, "The Constructivist Challenge to Structural Realism: A Review Essay," *International Security* 25, no. 2 (2000): 199–200, 202–3; Mark L. Haas, "The United States and the End of the Cold War: Reactions to Shifts in Soviet Power, Policies, or Domestic Politics?" *International Organization* 61, no. 1 (2007): 148–49.

57. See Andrew H. Kydd, *Trust and Mistrust in International Relations* (Princeton, NJ: Princeton University Press, 2005); Glaser, *Rational Theory of International Politics*.

58. John J. Mearsheimer, *The Tragedy of Great Power Politics* (New York: W. W. Norton and Company, 2001), 31.

59. Mearsheimer distinguishes between military power and latent power. The former captures the size and strength of the army along with its various types of fighting forces, while the latter refers to the socioeconomic ingredients (such as wealth and population) that go into building military power (ibid., 83–137). Offensive realists believe that distinctions between offensive and defensive weapons are not meaningful, and strategies resting on the idea that intentions can be discerned through the kinds of weapons a state deploys are neither effective nor prudent. Harry Kreisler, *Conversations with History: John J. Mearsheimer* (Berkeley: Institute of International Studies, University of California at Berkeley, April 8, 2002), http://globetrotter.berkeley .edu/people2/Mearsheimer/mearsheimer-con0.html (accessed July 14, 2008); John J. Mearsheimer, "Conversations in International Relations: Interview with John J. Mearsheimer (Part I)," *International Relations* 20, no. 1 (2006): 105–23.

60. Kydd argues that security seekers can reduce the security dilemma and effectively signal their benign foreign policy intentions by sending reassuring costly signals. According to Kydd, both costly changes in the aggregation of capabilities and the types of forces that a country deploys are consistent with this logic, although his typology of costly signaling is not restricted to changes in military capabilities per se. He claims, for example, that security-seeking states can communicate their benign intentions through ideology, policy toward domestic minorities, or policy toward weaker neighbors. These points are relevant to the discussion later in this chapter of the behavioral signal thesis. Andrew H. Kydd, "Sheep in Sheep's Clothing: Why Security Seekers Do Not Fight Each Other," *Security Studies* 7, no. 1 (1997): 114–55; Glaser, "Realists as Optimists," 67–68.

61. Glaser, *Rational Theory of International Politics*, 76–77.

62. See, for example, Robert Jervis, "Cooperation under the Security Dilemma," *World Politics* 30, no. 2 (1978): 167–214; Charles L. Glaser, *Analyzing Strategic Nuclear Policy* (Princeton, NJ: Princeton University Press, 1991); Charles L. Glaser and Chaim D. Kaufmann, "What Is the Offense-Defense Balance and Can We Measure It?" *International Security* 22, no. 4 (1998): 44–82; Stephen Van Evera, "Offense, Defense, and the Causes of War," *International Security* 22, no. 4 (1998): 5–43.

63. Nevertheless, when offensive weapons cannot be distinguished from defensive ones, some offense-defense theorists have argued that an increase or decrease in the quantity of military forces deployed may serve as a signal about intentions. The more resources a state spends on increasing (or decreasing) the scale of its military forces, the clearer the signal about its intentions. Evan Montgomery has pointed out, correctly I think, that when offense and defense cannot be distinguished, a reduction in a state's ability to attack is likely to make it more vulnerable to attack by aggressive states. This is one explanation why reassurance under these conditions is an extremely risky strategy and therefore a costly signal. Evan Braden Montgomery, "Breaking out of the Security Dilemma: Realism, Reassurance, and the Problem of Uncertainty," *International Security* 31, no. 2 (2006): 151–85.

64. Critics of the offense-defense theory assert that weapons cannot be usefully characterized as either offensive or defensive, and that most weapons can be used to support both defensive or offensive operations and objectives. For a good summary of this debate and the counterclaims that have been offered by proponents of the offense-defense theory, see Sean M. Lynn-Jones, "Offense-Defense Theory and Its Critics,"

Security Studies 4, no. 4 (1995): 660–91; Keir A. Lieber, *War and the Engineers: The Primacy of Politics over Technology* (Ithaca, NY: Cornell University Press, 2005).

65. Most offense-defense scholars characterize the period after 1945 as one of "defense dominance," even though they acknowledge that in a nuclear war, defense is impossible and it is deterrence that really has the advantage. Other scholars have contended that this characterization is inaccurate and misleading, and we should distinguish between periods of defense versus deterrence dominance. See Richard K. Betts, "Must War Find a Way? A Review Essay," *International Security* 24, no. 2 (1999): 179–80; Karen Ruth Adams, "Attack and Conquer? International Anarchy and the Offense-Defense-Deterrence Balance," *International Security* 28, no. 3 (2003–4): 45–83.

66. Offensive weapons in this context include those that can destroy the adversary's nuclear warheads before they are launched along with those that can destroy the adversary's retaliating warheads in flight toward one's own cities or limit the damage these warheads do to those cities. Accordingly, in the nuclear context, offense-defense theorists have classified the following as conveying hostile intentions: highly accurate intercontinental ballistic missiles (ICBMs) and submarine-launched ballistic missiles (SLBMs), which can destroy enemy ICBMs and bombers on the ground; antisubmarine forces that can destroy enemy ballistic missile submarines; area defense systems that can shoot down retaliating bombers; areawide missile defenses that could protect cities against retaliating ICBMs and SLBMs; and civil defenses, which limit the damage inflicted by the enemy's warheads that get through. See Glaser, *Analyzing Strategic Nuclear Policy*, 207–11; Barry R. Posen and Stephen Van Evera, "Defense Policy and the Reagan Administration: Departure from Containment," *International Security* 8, no. 1 (1983): 3–45; Alan Collins, *The Security Dilemma and the End of the Cold War* (Edinburgh: Keele University Press, 1997).

67. Glaser, *Analyzing Strategic Nuclear Policy*, 73–75. This assumption is overstated because limited countervalue options could have coercive uses as well. Robert Jervis, *The Meaning of the Nuclear Revolution: Statecraft and the Prospect of Armageddon* (Ithaca, NY: Cornell University Press, 1989), 209–10.

68. In categorizing types of weapon systems and technologies as defensive, offensive, or both, I use the classifications developed by proponents of offense-defense theory. See, for example, Barry R. Posen, *The Sources of Military Doctrine: France, Britain, and Germany between the World Wars* (Ithaca, NY: Cornell University Press, 1984); Van Evera, "Offense, Defense, and the Causes of War"; Jervis, *The Meaning of the Nuclear Revolution*. By defining the explanatory variable as perceptions of the offense-defense balance, I essentially test the offense-defense theory not at the systemic level but instead at the state level.

69. This distinction is important since other studies have already demonstrated that states sometimes misperceive the real balance and as a result adopt misguided strategies. See, for example, Robert Jervis, "Realism, Game Theory, and Cooperation," *World Politics* 40, no. 3 (1988): 317–49; Bernard Brodie, "Technological Change, Strategic Doctrine, and Political Outcomes," in *Historical Dimensions of National Security Problems*, ed. Klaus Knorr (Lawrence: University Press of Kansas, 1976); Jack S. Levy, "The Offensive/Defensive Balance of Military Technology: A Theoretical and Historical Analysis," *International Studies Quarterly* 28 no. 2 (1984): 219–38; Lynn-Jones, "Offense-Defense Theory and Its Critics," 679.

70. Posen, *The Sources of Military Doctrine*, 17.

71. This offense, defense, and deterrence typology is taken from ibid. On the role of doctrinal differences in complicating signaling and assessments of credibility in crises, see Christopher P. Twomey, *The Military Lens: Doctrinal Difference and Deterrence Failure in Sino-American Relations* (Ithaca, NY: Cornell University Press, 2010).

72. A classic example of an offensive doctrine is the blitzkrieg, as invented by the Germans in the 1930s.

73. French doctrine on the eve of World War II is one good illustration of a defensive doctrine.

74. China's doctrine of a people's war is an example of a deterrent doctrine that is achieved with conventional means.

75. The two ideal types of nuclear doctrines essentially mirror the arguments proposed by two prominent schools of thought about nuclear strategy since World War II: the assured destruction school and the war-fighting doctrine school that advocated an approach associated with the concept of a *flexible response*. See Robert Jervis, "Why Nuclear Superiority Doesn't Matter," *Political Science Quarterly* 94, no. 4 (1979–80): 617–33; Glaser, *Analyzing Strategic Nuclear Policy*; Robert J. Art, "Between Assured Destruction and Nuclear Victory: The Case for the 'Mad-Plus' Posture," *Ethics* 95, no. 3 (1985): 497–516. The punishment school is associated with Robert McNamara, McGeorge Bundy, Bernard Brodie, Jervis, and Glaser; the denial school is associated with Colin Gray, Keith Payne, secretaries of defense Harold Brown and Caspar Weinberger, and other US officials in the 1970s and 1980s.

76. Glaser, *Analyzing Strategic Nuclear Policy*, 97.

77. While this study centers on several types of actions that have been treated in the recent rationalist literature as costly signals, this is by no means an exhaustive list of potential behavioral indicators of intentions.

78. See James D. Fearon, "Signaling Foreign Policy Interests: Tying Hands versus Sinking Costs," *Journal of Conflict Resolution* 41, no. 1 (1997): 68–90. These insights originated with Thomas C. Schelling, *The Strategy of Conflict* (Cambridge, MA: Harvard University Press, 1960); Thomas C. Schelling, *Arms and Influence* (New Haven, CT: Yale University Press, 1966).

79. See Robert O. Keohane and Lisa L. Martin, "The Promise of Institutionalist Theory," *International Security* 20, no. 1 (1995): 39–51; Philip E. Tetlock, Jo L. Husbands, Robert Jervis, Paul C. Stern, and Charles Tilly, eds., *Behavior, Society, and Nuclear War* (New York: Oxford University Press, 1989); Lisa L. Martin, *Democratic Commitments: Legislatures and International Cooperation* (Princeton, NJ: Princeton University Press, 2000); Seth Weinberger, "Institutional Signaling and the Origins of the Cold War," *Security Studies* 12, no. 4 (2003): 114–55; Celeste A. Wallander, *Mortal Friends, Best Enemies: German-Russian Cooperation after the Cold War* (Ithaca, NY: Cornell University Press, 1999); Stephen D. Krasner, *International Regimes* (Ithaca, NY: Cornell University Press, 1983); Kydd, "Sheep in Sheep's Clothing"; Celeste A. Wallander and Robert O. Keohane, "Risk, Threat, and Security Institutions," in *Imperfect Unions: Security Institutions over Time and Space*, ed. Helga Haftendorn, Robert O. Keohane, and Celeste A. Wallander (New York: Oxford University Press, 1999); Morrow, "The Strategic Setting of Choices"; James D. Morrow, "Alliances: Why Write Them Down?" *Annual Review of Political Science* 3 (2000): 63–81; Jana von Stein, "The International Law and Politics of Climate Change: Ratification of the United Nations Framework

Convention and the Kyoto Protocol," *Journal of Conflict Resolution* 52, no. 2 (2008): 243–68; Alexander Thompson, *Channels of Power: The UN Security Council and US Statecraft in Iraq* (Ithaca, NY: Cornell University Press, 2009).

80. This literature has advanced several ways in which international institutions can generate costly signals. As Seth Weinberger notes, "Institutions can create obligations to which their members commit themselves, such as eliminating certain types of weapons from national arsenals, or agreeing to international inspection processes. Institutions can create external veto points or decisions that exist above the actions of states. . . . Institutions may require states to transform their domestic political institutions in order to obtain membership. . . . Institutions can exact more subtle costs as well, as international norms and laws may be internalized, changing the preferences and altering the beliefs of member states." Weinberger, "Institutional Signaling," 88.

81. Ibid., 27.

82. John M. Owen, "How Liberalism Produces Democratic Peace," *International Security* 19, no. 2 (1994): 87–125.

83. For a study of differences in domestic institutions and political ideologies between states as a source of threat, see Mark Haas, *The Ideological Origins of Great Power Politics, 1789–1989* (Ithaca, NY: Cornell University Press, 2005).

84. Kenneth A. Schultz, *Democracy and Coercive Diplomacy* (Cambridge: Cambridge University Press, 2001); Fearon, "Signaling Foreign Policy Interests"; Jessica L. Weeks, "Autocratic Audience Costs: Regime Type and Signaling Resolve," *International Organization* 62, no. 1 (2008): 35–64.

85. The work of Edward Mansfield and Jack Snyder, however, indicates the opposite. Since democratizing states during the transition period are prone to conflict, other counties are likely to be more wary of their intentions. See Edward D. Mansfield and Jack L. Snyder, *Electing to Fight: Why Emerging Democracies Go to War* (Cambridge, MA: MIT Press, 2005).

86. Kydd, "Sheep in Sheep's Clothing," 143.

87. Kydd, *Trust and Mistrust*, 230.

88. Charles L. Glaser, "The Security Dilemma Revisited," *World Politics* 50, no. 1 (1997): 171–201; Glaser, *Analyzing Strategic Nuclear Policy*.

89. Schelling, *The Strategy of Conflict*; Schelling, *Arms and Influence*. Reputation also plays a central role in theories of deterrence: leaders have an incentive to follow through on their commitments because a failure to do so will diminish their credibility in the future. Anne E. Sartori, *Deterrence by Diplomacy* (Princeton, NJ: Princeton University Press, 2005). On the importance of reputation in international political economy, see Michael Tomz, *Reputation and International Cooperation: Sovereign Debt across Three Centuries* (Princeton, NJ: Princeton University Press, 2007).

90. See Snyder and Diesing, *Conflict among Nations*; Richard Ned Lebow, *Between Peace and War: The Nature of International Crisis* (Baltimore: Johns Hopkins University Press, 1981); Ted Hopf, *Peripheral Visions: Deterrence Theory and American Foreign Policy in the Third World, 1965–1990* (Ann Arbor: University of Michigan Press, 1994). More recent qualitative works have questioned whether decision makers actually rely on the adversary's past actions to infer their credibility in crises. See, for instance, Jonathan Mercer, *Reputation and International Politics* (Ithaca, NY: Cornell University Press, 1996); Daryl G. Press, *Calculating Credibility: How Leaders Assess Military Threats* (Ithaca, NY: Cornell University Press, 2005); Shiping Tang,

"Reputation, Cult of Reputation, and International Conflict," *Security Studies* 14, no. 1 (2005): 34–62.

91. See, for example, Richard E. Neustadt and Ernest R. May, *Thinking in Time: The Uses of History for Decision-Makers* (New York: Free Press, 1986); Ernest R. May, *"Lessons" of the Past: The Use and Misuse of History in American Foreign Policy* (New York: Oxford University Press, 1973); Jack S. Levy, "Learning and Foreign Policy: Sweeping a Conceptual Minefield," *International Organization* 48, no. 2 (1994): 279–312; Yuen Foong Khong, *Analogies at War: Korea, Munich, Dien Bien Phu, and the Vietnam Decisions of 1965* (Princeton, NJ: Princeton University Press, 1992); Jervis, *Perception and Misperception*. According to Jervis, there is a tendency to learn from events that have a major impact, affect the individual or their society directly, occur recently in time, and are observed firsthand and at a formative period in a person's life. Still, it remains unclear exactly what decision makers learn, the process by which they learn, and the impact of these lessons on their subsequent decisions. Some have also suggested that the causal arrow may be reversed or spurious—that is, current assessments about intentions might lead decision makers to refer selectively to past actions or events that support their position, either subconsciously because of cognitive or motivated biases, or deliberately for leverage in political debates. Jack Levy, "Political Psychology and Foreign Policy," in *Oxford Handbook of Political Psychology*, ed. David O. Sears, Leonie Huddy, and Robert Jervis (New York: Oxford University Press, 2003), 267–68.

92. The adversary's past actions can shape the beliefs that observers form *prior* to the interaction I capture. Here, however, I am interested only in whether observers explicitly rely on past actions to support their *current* assessments of the adversary's long-term intentions.

93. Charles L. Glaser, *Rational Theory of International Politics: The Logic of Competition and Cooperation* (Princeton, NJ: Princeton University Press, 2010), 23, 30, 270.

94. Kydd, *Trust and Mistrust*, 18–19 (emphasis in original). Glaser's (*Rationalist Theory of International Politics*, 161) rationalist theory, though, is more skeptical about the ability of security seekers to reveal their intentions.

95. This last aspect of decision making is applicable when exploring the assessments of decision makers, but not in the discussion of the intelligence community's views, because intelligence communities rarely offer foreign policy suggestions, and such suggestions are still rarer in written documents.

96. See, for example, Miron Zuckerman, "Attribution of Success and Failure Revisited, or: The Motivational Bias Is Alive and Well in Attribution Theory," *Journal of Personality* 47, no. 2 (1979): 245–87.

97. Vertzberger, *The World in Their Minds*, 67.

98. Intelligence organizations are, like decision makers, influenced by motivational bias to reduce trade-offs, avoid ambiguity, and decrease inconsistencies, and may as a result use just one set of indicators to reach conclusions about the adversary's intentions. Consider the case of the Israeli Defense Force's failure to anticipate Anwar el-Sādāt's planned attack against Israel in October 1973. The evidentiary record makes it clear that the Israeli Defense Forces relied on one overriding indicator to assess the probability of attack: it assumed that Egypt would not attack unless it acquired a capability to strike Israel in depth and its airfields in particular. Thus, the principal indicator of the probability of an Egyptian attack would be an increase in Egypt's aerial

strike capability. Janice Gross Stein, "Calculation, Miscalculation, and Conventional Deterrence I: The View from Cairo," in *Psychology and Deterrence*, ed. Robert Jervis, Richard Ned Lebow, and Janice Gross Stein (Baltimore: Johns Hopkins University Press, 1985).

99. If the documents contain extensive analysis of or opinions about the adversary's intentions, this indicates that this issue was prominent for the observer. Alternatively, if a discussion about intentions is absent, this could either mean that this issue was not relevant for the observer at the time or that there was a well-established consensus among observers about the adversary's intentions.

100. When possible, I looked for evidence indicating a decision maker's perception of the adversary's intentions in the period just before the one I analyzed. Yet this might be misleading, because as decision makers assume office, they are exposed to new, important, and secret information about the adversary, and this may affect their beliefs or assessments.

101. Decision makers may use several different strategies when they believe an adversary's intentions are hostile, including balancing, bandwagoning, binding, appeasing, or buck-passing. For a good summary of these strategies, see Randall L. Schweller, *Deadly Imbalances: Tripolarity and Hitler's Strategy of World Conquest* (New York: Columbia University Press, 1998).

102. For more on this logic, see Edelstein, "Managing Uncertainty."

103. This study does not attempt to offer a thorough account of the evolution in British or US policies; the many intertwined factors that affect a state's policies toward an adversary go well beyond the scope of this book.

104. An alternative way to analyze the documents would be to perform content analysis on archival data and public statements. Yet such an analysis would be potentially misleading because I am interested in capturing how observers discussed different indicators in association with assessments of intentions, not the overall threat posed by the adversary. Such a contextualized understanding of the inference process might be extremely hard to grasp using the content analysis method. See Barbara M. Montgomery and Steve Duck, *Studying Interpersonal Interaction* (New York: Guilford Press, 1991); Stuart J. Sigman, Sheila J. Sullivan, and Marcley Wendell, "Conversation: Data Acquisition and Analysis," in *A Handbook for the Study of Human Communication: Methods and Instruments for Observing, Measuring, and Assessing Communication Processes*, ed. Charles H. Tardy (Norwood, NJ: Ablex, 1988); Deborah Welch Larson, "Problems of Content Analysis in Foreign-Policy Research: Notes from the Study of the Origins of Cold War Belief Systems," *International Studies Quarterly* 32, no. 2 (1988): 241–55.

105. Richard E. Nisbett and Timothy D. Wilson, "Telling More Than We Can Know: Verbal Reports on Mental Processes," *Psychological Review* 84, no. 3 (1977): 231–58. See also Timothy D. Wilson, *Strangers to Ourselves: Discovering the Adaptive Unconscious* (Cambridge, MA: Belknap Press, 2002).

106. After coding the documents according to the standardized questions, I randomly selected 10 percent of the documents and recoded them. There were no inconsistencies in the results.

107. Mark Lowenthal, "Tribal Tongues: Intelligence Consumers, Intelligence Producers," *Washington Quarterly* 15, no. 1 (1992): 157–68.

108. On the politicization of intelligence, see Richard K. Betts, "Incorruptibility or Influence? Costs and Benefits of Politicization," in *Enemies of Intelligence: Knowledge and Power in American National Security* (New York: Columbia University Press, 2007); Robert Jervis, "The Iraq WMD Intelligence Failure: What Everyone Knows Is Wrong," in *Why Intelligence Fails: Lessons from the Iranian Revolution and the Iraq War* (Ithaca, NY: Cornell University Press, 2010); Rovner, *Fixing the Facts*.

109. Policy makers rarely engage in direct manipulation of intelligence analysis to deliver products that support their preferred policies. But more subtle kinds of politicization, such as tacit signals that indicate the desired course of intelligence findings, are far more common and harder to prove. Alternatively, at the opposite extreme we may envision a scenario in which estimates put forward by the intelligence community heavily influence a key decision maker's assessment of the adversary's intentions. We should be able to detect such cases in the reasoning decision makers put forth to support their assessments.

110. When possible, I also conducted interviews with intelligence analysts and policy makers to explore the relationship between the intelligence community and policy makers during that time period. Public hearings (such as the confirmation hearings of Robert Gates in 1994) or secondary literature (for instance, on the effects of the Team B report on subsequent assessments of Soviet intentions) also serve as important resources, allowing examination of the views of intelligence analysts and policy makers who concurred with the estimates' conclusions at the time as well as those who objected to them.

Chapter 2: Indicators of Nazi Germany's Intentions and the Coming of World War II, 1934–39

1. Although this case study is not interested in how British assessments of intentions drove policy, I do examine the policies that British decision makers collectively or individually advocated as corroborating evidence of their assessments of intentions.

2. Robert C. Self, *Neville Chamberlain: A Biography* (Aldershot, UK: Ashgate Publishing Limited, 2006), 317.

3. Anthony R. Peters, *Anthony Eden at the Foreign Office, 1931–1938* (New York: St. Martin's Press, 1986), 46.

4. Ibid., 88.

5. Adam Roberts, *The Holy Fox: A Biography of Lord Halifax* (London: Weidenfeld and Nicolson, 1991), 72–74.

6. Michael Lawrence Roi, *Alternative to Appeasement: Sir Robert Vansittart and Alliance Diplomacy, 1934–1937* (Westport, CT: Praeger, 1997), 12.

7. Aaron L. Goldman, "Two Views of Germany: Nevile Henderson vs. Vansittart and the Foreign Office, 1937–1939," *British Journal of International Studies* 6, no. 3 (October 1980): 253.

8. Wesley K. Wark, *The Ultimate Enemy: British Intelligence and Nazi Germany, 1933–1939* (Ithaca, NY: Cornell University Press, 1985), 18.

9. Ibid., 36.

10. Unlike the capabilities thesis, the organizational expertise hypothesis does not predict what conclusions British intelligence would reach about German's intentions

from its military capabilities. The hypothesis simply predicts that the COS would rely on "bean-counting" practices in order to assess German intentions.

11. "Progress in German Military Rearmament, July to September 1934," October 19, 1934, War Office (WO), 32/6594, 1–5.

12. This calculation reflected the prevailing assumption that Hitler intended only to achieve air parity with France. As a memo by the Joint Intelligence Subcommittee noted, "Germany appears still to adhere to her intention, expressed in 1935, to achieve air parity with France and there has been nothing to indicate either a slackening or increase in the progress of expanding and increasing the potency of her Air Force." Joint Intelligence Subcommittee, "Foreign Armament," January 22, 1937, cabinet files (CAB) 56/2.

13. Wark, *The Ultimate Enemy*, 64. The Committee of Imperial Defence (CID), a standing advisory committee to the prime minister, was concerned by reports of the rapid increase in the German monthly rate of aircraft production. As a result, in late 1936 the British began to envision a scenario of a German knockout blow from the air. This led British decision makers to conclude that Britain should avoid war until its air defenses were improved. See Minutes of the 283rd Meeting of the CID, October 29, 1936, CAB 2/6, 176; "Estimated Scale of Air Attack on England in the Event of War with Germany," CID Memorandum by the COS Subcommittee, enclosure 2, June 16, 1937, CAB 3/6, 310. See also Gerald Lee, " 'I See Dead People': Air-Raid Phobia and Britain's Behavior in the Munich Crisis," *Security Studies* 13, no. 2 (Winter 2003–4): 230–72; Uri Bialer, *The Shadow of the Bomber: The Fear of Air Attack in British Politics, 1932–1939* (London: Royal Historical Society Press, 1980); G. Bruce Strang, "The Spirit of Ulysses? Ideology and British Appeasement in the 1930s," *Diplomacy and Statecraft* 19, no. 3 (September 2008): 491.

14. COS Committee, "Comparison of the Strength of Great Britain with That of Certain Other Nations," February 9, 1937, CAB 24/41. The COS repeated these conclusions in the report it circulated to the cabinet in November 1937. Ibid., November 12, 1937, CAB 24/296.

15. Norman Henry Gibbs, *Grand Strategy*, vol. 1, *Rearmament Policy* (London: Her Majesty's Stationery Office, 1976), 567. See also Minutes of the 298th Meeting of the CID, July 29, 1937, CAB 2/6, 275.

16. Minutes of the 316th Meeting of the CID, March 31, 1938, CAB 2/7, 151–152.

17. Fourth Strategic Appreciation report, quoted in Wark, *The Ultimate Enemy*, 214.

18. Still, the British air attaché concluded optimistically that "the disparity between the British and German outputs must be steadily growing less, and, even if the British air force cannot catch up with the German air force in actual numbers, the difference in the rate at which the two are expanding must be diminishing."

19. Wark, *The Ultimate Enemy*; David Dilks, "Appeasement and 'Intelligence,' " in *Retreat from Power, 1906–39*, vol. 1, *Studies in Britain's Foreign Policy of the Twentieth Century*, ed. David Dilks (London: Macmillan Press, 1981), 141–42; Barton Whaley, "Covert Rearmament in Germany, 1919–1939: Deception and Misperception," *Journal of Strategic Studies* 5, no. 1 (March 1982): 3–39.

20. Ministerial Subcommittee, "Report of the Ministerial Subcommittee on German Rearmament," November 23, 1934, CAB 24/268.

21. "The German Army: Its Present Strength and Possible Rate of Expansion in Peace and War," War Office Memorandum, January 1936, WO 190/379, 3–14. Hitler's

announcement surprised but did not alarm the War Office, given Germany's strategic requirements and Hitler's assurances that Germany had no intention of exceeding these figures. The Foreign Office, however, differed over the significance of this military buildup for the future balance of power and stability of Europe. The War Office expected an eastward German expansion driven largely by security concerns; since this region did not constitute a vital British interest, it did not object to giving Hitler a free hand to pursue this path. The Foreign Office, in contrast, argued that the expansion of the German army posed serious challenges to European stability.

22. War Office Note on Cabinet Paper No. CP 13(36), "The German Danger," January 27, 1936, WO 32/3593; "Suggested Amendments to Table 'A' of J.P. 111," Directorate of Military Intelligence Memorandum, May 13, 1936, WO 190/428, 2. Military Intelligence Section 3 (MI3b) also observed that German reequipment was proceeding so quickly that fifteen new divisions could be added each year. "The German Army: Its Present Strength and Possible Rate of Expansion in Peace and War," Directorate of Military Intelligence MI3b Memorandum, July 15, 1937, WO 190/555, 7–8; "Expansion of the German Army in 1936–1937," Directorate of Military Intelligence Memorandum, September 19, 1936, WO 190/459, 4; untitled document, Directorate of Military Intelligence Memorandum, November 26, 1936, WO 190/486, 2.

23. In November 1937, the COS Committee estimated that by January 1938, Germany would be able to put thirty-nine divisions into the field on the first day of war, with fifteen reserve divisions available in the first four days. COS Committee, "Comparison of the Strength of Great Britain with That of Certain Other Nations as of January 1938," November 12, 1937, CAB 24/296; "Developments in Germany's Military Organization," Directorate of Military Intelligence Memorandum, November 3, 1937, WO 190/543, 3.

24. COS Committee, "The German Army: Its Present Strength and Possible Rate of Expansion in Peace and War," April 28, 1938, CAB 24/276. Furthermore, Britain saw that as a result of the Anschluss, the German Army overall grew considerably. The Anschluss, to some extent at least, alleviated economic and raw material limitations on the pace of German rearmament. See "Germany: Economic Effect of Absorption of Austria," Directorate of Military Intelligence MI3b Memorandum, May 31, 1938, WO 190/629, 1–2. By mid-1938, Britain expected that the Germans would have 240 battle-ready divisions by 1942. See "The German Army: Its Present Organization and Strength," Directorate of Military Intelligence MI3b Memorandum, June 15, 1938, WO 190/634, 1.

25. Minutes of the 320th Meeting of the CID, April 28, 1938, CAB 2/7, 174. See also "Strength of the German Army," Directorate of Military Intelligence MI3b Memorandum, May 1938, WO 190/630, 43.

26. The War Office estimated Germany's total peacetime army at 52 divisions, and the potential wartime army at somewhere between 121 and 130 divisions. Wark, The Ultimate Enemy, 111.

27. The Foreign Office doubted the accuracy of these long-term estimates and whether Germany would respect the limits on its naval rearmament, but with no intelligence to support this speculation, the Foreign Office accepted the NID reports about the future rate of growth of the German fleet. Wark, The Ultimate Enemy, 135–40.

28. Ibid., 140.

29. By 1939, the Allies would possess marked air superiority in total first-line strength (4,560 versus 2,400), though only about 20 percent superiority in bombers (1,600 versus 1,200). The report indicated that the "combined British and French Fleets would be markedly superior to that of Germany." In 1935, the MI3b General Staff was optimistic about the Allied chances of victory against Germany in the event of war: "We do not think that by 1939 Germany will be in such a state of war-preparedness that she can engage in war against the United Kingdom, France, Belgium and possibly Holland with a reasonable chance of success." Note by the General Staff of MI3b, February 28, 1935, WO 190/303, 2.

30. COS Committee, "Appreciation of the Situation in the Event of War against Germany in 1939 by the Joint Planning Subcommittee," October 26, 1936, CAB 53/29. The report indicated that due to France's industrial limitations, Germany might maintain slight ground superiority through the first six months of a war in 1939, but after 1939, Germany's position was likely to be stronger. This report concluded that the Allies' current air rearmament programs were intended to attain numerical parity with Germany, but warned that French rearmament programs might lag. Consequently, the "Allies might have to face a German air striking force which had not only the great advantage of being under single control, but which was also superior in striking power" (ibid.).

31. COS Committee, "Draft Appreciation of the Situation in the Event of War against Germany in April 1939," July 1938, CAB 53/40.

32. Specifically, the February 1939 Strategic Appreciation report indicated that the German public was reluctant to go to war with Britain over Czechoslovakia and that there would be high morale among the British people in case of an attack on their homeland. The COS argued that during wartime, Germany's economy would have less capacity for expansion and endurance than Britain's. The War Office Directorate of Military Intelligence observed by January 1939 that the pace of German rearmament had exceeded the capacity of the German economy to sustain it. As a result, both British intelligence and many members of the cabinet believed that the German war machine could have great difficulty fighting a protracted war against Britain, which would use its naval superiority to impose a strategic blockade. See "Note on Germany's Present Position and Future Aims," Directorate of Military Intelligence Memorandum, January 7, 1939, WO 190/745; "Germany," Directorate of Military Intelligence Memorandum, January 23, 1939, WO 190/746, 1; "Germany," Directorate of Military Intelligence Memorandum, March 2, 1939, WO 190/753, 1; Minutes of the 35th Meeting of the Cabinet Foreign Policy Committee, F.P. (36) 35th Mtg., January 23, 1939, CAB 27/624, 104.

33. Norrin M. Ripsman and Jack S. Levy, "Playing It Straight or Politicized Process? British Military Intelligence and the Nazi Threat, 1933–39" (paper presented at Princeton University, April 28–29, 2011), 18; Norrin M. Ripsman and Jack S. Levy, "Wishful Thinking or Buying Time? The Logic of British Appeasement in the 1930s," *International Security* 33, no. 2 (2008): 177–80. Michael Howard disagrees, suggesting that at this time British deficiencies had still not been remedied, but he acknowledges that some improvement in British air defenses had been achieved. Michael Howard, "British Military Preparations for the Second World War," in *Retreat from Power, 1906–39*, vol. 1, *Studies in Britain's Foreign Policy of the Twentieth Century*, ed. David Dilks (London: Macmillan Press, 1981), 116–17.

34. British intelligence underwent yet another change in its assessments—this time from extreme pessimism to relative optimism—in early 1939. This shift occurred even though British intelligence continued to report an unabated expansion of German capabilities. Both the numerical balance of military capabilities and deployment of these capabilities—the dimensions of power most relevant for deriving predictions from the capabilities thesis—were reported to have *worsened* from the perspective of British policy makers. Wark (*The Ultimate Enemy*, 231) contends that the roots of this peculiar optimism came not from calculation of the numerical balance of power but rather from perceptions that German economic potential could not sustain this massive buildup in the event of war and that the morale of the German soldiers had decreased. These are not considerations relevant to the narrow perspective of the capabilities thesis, however.

35. Thomas J. Christensen, "Perceptions and Alliances in Europe, 1865–1940," *International Organization* 51, no. 1 (1997): 65–97; Stephen Van Evera, "Offense-Defense and the Causes of War," *International Security* 22, no. 4 (1998): 5–43. In Christensen's view, British decision makers' belief that defense was dominant enabled them to avoid a trade-off between arms and allies, and to believe that no state could accomplish quick victories in land warfare. In light of these expectations, Britain reinforced its naval and air defenses, trusting the French to provide an effective ground defense (with the Maginot Line) to stem any German military advance, at least in the short term. As Christensen and Snyder note, "Confidence in the Maginot line and the extra cushion provided by Britain's off-shore position gave the British the luxury of *waiting until the evidence of Hitler's intentions was all in*" (emphasis added). Thomas J. Christensen and Jack Snyder, "Chain Gangs and Passed Bucks: Predicting Alliance Patterns in Multipolarity," *International Organization* 44, no. 2 (1990): 163.

36. Barry R. Posen, *The Sources of Military Doctrine: France, Britain, and Germany between the World Wars* (Ithaca, NY: Cornell University Press, 1984), 179.

37. See Matthew Cooper, *The German Army, 1933–1945* (Chelsea, MI: Scarborough House, 1997), 115–16; Posen, *The Sources of Military Doctrine*, 210–12.

38. Posen, *The Sources of Military Doctrine*, 210.

39. Dispatch by Colonel Frederick Hotblack, August 31, 1937, Foreign Office (FO) 371/20731. See also Hotblack Memo, February 23, 1938, WO 216/189. Quoted in Wark, *The Ultimate Enemy*, 97.

40. See Donald C. Watt, "British Intelligence and the Coming of the Second World War in Europe," in *Knowing One's Enemies: Intelligence Assessment before the Two World Wars*, ed. Ernest R. May (Princeton, NJ: Princeton University Press, 1984), 252; F. H. Hinsley, *British Intelligence in the Second World War*, abr. (New York: Cambridge University Press, 1993), 77–79.

41. Wark, *The Ultimate Enemy*, 97.

42. Colonel Noel Mason-Macfarlane, July 15, 1938, WO 190/640.

43. Cooper, *The German Army*, 113–17; Wark, *The Ultimate Enemy*, 98.

44. Hinsley, *British Intelligence in the Second World War*, 76.

45. Indeed, as Posen (*The Sources of Military Doctrine*, 86) argues, "By 1940 elements within the German Army had created (though the army had not yet fully adopted) a new doctrine—Blitzkrieg." Moreover, the War Office at the time deferred questions relating to the German Army to the French, who at the time did not anticipate Germany's blitzkrieg. Hinsley, *British Intelligence in the Second World War*, 76–77.

46. British decision makers were still alarmed when, in September, Germany rejected an eastern Locarno pact that would resolve ongoing territorial disagreements with Poland. In March 1935, Hitler announced that Germany had already achieved parity in air strength with France and reintroduced compulsory military service as part of his effort to rebuild the German military. During the next month Germany expressed its willingness to sign an eastern nonaggression pact. In May, in an important foreign policy statement to the Reichstag, Hitler declared Germany's desire for peace while making demands for a peaceful revision of the status quo. In the same speech, Hitler also promised not to impinge on Austrian sovereignty, renounced the armaments clauses of the Treaty of Versailles, promised to scrupulously fulfill treaties voluntarily undertaken, and expressed willingness for Germany to participate in systems of collective cooperation for safeguarding European peace. He also expressed the rejection of unilateral imposition of terms, a willingness to enter an air agreement, a willingness to agree on arms limitations, and an insistence on an agreement to prevent interference in the internal affairs of other states. Put together, the signals that Germany was sending were mixed, though arguably more negative than positive.

47. Zach Shore, "Hitler, Intelligence, and the Decision to Remilitarize the Rhine," *Journal of Contemporary History*, 34, no. 1 (1999): 5–18. Britain condemned German actions and reaffirmed its commitment to France two days later. The same day it remilitarized the Rhineland, Germany also offered to enter negotiations to create a mutually demilitarized zone with France, Belgium, and the Netherlands; conclude twenty-five-year nonaggression pacts with France and Belgium; ask Britain and Italy to sign the pacts as guarantors; conclude an air pact; conclude nonaggression pacts with countries on Germany's eastern border; and reenter the League of Nations.

48. As 1936 ended, Germany renounced its acceptance of the international control of the Rhine, Elbe, Oder, and Danube rivers provided in the Treaty of Versailles. Eden expressed "regrets" over the steps taken by Germany, claiming that "the German Government would once again have abandoned procedure by negotiation in favour of unilateral action." Eden, House of Commons, November 16, 1936.

49. In October, Germany notified Belgium that it intended to respect its integrity and lend its support if Belgium were attacked so long as Belgium did not participate in joint military action against Germany.

50. See, for example, Report by William Strang, July 6, 1937, Documents on British Foreign Policy (*DBFP*), part II, vol. XIX, no. 21; Letter from Alexander Cadogan to Nevile Henderson, July 8, 1937, *DBFP*, part II, vol. XIX, o. 26.

51. On March 11, Germany declared that two hundred thousand German troops would cross the Austrian frontier unless the following conditions were met: that Austrian chancellor Kurt Schuschnigg resign; that Arthur SeyssInquart assume the chancellorship; that Nazis would be appointed to at least two-thirds of the positions in the new cabinet; that full and unrestricted liberty would be granted to the Austrian Nazi Party; and that the "Austrian Legion" of Nazi exiles would be readmitted to Austria. Schuschnigg resigned later that day, and SeyssInquart requested that German troops be sent to Austria. SeyssInquart appealed to the Austrian public for peace and order along with nonresistance to the German Army. German troops entered Austria on March 12, 1938. After this episode, Germany again sent reassuring signals aimed at Hungary, Italy, Switzerland, and Yugoslavia that their frontiers would be respected, and claimed that German policy had no aims beyond Austria.

52. Prime Minister Chamberlain said that the Anglo-French Munich guarantee did not apply because it had not been ratified.

53. US House of Representatives, 78th Cong., 2d Sess., "Events Leading Up to World War II: Chronological History of Certain Major International Events Leading Up to and during World War II with the Ostensible Reasons Advanced for their Occurrence, 1931–1944," House Document No. 541, *British*, No. 22, 69; *German*, No. 294, 313f, http://www.ibiblio.org/pha/events/index.html (accessed May 7, 2008).

54. The list of costly actions considered here does not include actions undertaken in the Reich and Austria by the Nazis against Jewish minorities and other declared "enemies of the state," such as the Night of the Long Knives and Kristallnacht. It is not clear to what extent such actions should be deemed costly signals. Changes in the nature of Germany's domestic institutions are also not discussed here at length. Arguably the most significant domestic political change took place in 1933, when the Reichstag passed the Enabling Acts that established Hitler's dictatorship. As we will see, British discussions over Germany's intentions did not focus on these indicators to gauge Germany's foreign policy intentions. In the following chapters, I do include instances in which they talked about these domestic actions.

55. Observers drew different inferences about Germany from the events before and during World War I, but this hypothesis merely expects British observers to link their current assessments of Hitler's intentions to Germany's costly actions before or during the First World War. See, for instance, Memo by Eric Phipps (British ambassador to Berlin and later to Paris) to Eden, April 13, 1937, *DBFP*, part II, vol. XIX, no. 399; COS Committee, "Annual Review for 1933 by the Chiefs of Staff," October 12, 1933, CAB 16/109.

CHAPTER 3: BRITISH DECISION MAKERS' PERCEPTIONS OF NAZI GERMANY'S INTENTIONS

1. Because I concentrate on British decision makers in the interwar period, I do not analyze how Winston Churchill assessed Nazi German intentions. Churchill is of historical interest not only because of the major role he played during the Second World War but also because he correctly judged Nazi intentions as incorrigibly hostile and revisionist. Nevertheless, I exclude him from this study for two reasons. First, he did not occupy an official cabinet post during the 1930s. Second, because he was a marginalized politician during much of that period, Churchill presumably had access to different information than that which actual decision makers at the time observed. Including Churchill in the analysis would therefore mean that I could not control for the information sets across decision makers. Churchill's views of Germany's intentions are well documented in Martin Gilbert, *Winston Churchill: The Wilderness Years, Speaking Out against Hitler in the Prelude to War* (London: Macmillan London Limited, 1981); William Manchester, *The Last Lion: Winston Spencer Churchill, Alone, 1932–1940* (Boston: Little, Brown and Company, 1988); Lynne Olson, *Troublesome Young Men: The Rebels Who Brought Churchill to Power and Helped Save England* (New York: Farrar, Straus and Giroux, 2007).

2. "The Foreign Policy of the Present German Government," May 16, 1933, CAB 24/241. The newly appointed British ambassador to Berlin, Phipps, shared these views. Memo by Eric Phipps, October 25, 1933, CAB 24/259.

3. Memo by John Simon, "Austria," January 22, 1934, CAB 24/247.

4. Quoted in Anthony R. Peters, *Anthony Eden at the Foreign Office, 1931–1938* (New York: St. Martin's Press, 1986), 47–48.

5. Quoted in Peters, *Anthony Eden at the Foreign Office*, 48–49; David Dutton, *Anthony Eden: A Life and Reputation* (New York: St. Gilbert's Press, 1997), 35; David Carlton, *Anthony Eden: A Biography* (New York: Viking, 1981), 45–47. Eden later wrote, "Perhaps I attach too much importance to Hitler's offer to me . . . because . . . I much doubt if Hitler and Musso would ever have held to any agreements we made with them." Quoted in Dutton, *Anthony Eden*, 36.

6. Since this chapter deals only with assessments by civilian decision makers, the analysis focuses on the perceptions of the three civil servants on the DRC: Vansittart, Warren Fisher, and Maurice Hankey.

7. On January 25, Vansittart argued that it was "quite a conceivable contingency" that Germany would initiate a war against Britain and France within the foreseeable future. Minutes of the Seventh DRC Meeting, January 25, 1934, 3–4, CAB 16/109.

8. Minutes of the Ninth DRC Meeting, January 30, 1934, 11–12, CAB 16/109.

9. Committee of Imperial Defence, Defence Requirements Subcommittee Report, February 28, 1934, CAB 16/109.

10. Memo by John Simon, "Germany's Illegal Rearmament and Its Effect on British Policy," March 21, 1934, CAB 24/247.

11. Hoare believed that Germany "would not be likely to risk an attack." He thought that Britain "might eventually be driven to it," but it was, in his opinion, not "yet at that point." Cabinet Meeting, March 19, 1934, CAB 23/78.

12. Ibid.

13. Simon asserted that Hitler's intentions were not to disarm his neighbors but rather to obtain formal recognition of Germany's illegal armaments, because such a move would strengthen Hitler's position at home and abroad. Yet Simon estimated that Hitler would not seek such recognition immediately given that German rearmament was "still insufficient to remove the fear of effective military intervention by France and especially to secure the defense." Memo by John Simon, "Germany's Illegal Rearmament and Its Effect on British Policy," March 21, 1934, CAB 24/247.

14. Memo by Robert Vansittart, "The Future of Germany," April 7, 1934, CAB 24/247.

15. The Ministerial Committee discussed the DRC report at thirteen meetings from early May to late July 1934. The committee consisted of Simon (foreign secretary), Chamberlain (chancellor of the exchequer), James Henry Thomas (secretary of state for dominion affairs), Bolton Eyres-Monsell (first lord of the admiralty), Douglass Hogg (secretary of state for war), Charles Vane-Tempest-Stewart (secretary of state for air), and Eden (lord privy seal). Chamberlain and Simon argued that the German "rate of re-armament in the air was increasing rapidly," and that Germany constituted "the maximum risk and the worst case so far as the army was concerned," whereas the German naval threat appeared more distant. Ministerial Committee Meeting, May 3, 1934, CAB 16/110. Hankey and Ernie Chatfield disagreed with this assessment, contending that it was Japan that represented the principal danger to Britain's interests. Minute by Maurice Hankey, June 22, 1934, CAB 63/49, quoted in Peter Bell, *Chamberlain, Germany, and Japan, 1933-4* (New York: St. Martin's Press, 1996), 125–27.

16. Because of his unwillingness to commit enough resources to the Expeditionary Forces, Chamberlain was accused of giving in to public pressure. The General Staff (as well as the Dominions Office) criticized Chamberlain's program, claiming that in

order to deter Germany and defend itself, Britain must also be able to protect the integrity of Belgium and Holland. For this, the army needed to be ready in less than five years. The only consensus at the time was the expectation that Germany would first attack in the East with some possibility of a subsequent attack in the West. Ministerial Committee Meeting, May 15, 1934, CAB 16/110. The Ministerial Committee's final report approved the DRC's case on its merits, but financial considerations and international developments led the committee to present a fresh defense program. Army requirements as well as the necessity to secure the Low Countries were conceded, with the reservation that public opinion might not endorse these continental commitments. Air defense against Germany was stressed, together with the assumption that the German air force posed the greatest threat to Britain's security. On July 31, the cabinet approved the DRC report as amended by the Ministerial Committee on Disarmament. Report by Ministerial Committee on Defence Requirements, July 31, 1934, CAB 25/250.

17. Eden believed that Britain could no longer play the role of an honest broker between Germany and France, and advocated the creation of a concerted front to oppose Germany. Peters, *Anthony Eden at the Foreign Office*, 88–91. Eden's diary account reads, "Simon toyed with the idea of letting G. expands eastwards. I am strongly against it. Apart from its dishonesty it would be our turn next." Quoted in Dutton, *Anthony Eden*, 50.

18. Cabinet Meeting, March 20, 1935, CAB 23/81.

19. Quoted in Peters, *Anthony Eden at the Foreign Office*, 98.

20. In March, Hitler also declared to British officials that Germany had already attained parity with Britain in the air and that he intended to achieve parity with France.

21. On the Naval Agreement, see Norman Henry Gibbs, *Grand Strategy*, vol. 1, *Rearmament Policy* (London: Her Majesty's Stationery Office, 1976), 155–70; Hines H. Hall III, "The Foreign Policy-Making Process in Britain and the Origins of the Anglo-German Naval Agreement," *Historical Journal* 19, no. 2 (1976): 477–99.

22. Programs of the Defense Services, Third Report, November 21, 1935, CAB 24/259.

23. Eden recommended that Britain hasten its rearmament while keeping open the option of reaching some modus vivendi with Germany. Memo by Anthony Eden, "The German Danger," January 17, 1936, CAB 27/599.

24. "German Ministers' Speeches; Memorandum by Secretary of State for Foreign Affairs," February 10, 1936, CAB 24/260.

25. "Letter from Sir E. Phipps (Berlin) to Sir R. Vansittart," January 22, 1936, C 585/4/18, *BDFP*, part II, vol. XV, 582–83.

26. Memo by Robert Vansittart, "Britain, France, and Germany," February 3, 1936, CAB 24/260.

27. "Memorandum by Mr. Wigram on the Rhineland Demilitarised Zone," C 291/4/18, *BDFP*, part II, vol. XV, 564–65. There were serious disagreements within the British military over the effectiveness of the zone. See "Memorandum by the Secretary of State of Air on the Rhineland Demilitarised Zone," January 27, 1936, *BDFP*, part II, vol. XV, 606–7; "Memorandum by the Secretary of State for War on the Rhineland Demilitarised Zone," January 27, 1936, *BDFP*, part II, vol. XV, 609–10. See also Gibbs, *Grand Strategy*, 230–32. Diplomatically, due to the "highly delicate and complicated" nature of this issue, British officials wished to avoid any discussions with the French over British policy toward the zone in case of a German reoccupation. Memo by Anthony Eden, "Rhineland Demilitarised Zone," February 14, 1936, CAB 27/599.

28. Memo by Anthony Eden, "Germany and the Locarno Treaty," March 8, 1936, CAB 24/261.
29. Memo by Eric Phipps to Anthony Eden, March 11, 1936, *BDFP*, part II, vol. XVI, no. 65.
30. Minutes by Robert Vansittart, March 17, 1936, *DBFP*, part II, vol. XVI, no. 121.
31. *DBFP*, part II, vol. XVI, no. 340. See also Foreign Office memos, *DBFP*, part II, vol. XVI, nos. 139, 306, 324, 328.
32. Note by Robert Vansittart, April 1936, *DBFP*, part II, vol. XVI, no. 204.
33. Memo by Anthony Eden, "Germany," April 25, 1936, CAB 24/262.
34. Ibid., July 20, 1936, CAB 24/263.
35. It was not, he continued, because "anyone, even Herr Hitler, was, so far as he knew, projecting warlike operations, but that the various nations were in such ferment that some episode might precipitate danger." Memo prepared by the Foreign Office for the Committee on Foreign Policy, July 13, 1936, CAB 27/626.
36. Germany's course of action was thought to depend on whether the moderate school in Germany, which included the army, the Foreign Office, and some officials, would be able to overcome the hawkish members of the Nazi Party. Cabinet Meeting, January 8, 1937, CAB 23/87.
37. Memo by Eric Phipps, January 4, 1937, *DBFP*, part II, vol. XVIII, no. 8.
38. Minutes by Orme Sargent on Remarks by Herr Ernst Woermann (German Diplomat), January 12, 1937, *DBFP*, part II, vol. XVIII, no. 59, n3.
39. The changes Eden demanded would include the entry of Germany into a new version of the Locarno Treaty that would redress the shortcomings of the 1925 Locarno Treaties in resolving territorial claims on Germany's eastern borders. These changes included the encouragement of an abandonment of Germany's policy of economic self-sufficiency and the corollary of territorial expansion, establishment of neighborly relations with Czechoslovakia, readiness to consider a means for putting a stop to the present armaments race, and Germany's return to the League of Nations. Memo by Anthony Eden to Sir Frederick Leith-Ross, January 19, 1937, *DBFP*, part II, vol. XVIII.
40. Memo by Anthony Eden, Anglo-German Relations with Particular Reference to the Colonial Question, March 15, 1937, CAB 27/626.
41. Letter by Robert Vansittart to Anthony Eden, January 25, 1937, *DBFP*, part II, vol. XVIII, no. 116.
42. Memo by Anthony Eden on the Colonial Question, March 22, 1937, *DBFP*, part II, vol. XVIII, no. 326, n7.
43. Committee on Foreign Policy Meeting, May 10, 1937, CAB 27/622.
44. Memo by Neville Chamberlain, Anglo-German Relations, April 2, 1937, CAB 27/626.
45. Memo by Lord Halifax to Eric Phipps, February 11, 1937, *DBFP*, part II, vol. XVIII, no. 167; Memo by Eric Phipps to Foreign Office, February 13, 1937, *DBFP*, part II, vol. XVIII, no. 175; Memo by Anthony Eden to Eric Phipps, March 23, 1937, *DBFP*, part II, vol. XVIII, no. 336.
46. Memo prepared by the Foreign Office for the Committee on Foreign Policy, July 13, 1936, CAB 27/626.
47. Memo by Eric Phipps to Anthony Eden, April 15, 1937, *DBFP*, part II, vol. XVIII, no. 404, n2. Phipps cautioned that as Germany's rearmament was nearing completion,

and "her entente with Italy has strengthened her position," there was no reason "to set a limit to German ambitions." In fact, the younger generation in Germany now believed, according to Phipps, that once-distant aims appeared "capable of realization." Memo by Eric Phipps to Anthony Eden, April 13, 1937, *DBFP*, part II, vol. XVIII, no. 399.

48. Letter from Orme Sargent to Eric Drummond, May 13, 1937, *DBFP*, part II, vol. XVIII, no. 493. The German air force reportedly began to "indulge in war games with England as the [inevitable] enemy." Adding to the concerns were reports from various sources of a decrease in the influence on Hitler of moderate voices and an overall heightened level of anxiety in Germany. Memo by Nevile Henderson to Foreign Office, May 25, 1937, *DBFP*, part II, XVIII, no. 538.

49. Letter from Nevile Henderson to Anthony Eden, July 1, 1937, *DBFP*, part II, vol. XIX, no. 10.

50. Memo by Nevile Henderson to Anthony Eden, July 5, 1937, *DBFP*, part II, vol. XIX, no. 16.

51. Nevile Henderson to Anthony Eden, July 8, 1937, *DBFP*, part II, vol. XIX, no. 27; Nevile Henderson to Alexander Cadogan, July 12, 1937, *DBFP*, part II, vol. XIX, no. 33.

52. Enclosed Memo by Nevile Henderson on British Policy toward Germany, May 10, 1937, *DBFP*, part II, vol. XIX, no. 53.

53. Memo of a Conversation with Hermann Göring, September 17, 1937, *DBFP*, part II, vol. XIX, annex IV to no. 160.

54. Letter from Neville Chamberlain to his sister Ida Chamberlain, November 26, 1937, *DBFP*, part II, vol. XIX, no. 349.

55. Minutes of the Cabinet Meeting (hereafter referred to as MCM), November 24, 1937, CAB 23/90.

56. MCM, March 9, 1938, CAB 23/92.

57. MCM, February 16, 1938, CAB 23/92.

58. MCM, March 12, 1938, CAB 23/92.

59. Ibid.

60. Memo by Nevile Henderson to Lord Halifax, March 24, 1939, *DBFP*, part III, vol. I, no. 115.

61. Minutes of the Committee on Foreign Policy, March 21, 1938, appendix I, CAB 27/623.

62. Ibid.

63. Report by the COS Committee, "Military Implications of German Aggression against Czechoslovakia," March 21, 1938, CAB 27/627.

64. Minutes of the Committee on Foreign Policy, March 18, 1938, appendix I, CAB 27/623.

65. Ibid.

66. Ibid. Addressing the assertion that it was Britain's duty to help France save Czechoslovakia, Halifax cited the COS report on the military's lack of readiness, which confirmed his contention that there was not really any genuine alternative to diplomacy. Ibid., March 21, 1938, appendix I, CAB 27/623.

67. Ibid., March 18, 1938, CAB 27/623.

68. Memo by Lord Halifax, "Possibility of Modifying Czechoslovakia's Treaties of Mutual Assistance with France and Russia," June 14, 1938, CAB 27/627.

69. MCM, July 13, 1938, CAB 23/94

70. The only policy Britain could adopt, as a practical matter, was to keep Hitler guessing about Britain's intentions while simultaneously putting pressure on Czechoslovakia's government to reach an agreement with Germany. Chamberlain as well as the rest of the cabinet agreed with Halifax's assessment. MCM, August 30, 1938, CAB 23/94.

71. MCM, September 17, 1938, CAB 23/95.

72. Ibid.

73. "Meeting of Ministers on 'The Situation in Czechoslovakia,'" September 16, 1938, CAB 27/646.

74. Quoted in Adam Roberts, *The Holy Fox: A Biography of Lord Halifax* (London: Weidenfeld and Nicolson, 1991), 115. See also David Dilks, ed., *The Diaries of Sir Alexander Cadogan, O.M., 1938–1945* (London: Cassell, 1971), 105 (September 25, 1938).

75. MCM, September 25, 1938, CAB 23/95.

76. Quoted in Roberts, *The Holy Fox*, 117–18.

77. MCM, September 17, 1938, CAB 23/95.

78. MCM, September 25, 1938, CAB 23/95. By contrast, although some in the cabinet, including the president of the Board of Education, acknowledged the variances between Hitler's past declarations and actions and the statements he had made personally to the prime minister, they did not explain why they still thought Hitler's assurances should be trusted.

79. Memo by Gladwyn Jebb, "Summary of Information from Secret Sources," January 19, 1939, circulated to the Committee on Foreign Policy by Lord Halifax, CAB 27/627.

80. Ibid.

81. Wesley K. Wark, "Something Very Stern: British Political Intelligence, Moralism, and Grand Strategy in 1939," *Intelligence and National Security* 5, no. 1 (1990): 157. Indeed, the Nazi Party's violent public assault on German Jews on November 10—Kristallnacht, the "night of broken glass"—may have served as a manifestation of Germany's hostile attitudes that disgusted Chamberlain.

82. "Germany: Factors, Aims, Methods, etc.," December 20, 1938, FO 1093/86.

83. Ibid.

84. Ibid.

85. Ibid. (emphasis in original).

86. Ibid.

87. Memo by Olivie-Forbes to Lord Halifax, December 6, 1938, *DBFP*, part III, vol. III, no. 403.

88. Memo by Gladwyn Jebb, "Summary of Information from Secret Sources," January 19, 1939, part II, CAB 27/627.

89. MCM, January 18, 1939, CAB 23/97.

90. Memo by Lord Halifax, "Possible German Intentions," January 19, 1938, CAB 27/627.

91. Minutes by Alexander Cadogan, January 6, 1939, FO 371/22690.

92. Another Foreign Office memo similarly predicted that Hitler would use military as well as nonmilitary means such as propaganda to achieve his objectives of world domination. "Two Memoranda Communicated to the Foreign Office by Prominent Germanophils," circulated to the Committee on Foreign Policy by Lord Halifax, CAB 27/627. Halifax believed that Hitler's change of plans was rooted in Germany's increasingly desperate financial and economic conditions, which compelled Hitler to conquer further territories. The objectives of such an "explosion," as Halifax put it, "would be to distract attention from the failure of his system to work in time of peace;

to provide an excuse for suppressing the German 'Moderates'; and no doubt also—perhaps mainly—to secure by physical force the vast supplies of raw material which Nazi Germany could no longer produce by legitimate methods of trade." Statement by Lord Halifax, "Germany," circulated to the cabinet on January 25, 1939, CAB 23/97.

93. Minutes by Alexander Cadogan, January 6, 1939, FO 371/22690.

94. MCM, February 8, 1939, CAB 23/97.

95. Henderson was absent from Germany from November to early February for medical reasons, but immediately on his return, he reported that the Germans were not contemplating an immediate attack.

96. Memo by Nevile Henderson to Lord Halifax, February 18, 1939, *DBFP*, part II, vol. XV, no. 118.

97. Henderson was certain that his information was correct. The head of the Central Department concurred that Henderson's assessment was supported by other independent sources. *DBFP*, part III, vol. IV, 160–61.

98. Henderson added a note at the end that the memo was written before the crisis in Czechoslovakia became acute, and therefore should be regarded as "academical" for the moment. Memo by Nevile Henderson to Lord Halifax, March 9, 1939, *DBFP*, part III, vol. IV, no. 195.

99. Robert C. Self, *Neville Chamberlain: A Biography* (Aldershot, UK: Ashgate Publishing Limited, 2006), 347.

100. Letter from Neville Chamberlain to his sister Hilda Chamberlain, February 19, 1939, quoted in *Neville Chamberlain*, 348; Kennedy Dispatch 246, February 17, 1939, quoted in Self, *Neville Chamberlain*, 348. See also Letter from Nevile Henderson to Alexander Cadogan, FO 800/294; Minutes by Orme Sargent, FO 800/294.

101. Roberts, *The Holy Fox*, 141.

102. Wark, "Something Very Stern," 161.

103. "Foreign Office Memo on the Situation after the Absorption of Czecho-Slovakia, and on the Policy of His Majesty's Government," March 29, 1939, *DBFP*, part III, vol. IV, appendix IV.

104. MCM, March 15, 1939, CAB 23/98.

105. *DBFP*, part III, vol. VII, 270–72.

106. Dilks, *The Diaries of Sir Alexander Cadogan*, 163, 151.

107. MCM, March 18, 1939, CAB 23/98. According to Self (*Neville Chamberlain*, 357–82), at this time Chamberlain still believed that Hitler might be persuaded to give up his ambitious designs. The change in tone and policies reflected Chamberlain's desire "to bring Hitler to his senses." In other words, Chamberlain still thought that Germany was an unlimited opportunistic power as opposed to an unlimited expansionist power. There is some evidence to support this conclusion: during spring and summer 1939, Chamberlain engaged in a series of secret and unofficial contacts with the Nazi leadership in an attempt to reach a negotiated settlement with Hitler.

108. In a letter to his sister Hilda, Chamberlain explained that he later regretted these words, and said that he had not had time to digest what had happened and had "no time to consider our attitudes." Letter to Hilda Chamberlain, March 19, 1939, quoted in Robert C. Self, *Neville Chamberlain Diary Letters: The Downing Street Years, 1934–1940* (Aldershot, UK: Ashgate Publishing Limited, 2005), 393.

109. On the evening of March 17, 1939, Chamberlain spoke at the annual meeting of the Birmingham Unionist Association and referred in strong terms to Hitler's violation of the Munich Agreement.

110. MCM, March 18, 1939, CAB 23/98.

111. MCM, March 20, 1939, CAB 23/98.

112. The analytic focus here is on certain key decision makers who were vocal in expressing their assessments about German intentions, somewhat explicit in their reasoning, and central to the process of formulating British foreign policy toward Germany during this time period: two secretaries of foreign affairs (Eden and Halifax), Prime Minister Chamberlain, and high-level officials in the Foreign Office, including the two permanent undersecretaries, Cadogan and Vansittart, and the British ambassadors to Berlin, Henderson and Phipps.

113. Surprisingly, I have found little proof to support the past actions hypothesis of the behavior thesis. The COS appeared to have looked to the history of World War I to estimate Germany's strategy and tactics, but not its intentions.

114. Before Hitler had signed the pact with Poland, Vansittart thought that the "Germans' ambitions had lain in the following order of preference: (i) Austria, (ii) Poland, and (iii) a Colonial Empire." The pact, if Hitler was indeed sincere about it, would mean that Britain's "difficulties might occur the sooner," and that Hitler would sooner be free to turn his attention to Austria and Czechoslovakia. Minutes of the Ninth DRC Meeting, January 30, 1934, CAB 16/109.

115. Defence Requirements Subcommittee Report, February 28, 1934, CAB 24/247.

116. Memo by Robert Vansittart, "The Future of Germany," April 7, 1934, *DBFP*, part II, vol. VI, appendix II.

117. Ibid.

118. Dutton, *Anthony Eden*, 35.

119. Peters, *Anthony Eden at the Foreign Office*, 89–90.

120. Minutes by William Strang, January 31, 1936, *DBFP*, part II, vol. XV, no. 490.

121. "Report by the Committee on German Re-armament," December 20, 1934, CAB 27/572.

122. Minutes of the First Meeting of the Foreign Policy Committee, November 22, 1934, CAB 27/572.

123. MCM, March 19, 1934, CAB 23/78.

124. MCM, July 4, 1934, CAB 23/79.

125. Memo by Eric Phipps to Samuel Hoare, November 13, 1935, *DBFP*, part II, vol. XV, no. 213. For example, the growing number of air defense schools and instructors signaled to the Foreign Office that Germany was not merely interested in equality of rights. Instead, such developments were taken as evidence that Germany's aim "was so clearly superiority." Ibid., November 18, 1935, *DBFP*, part II, vol. XV, no. 228, n1. "Germany may be said without exaggeration to be living in a state of war." Ibid., November 13, 1935, *DBFP*, part II, vol. XV, no. 213. To be sure, German military capabilities, as we will see in the next chapter, were intimately linked to assessments of Germany's *military* intentions in a manner that is consistent with the capabilities thesis. Further, decision makers during that period debated whether the German buildup was offensive or defensive in nature. See Meeting of Committee on German Rearmament, November 22, 1934, CAB 27/572.

126. Memo by Anthony Eden, "Germany and the Locarno Treaty," March 8, 1936, CAB 24/261.

127. MCM, March 11, 1936, CAB 23/83. Vansittart proposed a test with different kinds of observable indicators. In a memo shortly after the Rhineland crisis, he cautioned that "the real test of Germany's intentions will be . . . whether Germany intends to

correct the systematic deformation of the German mind before it is too late." But he too endorsed Eden's questionnaire. On Vansittart's rationale and litmus test, see Michael Lawrence Roi, *Alternative to Appeasement: Sir Robert Vansittart and Alliance Diplomacy, 1934–1937* (Westport, CT: Praeger, 1997), 129.

128. Memo by Anthony Eden, "Germany," July 20, 1936, CAB 24/263.

129. Ibid., April 25, 1936, CAB 24/262.

130. Vansittart also justified his perceptions of Germany's intentions by referring to his own observations of Hitler's domestic policies, especially "the militarization of the whole nation in all its aspects," which he saw as a means by which Hitler sought to achieve his foreign policy goals, including "the destruction of the peace settlement and the establishment of Germany as the dominant power in Europe." Memo by Robert Vansittart, "The German Danger," January 17, 1936, CAB 24/259.

131. Memo by Orme Sargent and Ralph Wigram on "Britain, France, and Germany," November 21, 1935, *BDFP*, part II, vol. XV, appendix I.

132. Memo by Anthony Eden, "German Ministers' Speeches," February 10, 1936, CAB 24/260.

133. Memo by Eric Phipps to Anthony Eden, October 22, 1936, *DBFP*, part II, vol. XVII, no. 318.

134. Memo by Nevile Henderson to Anthony Eden, July 5, 1937, *DBFP*, part II, vol. XIX, no. 16, n4.

135. Memo by Nevile Henderson to Lord Halifax, May 14, 1938, *DBFP*, part III, vol. I, no. 218.

136. Ibid., no. 121.

137. Ibid., no. 218.

138. For example, after Goebbels's reported declarations in November 1936 that nothing was further from Hitler's mind than war, Wigram, Sargent, and Vansittart wrote in a comment: "We must not forget that German leaders have constantly emphasized the pacific intentions of Germany and of Herr Hitler himself. . . . Therefore this action on the part of Dr. Goebbels need not surprise us. It is accompanied, as we know, by wholesale preparations for war and in particular, by the extraordinary campaign for 'Wehrfreudigkeit' [the joy of war]." Memo by Eric Phipps to Anthony Eden, November 27, 1936, *DBFP*, part II, vol. XVII, no. 416, n2.

139. Memo by Eric Phipps to Anthony Eden, April 13, 1937, *DBFP*, part II, vol. XIX, no. 399.

140. The Night of the Long Knives refers to a purge that took place in Nazi Germany between June 30 and July 2, 1934, when the Nazi regime carried out a series of political murders of officials who objected to Hitler and his policies.

141. MCM, November 24, 1937, CAB 23/90; Roberts, *The Holy Fox*, 72–75.

142. Letter from Neville Chamberlain to his sister Ida Chamberlain, November 26, 1937, *DBFP*, part II, vol. XIX, no. 349.

143. Minutes of the Visit of French Ministers to London, December 6, 1937, CAB 27/626.

144. Memo by Nevile Henderson to Anthony Eden, November 7, 1937, *DBFP*, part II, vol. XIX, no. 298.

145. Draft Memo for the French Government, "Situation in Central Europe: Czechoslovakia," March 21, 1938, CAB 27/627.

146. Letter from Nevile Henderson to Anthony Eden, July 1, 1937, *DBFP*, part II, vol. XIX, no. 10.

147. Quoted in Self, *Neville Chamberlain*, 348.

148. "Meeting of Ministers on 'the Situation in Czechoslovakia,'" September 16, 1938, CAB 27/646.

149. Quoted in Self, *Neville Chamberlain*, 350.

150. Ibid., 347–48.

151. Letter from Secretary of the Board of Trade to Neville Chamberlain, October 3, 1938, private papers, PREM, 1/266A.

152. The primary sources were intelligence reports from "reliable sources," some of which were identified in the documents as, for example, "a prominent member of the German Foreign Office," an "important member of the Nazi Party in Berlin," a "prominent young Nazi press leader," or "a high and trustworthy German source." These sources transmitted information obtained from Hitler's private statements and declarations, conversations among top German officials, and written documents from the German Foreign Office, German intelligence, and leading Nazi officials about Germany's attitude regarding relations with Britain as well as its more specific plans to attack in the West before turning to the East.

153. Memo by Lord Halifax to Mr. Mallet, *DBFP*, part III, vol. IV, no. 5. Henderson, however, questioned the reliability of these sources, claiming that these reports lacked credibility because they came from elements opposed to the Nazi regime. See Memo by Nevile Henderson to Lord Halifax, February 28, 1939, *DBFP*, part II, vol. XV, no. 162.

154. Memo by Lord Halifax to Mr. Mallet, *DBFP*, part III, vol. IV, no. 5. "Colour was lent to [this] theory," Halifax said, "by the vigour with which the Nazis seemed to be championing the cause of Ukrainian independence; by the obvious nervousness of the Poles, who even made approaches to Soviet Russia; and by the fact that it would be more logical, and more in accordance with the principles of 'Mein Kampf,' for the Nazis first to exploit the East and then turn, reinforced, upon the West." "Statement by Halifax to the Cabinet," January 25, 1939, CAB 23/97.

155. Memo by Robert Vansittart, January 16, 1939, circulated to the Committee on Foreign Policy by Lord Halifax, CAB 27/627. Similarly, Halifax pointed to changes within the Nazi Party as proof that the more radical members of the party now influenced Hitler. "The removal of moderates such as Schacht and Wiedmann," Halifax wrote, "are symptomatic." Memo by Lord Halifax to Mr. Mallet, *DBFP*, part III, vol. IV, no. 5.

156. Memo by Olivie-Forbes to Lord Halifax, December 6, 1938, *DBFP*, part III, vol. III, no. 403.

157. Quoted in Dilks, *The Diaries of Sir Alexander Cadogan*, 132.

158. Memo by Nevile Henderson to Lord Halifax, March 9, 1939, *DBFP*, part III, vol. IV, no. 195.

159. Ibid.

160. MCM, February 1, 1939, CAB 23/97.

161. MCM, March 18, 1939, CAB 23/98.

162. "Foreign Office Memo on the Situation after the Absorption of Czecho-Slovakia, and on the Policy of His Majesty's Government," March 29, 1939, *DBFP*, part III, vol. IV, appendix IV.

163. Letter from Neville Chamberlain to his sister Hilda Chamberlain, March 19, 1939, quoted in Self, *Neville Chamberlain Diary Letters*, 393.

164. Letter from Neville Chamberlain to his sister Ida Chamberlain, March 26, 1939, quoted in Self, *Neville Chamberlain Diary Letters*, 395.

165. For reviews of this literature, see Donald Watt, "The Historiography of Appeasement," in *Crisis and Controversy: Essays in Honour of A.J.P. Taylor*, ed. Alan Sked and
Chris Cook (London: Macmillan, 1976), 110–29; Robert J. Caputi, *Neville Chamberlain and Appeasement* (Selinsgrove, PA: Susquehanna University Press, 2000). For
scholarly works that critically reexamine the logic of appeasement, some of which
offer revisionist accounts of British policy during the interwar period, see James P.
Levy, *Appeasement and Rearmament, Britain, 1936–1939* (Lanham, MD: Rowman
and Littlefield, 2006); Peter Neville, *Hitler and Appeasement: The British Attempt
to Prevent the Second World War* (London: Hambledon Continuum, 2006); Gustav
Schmidt, *The Politics and Economics of Appeasement: British Foreign Policy in the 1930s*,
trans. Jackie Bennett-Ruete (Leamington Spa, UK: Berg, 1986); Wesley K. Wark, *The
Ultimate Enemy: British Intelligence and Nazi Germany, 1933–1939* (Ithaca, NY: Cornell University Press, 1985).

166. This section, however, does not examine the significance of perceived intentions on
policies relative to other variables.

167. Following Ripsman and Levy, I define appeasement as a systematic strategy of concessions in response to threat. According to Ripsman and Levy, appeasement could
be designed for many reasons, such as to avoid war by eliminating grievances. It could
also be designed "to reduce tensions with one adversary in order to convert resources
for deterrence and/or defense against another adversary." Appeasement could be intended to buy time to rearm and prepare for a likely future war. See Norrin Ripsman
and Jack S. Levy, "Wishful Thinking or Buying Time? The Logic of British Appeasement in the 1930s," *International Security* 33, no. 2 (2008): 150; Norrin Ripsman and
Jack S. Levy, "The Realism of Appeasement in the 1930s: Buying Time for Rearmament" (paper presented at the annual meeting of the American Political Science Association, Washington, DC, September 1, 2005).

168. Wark, "Something Very Stern," 162.

169. For recent studies supporting the revisionist account, see Ripsman and Levy, "The
Realism of Appeasement in the 1930s"; Norrin Ripsman and Jack S. Levy, "The Preventive War That Never Happened: Britain, France, and the Rise of Germany in the
1930s," *Security Studies* 16, no. 1 (2007): 32–67; Christopher Layne, "Security Studies and the Use of History: Neville Chamberlain's Grand Strategy Revisited," *Security
Studies* 17, no. 3 (2008): 397–437; David Dilks, "Appeasement Revisited," *University of
Leeds Review* 15 (1972): 28–56.

170. This is not to argue that systemic and domestic constraints did not play an important role in shaping British policies. This study stresses how uncertainty about
the scope and nature of Hitler's intentions led decision makers to settle on the dual
policy. For systemic and domestic-level explanations for British policies, see John J.
Mearsheimer, *The Tragedy of Great Power Politics* (New York: W. W. Norton and
Company, 2001), 269–72; Thomas J. Christensen and Jack Snyder, "Chain Gangs and
Passed Bucks: Predicting Alliance Patterns in Multipolarity," *International Organization* 44, no. 2 (1990): 137–68; Kenneth Waltz, *Theory of International Politics* (New
York: McGraw-Hill, 1979), 165–69. Walt supplements this analysis by incorporating
perceived intentions into his analysis. Because Hitler tried to hide his hegemonic ambitions from the West, Walt says, the British and French limited balancing response
was appropriate. Stephen M. Walt, "Alliances, Threats, and U.S. Grand Strategy: A
Reply to Kaufman and Labs," *Security Studies* 1, no. 3 (spring 1992): 448–82; Ran-

dall L. Schweller, *Unanswered Threats: Political Constraints on the Balance of Power* (Princeton, NJ: Princeton University Press, 2006).

171. When Hitler announced in March 1935 that he had achieved air parity with Britain, the cabinet authorized a new plan, known as Scheme C, to further expand and expedite the buildup of the Royal Air Force. Robert P. Shay, *British Rearmament in the Thirties: Politics and Profits* (Princeton, NJ: Princeton University Press, 1977), 48–60.

172. Peters, *Anthony Eden at the Foreign Office*, 97–99. See memo by Anthony Eden, April 7, 1935, *DBFP*, part II, vol. XII, no. 701; MCM, March 27 and April 8, 1935, CAB 23/81. Vansittart, along with other senior Foreign Office officials, believed that Britain should balance externally as well. Given the expected requirements of alliance building, he urged DRC members to allow for a building up of all three services. Vansittart supported a continental commitment to Europe in the form of a British Expeditionary Force that could protect the Low Countries in case of a German invasion.

173. Vansittart argued that while ready to offer Germany significant concessions, Britain "must give away nothing (a) until we have made up our minds that we will approach Germany on terms that promise lasting success, (b) till we are sure, having made that approach, that such a political settlement is really possible." Memo by Robert Vansittart, February 3, 1936, quoted in *DBFP*, part II, vol. XV, 620.

174. To make Germany's expansion toward Central and Southeast Europe more peaceful, the Foreign Office contended, Britain should moderate or reverse its present commercial policy, and find alternatives to satisfy Germany's ambitions, perhaps through the return of former German colonies or by eliminating discrimination against the import of German goods into the colonial British Empire. "Memorandum by Messrs. F.T.A. Ashton-Gwatkin and H.M.G. Jebb Respecting German 'Expansion,'" January 31, 1936, *DBFP*, part II, vol. XV, 762–68.

175. "Germany: Memorandum by the Secretary of State for Foreign Affairs," February 11, 1936, CAB 24/260.

176. Memo by Robert Vansittart, "Britain, France, and Germany," February 3, 1936, CAB 24/260.

177. In the immediate aftermath of German actions in the Rhineland, Eden suggested opening conversations with Belgium and France about possible military coordination. The cabinet, however, rejected this proposal because of opposition from the public and because strategic reports indicated that Britain was not in a position to conduct a successful military campaign against Germany. See MCM, March 16 and 18, 1936, CAB 23/86.

178. Memo by Anthony Eden, "The German Danger," January 17, 1936, CAB 27/599.

179. Minutes by Orme Sargent on Possible Policies toward Germany, March 18, 1936, *DBFP*, part II, vol. XVI, no. 135, n6.

180. The Foreign Office considered alternatives to the established British policy of "general settlement," such as an immediate agreement confined to Western Europe alone. This was rejected due to the recognition that no bilateral détente could be reached with Germany unless Britain was willing to sacrifice colonies. Even then, Britain could not be certain that Germany would be satisfied. Memo prepared by the Foreign Office for the Committee on Foreign Policy, July 13, 1936, CAB 27/626.

181. MCM, July 6, 1936, CAB 23/85.

182. Memo prepared by the Foreign Office for the Committee on Foreign Policy, July 13, 1936, CAB 27/626.

183. Report of the Plymouth Committee on the Transfer of a Colonial Mandate to Germany, June 9, 1936, *DBFP*, part II, vol. XVI, appendix III. Even after this report, Committee on Foreign Policy members continued to debate the colonial issue throughout 1937. Some, like Hoare and MacDonald, claimed that the "prestige" of social equality was "the mainspring of Germany's demands for colonies," while others believed that the economic value of the colonies, although exaggerated, was the source of its demands. Committee on Foreign Policy, July 21, 1936, CAB 27/622. See also Memo by Eric Phipps to Anthony Eden, October 22, 1936, *BDFP*, part II, vol. XVII, no. 318; ibid., November 4, 1936, *BDFP*, part II, vol. XVII, no. 318, n6; Committee on Foreign Policy, July 27, 1936, CAB 27/622.

184. Roi, *Alternative to Appeasement*, 127.

185. Ibid.

186. Quoted in Robert A. C. Parker, *Chamberlain and Appeasement: British Policy and the Coming of the Second World War* (Bedford, UK: St. Martin's, 1993), 96. See Self, *Neville Chamberlain*, 282; Peters, *Anthony Eden*, 307–9. On Eden's resignation, see Self, *Neville Chamberlain*, 280–89; Peters, *Anthony Eden*; Norman Rose, "The Resignation of Anthony Eden," *Historical Journal* 25, no. 4 (1982): 911–31. The differences between Chamberlain and Eden had to do mainly with relations toward Italy, not Germany.

187. Minutes by Anthony Eden, October 27, 1937, *DBFP*, part II, vol. XIX, no. 273.

188. At the same time, Britain wanted to make it clear that it would not contemplate "any settlement at the expense of the political independence of the nations of Eastern and Central Europe." Memo by Anthony Eden to Nevile Henderson, November 6, 1937, *DBFP*, part II, vol. XIX, no. 295.

189. Chamberlain believed that Germany would neither use force nor commit an act of aggression in Czechoslovakia and instead would encourage, through propaganda, the local Sudeten Germans to establish some form of local government.

190. Minutes of Anglo-French Conversations, November 29 and 30, 1937, CAB 27/626.

191. Memo by Nevile Henderson to Anthony Eden, November 8, 1937, *DBFP*, part II, vol. XIX, no. 301. In a later memo, Henderson clarified that he did not mean Britain should actually make such concessions to Germany but instead merely "concede the possibility" that a change in the status quo in Austria and Czechoslovakia would be required to achieve peace. See Letter from Nevile Henderson to Orme Sargent, November 23, 1937, *DBFP*, part II, vol. XIX, no. 344.

192. Quoted in Self, *Neville Chamberlain*, 304.

193. Chamberlain was still reluctant to commit Britain to assist Poland if its independence was threatened. Halifax and Cadogan had to work to persuade Chamberlain in late March of the accuracy of the intelligence that Hitler's immediate next step would be Poland. Chamberlain, reluctant at first to trust these intelligence sources, was eventually convinced by additional confirming evidence from the British military attaché in Berlin. Self, *Neville Chamberlain*, 356–57.

194. Quoted in Dilks, *The Diaries of Sir Alexander Cadogan*, 161.

195. MCM, March 18, 1939, CAB 23/98.

196. Chamberlain's resistance can be seen as motivated defensive avoidance bias. Defensive avoidance is a type of motivated bias characterized by efforts to avoid, dismiss, and deny warnings that increase the decision maker's anxiety and fear. Irving Janis

and L. Mann, *Decision Making: A Psychological Analysis of Conflict, Choice, and Commitment* (New York: Free Press, 1977), 57–58, 107–33.

197. Roberts, *The Holy Fox*, 143.

198. Self, *Neville Chamberlain*, 361.

199. See Frank McDonough, *Neville Chamberlain, Appeasement, and the British Road to War* (Manchester: Manchester University Press, 2010); Parker, *Chamberlain and Appeasement*. Parker argues that Chamberlain continued to pursue appeasement even after it became a deeply unpopular and discredited policy. Scholars have differed on the impact of British public opinion on Chamberlain's decision to shift his policies. Williamson Murray contends that "an unwilling Chamberlain" abandoned appeasement for resistance only because of "intense pressure from public opinion." Williamson Murray, "Britain," in *The Origins of World War Two: The Debate Continues*, ed. Robert Boyce and Joseph A. Maiolo (Basingstoke, UK: Palgrave Macmillan 2003), 124.

CHAPTER 4: THE BRITISH INTELLIGENCE COMMUNITY'S ASSESSMENTS OF NAZI GERMANY'S INTENTIONS

1. The COS Annual Reviews, Strategic Reviews, and Strategic Appreciations are the most similar to the NIEs that I analyze in the chapters discussing the US intelligence community's assessments of Soviet intentions. The main difference between these reports and the US NIEs is that with the exception of two Strategic Appreciations, the British documents did not incorporate the views of the Foreign Office (the equivalent of the US Department of State). The Foreign Office was the sole agency responsible for providing long-term assessments of Germany's intentions.

2. Wesley K. Wark, *The Ultimate Enemy: British Intelligence and Nazi Germany, 1933–1939* (Ithaca, NY: Cornell University Press, 1985), 188–89. This study covers only a small part (though substantial in volume) of the entire body of intelligence documents generated by the Air Ministry, War Office, British Admiralty, Industrial Intelligence Center, and all the COS committees. For a more comprehensive study of the intelligence community's work in this period, see Wark, *The Ultimate Enemy*; Ernest R. May, ed., *Knowing One's Enemies: Intelligence Assessment before the Two World Wars* (Princeton, NJ: Princeton University Press, 1984); F. H. Hinsley, *British Intelligence in the Second World War*, abr. (New York: Cambridge University Press, 1993); Williamson Murray and Allan R. Millett, eds., *Calculations: Net Assessment and the Coming of World War II* (New York: Free Press, 1992).

3. Murray and Millett, *Calculations*, 39–43.

4. In January 1936, the CID created the Interservice Intelligence Committee, which by July of that year evolved into the Joint Intelligence Subcommittee. Between July 1936 and August 1939, the Joint Intelligence Subcommittee was composed of the deputy directors of intelligence of the three services, and also frequently included a representative from the Industrial Intelligence Center and, from November 1938, Foreign Office representation. At the outbreak of war in September 1939, the CID was dissolved, but the Joint Intelligence Subcommittee continued as one of the principal subordinate bodies of the COS Committee. Since the subcommittee remained a peripheral body until summer 1939, its assessments are not analyzed here. On the role of the Joint

Intelligence Subcommittee in the years leading up to World War II, see Hinsley, *British Intelligence in the Second World War*, 10–11, 35–43.

5. COS Committee, "Annual Review for 1933 by the Chiefs of Staff," October 12, 1933, 9, CAB 16/109.

6. Ibid.

7. Wark, *The Ultimate Enemy*, 193–94.

8. CAB 53/25, COS 401 (JP), "Defense Plans for the Event of War against Germany," quoted in Ohad Leslau, "The Role of Intelligence in National Security Decision-Making" (PhD diss., University of Haifa, 2009), 181.

9. Joint Planning Subcommittee of the COS Committee, "Strategic Review," July 3, 1936, CAB 53/28 (emphasis added). The task of assessing Germany's future plans was further complicated by the British perception that the German General Staff and Nazi Party disagreed on Hitler's foreign policy objectives. Available documents did not indicate that the army opposed Hitler's expansionist designs; rather, British intelligence thought that the army merely disagreed with Hitler's views about when and how to achieve these objectives. Colonel Hotblack, the British military attaché at the time, wrote, "The steadying action of the German army is one of time rather than principle." Memo regarding the Aims of the German General Staff, April 9, 1936, *DBFP*, part II, no. 228.

10. COS Committee, "Imperial Conference 1937: Chiefs of Staff Review of Imperial Defence," November 17, 1936, CAB 56/2.

11. Ibid. Domestic economic difficulties, along with the interdependence between Germany's intensive rearmament efforts and its economic welfare, were the most significant factors motivating German expansion. The COS thought Hitler might be forced into foreign action to distract attention from Germany's domestic economic difficulties and that Germany would insist at least on regaining her colonies.

12. Wark, *The Ultimate Enemy*, 195, referring to Joint Planning Subcommittee, "Appreciation of the Situation in the Event of War against Germany in 1939 by the Joint Planning Subcommittee," October 26, 1936, CAB 53/29.

13. Joint Planning Subcommittee, "Appreciation of the Situation in the Event of War against Germany in 1939 by the Joint Planning Subcommittee," October 26, 1936, CAB 53/29.

14. Wark, *The Ultimate Enemy*, 195.

15. Joint Planning Subcommittee, "Appreciation of the Situation in the Event of War against Germany in 1939 by the Joint Planning Subcommittee," October 26, 1936, CAB 53/29. Despite the alarming nature of the COS report, British decision makers did not give it much consideration in cabinet discussions.

16. COS Committee, "Review of Imperial Defence by the Chiefs of Staff Committee," February 22, 1937, COS 560.

17. COS Committee, "Comparison of the Strength of Great Britain with That of Certain Other Nations as at May 1937," February 9, 1937, CAB 56/3.

18. Ibid.

19. Memo by Colonel Hotblack on German Military Preparedness, August 1937, *DBFP*, part II, vol. XIX, no. 112.

20. This was reiterated in the report's conclusion: "the German Army with its increasing influence is likely to try to put a brake on Hitler undertaking any foreign adventure until the armed forces are fit to deal with all eventualities." "Review of the World Situ-

ation in Relation to Possible Causes of War," WO 190/586. See also Christopher M. Andrew, *Her Majesty's Secret Service: The Making of the British Intelligence Community* (New York: Viking, 1986), 390; Peter Neville, "Rival Foreign Office Perceptions of Germany, 1936–1939," *Diplomacy and Statecraft* 13, no. 3 (2002): 142–43; Wark, *The Ultimate Enemy*, 87; Donald Cameron Watt, "British Intelligence and the Coming of the Second World War in Europe," in Ernest R. May, ed., *Knowing One's Enemy: Intelligence Assessment before the Two World Wars* (Princeton, NJ: Princeton University Press, 1984), 266.

21. COS Committee, "Comparison of the Strength of Great Britain with That of Certain Other Nations as at January 1938," November 12, 1937, CAB 24/296. The COS used this line of reasoning in another report: "None of the countries specified [Germany and Italy], considered individually, will be in a position by January 1938 to embark on a major land offensive with any great prospect of success in Europe. . . . Germany is unlikely to embark on a war in which she cannot foresee a good prospect of gaining a decision in a short time. . . . We therefore conclude that, even if assured of the co-operation of Italy, Germany would hesitate to embark, early in 1938, on hostilities against us." *DBFP*, vol. XIX, no. 316. See also John R. Ferris, "Indulged in All Too Little: Vansittart, Intelligence, and Appeasement," *Diplomacy and Statecraft* 6, no. 1 (1995): 122–75.

22. Vansittart received intelligence in March 1938 that was more alarming, stating that in order to alleviate internal tensions and external ambitions, Hitler would attack Czechoslovakia. Ferris, "Indulged in All Too Little," 152.

23. COS Committee, "Appreciation of the Situation in the Event of War against Germany," September 14, 1938, CAB 24/278. In retrospect, this pessimist view was far from accurate. As Wark points out, "The military balance in Europe in September 1938 was simply not favorable for Hitler as was so devoutly believed in London and Paris." Wark, *The Ultimate Enemy*, 210. The COS view was somewhat modified a week later as a result of further intelligence from the War Office claiming that Germany was holding its Western frontier with only a small number of divisions. Consequently, the COS determined that "until such time as we can build up our fighting potential, we cannot hope for quick results. Nevertheless, the latent resources of the Empire and the doubtful morale of our opponents under the stress of war, gives us confidence as to the ultimate outcome." COS Committee, "The Czechoslovakian Crisis," September 24, 1938, CAB 53/41.

24. Paul Kennedy, "British 'Net Assessment' and the Coming of the Second World War," in *Calculations: Net Assessment and the Coming of World War II*, ed. Williamson Murray and Allan R. Millett, eds. (New York: Free Press, 1992), 31.

25. The protocol of a cabinet meeting from March suggested that Chamberlain and Halifax were significantly influenced by the COS reports: "Several Members . . . including the Prime Minister and the Foreign Secretary, admitted that they had approached the question with a bias in favour of some kind of guarantee to Czecho-Slovakia, but that the investigation [the COS report] . . . had changed their views." CAB 23/93/6755, "Conclusions of the Cabinet of 22 March 1938." Yet as discussed in chapter 3 we now know that Chamberlain had other reasons for not committing Britain to the defense of Czechoslovakia in both crises.

26. COS Committee, "The German Army: Its Present Strength and Possible Rate of Expansion in Peace and War," April 22, 1938, CAB 24/276.

27. Memo by Noel Mason-Macfarlane, November 30, 1938, *DBFP*, part III, vol. III, no. 389.

28. Memo by Noel Mason-Macfarlane, "Memorandum Respecting the Military Possibilities in 1939," December 26, 1938, *DBFP*, part III, vol. III, no. 505.

29. Wesley K. Wark, "Something Very Stern: British Political Intelligence, Moralism, and Grand Strategy in 1939," *Intelligence and National Security* 5, no. 1 (1990): 150–70.

30. David Dilks, "Appeasement and 'Intelligence,'" *Retreat from Power, 1906–39*, vol. 1, *Studies in Britain's Foreign Policy of the Twentieth Century*, ed. David Dilks (London: Macmillan, 1981), 157–58.

31. Wark, "Something Very Stern," 156.

32. Historians have suggested that Germans who wanted Britain to balance against Germany more effectively planted reports warning of an attack on London or Holland. Dilks, "Appeasement and 'Intelligence'"; Richard Overy, "Strategic Intelligence and the Outbreak of the Second World War," *War in History* 5 (1998): 465; Andrew, *Her Majesty's Secret Service*, 412–15. Military intelligence was highly skeptical of Foreign Office reports warning of a potential invasion of Holland or an aerial knockout blow against London. Moreover, the War Office believed that in early 1939, the German Army was not ready to fight a major war on two fronts and therefore would not risk a confrontation with the West. A reading of Hitler's mood or intentions did not factor into its assessment of Germany's military intentions, which instead were inferred primarily from the current state of German military activities. See Wark, *The Ultimate Enemy*, 113–14; "Notes on Germany's Present Position and Future Aims," January 17, 1939, WO 190/745.

33. "Notes on Germany's Present Position and Future Aims," January 17, 1939, WO 190/745, 1–16; Overy, "Strategic Intelligence."

34. Memo by Gladwyn Jebb, "Summary of Information from Secret Sources," January 19, 1939, part II, CAB 27/627.

35. Wesley K. Wark, "Possible German Intentions," January 19, 1939, CAB 27/627, 159. Vansittart was the chief diplomatic adviser at the time; his most important source of information outside the SIS was Malcolm Graham Christie. Christie had been the air attaché in Berlin and enjoyed many close contacts in Germany. Indeed, during the period from October 1938 through the end of January, based in part on information from Christie, Vansittart acquired new credibility within the Foreign Office, and his reports finally began to influence Cadogan and Halifax. Dilks, "Appeasement and 'Intelligence,'" 145; Ferris, "Indulged in All Too Little?"

36. This was partly because of Henderson's reassuring reports from Germany at the time as well as Hitler's unpredictability and a lack of hard evidence pointing to an imminent attack on Czechoslovakia. In fact, even the head of the Foreign Office's Central Office (who cannot be described as a dove) wrote in response to Henderson's optimistic reports in February that his "view is supported by our most recent summary of information from other sources." Dilks, "Appeasement and 'Intelligence,'" 159–60.

37. Wark, "Something Very Stern." On Vansittart's intelligence sources, see Ferris, "Indulged in All Too Little?"

38. The report makes it clear, however, that improvements in the military balance would show only in the following year, 1939–40.

39. The British Appreciation report from early 1939 did not include qualitative assessments based on Germany's military doctrine, and thus did not discuss issues such as mobility, firepower, or the overall efficiency of the German Army.

40. Kennedy, "British 'Net Assessment' and the Coming of the Second World War," 30, 29.
41. The COS Strategic Appreciation was written in February 1939 during a lull between war scares. This lull gave some basis for optimism, as the COS and some decision makers believed it to be a sign that Hitler perceived British and US warnings as credible. The War Office similarly perceived the situation as more relaxed, and its reports pointed to German military deficiencies. The Foreign Office and SIS, however, issued estimates pertaining to German political intentions that indicated alarming changes. Ibid., 33.
42. COS Committee, "German Colonial Claims: French Security," January 30, 1939, CAB 53/44.
43. Norman Henry Gibbs, *Grand Strategy*, vol. 1, *Rearmament Policy* (London: Her Majesty's Stationery Office, 1976), 701; Wesley K. Wark, "Conclusion: The Four Phases of Intelligence," in *The Ultimate Enemy: British Intelligence and Nazi Germany, 1933–1939* (Ithaca, NY: Cornell University Press, 1985); Kennedy, "British 'Net Assessment' and the Coming of the Second World War," 49–55.
44. Memo by Noel Mason-Macfarlane, March 29, 1939, *DBFP*, part III, vol. IV, appendix V.
45. It had become clear by early September 1938 that the COS and Foreign Office should have collaborated more closely on strategic matters. The COS thus concluded a memo with a cautionary note: "We invite attention to the close relationship which, in our view, foreign policy bears to strategy and war planning. We suggest that it would be of advantage from both the political and military point of view if, when the Foreign Office are asked to draw up political appreciations as to the possibilities of wars and the circumstances in which they were liable to break out, they should invite a preliminary discussion with the Chiefs of Staff Committee." See COS Committee, "Planning for War with Germany," September 2, 1938, CAB 53/40.
46. Wark, *The Ultimate Enemy*, 123. For a similar argument, see Janice Gross Stein, "Building Politics into Psychology: The Misperception of Threat," *Political Psychology* 9, no. 2 (1988): 379. Murray contends that British intelligence reports on the eve of the Sudeten crisis "represented a deliberate skewing of the evidence." See Williamson Murray, "Appeasement and Intelligence," *Intelligence and National Security* 3, no. 3 (1987): 61.
47. There is some evidence to suggest that Chamberlain did manipulate intelligence indirectly on the eve of the Czechoslovakia crisis by providing his military advisers with extremely restrictive terms of reference. He directed the COS to address British military ability to defend the sovereignty of Czechoslovakia in the event of war, not to examine how the overall strategic balances would look in a year if Germany conquered Czechoslovakia. Chamberlain also did not present to the cabinet the more optimistic COS reports of September 1938, which suggested more confidence in Britain's ability to engage in war over Czechoslovakia. Correlli Barnett, *The Collapse of British Power* (London: Eyre Methuen, 1972); Williamson Murray, *Change in the European Balance of Power, 1938–1939: The Path to Ruin* (Princeton, NJ: Princeton University Press, 1984); Murray, "Appeasement and Intelligence," 53–58. Murray ("Appeasement and Intelligence," 61–62) did not view the shift in mood of British estimates from 1938 to 1939 as intellectually dishonest.
48. The available evidence from additional sources and the SIS reports on Hitler's political intentions point to the importance of military calculations and reports from "credible" human intelligence sources.
49. Hinsley, *British Intelligence in the Second World War*, 79–80.

CHAPTER 5: THE CARTER ERA AND THE COLLAPSE OF DÉTENTE, 1977–80

1. Zbigniew Brzezinski, *Power and Principle: Memoirs of the National Security Advisor, 1977–1981* (New York: Farrar, Straus and Giroux, 1983), 343. According to Vance, the exchange in Vienna was less extensive than would have been desirable. It was confined largely to winding up the final details on SALT II and a somewhat-sharp exchange on Soviet activities in the third world. Cyrus R. Vance, *Hard Choices: Critical Years in America's Foreign Policy* (New York: Simon and Schuster, 1983), 139.
2. Jimmy Carter, *Keeping Faith: Memoirs of a President* (New York: Bantam, 1982), 245.
3. Vance, *Hard Choices*, 56.
4. Steven Jay Campbell, "Brzezinski's Image of the USSR: Inferring Foreign Policy Beliefs from Multiple Sources over Time" (PhD diss., University of South Carolina, 2003), 74–75. See also Betty Glad, *An Outsider in the White House: Jimmy Carter, His Advisors, and the Making of American Foreign Policy* (Ithaca, NY: Cornell University Press, 2009).
5. Melchiore J. Laucella, "A Cognitive-Psychodynamic Perspective to Understanding Secretary of State Cyrus Vance's Worldview," *Presidential Studies Quarterly* 34, no. 2 (June 2004): 227–71.
6. Jerel A. Rosati, *The Carter Administration's Quest for Global Community: Beliefs and Their Impact on Behavior* (Columbia: University of South Carolina Press, 1987); Gaddis Smith, *Morality, Reason, and Power: American Diplomacy in the Carter Years* (New York: Farrar, Straus and Giroux, 1987).
7. The intelligence community produced several relevant NIEs on the Soviet Union during these two years: NIE 11-4-77, "Soviet Strategic Objectives," January 1977; NIE 11-3/8-77, "Soviet Capabilities for Strategic Nuclear Conflict through the Late 1980s," February 1978; NIE 4-1-78, "Warsaw Pact Concepts and Capabilities for Going to War in Europe: Implications for NATO Warning of War," April 1978; NIE 11-4-78, "Soviet Goals and Expectations in the Global Power Arena," May 1978; NIE 11-6-78, "Soviet Forces for Peripheral Attack," September 1978; NIE 11-3/8-78, "Soviet Capabilities for Strategic Nuclear Conflict through the Late 1980s," January 1979; NIE 11-14-79, "Warsaw Pact Forces Opposite NATO," January 1979; NIE 11-10-79, "Soviet Military Capabilities to Project Power and Influence in Distant Areas," October 1979; NIE 11-3/8-79, "Soviet Capabilities for Strategic Nuclear Conflict through the Late 1980s," March 1980; NIE 11-3/8-80, "Soviet Capabilities for Strategic Nuclear Conflict through 1990," December 1980. Several additional NIEs were much narrower in scope, and related to specific or pressing policy issues: NIE 15-79, "Prospects for Post-Tito Yugoslavia," September 1979; NIE 11/13-80, "Sino-Soviet Relations in the Early 1980s," June 1980; SNIE 11-34/36.2-80, "Soviet Interests, Policies, and Prospects with Respect to the Iran-Iraq War," December 1980.
8. See Raymond L. Garthoff, "Estimating Soviet Intentions and Capabilities," in *Watching the Bear: Essays on CIA's Analysis of the Soviet Union*, ed. Gerald K. Haines and Robert E. Leggett (Washington, DC: Center for the Study of Intelligence Publications, 2003), chapter 5, https://www.cia.gov/library/center-for-the-study-of-intelligence/csi-publications/books-and-monographs/watching-the-bear-essays-on-cias-analysis-of-the-soviet-union/index.html (accessed August 20, 2013).
9. Quoted in Raymond L. Garthoff, "Speeches Delivered at the Conference," in *Watching the Bear: Essays on CIA's Analysis of the Soviet Union*, ed. Gerald K. Haines and Robert

E. Leggett (Washington, DC: Center for the Study of Intelligence Publications, 2003), chapter 8.

10. For example, the NSC's Comprehensive Net Assessment (CNA) in 1978 stated that this trend had become significantly more pronounced in the previous two years. But when evaluating the general causes of these changes, the 1978 CNA judged that virtually all the major changes in the global balance in 1977 and 1978 did *not* derive from Soviet initiatives, claiming that "Soviet policy, particularly with respect to its military programs, was characterized by *substantial continuity.*" Thus, the CNA concluded, "both positive and negative changes in the global balance during the last two years have been due less to what the Soviets have done than to what we and others have done." Comprehensive Net Assessment, 1978, 8 (emphasis added). Les Aspin's study on the Soviet military buildup reaches similar conclusions—namely, that "the gap [in strategic forces] is caused more by a drop in the American side than by a Soviet jump." See Les Aspin, "What Are the Russians Up To?" *International Security* 3, no. 1 (1978): 30–54.

11. Report of Secretary of Defense Harold Brown on the FY 1979 Budget, FY 1980 Authorization Request, and FY 1979–83 Defense Programs, January 23, 1978, 65–66; NIE 11-3/8-77; NE 11-4-77; NIE 11-3/8-78; NIE 11-3/8-79. Throughout the 1970s, the United States had about 1,050 ICBM launchers, while the USSR maintained about 400 to 500 more. The decline in the number of Soviet ICBMs in the 1970s, however, had been more than offset, US policy makers reasoned, by the significantly greater throw weight and accuracy of the new generation of Soviet missiles. For a good discussion of US perceptions of Soviet capabilities during this period, see Raymond L. Garthoff, *Perspectives on the Strategic Balance: A Staff Paper* (Washington, DC: Brookings Institution, 1983); John M. Collins, *U.S.-Soviet Military Balance* (New York: Pergamon-Brassey's, 1985); Lawrence Freedman, *US Intelligence and the Soviet Strategic Threat* (Basingstoke, UK: Macmillan, 1977); John Prados, *The Soviet Estimate: U.S. Intelligence Analysis and Russian Military Strength* (Princeton, NJ: Princeton University Press, 1986); Pavel Podvig, "The Window of Vulnerability That Wasn't: Soviet Military Buildup in the 1970s—A Research Note," *International Security* 33, no. 1 (2008): 118–38. According to Podvig, the US intelligence community overestimated the accuracy of the Soviet strategic forces in the late 1970s and early 1980s.

12. The United States was still believed to have an advantage in the number of weapons throughout the 1970s and number of targets that could be hit by a US delivery vehicle carrying more than one weapon, although the Soviets were believed to be slowly closing this gap. See NIE 11-3/8-80, A-4, A-5, B-10, B-11.

13. NIE 11-3/8-79, 2, 4. In NIE 11-3/8-80, the intelligence community claimed that the Soviets were now able to destroy 60 percent of US ICBMs, and would be able to destroy about 90 percent by 1985. Still, it was believed that US deployment of MX missiles in multiple protective shelters in the late 1980s would make the accomplishment of the Soviet counterforce mission a much more challenging and expensive proposition. See NIE 11-3/8-80, B-12.

14. Until the late 1980s, according to NIE 11-3/8-80, 5–6, 11, the "Soviet ICBM force would be capable of destroying most US ICBM silos and still have many warheads remaining for other purposes." Soviet advantages in this regard were estimated to be higher if the Soviets were not bound by SALT II limits. It was nonetheless always

acknowledged that even under the most unfavorable circumstances, the United States would retain significant retaliatory potential. This was repeated in all the NIEs that were dedicated to estimating Soviet capabilities—the 11-3/8 NIEs.

15. Intelligence Assessment, "The Development of Soviet Military Power: Trends since 1965 and Prospects for the 1980s," Special Report (SR) 81-10035X, xiii–xv.

16. Because of their accuracy, MIRV capability, and survivability, the defense and intelligence communities believed that these mobile SS-20 intermediate-range ballistic missiles would become the backbone of Soviet land-based ballistic missile forces for peripheral nuclear attack. NIE 11-6-78, 2–3. See also Falk Bomsdorf, "Western Perceptions of Soviet Military Power and Its Political Unity toward Western Europe," in *Soviet Military Doctrine and Western Policy*, ed. Gregory Flynn (London: Routledge, 1989), 123–26.

17. Intelligence Assessment, "The Balance of Nuclear Forces in Central Europe," SR 78-10004, 1. Soviet improvement efforts were perceived as rapidly undermining NATO's monopoly on nuclear artillery in Central Europe and providing the Soviets with the "capability for conducting theater nuclear war at higher levels of intensity before having to resort to the peripheral strike forces based on Soviet territory." Ibid., 1–2.

18. The Soviet buildup was such that analysts debated its possible parallels with the Nazi buildup in the late 1930s. See, for example, Aspin, "What Are the Russians Up To?"; Charles Tyroler, ed., *Alerting America: The Papers of the Committee on the Present Danger* (Washington, DC: Potomac Books, 1984); David Holloway, *The Soviet Union and the Arms Race*, 2nd ed. (New Haven, CT: Yale University Press, 1984); Tom Gervasi, *The Myth of Soviet Military Supremacy* (New York: Harper and Row, 1986); Robbin F. Laird and Dale R. Herspring, *The Soviet Union and Strategic Arms* (Boulder, CO: Westview Press, 1984).

19. In 1978, the CNA stated that the "1975 projections in the key indicators of the strategic balance generally showed adverse trends for the U.S. into the early 1980s and then, on most key indicators, a reversal in favor of the U.S. by 1985." Still, the 1978 projections showed a steady decline for the United States on almost all key indicators into the 1990s.

20. If the United States decided to build the MX, though, the adverse trend would level off in the mid-1980s at a much smaller Soviet advantage. In June 1978, Brzezinski reported that according to new data received by DOD's Office of Net Assessment the adverse trend was expected to last through the 1980s, largely due to changes in projected US forces.

21. Nevertheless, when the NSC evaluated the political, economic, and diplomatic capabilities of the two superpowers, the United States was perceived to be at a great advantage, making the overall assessment of the strategic balance for the rest of the 1970s one of asymmetrical equivalence. In his public statements, Carter also described the balance of capabilities as one of "essential equivalence." See, for example, *Public Papers of the Presidents of the United States* (hereafter referred to as *PPP*) (Washington, DC: US Government Printing Office, 1978), January 19, 1978, 122–33. See also *PPP*, March 17, 1978, 532.

22. Indeed, in 1976 the CIA published a major revision of its spending estimates, revealing, first, that Soviet defense industries were far less efficient than the CIA had formerly believed, and second, that the USSR was more willing to sacrifice civilian consumption and production in the pursuit of military power than the CIA and many

outside analysts had believed. Growing evidence of a sharp deterioration in Soviet economic growth, though, did not prevent the intelligence community from estimating a continuous increase of 4–5 percent in defense spending. Stansfield Turner, "Intelligence for a New World Order," *Foreign Affairs* 71, no. 4 (1991): 162; Noel E. Firth, *Soviet Defense Spending: A History of CIA Estimates, 1950–1990* (College Station: Texas A&M University Press, 1998), 76. For more on Soviet defense spending in this period, see Aaron Lobel, ed., *Presidential Judgment: Foreign Policy Decision Making in the White House* (Hollis, NH: Hollis Press, 2001); Franklyn D. Holzman, "Politics and Guesswork: CIA and DIA Estimates of Soviet Military Spending," *International Security* 14, no. 2 (1989): 101–31.

23. NSC meeting, June 4, 1979, quoted in Brzezinski, *Power and Principle*, 334–36. Carter similarly commented on February 8, 1977, "I think we are roughly equivalent, even though I think we are superior." *PPP*, May 22, 1977, 95. To be sure, throughout this period the administration recognized that neither the United States nor the USSR could launch a disarming first strike that would prevent the other side from launching a retaliatory strike of devastating proportions. The US leadership continued to characterize the strategic balance as one of parity, essential equivalence, or asymmetrical equivalence. See Report of Secretary of Defense Harold Brown, on the FY 1979 Budget, FY 1980 Authorization Request, and FY 1979–1983 Defense Programs, January 23, 1978; Report of Secretary of Defense Harold Brown, on the FY 1980 Budget, FY 1981 Authorization Request, and FY 1980–1984 Defense Programs, January 25, 1979.

24. Raymond L. Garthoff, *Deterrence and the Revolution in Soviet Military Doctrine* (Washington, DC: Brookings Institution, 1990), 40.

25. The US conception of mutual assured destruction was often expressed in terms of countervalue capabilities for destroying a specified percentage of the opponent's industry and population. In comparison, the Soviet understanding of mutual assured destruction was broader, expressed instead in terms of assured retaliatory capability that would disarm the aggressor. These scholars claimed that statements by Soviet leaders proved that they did in fact endorse the concept of deterrence, which in the Soviet view required strong and ready combat capabilities. Raymond L. Garthoff, "Mutual Deterrence and Strategic Arms Limitation in Soviet Policy," *International Security* 3, no. 1 (1978): 112–47.

26. Richard Pipes, "Why the Soviet Union Thinks It Could Fight and Win a Nuclear War," *Commentary* 64, no. 1 (1977): 21–34.

27. Richard Pipes, "Soviet Strategic Doctrine: Another View," *Strategic Review* 10, no. 4 (1982): 36–63; Richard Soll, "The Soviet Union and Protracted Nuclear War," *Strategic Review* 8, no. 4 (1980): 15–28.

28. John G. Hines, Ellis Mishulovich, and John F. Shull, *Soviet Intentions, 1965–1985, Volume I: An Analytical Comparison of US-Soviet Assessments during the Cold War* (McLean, VA: BDM Federal Inc., 1995), 14 (hereafter referred to as Hines, Mishulovich, and Shull, *Volume I* or *Volume II*). See also Hines, Mishulovich, and Shull, *Volume II*, 16.

29. Brzezinski held the view that the Soviets considered their war-fighting capabilities as a means to enhance deterrence. As for the question of Soviet adherence to mutual assured destruction, Brzezinski claims that it was a purely academic question, but notes that the "Soviets did not believe in MAD in the sense of accepting the logic of mutual deterrence based on fear as a substitute for developing a credible warfighting

capability." Brown expressed the conviction that the Soviet deterrent rested on the capacity to inflict unacceptable damage on the United States, but he believed that the Soviet leadership did not embrace mutual assured destruction to the extent of renouncing efforts to limit damage or relying entirely on a capacity to kill only civilians to deter the United States. Hines, Mishulovich, and Shull, *Volume II*, 13, 15; Report of Secretary of Defense Harold Brown, on the FY 1980 Budget, FY 1981 Authorization Request, and FY 1980–84 Defense Programs, January 25, 1979, 83. For the views of Fritz Ermarth, a member of Carter's NSC staff, see Fritz W. Ermarth, "Contrasts in American and Soviet Strategic Thought," *International Security* 3, no. 2 (1978): 145.

30. The debate between Garthoff and Pipes, for instance, reflects these opposite interpretations. Raymond L. Garthoff, "A Garthoff–Pipes Debate on Soviet Strategic Doctrine," *Strategic Review* 10, no. 4 (1982): 36–63.

31. Hines, Mishulovich, and Shull, *Volume II*, 16–17.

32. Ibid., 13.

33. Ermarth, "Contrasts in American and Soviet Strategic Thought," 144–45.

34. Western analysts, however, interpreted these changes differently. One school of thought underscored the Soviet preference for preemption, while others alleged that the Soviets based their own policy of deterrence on a launch-on-warning capability with ride out (assured second strike) as the backup, much like Western declaratory policy. For examples of this school, see Benjamin S. Lambeth, *How to Think about Soviet Military Doctrine* (Santa Monica: Rand, 1978); Joseph D. Douglass, *Soviet Military Strategy in Europe* (New York: Pergamon Press, 1980). The second school of thought characterized the Soviet adoption of these new options as a "step toward stability from preemption" and considered the Soviet pledge for "no first use" substantive as opposed to mere propaganda. Honore Catudal, *Soviet Nuclear Strategy from Stalin to Gorbachev* (Berlin: Spitz, 1988), 112–15. For a detailed discussion of the evolution in Soviet doctrine with regard to the first use of nuclear weapons, see Garthoff, *Deterrence and the Revolution in Soviet Military Doctrine*.

35. Quoted in Hines, Mishulovich, and Shull, *Volume I*, 28; Hines, Mishulovich, and Shull, *Volume II*, 14.

36. Hines, Mishulovich, and Shull, *Volume II*, 28.

37. Ibid., 17.

38. According to Rosati, events in Africa in 1978 lifted Cuba and the Soviet Union from minor players in the region to two of the area's most important actors in the eyes of the Carter administration. Rosati, *The Carter Administration's Quest for Global Community*, 58–60.

39. Thirteen of these crises took place in Africa (six in South Africa, three in North Africa, two in Central Africa, and two in East Africa), six in the Middle East, four in South and East Asia (one in East Asia, two in Southeast Asia, and one in South Asia), one in Central Asia, one in East Europe, and another in South Europe. The Soviet Union exhibited low-level involvement in eleven of these crises, and showed covert or semi-military activities in thirteen of them. For a quick summary of these crises, see the International Crisis Behavior data set, http://www.cidcm.umd.edu/icb/ (August 21, 2013).

40. Memorandum for the President by Zbigniew Brzezinski, "Strategic Reactions to the Afghanistan Problem," January 3, 1980.

41. The 1977 "Shaba I" incident in Zaire, for example, was treated as an "African problem" and not as an East-West one. It began when the leftist Front for the National Lib-

eration of the Congo crossed into Zaire from Angola. The administration was not able to establish that the Soviets were directly involved in the crisis. See Raymond L. Garthoff, *Détente and Confrontation: American-Soviet Relations from Nixon to Reagan*, rev. ed. (Washington, DC: Brookings Institution Press, 1994), 687–88; Vance, *Hard Choices*, 69–75. Brzezinski does not even mention the Shaba I crisis in his memoirs.

42. On the crisis in the Horn of Africa, see, for example, Garthoff, *Détente and Confrontation*, 695–719; Bruce D. Porter, *The USSR in Third World Conflicts: Soviet Arms and Diplomacy in Local Wars, 1945–1980* (Cambridge: Cambridge University Press, 1984); Stephen S. Kaplan, *Diplomacy of Power: Soviet Armed Forces as a Political Instrument* (Washington, DC: Brookings Institution, 1981); James E. Dougherty, *The Horn of Africa: A Map of Political-Strategic Conflict* (Cambridge, MA: Institute for Foreign Policy Analysis, 1982).

43. Finally, the International Crisis Behavior data set codes 1977 as the year that hostilities between Vietnam and Cambodia began. Yet Soviet semi-military involvement in this crisis started in 1978 with the Vietnamese invasion of Cambodia. After Vietnam joined the Soviet-led Council of Mutual Economic Assistance in January 1978, Brzezinski called the Vietnamese a "Soviet proxy." Thus when Vietnam moved into Cambodia later in 1978, the move was seen as Soviet sponsored. See Garthoff, *Détente and Confrontation*, 729.

44. See Vance, *Hard Choices*, 360–61; Brzezinski, *Power and Principle*, 347; *NSC Weekly Report*, no. 98, May 25, 1979; *NSC Weekly Report*, no. 103, July 20, 1979; *NSC Weekly Report*, no. 104, July 27, 1979; *NSC Weekly Report*, no. 109, September 13, 1979; David D. Newsome, *The Soviet Brigade in Cuba: A Study in Political Diplomacy* (Bloomington: Indiana University Press, 1987); Robert Strong, *Working in the World: Jimmy Carter and the Making of American Foreign Policy* (Baton Rouge: Louisiana State University Press, 2000), 208–32.

45. Quoted in *NSC Weekly Report*, no. 95, March 3, 1979.

46. Quoted in *NSC Weekly Report*, no. 98, May 25, 1979.

47. Brzezinski, *Power and Principle*, 347.

48. Vance, *Hard Choices*, 360–61; Brzezinski, *Power and Principle*, 347.

CHAPTER 6: US DECISION MAKERS' PERCEPTIONS OF SOVIET INTENTIONS: THE COLLAPSE OF DÉTENTE

1. Jerel A. Rosati, *The Carter Administration's Quest for Global Community: Beliefs and Their Impact on Behavior* (Columbia: University of South Carolina Press, 1987), 183.

2. I do not discuss the views of Secretary of Defense Brown because he was not nearly as involved with US foreign policy as Brzezinski or Vance, and certainly did not have as much influence on Carter. The evidence available contains few references by Brown to Soviet intentions.

3. Author's interview with Zbigniew Brzezinski, Washington, DC, October 2006.

4. According to Rosati (*The Carter Administration's Quest for Global Community*), during Carter's term in office the NSC rarely met and was not regarded as a decision-making entity.

5. Ibid., 226.

6. Brzezinski certainly held a more negative image of the USSR before coming to office, but during 1977 he appears sincerely to have shared some of Carter and Vance's

dovish views. For a similar interpretation based on public documents, see ibid., 55–57; Rosati, "Jimmy Carter, a Man Before His Time? The Emergence and Collapse of the First Post–Cold War Presidency," *Presidential Studies Quarterly* 23, no. 3 (Summer 1993): 471; Steven Jay Campbell, *Brzezinski's Image of the USSR: Inferring Foreign Policy Beliefs from Multiple Sources over Time* (Columbia: University of South Carolina Press, 2003); Erwin C. Hargrove, *Jimmy Carter as President: Leadership and the Politics of the Public Good* (Baton Rouge: Louisiana State University Press, 1988); Raymond A. Moore, "The Carter Presidency and Foreign Policy," in *The Carter Years: The President and Policy Making*, ed. M. Glenn Abernathy, Dilys M. Hill, and Phil Williams (New York: St. Martin's Press, 1984); John Dumbrell, *The Carter Presidency: A Re-evaluation*, 2nd ed. (New York: Manchester University Press, 1995). For a different interpretation, see Martha L. Cottam, "The Carter Administration's Policy toward Nicaragua: Images, Goals, and Tactics," *Political Science Quarterly* 107, no. 1 (1992): 123–46; Gaddis Smith, *Morality, Reason, and Power: American Diplomacy in the Carter Years* (New York: Hill and Wang, 1986).

7. Letter from Jimmy Carter to Leonid Brezhnev, January 26, 1977, Zbigniew Brzezinski Collection, box 18, file USSR-Carter/Brezhnev Correspondence 1/77–5/77.

8. Letter from Jimmy Carter to Leonid Brezhnev, February 14, 1977, Zbigniew Brzezinski Collection, box 18, file USSR-Carter/Brezhnev Correspondence 1/77–5/77.

9. Letter from Leonid Brezhnev to Jimmy Carter, February 25, 1977, Zbigniew Brzezinski Collection, box 18, file USSR-Carter/Brezhnev Correspondence 1/77–5/77.

10. Brezhnev's letter on the US offer for SALT II struck Vance as "good, hard hitting, to the point," while Brzezinski viewed it as "brutal, cynical, sneering and even patronizing." Zbigniew Brzezinski, *Power and Principle: Memoirs of the National Security Advisor, 1977–1981* (New York: Farrar, Straus and Giroux, 1983), 154–55; Jimmy Carter, *Keeping Faith: Memoirs of a President* (Fayetteville: University of Arkansas Press, 1995), 150–51, 223–25.

11. See, for example, *Public Papers of the Presidents of the United States* (hereafter referred to as *PPP*) (Washington, DC: US Government Printing Office, 1978), May 22, 1977, 54.

12. *PPP*, March 24, 1977, 497, 237.

13. *PPP*, June 30, 1977, 1198.

14. Ibid.

15. *PPP*, July 12, 1977, 1239.

16. *PPP*, July 15, 1977, 1270; *PPP*, September 29, 1977, 1689.

17. *PPP*, October 15, 1977, 1800.

18. *PPP*, December 15, 1977, 2119.

19. Quoted in *NSC Weekly Report*, no. 2, February 26, 1977.

20. Brzezinski, *Power and Principle*, 165–76.

21. Quoted *NSC Weekly Report*, no. 18, June 24, 1977.

22. But Brzezinski also believed that the Soviets were "taking our measure and assessing our steadfastness," and therefore thought the United States should not bow to Soviet pressure to accept their SALT proposal. On July 8, 1977, Brzezinski indicated that he "did not believe that any significant alteration in [the administration's] approach [would be] required." *NSC Weekly Report*, no. 20, July 8, 1977.

23. Melchiore J. Laucella, "A Cognitive-Psychodynamic Perspective to Understanding Secretary of State Cyrus Vance's Worldview," *Presidential Studies Quarterly* 34, no. 2 (June 2004): 244–46.

24. Quoted in Rosati, *The Carter Administration's Quest*, 54
25. Yael Aronoff interview with Zbigniew Brzezinski, Washington, DC, March 29, 2000, quoted in Yael Aronoff, "Making the Impossible Possible: When and Why Do Hardliners Become Soft?" (PhD diss., Columbia University, 2001), 437. Further, an operational code analysis based on Carter's public speeches alone shows that his approach toward the Soviet Union did not change prior to the invasion of Afghanistan. Stephen G. Walker, Mark Schafer, and Michael D. Young, "Systematic Procedures for Operational Code Analysis: Measuring and Modeling Jimmy Carter's Operational Code," *International Studies Quarterly* 42, no. 1 (1998): 175–89.
26. Cyrus R. Vance, *Hard Choices: Critical Years in America's Foreign Policy* (New York: Simon and Schuster, 1983), 84.
27. Quoted in *NSC Weekly Report*, no. 42, January 13, 1978.
28. Ibid.
29. Memorandum for the President by Zbigniew Brzezinski, quoted in Brzezinski, *Power and Principle*, 181.
30. *NSC Weekly Report*, no. 47, February 17, 1978.
31. Quoted in *NSC Weekly Report*, no. 47. See also Brzezinski, *Power and Principle*, 188–89.
32. Brzezinski suggested that the Soviet Union was "pursuing deliberately a policy on which it embarked some fifteen years ago: to structure a relationship of stability with the United States in those areas that are congenial or convenient to the USSR, while pursuing assertively every opportunity for the promotion of Soviet influence." Memorandum for the President by Zbigniew Brzezinski, "The USSR and Ethiopia: Implications for US Soviet Relations," March 3, 1978.
33. Quoted in *NSC Weekly Report*, no. 53, April 7, 1978.
34. Quoted in *NSC Weekly Report*, no. 57, May 5, 1978.
35. Vance, *Hard Choices*, 84–85.
36. Ibid., 101–3.
37. Memorandum for the President by Cyrus Vance, May 29, 1978, released to author under FOIA Request no. 200604709 on June 26, 2007. According to Vance (*Hard Choices*, 91), "The government wide study led most participants to reject the 'grand design' interpretation of Soviet behavior. It concluded that Soviet policy in Africa could best be described as an exploitation of opportunity, and attempt to take advantage of African conflicts to increase Soviet influence."
38. Brzezinski's close relationship with Carter and his ability to present his views to the president with clarity as well as simplicity put him at a great advantage in shaping Carter's understanding of the conflict in the Horn. Betty Glad claims that Brzezinski's advantage over Vance arose from the way in which Brzezinski presented information to Carter, and as a result, Brzezinski ultimately controlled the foreign policy process and was able "to lead the president in the direction he thought best." Betty Glad, *An Outsider in the White House: Jimmy Carter, His Advisors, and the Making of American Foreign Policy* (Ithaca, NY: Cornell University Press, 2009), 40.
39. Ibid., 84–85. On Brzezinski's advantage, see ibid., 29–40.
40. *PPP*, May 20, 1978, 872, 940; *PPP*, May 25, 1978, 977. Carter's address at Wake Forest University on March 17, 1978, also reflected his concerns over Soviet actions in Africa. *PPP*, 1978, 529–38.
41. *PPP*, June 7, 1978, 1054; *PPP*, September 28, 1978, 1656.
42. The Helsinki Accords provided that signatories should respect human rights, resolve disputes peacefully, refrain from the use of force, and not intervene in the domestic

affairs of other states. *PPP*, June 7, 1978, 1054. Brzezinski (*Power and Principle*, 320–21) insists that many of the toughly worded statements were Carter's own. Vance (*Hard Choices*, 102) says that the speech was a pastiche of ideas both he and Brzezinski had suggested.

43. Quoted in *NSC Weekly Report*, no. 62, June 9, 1978. Vance, however, believed the speech underlined the inconsistency in the administration.

44. According to Vance (*Hard Choices*, 106), "On the eve of Gromyko's visit" in September 1978, there were "modest grounds" for hope that the erosion in US-Soviet relations could be halted: "African issues had receded, and the Soviets had taken several steps that suggested they wished to reduce the strain between us. The US businessman who had been jailed was released; Jewish emigration levels rose to the highest number in five years; recent trials of Soviet dissidents ended in relatively light sentences; and restrictions on US newsmen in Moscow were eased. The Soviets also indicated through various channels that they expected and would not object to our establishment of a diplomatic relationship with China, so long as normalization was not portrayed as a move against the Soviet Union." Carter shared this optimism and confessed that this meeting with Gromyko was "the most productive one" thus far. Carter, *Keeping Faith*, 238–39; Brzezinski, *Power and Principle*, 326–27. Progress on SALT, however, slowed down at year's end when the US normalization of diplomatic relations with China was announced on the eve of a critical SALT meeting between Gromyko and Vance. Carter, *Keeping Faith*, 239; Vance, *Hard Choices*, 111–12.

45. Quoted in *NSC Weekly Report*, no. 65, June 30, 1978. The group then attempted to determine how the Soviets assessed US resolve and their approach toward the United States. There was a considerable consensus, which according to Brzezinski, was "especially interesting given the difference of views on the first issue." The group concluded that "the Soviets will seek to influence our conduct while staying on their present track and not showing much flexibility. In Africa, they *may* watch their steps for a time in this situation, but will not do anything to accommodate us. They will be leery of exposing themselves to more charges from the segment of US public opinion that believes they broke the rules in Africa. But their greatest concern is with China and US behavior might be affected by the current context."

46. *PPP*, November 13, 1978, 2017.

47. *PPP*, January 26, 1979, 171; *PPP*, February 12, 1979, 260; *PPP*, February 23, 1979, 317.

48. Smith, *Morality, Reason, and Power*, 210.

49. Jimmy Carter, *White House Diary* (New York: Farrar, Straus and Giroux, 2010), 324.

50. Memorandum of Conversation, "Fourth Plenary Meeting between President Carter and General Secretary Brezhnev," June 18, 1979.

51. Melvyn P. Leffler, *For the Soul of Mankind: The United States, the Soviet Union, and the Cold War* (London: Macmillan, 2007), 318.

52. Carter, *Keeping Faith*, 263–66.

53. *PPP*, June 18, 1979, 1092.

54. Quoted in *NSC Weekly Report*, no. 95, May 3, 1979.

55. Quoted in *NSC Weekly Report*, no. 98, May 25, 1979.

56. Quoted in *NSC Weekly Report*, no. 102, July 6, 1979.

57. Quoted in *NSC Weekly Report*, no. 104, July 27, 1979.

58. Vance, *Hard Choices*, 360–61; Brzezinski, *Power and Principle*, 347.

59. Vance, *Hard Choices*, 360.
60. Brzezinski, *Power and Principle*, 351.
61. *PPP*, October 1, 1979, 1805.
62. Message for Leonid Brezhnev from Jimmy Carter regarding Afghanistan, sent December 28, 1979, Zbigniew Brzezinski Collection, box 18, file USSR-Carter/Brezhnev Correspondence 9/79–2/80. See also Brzezinski, *Power and Principle*, 429.
63. Transcript of President's Interview on Soviet Reply, Jimmy Carter interview with Frank Reynolds, ABC NEWS, January 1, 1980.
64. *PPP*, 1980, 40, 108; *PPP*, 1980, 329, 308, 196.
65. Quoted in *NSC Weekly Report*, no. 134, March 28, 1980.
66. Ibid.
67. Ibid.
68. Memorandum for Zbigniew Brzezinski and David Aaron by Marshall Berment, "Response to the Soviets regarding Afghanistan: A Menu of Possible Options," December 28, 1979.
69. Memorandum for the President by Zbigniew Brzezinski, "Strategic Reactions to the Afghanistan Problem," January 3, 1980.
70. Quoted in *NSC Weekly Report*, no. 134, March 28, 1980.
71. Memorandum for Vance's Deputy, Warren Christopher, by Marshall Shulman, "Notes on SU/Afghanistan," January 22, 1980. A month later, Shulman handed Vance a memorandum about the "present Soviet outlook" that spelled out what he interpreted to be the Soviet Union's rather-benign and defensive intentions. In this document, he judged US reactions to be exaggerated and largely counterproductive. Shulman claimed that in assessing Soviet intentions in the longer term, "while the Soviet leadership may conclude that the entire Brezhnev 'peace policy' has failed, and that we may have a period of greater assertiveness in the exploitation of their increased military capabilities, the logic that led them to seek to advance their interests through low-tension policies is likely to assert itself again." Memorandum for Cyrus Vance by Marshall Shulman, "Some Observations of Present Soviet Outlook," February 15, 1980.
72. Quoted in *Department of State Bulletin* (hereafter referred to as *DSB*), March 1980, 38.
73. Quoted in *DSB*, April 1980, 12.
74. Quoted in *DSB*, March 1980, 37–38.
75. Interview with Cyrus Vance, in Melchiore J. Laucella, "Cyrus Vance's Worldview: The Relevance of the Motivated Perspective" (PhD diss., Union Institute, 1996) (emphasis added).
76. Ibid.
77. Interview with Marshall Shulman, in Melchiore J. Laucella, "Cyrus Vance's Worldview: The Relevance of the Motivated Perspective" (PhD diss., Union Institute, 1996).
78. *PPP*, March 24, 1977, 503, 513.
79. *PPP*, April 8, 1977, 603.
80. *PPP*, May 3, 1977, 781.
81. *PPP*, May 30, 1977, 1043. He said, "We felt . . . that they genuinely wanted to have discussions leading to an agreement."
82. *PPP*, December 15, 1977, 2119; *PPP*, October 29, 1936; *PPP*, October 29, 1977, 1939.
83. *PPP*, December 15, 1977, 2119.

84. *PPP*, July 28, 1977, 1367–68.
85. Memorandum to Harold Brown by the President, February 8, 1979, obtained through the Declassified Documents Reference System.
86. From a narrow cognitive perspective, this dramatic and comprehensive change in Carter's beliefs presents somewhat of a puzzle. Cognitive models expect decision makers to be cognitive misers who discount inconsistent information and respond to new evidence only incrementally. Yet Carter's statements indicate that the transformation of his beliefs was genuine. Carter could, like Vance, have chosen to view the invasion of Afghanistan as a manifestation of opportunistic behavior rather than expansionism. This interpretation would have been consistent with his existing beliefs about Soviet intentions and have allowed him to pursue his established policy objectives of arms control. His statements clearly indicate that this was not the case. For an excellent analysis of the sources of Carter's reaction to Afghanistan, see Richard Ned Lebow and Janice Gross Stein, "Afghanistan, Carter, and Foreign Policy Change: The Limits of Cognitive Models," in *Diplomacy, Force, and Leadership: Essays in Honor of Alexander L. George*, ed. Dan Caldwell and Timothy J. McKeown (Boulder, CO: Westview, 1993), 95–128. The analysis here draws on their interpretation.
87. *PPP*, January 20, 1980, 11. For a similar line of reasoning, see also ibid., 308, 329.
88. *PPP*, January 21, 1980, 164.
89. Letter from President Jimmy Carter to Chancellor Helmut Schmidt, February 9, 1980. Obtained through the Declassified Documents Reference System.
90. *DSB*, January 1980, vol. 80.
91. Rosalynn Carter, *First Lady from Plains* (New York: Fawcett, 1984), 298.
92. Lebow and Stein, "Afghanistan, Carter, and Foreign Policy Change," 112.
93. Raymond L. Garthoff, *Détente and Confrontation: American-Soviet Relations from Nixon to Reagan*, rev. ed. (Washington, DC: Brookings Institution Press, 1994), 1059.
94. Hamilton Jordan, *Crisis: The Last Year of the Carter Presidency* (New York: G. P. Putnam's Sons, 1982), 99.
95. Carter, *White House Diary*, 383.
96. Carter, *Keeping Faith*, 481.
97. See, for example, *PPP*, January 20, 1980, 111.
98. *NSC Weekly Report*, no. 47, February 17, 1978.
99. Other NSC staff members were also influenced by recent Soviet actions in the Horn of Africa, and viewed them as indicative of intentions. See, for instance, Memorandum for Zbigniew Brzezinski by Paul Henze (Brzezinski's Deputy), "Realities and Lessons of History in the Horn of Africa," January 12, 1978; Memorandum for Zbigniew Brzezinski by Paul Henze, "Fundamentals in the Horn of Africa Situation," January 16, 1978. The US ambassador to Moscow used similar language. See Telegram for Cyrus Vance from US Ambassador in Moscow Michael Toon, "Prospects for US-Soviet Cooperation on Horn," February 1978.
100. Memorandum for the President by Zbigniew Brzezinski, "The Soviet Union and Ethiopia: Implications for US Soviet Relations," March 3, 1978.
101. *NSC Weekly Report*, no. 65, June 30, 1978.
102. In his memoirs, Brzezinski said that several actions that the Soviets took in 1978 caused great concern in the administration about Soviet objectives and the possibility of ratifying SALT: "they continued the buildup of their military presence in Vietnam and increased their support for Vietnamese aggressiveness in Cambodia"; these con-

cerns were "compounded by the persisting irritation over the Soviet sponsorship of the Cuban military proxy in Africa"; indicators of Soviet involvement in Afghanistan further aggravated these concerns; and the issue of Soviet troops in Cuba "almost fatally" destroyed any chance of ratifying SALT. See Brzezinski, *Power and Principle*, 345–46.

103. *NSC Weekly Report*, no. 95, May 3, 1979. Brzezinski referred to past Cuban and Soviet actions on several different occasions in the following months. Throughout the Soviet brigade affair, Brzezinski's objective was to convince Carter to look at Soviet actions worldwide and across time, and not focus solely on the particularities of the brigade affair.

104. Quoted in *NSC Weekly Report*, no. 109, September 13, 1979.

105. Brzezinski, *Power and Principle*, 430.

106. Memorandum for the President by Zbigniew Brzezinski, "Strategic Reaction to the Afghanistan Problem," January 3, 1980.

107. Quoted in *NSC Weekly Report*, no. 134, March 28, 1980.

108. Ibid.

109. Remarks by Zbigniew Brzezinski to the 1980 American Society of Newspaper Editors Convention, "SP 3–288 Executive 1/2/77–1/20/81," box SP27, subject file, Jimmy Carter Library.

110. Quoted in *NSC Weekly Report*, no. 134, March 28, 1980.

111. Quoted in *NSC Weekly Report*, no. 75, October 13, 1978.

112. Quoted in *NSC Weekly Report*, no. 33, October 21, 1977.

113. In one instance, Brzezinski did link the issue of Soviet capabilities to an assessment of intentions. In September 1979, Brzezinski reported that "several Soviet military activities observed in recent weeks provide further evidence that Soviet force posture is designed for the conduct of a long-term campaign even under conditions of nuclear war." Brzezinski's list of military activities, though, does not provide conclusive evidence to support the capabilities thesis for two reasons. First, most of the indicators mentioned refer to the deployment of capabilities and military exercises; my study characterizes these factors as indicators the strategic military doctrine thesis. Second, the passage does not seem to constitute an assessment of Soviet intentions per se; Brzezinski did not conclude this section with any insights regarding what these trends in Soviet deployed forces actually mean in terms of the ultimate foreign policy objectives of the Soviet Union or its inclination to use force. *NSC Weekly Report*, no. 108, September 6, 1979.

114. Quoted in *NSC Weekly Report*, no. 2, February 26, 1977.

115. Quoted in *NSC Weekly Report*, no. 75, October 13, 1978.

116. "Meeting the Challenge in Southwest Asia," February 1, 1980, *State Bulletin* 80 (March 1980): 35. See also Vance, *Hard Choices*, 391.

117. Cyrus Vance, Statement of US Foreign Policy before the Senate Foreign Relations Committee, March 27, 1980, quoted in Vance, *Hard Choices*, 502.

118. Quoted in *NSC Weekly Report*, no. 134, March 28, 1980.

119. Cyrus Vance, Statement of US Foreign Policy before the Senate Foreign Relations Committee, March 27, 1980, quoted in Vance, *Hard Choices*, 503.

120. Some may argue that Vance's bureaucratic position as a secretary of state colored his interpretation of Soviet intentions, and that because of bureaucratic interests, he did not wish to claim Soviet intentions were expansionist. This interpretation is plausible, but

I find it unconvincing because there is no evidence to suggest that portraying Soviet intentions as expansionist would have had significant ramifications for the State Department. Also, Vance continued to hold these beliefs long after leaving office. See Laucella, "Cyrus Vance's Worldview."

121. For a similar finding, see Rosati, *The Carter Administration's Quest*, 151–53. Vance's resignation stemmed primarily from his opposition to the US rescue operations to free the hostages held in Iran, but also from his pessimism about the future course of US-Soviet relations. Glad, *An Outsider in the White House*, 215.

122. On the role of different domestic political considerations in shaping the change in Carter's policies, see Dan Caldwell, *The Dynamics of Domestic Politics and Arm Control: The SALT II Treaty Ratification Debate* (Columbia: University of South Carolina Press, 1991), 114–15; David Skidmore, *Reversing Course: Carter's Foreign Policy, Domestic Politics, and the Failure to Reform* (Nashville, TN: Vanderbilt University Press, 1996).

123. Brzezinski, *Power and Principle*, 148.

124. Quoted in *NSC Weekly Report*, no. 7, April 1, 1977.

125. *NSC Weekly Report*, no. 18, June 24, 1977.

126. Quoted in *NSC Weekly Report*, no. 20, July 8, 1977.

127. Brzezinski, *Power and Principle*, 175–76.

128. Quoted in *NSC Weekly Report*, no. 37, November 18, 1977.

129. Vance, *Hard Choices*, 46.

130. On Carter's use of the human rights issue in dealing with the Soviets, see Brzezinski, *Power and Principle*, 587, 155–56; Garthoff, *Détente and Confrontation*, 1206.

131. Possible areas for a tougher stance included defense (deployment of MX missiles in multiple protective shelters), trade (a cutoff in the transfer of petroleum technology to the USSR), arms control ("a specific trade-off proposal regarding the ERW," the enhanced radiation weapon or neutron bomb, and "not to budge on the Backfire issue"), or China ("open up access to our technology"). *NSC Weekly Report*, no. 54, April 14, 1978.

132. Quoted in *NSC Weekly Report*, no. 53, April 7, 1978.

133. Quoted in *NSC Weekly Report*, no. 66, July 7, 1978.

134. Brzezinski, *Power and Principle*, 323–25.

135. *NSC Weekly Report*, no. 66, July 7, 1978.

136. Quoted in *NSC Weekly Report*, no. 75, October 13, 1978.

137. *NSC Weekly Report*, no. 55, April 21, 1978. The paragraph that deals with this specific idea was redacted, but Carter's comments on the margins say "proxy war???" Next to the following paragraph where Brzezinski indicated his intention to "develop some ideas regarding the above," Carter wrote, "You will be wasting your time."

138. *NSC Weekly Report*, no. 66, July 7, 1978; *NSC Weekly Report*, no. 69, August 4, 1978. Brzezinski's final weekly report of 1978 provided Carter with an overview of the administration's foreign policy as it had evolved. Brzezinski said that US foreign policy vis-à-vis the USSR was *not*: "confrontational" or a "renewed Cold War"; a "condominium" based on "a balance of power to preserve the status quo"; or "simply a partnership," according to which "a US Soviet partnership on a broad front, starting with SALT, will be the basis for world peace, and hence it ought to be the centerpiece of US foreign policy." Instead, Brzezinski said, the US policy was one of "reciprocal accommodation," meaning "containment . . . resistance to indirect expansion . . . ideological

competition, and most important and above all . . . creation of a framework within which the Soviet Union can accommodate with us, or face the prospect of isolating itself globally." Quoted in *NSC Weekly Report*, no. 83, December 28, 1978.

139. Special Coordination Committee Meeting on the Horn of Africa, March 2, 1978.

140. Quoted in Rosati, *The Carter Administration's Quest*, 61.

141. Vance, *Hard Choices*, 91–93.

142. Memorandum for the President by Cyrus Vance, May 29, 1978.

143. Brzezinski, *Power and Principle*, 335–36. Between 1977 and 1979, the president kept pressing his secretary of defense on whether the United States still needed a strategic triad. Brown assured the president that the triad was essential to US security and that the United States should not move into a defense posture in which its nuclear deterrent would be predominantly sea based. The decision to develop the new land-based deterrent (the MX missile) in May 1979 resulted from shared pessimistic views on trends in the balance of strategic forces. Initially, the president expressed doubts about the threat posed by the Soviet military buildup, and consequently, questioned the request to modernize the US nuclear arsenal, indicating that much of the perception of Soviet superiority had been created by "this [NSC] group." Nevertheless, the president was ultimately persuaded to authorize the development of the MX, but he deferred a decision on deployment until September. Brzezinski, *Power and Principle*, 335–36.

144. Quoted in *NSC Weekly Report*, no. 98, May 25, 1979.

145. Quoted in *NSC Weekly Report*, no. 84, January 12, 1979.

146. Ibid.

147. Quoted in *NSC Weekly Report*, no. 109, September 13, 1979.

148. Quoted *NSC Weekly Report*, no. 110, September 21, 1979.

149. Ibid.

150. At the same time, Brzezinski also thought that the threat posed by the USSR was different from the Cuban Missile Crisis and more like what John Fitzgerald Kennedy confronted when the Soviets suddenly put up the Berlin Wall in 1961. "That situation was 'unacceptable,'" he continued, "but we had no choice except to live with it. Kennedy was not prepared to knock it down. Neither are we prepared to create a military situation in order to get the Soviets to remove their troops from Cuba." Quoted in *NSC Weekly Report*, no. 110, September 21, 1979.

151. Vance, *Hard Choices*, 363–64.

152. Brzezinski's suggestions included the following: do more on defense; show less hesitation in explicitly condemning the Soviet/Cuban exploitation of third world turbulence; adopt a "forceful policy of ostracizing Cuba"; strengthen relations with China; instruct Radio Liberty/Voice of America to "step up their broadcasts to Soviet national minorities, notably the Moslems and Ukrainians"; and convey to Brezhnev the message that the United States is prepared to "take steps that they do not like." Brzezinski noted that he realizes the above would trouble and perhaps even irritate Carter. The president wrote "good" on the first page of the document, although he did not offer his opinion regarding any of Brzezinski's suggestions. *NSC Weekly Report*, no. 109, September 13, 1979; Brzezinski, *Power and Principle*, 346–51.

153. Memorandum for Cyrus Vance and Harold Brown by the President, July 11, 1979, quoted in Brzezinski, *Power and Principle*, 420.

154. Memorandum for the President by Zbigniew Brzezinski, "Secretary Brown's Visit to China: Conflicting Memoranda from Vance and Brown," September 18, 1979. Vance's memo is quoted in part in Vance, *Hard Choices*, 390.
155. Memorandum for the President by Zbigniew Brzezinski, "Secretary Brown's Visit to China: Conflicting Memoranda from Vance and Brown," September 18, 1979. See also Brzezinski, *Power and Principle*, 421–22.
156. Vance, *Hard Choices*, 390–91; Brzezinski, *Power and Principle*, 423–24.
157. For an excellent account of US policies following the invasion of Afghanistan, see Gabriella Grasselli, *British and American Responses to the Soviet Invasion of Afghanistan* (Brookfield, VT: Dartmouth Publishing Co., 1996).
158. On the domestic political price Carter paid for adopting these policies, see Glad, *An Outsider in the White House*, 206–11.
159. Brzezinski, *Power and Principle*, 430.
160. "Foreign Policy: Coherence and Sense of Direction," Meeting of the Special Coordination Committee 293: 3/25/80, box 32, Zbigniew Brzezinski Collection, Jimmy Carter Library.
161. Carter, *Keeping Faith*, 482–86; Brzezinski, *Power and Principle*, 428.
162. Glad, *An Outsider in the White House*, 203–4.
163. Carter nonetheless wrote "no" next to each of the following suggestions by Brzezinski: "1) restrict social contacts with Soviets, and have our officials worldwide keep official contacts with Soviet counterparts to the minimum; 2) expel Soviet intelligence agents from the US; 3) consider raising levels of our human rights criticism of the USSR; 4) [increase] US military alert."
164. Memorandum for the President by Zbigniew Brzezinski, "A Long Term Strategy for Coping with the Consequences of the Soviet Action in Afghanistan," January 9, 1980.
165. Ibid. (emphasis in original). Next to the first comment, Carter wrote, "I agree."
166. Quoted in *NSC Weekly Report*, no. 123, December 14, 1979.
167. Brzezinski, *Power and Principle*, 454. Archival documents reveal that until 1980, Carter had rejected Brzezinski's repeated attempts (which lasted more than a year) to implement this doctrine of containment. After the invasion, on January 16, 1980, Carter informed Brzezinski that he had decided to make the Soviet regional challenge the main theme of his forthcoming State of the Union address. Garthoff, *Détente and Confrontation*, 1084.
168. Most notorious was Presidential Directive 59, announced in July 1980. It was "an attempt to replicate what at least some in the Carter administration believed to be the Soviet war-fighting strategic concept—on the assumption that such a concept would better deter the Soviet Union as well as provide a recourse for waging 'slow-motion' limited nuclear war if deterrence failed." The formulation of this policy had begun in 1977, following the alarming conclusions reached in Presidential Review Memorandum 10. According to Brzezinski (*Power and Principle*, 869), though, Carter increasingly came to support these policies only in the "period from 1978 to 1980 as relations with the USSR deteriorated and the prospects of military détente receded." See also Garthoff, *Détente and Confrontation*, 869.
169. Vance objected to this and other initiatives that Brzezinski and Carter pursued with regard to China. *DSB*, March 1980, vol. 80, 39, 45; Brzezinski, *Power and Principle*, 424–25; Memorandum for the President by Zbigniew Brzezinski, "Strategic Reaction to the Afghanistan Problem," January 3, 1980.

170. Brian Auten attributes the hardening of Carter's defense policy during late 1978 and early 1979 to changes in the administration's strategic assessments, interallied relations, and arms control negotiations. See Brian Auten, *Carter's Conversion: The Hardening of American Defense Policy* (Columbia: University of Missouri Press, 2008), 2–3. For a similar argument, see Nichols Thomas, "Carter and the Soviets: The Origins of U.S. Return to a Strategy of Confrontation," *Diplomacy and Statecraft* 13 (2002): 21–42.

171. These reports pointed to important adverse strategic trends and deficiencies across the board, and thus they helped to convince members of the Carter administration of the need to adopt a countervailing strategy against the Soviet Union. Auten, *Carter's Conversion*, 271–304.

172. According to David Skidmore, for instance, "public skepticism and elite opposition to reform raised the political costs of policy change to intolerable levels, prompting the administration to retreat from its initial liberal internationalist orientation. Each of these constraints can be traced back to the domestic politics of the Cold War era." David Skidmore, *Reversing Course: Carter's Foreign Policy, and the Failure of Reform* (Nashville, TN: Vanderbilt University Press, 1996), xvi. A more recent study criticizes Skidmore's findings by pointing to Carter's heated disagreements, late in his administration, with the military and Congress over defense budgets. See John D. Mini, "Forced Conversion: Civil-Military Relations and National Security Policy in the Carter Administration, 1977–1981" (PhD diss., University of North Carolina at Chapel Hill, 2010). For an additional critique of Skidmore's book, see Auten, *Carter's Conversion*, 3–10.

173. *NSC Weekly Report*, no. 66.

174. Memorandum for the President by Zbigniew Brzezinski, September 29, 1979, Staff Offices, Office of the Staff Secretary, handwriting file, box 149, file President's Address to the Nation re: Soviet Brigade in Cuba.

175. Quoted in Glad, *An Outsider in the White House*, 192. In addition, there is evidence to suggest that some of Carter's decisions on defense were driven, to some extent, by a desire to appease domestic actors who objected to SALT II. Auten, *Carter's Conversion*, 275–83. On Carter's domestic struggle to ratify SALT in the face of pressure from right-wing domestic political groups, see Skidmore, *Reversing Course*, 135–48.

CHAPTER 7: THE US INTELLIGENCE COMMUNITY'S ASSESSMENTS OF SOVIET INTENTIONS: THE COLLAPSE OF DÉTENTE

1. See Douglas F. Garthoff, "Analyzing Soviet Politics and Foreign Policy," in *Watching the Bear: Essays on CIA's Analysis of the Soviet Union*, ed. Gerald K. Haines and Robert E. Leggett (Washington, DC: Center for the Study of Intelligence Publications, 2003), chapter 3, https://www.cia.gov/library/center-for-the-study-of-intelligence/csi-publications/books-and-monographs/watching-the-bear-essays-on-cias-analysis-of-the-soviet-union/index.html (accessed July 9, 2008).

2. Thomas Fingar, *Reducing Uncertainty: Intelligence Analysis and National Security* (Stanford, CA: Stanford Security Studies, 2011), 71.

3. Some sections of the available NIEs are still classified, but these do not appear to pertain to assessments about intentions.

4. Evidence of reasoning in coordinated intelligence estimates might not accurately reflect the assessments of individual intelligence agencies. To the extent that I am interested in the assessment of the community as a whole, however, the final product should accurately reflect the collective assessment or at least the lowest common denominator language resulting from intellectual compromises. Nonetheless, in the US system, individual agencies can write a dissent, and explain how and why they disagree with the coordinated analysis. It is thus important to look at the reasoning that the individual agencies provide in these dissenting footnotes. In the words of Sherman Kent, a former director of ONE and chair of the Board of National Estimates, "Although many experts from perhaps all intelligence components of the community *participated in the production of the papers in the NIE* series, and although the intelligence chiefs themselves formally passed on the final text, *they could not bend its findings to suit their* own judgments. They could try to win him [DCI] to their sides by full and free discussions, but they could not outvote him and force him to join them, *nor could they make him dissent from them.* . . . They could of their own accord concur with his findings or, not being able to, they could dissent and make their alternative views known in footnotes to his text." Sherman Kent, *Sherman Kent and the Board of National Estimates: Collected Essays* (Washington, DC: Center for the Study of Intelligence Publications, 1994) (emphasis added). Yet the absence of a dissenting view might not necessarily mean that all agencies agreed with the estimate, because the National Foreign Intelligence Board (which reviewed and approved NIEs) or even the DCI himself might have decided not to include a particular dissenting footnote in the text.

5. Ibid.

6. NIE 11-3/8-74, 4.

7. Anne H. Cahn, *Killing Détente: The Right Attacks the CIA* (University Park: Penn State Press, 1998), 115. For an excellent review of this episode, see ibid., 115–20.

8. Colby urged Ford to wait until the next NIE (11-3/8-75) before making any further decisions. The president agreed, but critics of the CIA were still not satisfied, and the call for a competitive estimate was renewed a year later. William Colby, letter to President Gerald Ford, November 21, 1975, quoted in Cahn, *Killing Détente*, 119.

9. Pipes was a Harvard University historian and member of the Executive Committee of the Committee on the Present Danger, whose hawkish views of the USSR were well known.

10. See Cahn, *Killing Détente*; Willard C. Matthias, *America's Strategic Blunders* (University Park: Penn State Press, 2007).

11. Memo by DCI George H. W. Bush for Recipients of National Intelligence Estimate 11-3/8-76; printed in Donald P. Steury, *Intentions and Capabilities: Estimates on Soviet Strategic Forces, 1950–1983* (Washington, DC: Central Intelligence Agency, 1996), 339.

12. "Intelligence Community Experiment in Competitive Analysis: Soviet Strategic Objectives: An Alternative View, Report of Team B, December 1976" (hereafter referred to as "Team B Report"), 45. Released by the CIA to the National Archive. For a copy of this report, see Steury, *Intentions and Capabilities*, 365–90.

13. "Team B Report," 45–46.

14. Ibid., 1, 9 (emphasis added).

15. Ibid., 1.

16. Ibid., 2–3. What seems to have driven the Team B analysis were the observable implications of the alleged Soviet war-fighting doctrine—that is, actual and projected changes in Soviet capabilities. Despite the frequent references to Soviet doctrine, the report stopped short of actually adducing evidence to justify its own assumptions about the Soviet doctrine; instead, its interpretation was essentially an essay asserting differences between the Soviet and US military doctrines. Pipes did cite a number of sources for his interpretation (including articles in the classified Soviet journal *Soviet Military Thought*) in a public article that was, in effect, an unclassified version of the Team B Report on Soviet objectives. See Richard Pipes, "Why the USSR Thinks It Could Fight and Win a Nuclear War," *Commentary* 64, no. 1 (1977): 21–34. Soon thereafter, Garthoff published an article drawing on the same sorts of Soviet sources—but citing different passages—to rebut the view propounded by Pipes. Garthoff's article was implicitly a defense of the record of the estimates attacked by Team B. Raymond L. Garthoff, "Mutual Deterrence and Strategic Arms Limitation in Soviet Policy," *International Security* 3, no. 1 (1978): 112–47. For a similar interpretation of Team B reasoning, see Richard K. Betts, "Politicization of Intelligence: Costs and Benefits," in *Paradoxes of Intelligence: Essays in Honor of Michael Handel*, ed. Richard K. Betts and Thomas Mahnken (London: Cass, 2003), 59–79.

17. See, for example, "Team B Report," 3, 19, 21, 46.

18. NIE 11-3/8-76, 15 ("Team A Report").

19. Ibid.

20. Ibid., 4.

21. Ibid.

22. Ibid., 5.

23. Quoted in Cahn, *Killing Détente*, 174–75.

24. Ibid.

25. Raymond L. Garthoff, "Estimating Soviet Military Intentions and Capabilities," in *Watching the Bear: Essays on CIA's Analysis of the Soviet Union*, ed. Gerald K. Haines and Robert E. Leggett (Washington, DC: Center for the Study of Intelligence Publications, 2003), chapter 5.

26. Matthias, *America's Strategic Blunders*, 314.

27. Robert Michael Gates, *From the Shadows: The Ultimate Insider's Story of Five Presidents and How They Won the Cold War* (New York: Simon and Schuster, 1996), 63. The Senate Intelligence Committee report on the Team A-B episode concluded by stating that "the B Team made some valid criticism of the NIEs . . . but those contributions were less valuable than they might have been because . . . the B Team reflected the views of only one segment of the spectrum of opinion." The committee went so far as to say that "the composition of the B Team . . . was so structured that the outcome of the exercise was predetermined." Quoted in Robert C. Reich, "Re-Examining the Team A–Team B Exercise," *International Journal of Intelligence and Counterintelligence* 3, no. 3 (1989): 387–403.

28. Quoted in Matthias, *America's Strategic Blunders*, 313.

29. Author interview with William Odom, July 2007.

30. Author interview with Zbigniew Brzezinski, October 2006.

31. The intelligence community produced four relevant NIEs during the first two years of the Carter administration: NIE 11-4-77, "Soviet Strategic Objectives," January 1977; NIE 11-3/8-77, "Soviet Capabilities for Strategic Nuclear Conflict through

the Late 1980s," February 1978; NIE 11-4-78, "Soviet Goals and Expectations in the Global Power Arena," May 1978; NIE 11-3-78, "Soviet Capabilities for Strategic Nuclear Conflict through the Late 1980s," January 1979.

32. NIE 11-4-77, 1.

33. Ibid., 1–2.

34. Ibid., 7.

35. Ibid., 3.

36. Ibid., 3.

37. Ibid., 11–12. See also ibid., 3. This view of the military intelligence agencies did not discuss Soviet economic or technological difficulties, or the Soviet conflict with China, as factors affecting the projected correlation of forces between the superpowers.

38. NIE 11-3/8-78, 24. These conclusions were repeated in NIE 4-1-78, titled "Warsaw Pact Concepts and Capabilities for Going to War in Europe." It nevertheless estimated that if the Soviets did decide to go to war with NATO, for whatever reason, it was highly likely that their principal military objective would be the rapid defeat of all NATO forces in Central Europe and possibly France as well. See NIE 4-1-78, 1–2.

39. Gates, *From the Shadows*, 74.

40. NIE 11-4-78, i.

41. Ibid., viii, v.

42. Ibid., ix.

43. NIE 11-4-78, x.

44. The CIA at that time did not expect a major Soviet military invasion and occupation of Afghanistan. Yet the community did report a steady build up of forces on the border. See Douglas MacEachin and Janne Nolan, "The Soviet Invasion of Afghanistan in 1979: Failure of Intelligence or Policy Process?" Institute for the Study of Diplomacy Working Group Report 111, September 26, 2005, 4. See also Richard Kerr, "The Track Record: CIA Analysis from 1950 to 2000," in *Analyzing Intelligence: Origins, Obstacles, and Innovations*, ed. Roger George and James Bruce (Washington, DC: Georgetown University Press, 2008), 39.

45. NIE 11-4-78, x.

46. Ibid., xii. The INR also disagreed with how the NIE characterized Soviet arms control behavior, stating that the "arms control motives attributed to the Soviets in the Estimate are essentially those which would apply to any participant in arms control negotiations," and the Soviets "probably see a range of potential benefits—political and economic as well as military—in arms control." See ibid., xiii.

47. NIE 11-10-79, NIE 11-3/8-79, and NIE 11-3/8-80. Unlike the NIEs of the prior years (11-4-77 and 11-4-78), those produced in 1979 and 1980 were not dedicated solely to addressing the question of Soviet objectives.

48. NIE 11-10-79, "Soviet Military Capabilities to Project Power and Influence in Distant Areas," October 1979, 7.

49. Ibid., 44.

50. Ibid., 6

51. NIE 11-3/8-79, "Soviet Capabilities for Strategic Nuclear Conflict through the 1980s," March 1980, 4.

52. Ibid.

53. Ibid., 3.

54. Ibid., 4 (emphasis added).
55. NIE 11-3/8-80, "Soviet Military Capabilities for Strategic Nuclear Conflict through the 1990s," December 1980. The significance of addressing these questions led DCI Turner to take on for himself the task of drafting two NIEs (11-3/8-79 and 11-3/8-80). The inability to resolve these questions led the DIA and each of the military agencies to disassociate themselves from the conclusions reached in NIE 11-3/8-79, and present a second set of "key judgments" in NIE 11-3/8-80.
56. NIE 11-3/8-80, A12. The motivation of the Soviets was seen, however, as offensive: to dissuade the United States from entering an arms race, and split the NATO allies plus lull them into a false sense of security.
57. Ibid., A18.
58. Ibid., B17.
59. Ibid., B18.
60. Proponents of this conclusion explained that the Soviets probably saw their "improvements in survivability and in counterforce capabilities, air defense and antiballistic missile (ABM) development, and broad hardening and civil defense programs in particular, and their improvements in conventional forces in general as contributing to this objective." NIE 11-4-77, 2.
61. Ibid., 3.
62. Ibid., 3–4.
63. According to Garthoff, this assessment reflected the opinions that US analysts had on the correlation of forces at the time. See Garthoff, "Estimating Soviet Military Intentions and Capabilities."
64. NIE 11-4-78, 6.
65. Ibid., xiii.
66. NIE 4-1-78, 1. Another consideration that was mentioned was the USSR's concern that its Eastern European allies might not fight loyally and effectively.
67. NIE 4-1-78 (17), however, recognized that changes in the military balance "would not likely lead to war so long as the Soviets perceived that their losses would be heavy and that the risk to the Soviet homeland would be high."
68. NIE 11-3/8-79, 4.
69. Ibid., 4.
70. Ibid., B17–18.
71. Ibid., 2.
72. This type of analysis, Turner explained, addressed, say, "the potential of one side's ICBMs to attack the retaliatory forces of the other side and then compare[d] the residual destructive potential. . . . The residuals are on-pad potentials, calculated without considering such factors as specific targeting doctrines, command and control degradation, attrition by air defense, and other operational variables." Ibid., 14.
73. Ibid., 3.
74. Ibid., 3.
75. NIE 11-6/8-79, 23.
76. NIE 11-4-77, 11.
77. Ibid., 7.
78. Starting in 1973, as we now know, Colonel Ryszard Kuklinski, a Polish staff officer, supplied important clandestine information on the Warsaw Pact. The intelligence community consequently was able, according to a recent CIA study, "to reconstruct

the main features of the Soviet plans for conflict with NATO in the central region of Europe." Kuklinski's information allowed the intelligence community to "gain more information about planning for offensive operations into Western Europe." Nevertheless, it is not clear from the available documents whether and to what degree this information was shared within the community, and how much and when those NIOs responsible for drafting NIE 11-3/8 and NIE 11-4 on the Soviet Union were familiar with this source. On Kuklinski's contribution, see https://www.cia.gov/library/pub lications/historical-collection-publications/the-warsaw-pact-forces/warsaw-pact -catalogue.pdf (accessed August 21, 2013).

79. NIE 11-4-77, 12.
80. Ibid., 7.
81. Ibid., 7 (emphasis added).
82. NIE 11-3/8-77, 4.
83. NIE 11-4-78, 12.
84. Ibid., 13.
85. Ibid.
86. NIE 11-3/8-79, 3–4.
87. NIE 11-3/8-80, 2.
88. Ibid., 3.
89. NIE 11-4-78, ix.
90. NIE 11-10-79, 11.
91. The conflicting interpretations in Team A and Team B, for example, reflected the essential political debate of the 1970s between hawks and moderates over the nature along with extent of the Soviet threat, and consequently on the possibility as well as desirability of pursuing détente and arms control. The doves were not represented in this competitive analysis.
92. For a discussion on this and other fallacies in estimating intentions during the 1970s, see Raymond L. Garthoff, "On Estimating and Imputing Intentions," *International Security* 2, no. 3 (1978): 23–24.
93. They may have been focusing on different questions; they may have thought the distinction between political and military intent was irrelevant; or they may have found it convenient to hone in on the one aspect of Soviet intentions that was more consistent with their preexisting beliefs. Betts makes a similar point in Richard K. Betts and Thomas Mahnken, eds., *Paradoxes of Intelligence: Essays in Honor of Michael Handel* (London: Cass, 2003).
94. Zbigniew Brzezinski, speech at conference, quoted in Gerald K. Haines and Robert E. Leggett, eds., *Watching the Bear: Essays on CIA's Analysis of the Soviet Union* (Washington, DC: Center for the Study of Intelligence Publications, 2003), chapter 8, https://www.cia.gov/library/center-for-the-study-of-intelligence/csi-publications/ books-and-monographs/watching-the-bear-essays-on-cias-analysis-of-the-soviet- union (accessed August 20, 2013).
95. Quoted in *NSC Weekly Report*, no. 95, May 18, 1978. Such efforts began sometime around spring 1978. *NSC Weekly Report*, no. 54, April 14, 1978.
96. National Security Archive Cold War Interviews, interview with Stansfield Turner, http:// www.gwu.edu/~nsarchiv/coldwar/interviews/episode-21/turner1.html (accessed August 20, 2013).

CHAPTER 8: INDICATORS OF SOVIET INTENTIONS
AND THE END OF THE COLD WAR, 1985–88

1. See, for example, Don Oberdorfer, *The Turn: From the Cold War to a New Era, 1983–1990* (New York: Poseidon Press, 1991); Raymond L. Garthoff, ed., *The Great Transition: American-Soviet Relations and the End of the Cold War* (Washington, DC: Brookings Institution Press, 1994); Michael R. Beschloss and Strobe Talbott, *At the Highest Levels: The Inside Story of the End of the Cold War* (Boston: Little, Brown and Company, 1993); William C. Wohlforth, *Witnesses to the End of the Cold War* (Baltimore: Johns Hopkins University Press, 1996); William C. Wohlforth, ed., *Cold War Endgame: Oral History, Analysis, Debates* (University Park: Pennsylvania State University Press, 2003); Richard Ned Lebow and Thomas Risse-Kappen, eds., *International Relations and the End of the Cold War* (New York: Columbia University Press, 1995); Andrew H. Kydd, *Trust and Mistrust in International Relations* (Princeton, NJ: Princeton University Press, 2005); Mark L. Haas, "The United States and the End of the Cold War: Reactions to Shifts in Soviet Power, Policies, or Domestic Politics?" *International Organization* 61, no. 1 (2007): 145–79; Lou Cannon, *President Reagan: The Role of a Lifetime* (New York: Simon and Schuster, 2000); Melvyn P. Leffler, *For the Soul of Mankind: The United States, the Soviet Union, and the Cold War* (London: Macmillan, 2007); Barbara Farnham, "Reagan and the Gorbachev Revolution: Perceiving the End of Threat," *Political Science Quarterly* 116, no. 2 (2001): 225–52; John Mueller, "What Was the Cold War About? Evidence from Its Ending," *Political Science Quarterly* 119, no. 4 (2004–5): 609–31.

2. *Public Papers of the Presidents of the United States* (hereafter referred to as *PPP*) (Washington, DC: US Government Printing Office, 1978), June 1, 1987, 594–95; *PPP*, June 11, 1987, 624; *PPP*, June 12, 1987, 635–36; *PPP*, August 29, 1987, 988; *PPP*, September 16, 1987, 1038.

3. George Shultz, *Turmoil and Triumph: My Years as Secretary of State* (New York: Charles Scribner's Sons, 1993), 993.

4. Keith L. Shimko, *Images and Arms Control: Perceptions of the Soviet Union in the Reagan Administration* (Ann Arbor: University of Michigan Press, 1991), 233.

5. Ibid., 235–37.

6. For a list of the currently declassified NIEs on the Soviet Union, see the CIA's Electronic Reading Room, http://www.foia.cia.gov/ (accessed August 20, 2013).

7. Neither Reagan nor Shultz had much experience or in-depth knowledge about nuclear weapons, and Weinberger, while enjoying an edge over these two, was also not knowledgeable about these issues before becoming secretary of defense. As none of the key decision makers were experts on this topic, we should not expect to see evidence that any of them inferred Soviet intentions from material capabilities. Shimko, *Images and Arms Control*, 241–42.

8. US Department of Defense, Office of the Secretary of Defense, *Soviet Military Power* (hereafter referred to as *SMP*, accompanied by the publication year) (Washington, DC: US Government Printing Office). Many Sovietologists and political scientists writing on Soviet capabilities sharply questioned the data reported in *SMP*, arguing that the DOD was inflating the threat posed by the Soviet Union. Since this book is concerned with how Soviet capabilities were *perceived* by various bureaucracies in the

United States, the periodical provides an important piece of evidence. On the Soviet ICBM arsenal, see, for instance, NIE 11-3/8-86; NIE 11-3/8-87; NIE 11-3/8-88.

9. See *SMP*, 1990.

10. Negotiations for the INF Treaty began in September 1981, resulting in an agreement signed in 1987 at the Washington summit between Reagan and Gorbachev. Under the INF, both superpowers agreed to eliminate all intermediate-range ground-launched missiles, nuclear and conventional, over a three-year period starting in 1988.

11. *SMP*, 1988. NIE 11-3/8-86 (8) concluded that "[Soviet] warheads are increasing. [Soviet ICBM] systems now being deployed . . . carry many more warheads than the systems they are replacing. . . . Force diversity is increasing. A growing proportion of Soviet intercontinental attack warheads will be deployed on SSBNs and mobile ICBMs, with a lower proportion in fixed silos." For similar conclusions, see NIE 11-3/8-87, 7.

12. NIE 11-3/8-88, 5.

13. The Soviet strategic bomber force was considered, for many decades, to be the least effective element of the Soviet strategic triad. Yet in the 1980s, the USSR began deploying new aircraft and weapon systems such as the long-range BEAR H and BLACKJACK aircraft along with the AS-15 long-range air-launched cruise missile. The US defense establishment perceived these improvements as part of an effort to increase the bomber force's capability and survivability for intercontinental nuclear strike missions. *SMP*, 1989, 5.

14. In 1985, DOD analysts reported that the Soviets were developing widespread ABM deployments beyond Moscow. Four years later, they reported that the Soviets had nearly completed construction of an expanded and upgraded system to defend selected leadership and strategic facilities near Moscow. *SMP*, 1989.

15. NIE 11-3/8-88, 4.

16. Noel E. Firth, *Soviet Defense Spending: A History of CIA Estimates, 1950–1990* (College Station: Texas A&M University Press, 1998), 98–112.

17. *SMP*, 1989, 7.

18. NIE 11-3/8-88, 5. Only in 1989, following the initial phases of the Soviet unilateral force reductions and Reagan's departure from office, did the US intelligence community and defense establishment report a noticeable change in Soviet military capabilities. Even then, they concluded that Warsaw Pact forces would "remain the largest aggregation of military power in the world" and the Soviets would "remain committed to the offensive as the preferred form of operation in war-time." NIE 11-4-89, April 1989, 12; Ben B. Fischer, *At Cold War's End: US Intelligence on the Soviet Union and Eastern Europe, 1989–1991* (Reston, VA: Central Intelligence Agency, 1999), xiii. By September 1989, the impact of the significant steps taken by Gorbachev began to be recognized by the US intelligence community. Memorandum for Holders of NIE 4-1-84, September 1989.

19. NIE 11-3/8-88, 7

20. US defense spending increased under Reagan from 4.9 percent of the gross domestic product in 1981 to 6.1 percent in 1985. After that, the rate of increase could not be sustained, but the administration seemed satisfied that US strength had been restored. The alarming window of vulnerability of US strategic missiles depicted in the late 1970s and early 1980s had been debunked by the Scowcroft Commission's 1983 report.

21. See Shimko, *Images and Arms Control*, 72–74.

22. As late as February 1989, Defense Secretary Dick Cheney warned that future improvements in Soviet strategic offensive and defensive forces "could tilt the strategic balance in Moscow's favor." See Dick Cheney, "Annual Report to the President and Congress, 1990," 16–17.

23. Secretary of Defense, "Annual Report to the President and Congress, 1989," 29.

24. The result of these changes would leave a total Soviet strength in Eastern Europe of approximately fifty thousand personnel and five thousand vehicles (e.g., tanks, assault landing vehicles, and assault river-crossing vehicles).

25. In January 1989, a month after Gorbachev's announcement of the deep cuts in Warsaw Pact personnel and capabilities, Cheney warned that the Warsaw Pact's continuous military production would still allow it to "maintain its quantitative advantage over NATO in most categories of weapon systems." He believed it was positioned to keep that advantage for at least the next five years even if Gorbachev's reductions were implemented. Cheney, "Annual Report to the President and Congress, 1990," 19. Only in mid-1990 were US assessments of the regional military balances significantly modified to reflect the unilateral Soviet cuts. *SMP*, 1990, 92–93.

26. *Department of State Bulletin* (hereafter referred to as *DSB*), April 1988, 39, quoted in Shimko, *Images and Arms Control*, 90.

27. See US Congress 1987, House Panel of the Committee on Armed Services, *Hearings on National Security Policy*, 100th Cong., 1st Sess., 845; *DSB*, April 1988, 6; *DSB*, June 1984, 29; *DSB*, May 1985, 27. All are quoted in Shimko, *Images and Arms Control*, 91–94.

28. Ronald Reagan, "Address to the Nation on National Security," February 26, 1986, http://reagan2020.us/speeches/address_on_national_security.asp (accessed August 30, 2013).

29. *Public Papers of the Presidents of the United States* (hereafter referred to as *PPP*) (Washington, DC: US Government Printing Office, 1978), 1986, 287; *PPP*, 1985, 1347. Both are quoted in Shimko, *Images and Arms Control*, 110–13.

30. Caspar Weinberger, *Annual Report to the Congress, Fiscal Year 1988*, January 1987, 116 (emphasis added).

31. Coit D. Blacker, *Hostage to Revolution: Gorbachev and Soviet Security Policy, 1985–1991* (New York: Council on Foreign Relations Press, 1993), 68. In 1987, during a meeting of the Warsaw Pact's Political Consultative Committee in Berlin, the Soviets issued a document declaring that the military doctrine of the Warsaw Treaty member states was "strictly a defensive one" and "subordinate to the task of preventing war, both nuclear and conventional." On the Berlin Declaration, see William C. Green and Theodore W. Karasik, *Gorbachev and His Generals: The Reform of Soviet Military Doctrine* (Boulder, CO: Westview Press, 1990), 38–39.

32. For a good summary of the main features of the new Soviet doctrine and controversy it generated during this period, see Stephen M. Meyer, "The Sources and Prospects of Gorbachev's New Political Thinking on Security," *International Security* 13, no. 2 (1988): 124–63; Raymond L. Garthoff, *Deterrence and the Revolution in Soviet Military Doctrine* (Washington, DC: Brookings Institution, 1990); Christoph Bluth, *The Collapse of Soviet Military Power* (Brookfield, VT: Dartmouth Publishing Company, 1995), 83–90; Alan Collins, *The Security Dilemma and the End of the Cold War* (Edinburgh: Keele University Press, 1997).

33. In each of its annual volumes from 1985 to 1990, *SMP* continued to depict the Warsaw Pact forces as aiming to defeat European NATO forces at any level of conflict, occupy NATO countries, use Europe's surviving economic power to assist Soviet recovery, neutralize China along with the United States and its allies separately by disrupting and destroying their military forces, and dominate the postwar world. Although they recognized the devastating nature of nuclear weapons, the Soviets sought to survive and prevail in a nuclear war, believing that victory in such a war was possible. Analysts thought that the Soviet doctrine of nuclear war still emphasized offensive operations, although the 1987 *SMP* recognized that defensive actions had begun to receive increasing attention from Soviet strategists. Nevertheless, the *SMP* (1987, 16) judged that these actions would be undertaken "either to support nearby offensive operations or to create favorable conditions for resuming the offensive."

34. NIE 11-3/8-85, 18–22. All these conclusions were reiterated in NIE 11-3/8-86, April 1986; see ibid., 15–16. In that NIE, the intelligence community also stated that the Soviets did not endorse mutual vulnerability as a desirable basis for establishing or preserving strategic stability.

35. NIE 11-3/8-87, 5.

36. Ibid.

37. Ibid., 8–9.

38. The 1988 volume of the *SMP*, published in April, noted for the first time a declared change in the orientation of Soviet military doctrine as well as Soviet references to achieving "parity at lower levels." Nonetheless, it saw "no reason to conclude that 'reasonable sufficiency' represent[ed] a renunciation or even an alteration of the inherently offensive Soviet military strategy." *SMP*, 1988, 12–13. Soviet doctrine was also still judged as placing emphasis on the defeat or neutralization of the United States and its allies, and achieving victory in all kinds and phases of warfare (including nuclear war). Ibid., 13. All this was reiterated in the 1989 volume; it again acknowledged the changes in Soviet declaratory policy and major effects these would have on Soviet posture, but still concluded that these effects would become clear "only if and when" the Soviets were to "change the size and character of deployed Soviet military forces." *SMP*, 1989, 17. These views were echoed in Secretary of Defense Frank Carlucci, *Annual Report to the Congress, Fiscal Year 1990*, January 1989, 11–12; Joint Chiefs of Staff, "1989 Joint Military Net Assessment," June 1989, ES-2.

39. Office of Soviet Analysis (SOVA), Directorate of Intelligence, CIA, "Soviet National Security Policy: Responses to the Changing Military and Economic Environment," SOV 88-10040CX, June 1988, v.

40. NIE 11-14-89, February 1989, iii. The DOD was more reluctant than the intelligence community as a whole to acknowledge these changes. *SMP*, 1990, 2830.

41. The DIA did not share these conclusions, claiming propaganda objectives for Soviet discussions of the concept of reasonable sufficiency. NIE 11-14-89, v, 2–3.

42. Ibid., 6.

43. These conclusions were reiterated in National Intelligence Council Memo 89-10002, "The Post-CFE Environment in Europe," September 1989 (referring to ongoing negotiations on Conventional Forces in Europe); National Intelligence Council Memo 89-10003, "Status of Soviet Unilateral Withdrawals," October 1989; National Intelligence Council Memo 89-10005, "Soviet Theater Forces in 1991: The Impact of the Unilateral Withdrawals on Structure and Capabilities," November 1989.

44. Quoted in *DSB*, January 1987, 32; Shimko, *Images and Arms Control*, 89–90.

45. Quoted in Shimko, *Images and Arms Control*, 109.

46. Ibid., 108–10.

47. Quoted in Jack F. Matlock Jr., *Reagan and Gorbachev: How the Cold War Ended* (New York: Random House, 2004), 151.

48. Quoted in ibid., 150–54.

49. See Garthoff, *The Great Transition*, 214–15.

50. Matlock, *Reagan and Gorbachev*, 116–17.

51. Ibid., 116–17.

52. Reagan himself liked the fact that the Soviet leader was proposing to get rid of nuclear weapons altogether and chose to respond to Gorbachev's offer with a positive statement. Yet he also stated that certain elements of the proposal caused the United States "serious concern." Ibid., 178.

53. The deal collapsed over the terms of observing the ABM Treaty and proposals to limit SDI development to the laboratory.

54. US suspicions were also aroused by several flare-ups of espionage in 1986, including the arrest of a US journalist in Moscow that received widespread media attention. See Garthoff, *The Great Transition*, 281–84. Additionally, the Soviets continued to support revolutionary socialist movements around the third world. See Richard K. Hermann, "Soviet Behavior in Regional Conflicts: Old Questions, New Strategies, and Important Lessons," *World Politics* 44, no. 3 (1992): 252–61.

55. For more on the arguments against the INF, see Matlock, *Reagan and Gorbachev*, 275–76; Garthoff, *The Great Transition*, 334.

56. Under the INF Treaty, the USSR was required to destroy a total of 1,846 missiles, more than double the number (848) that the United States was required to destroy. See Garthoff, *The Great Transition*, 327.

57. Robert M. Gates, *From the Shadows: The Ultimate Insider's Story of Five Presidents and How They Won the Cold War* (New York: Simon and Schuster, 1996), 427–37. See also Richard K. Herrmann, "Regional Conflicts as Turning Points: The Soviet and American Withdrawal from Afghanistan, Angola, and Nicaragua," in *Ending the Cold War: Interpretations, Causation, and the Study of International Relations*, ed. Richard K. Herrmann and Richard Ned Lebow (Basingstoke, UK: Palgrave Macmillan, 2004), 59–83.

58. Even Gates (*From the Shadows*, 436–37) saw Gorbachev's withdrawals from Afghanistan and Angola as "the final proof that, at least in foreign policy," Gorbachev was "a very different Soviet leader"; he asserted that this impression was shared by many in the CIA, DOD, and NSC at the time.

59. Shultz, *Turmoil and Triumph*, 1092, 1086.

60. This took place in the plenary session of the Central Committee meeting in January 1987. See Haas, "The United States and the End of the Cold War," 162–63; Garthoff, *The Great Transition*, 303; Archie Brown, *The Gorbachev Factor* (New York: Oxford University Press, 1997), 34–36.

61. According to Haas, as late as February 1988, Gorbachev himself was still reluctant to say explicitly that he aimed at fundamental ideological changes in the Soviet Union. Some Soviet scholars, similarly, claim that it was only from spring 1988 onward that Gorbachev was willing to transform the Soviet system, not merely reform it. See Brown, *The Gorbachev Factor*, 200.

62. Mark L. Haas, *The Ideological Origins of Great Power Politics, 1789–1989* (Ithaca, NY: Cornell University Press, 2005), 200; Haas, "The United States and the End of the Cold War," 163–64; Frances Fitzgerald, *Way Out There in the Blue: Reagan, Star Wars, and the End of the Cold War* (New York: Simon and Schuster, 2001), 454; Jack F. Matlock Jr., *Autopsy of an Empire: The American Ambassador's Account of the Collapse of the Soviet Union* (New York: Random House, 1995), 122; Susanne Sternthal, *Gorbachev's Reforms: De-Stalinization through Demilitarization* (Westport, CT: Praeger 1997), 110–11.

63. Sternthal, *Gorbachev's Reforms*, 114–15.

64. See Matlock, *Reagan and Gorbachev*, 295–96; Sternthal, *Gorbachev's Reforms*, 1101–11.

CHAPTER 9: US DECISION MAKERS' PERCEPTIONS OF SOVIET INTENTIONS: THE END OF THE COLD WAR

1. Quoted in Raymond L. Garthoff, *The Great Transition: American-Soviet Relations and the End of the Cold War* (Washington, DC: Brookings Institution, 1994), 352.

2. Ronald Reagan, news conference, Spaso House, Moscow, *Department of State Bulletin* (hereafter referred to as *DSB*), June 1988, 32.

3. Fred Greenstein, "Ronald Reagan: Another Hidden-Hand Ike?" *PS: Political Science and Politics* 23, no. 1 (1990): 7–13.

4. Shultz notes that Reagan had a "serious weakness: a tendency to rely on his staff and friends to the point of accepting uncritically—even wishfully—advice that was sometimes amateurish and even irresponsible," such as the notion of the potential effectiveness of the SDI ("Star Wars"). George Shultz, *Turmoil and Triumph: My Years as Secretary of State* (New York: Charles Scribner's Sons, 1993), 263.

5. See Beth A. Fischer, *The Reagan Reversal: Foreign Policy and the End of the Cold War* (Columbia: University of Missouri Press, 2000), 69–84; Cecil V. Crabb Jr. and Kevin V. Mulcahy, *Presidents and Foreign Policy Making: From FDR to Reagan* (Baton Rouge: Louisiana State University Press, 1986), 272–303.

6. Fischer, *The Reagan Reversal*, 77–82. See also Lou Cannon, *President Reagan: The Role of a Lifetime* (New York: Simon and Schuster, 1992), 182–86.

7. Shultz, *Turmoil and Triumph*, 532.

8. Memorandums of Conversations, Reagan-Thatcher Meeting at Camp David, December 28, 1984, www.margaretthatcher.org/archive/displaydocument.asp?docid=109185 (accessed July 14, 2008).

9. Ronald Reagan, *An American Life* (New York: Simon and Schuster, 1990), 614–15.

10. Reagan's letter of April 30, 1985 to Gorbachev was dedicated to this incident; see www.gwu.edu/~nsarchiv/NSAEBB/NSAEBB172/Doc9.pdf (accessed July 14, 2008).

11. Reagan, *An American Life*, 629.

12. Garthoff, *The Great Transition*, 227.

13. *DSB*, November 1985, 11.

14. Keith L. Shimko, *Images and Arms Control: Perceptions of the Soviet Union in the Reagan Administration* (Ann Arbor: University of Michigan Press, 1991), 87.

15. On Reagan's public references to Soviet global expansionism during his first administration, see ibid., 103–5.

16. *Public Papers of the President of the United States* (hereafter referred to as *PPP*) (Washington, DC: US Government Printing Office, 1985), 415.

17. Quoted in Garthoff, *The Great Transition*, 236.

18. Quoted in Jack F. Matlock Jr. files, Ronald Reagan Presidential Library, Simi Valley, CA; also quoted in Jack F. Matlock Jr., *Reagan and Gorbachev: How the Cold War Ended* (New York: Random House, 2004), 151.

19. Memo by George Shultz to the President, "Your Meeting with Gorbachev in Geneva," November 7, 1985. A few days prior to the summit, Shultz sent a memo to Reagan, noting that a number of Russian citizens whose cases were on the US list of separated spouses, dual nationals, and divided families had received Soviet permission to emigrate. According to Shultz, this signified that "the Soviets are clearly sending a signal prior to the Geneva meeting expressing a willingness to move forward." Although this was a significant step, Shultz concluded, the Soviets were still a long way from resolving all the cases of separated spouses. Memo by George Shultz to the President, "Recent Resolution of US-Soviet Separated Spouse, Dual National, and Divided Family Cases," November 15, 1985.

20. Memo by Robert McFarlane to the President, "Your Meetings with Gorbachev in Geneva," November 8, 1985.

21. Shultz, *Turmoil and Triumph*, 601.

22. Reagan, *An American Life*, 635, 639.

23. Quoted in Cannon, *President Reagan*, 672.

24. Quoted in Geneva Plenary Session, 11:27–12:15 p.m., November 19, 1985, 6–7, http://www2.gwu.edu/~nsarchiv/NSAEBB/NSAEBB172/ (accessed October 3, 2013).

25. During a private meeting with Gorbachev, Reagan promised that if the Soviets were to change their policies on human rights and emigration, he would never take credit in public for persuading Gorbachev to do this. He explained that he shared Gorbachev's concerns about his domestic political image and reassured the Soviet leader that he would not give the impression that Gorbachev was caving in to outside influence. See Memorandum of Conversation, "Reagan-Gorbachev Morning Tête-à-Tête," November 20, 1985, 10:15 a.m.–11:25 a.m., 5–6, http://www2.gwu.edu/~nsarchiv/NSAEBB/NSAEBB172/ (accessed October 3, 2013).

26. On the significance of the summit's joint communiqué, see Shultz, *Turmoil and Triumph*, 599–606; Matlock, *Reagan and Gorbachev*, 165–60.

27. Reagan, *An American Life*, 641.

28. For a copy of Reagan's letter to Gorbachev, see www.gwu.edu/~nsarchiv/NSAEBB/NSAEBB172/Doc29.pdf (accessed July 14, 2008).

29. Ronald Reagan, "Address before a Joint Session of the Congress following the Soviet–United States Summit Meeting in Geneva," November 21, 1985, www.reagan.utexas.edu/archives/speeches/1985/112185c.htm (accessed September 3, 2009).

30. Matlock, *Reagan and Gorbachev*, 177–78.

31. Reagan, *An American Life*, 650–51.

32. Letter from Ronald Reagan to Mikhail Gorbachev, February 6, 1986, quoted in Reagan, *An American Life*, 652–56. During the following months, Reagan would deliver a series of public statements on regional conflicts and "Soviet expansionism." Ronald Reagan, "Message to Congress on Freedom, Regional Security, and World Peace," March 14, 1986, www.reagan.utexas.edu/archives/speeches/1986/31486d.htm (accessed July 14, 2008).

33. Shultz, *Turmoil and Triumph*.

34. Ibid., 706–7.

35. *PPP*, June 11, 1986, 750.

36. *PPP*, July 25, 1986, 1008; see also *PPP*, August 12, 1986, 1082.

37. NSC Paper, "Gorbachev's Goals and Tactics at Reykjavik," October 1986.

38. Shultz, *Turmoil and Triumph*, 771.

39. Reagan, *An American Life*, 676–77.

40. Ibid., 677, 679.

41. Matlock, *Reagan and Gorbachev*, 250.

42. Sidney D. Drell and George P. Shultz, eds., *Implications of the Reykjavik Summit on Its Twentieth Anniversary: Conference Report* (Stanford, CA: Hoover Institution Press, 2007), 99. See also George Shultz, Sidney D. Drell, and James E. Goodby, eds., *Reykjavik Revisited: Steps toward a World Free of Nuclear Weapons* (Stanford, CA: Hoover Institution Press, 2008).

43. *PPP*, October 13, 1986, 1369.

44. White House, "National Security Strategy," 1987.

45. Garthoff, *The Great Transition*, 308.

46. *PPP*, April 10, 1987, 367.

47. *PPP*, May 27, 1987, 571.

48. *PPP*, June 11, 1987, 626–27. Reagan was fond of this Russian proverb; he repeated it on nearly every occasion he was asked about his relations with Gorbachev during his tenure.

49. *PPP*, July 24, 1987, 868. See also *PPP*, June 1, 1987, 594–95; *PPP*, June 11, 1987, 624; *PPP*, June 12, 1987, 635–36; *PPP*, August 29, 1987, 988; *PPP*, September 16, 1987, 1038.

50. Reagan, *An American Life*, 691.

51. Ibid., 686.

52. *PPP*, September 28, 1987, 1088.

53. *PPP*, October 28, 1987, 1239.

54. Memo to the Vice President, Secretary of State, Secretary of Defense, National Security Advisor and Chairman, and Joint Chiefs of Staff from William Webster, November 24, 1987, NSA box 3.

55. Shultz, *Turmoil and Triumph*, 1003. See also Matlock, *Reagan and Gorbachev*, 269–70.

56. Author interview with Jack F. Matlock Jr., June 2007.

57. Matlock, *Reagan and Gorbachev*, 269–70. Shultz told Reagan that the administration should not speculate on the sources of Soviet conduct. Since "our knowledge was thin," he wrote, basing US policies on speculation or beliefs about what is going on in the Soviet Union "could be wrong." Instead, he suggested, the United States should continue to maintain its strength while seeking agreements that served its interests. Later, both Shultz and Matlock attributed Gorbachev's conduct during the meeting with Shultz on October 22 to the Soviet leader's struggles with growing domestic opposition from such party figures as Boris Yeltsin and Yegor Ligachev. See Shultz, *Turmoil and Triumph*, 1002, 1004; Matlock, *Reagan and Gorbachev*, 266–67.

58. Matlock, *Reagan and Gorbachev*, 274.

59. Cannon, *President Reagan*, 696.

60. Melvyn P. Leffler, *For the Soul of Mankind: The United States, the Soviet Union, and the Cold War* (London: Macmillan, 2007), 401.

61. Reagan, *An American Life*, 701.

62. Jack F. Matlock Jr., *Autopsy of an Empire: The American Ambassador's Account of the Collapse of the Soviet Union* (New York: Random House, 1995), 148.

63. *PPP*, 1987, 1508–9.

64. Ibid., 1510.

65. Caspar W. Weinberger, *Fighting for Peace: Seven Critical Years in the Pentagon* (New York: Warner Books, 1990), 332. In his memoir, Weinberger asserted that the fundamental difference between Gorbachev and his predecessors was that Gorbachev "seeks favorable world opinion." He acknowledged that Gorbachev made significant concessions in signing the INF, but was highly skeptical of Gorbachev's declaration of a unilateral withdrawal of conventional forces, noting that the USSR could still retain a large imbalance in conventional arms in its favor. Weinberger (ibid., 348) argued that Soviet military power "not only has not declined, but is still increasing, even though there may be occasional leveling off of their total spending as they complete production runs on some models and must retool before they start their latest series. The important thing to watch is their output, and that continues to outstrip ours each month in virtually all categories."

66. Quoted in *DSB*, January 1988, 6–7. Official publications by the White House, such as the "National Security Strategy" (published in January 1988), evidence a gradual but still-incomplete shift in the characterization of Soviet intentions. Garthoff, *The Great Transition*, 339.

67. Quoted in *DSB*, April 1988, 41.

68. Quoted in *DSB*, May 1988, 4.

69. President Ronald Reagan, Remarks to the World Affairs Council of Western Massachusetts, Springfield, April 21, 1988, www.reagan.utexas.edu/archives/speeches /1988/042188c.htm (accessed August 10, 2009). Like Shultz, Reagan explained that the issues of regional conflicts and human rights were "closely intertwined," because "when a government abuses the rights of its own people, it is a grim indication of its willingness to commit violence against others." See ibid.

70. Matlock, *Reagan and Gorbachev*, 291.

71. Ibid., 294–95.

72. Ronald Reagan interview with Soviet television journalists Valentin Zorin and Boris Kalyagin, May 20, 1988.

73. Ibid., May 19, 1988.

74. Ibid.

75. Written responses by Ronald Reagan to questions submitted by the Soviet magazine *Ogonyok*, May 19, 1988.

76. Shultz, *Turmoil and Triumph*, 1086.

77. *PPP*, May 23, 1988, 632; *PPP*, June 3, 1988, 726.

78. Weinberger, *Fighting for Peace*, 348–49.

79. Matlock, *Reagan and Gorbachev*, 295–96.

80. Ronald Reagan's First One-on-one Meeting with Mikhail Gorbachev, Moscow, May 29, 1988, www.margaretthatcher.org/commentary/displaydocument.asp?docid =110610 (accessed August 21, 2013).

81. Reagan, *An American Life*, 706–7.
82. President's News Conference, Spaso House, Moscow, June 1, 1988, *US Department of State Bulletin* 88, 2137:31–35.
83. Shultz, *Turmoil and Triumph*, 1131.
84. See Weinberger, *Fighting for Peace*, 348–49.
85. *PPP*, November 12, 1985, 1370.
86. Ronald Reagan, "Message to Congress on Freedom, Regional Security, and World Peace," March 14, 1986, www.reagan.utexas.edu/archives/speeches/1986/31486d.htm (accessed July 12, 2008).
87. *PPP*, August 24, 1985, 1010.
88. Ronald Reagan to Mikhail Gorbachev, April 30, 1985.
89. Plenary Session, Geneva, November 19, 1985, 11:27–12:15 p.m.
90. *PPP*, September 22, 1986, 1230–31.
91. *PPP*, October 29, 1985, 1313; see also statement in *PPP*, November 12, 1985, 1373.
92. *PPP*, August 24, 1985, 1010.
93. *PPP*, February 11, 1986, 204.
94. *PPP*, March 12, 1986, 330. Reagan did not treat all proposals equally, however. On the Soviet proposal for a nuclear testing moratorium, Reagan (ibid., 331) said, "Their proposal is unfair to us." Similarly, in June, while declaring the US withdrawal from SALT II, Reagan stated, "Based on Soviet conduct since my June 1985 decision [to continue to abide by SALT II], I can only conclude that the Soviet Union has not, as yet, taken those actions that would indicate its readiness to join us in an interim framework of truly mutual restraint." *PPP*, May 27, 1986, 679.
95. *PPP*, July 8, 1986, 931. In their private meeting in Reykjavik, Reagan pushed Gorbachev to move beyond rhetoric, reiterating the logic that Soviet behavior was the source of US fears and concerns over Soviet intentions. He thus reminded Gorbachev that the Soviet refusal to respond to US calls after World War II to eliminate nuclear weapons proved that "Soviet behavior reveal[s] a belief on the Soviets' part in a worldwide mission, which gives us legitimate ground to suspect Soviet motives." Quoted in Drell and Shultz, *Implications of the Reykjavik Summit on Its Twentieth Anniversary*, 135.
96. *PPP*, November 4, 1987, 1271.
97. Specifically, in terms of glasnost, Reagan demanded that Gorbachev "publish a valid budget of Soviet military expenditure; reveal the size and composition of Soviet armed forces; and open for debate the big issues of military policy and weapons." These steps, according to Reagan, "would contribute to greater understanding between us and also to the good sense of your own decisions on the grave matters of armaments and military posture." *PPP*, August 26, 1987, 980. On renouncing the Brezhnev Doctrine, Reagan reiterated these demands on numerous occasions. See, for example, *PPP*, 1987, 868; *PPP*, July 24, 1987, 980; *PPP*, August 26, 1987, 988; *PPP*, August 29, 1987, 1038; *PPP*, September 16, 1987; *PPP*, November 4, 1987, 1271–72.
98. *PPP*, October 28, 1987, 1239.
99. *PPP*, December 1, 1987, 1404, 1406.
100. *PPP*, December 3, 1987, 1426.
101. *PPP*, January 27, 1988, 128.
102. *PPP*, March 26, 1988, 326.
103. *PPP*, May 4, 1988, 555.

104. *PPP*, May 24, 1988, 649.

105. Reagan, *An American Life*, 707.

106. The list requested "the release from labor camps or exile of [some] people . . . [including] prisoners of conscience; the publication of books like 'Dr. Zhivago' and 'Children of the Arbat'; the distribution of movies like 'Repentance' that are critical of aspects of the Soviet past and present; allowing higher levels of emigration; greater toleration of dissent; General Secretary Gorbachev's recent statements on religious toleration; the beginning of Soviet withdrawal from Afghanistan." Reagan, *An American Life*, 659. "Although Soviet troops were still fighting in Afghanistan and the Soviets were still supporting guerillas in Central America and elsewhere, we were at least seeing real deeds from Moscow." Ibid., 686–87. During the Washington summit, Reagan was satisfied that Gorbachev had promised him in private that he would end the shipment of Soviet military weapons to Nicaragua. Ibid., 701.

107. Transcripts of National Security Planning Group meeting, September 8, 1987, 8.

108. Reagan's reference was to Mikhail Gorbachev, *Perestroika: New Thinking for Our Country and the World* (New York: HarperCollins, 1987). Ronald Reagan, news conference following the Moscow summit, June 1, 1988, quoted in *PPP*, 1988, 708–9. In that press conference Reagan (ibid., even defended Gorbachev's emigration policies, blaming issues on Soviet bureaucracy rather than Gorbachev's policies. Ibid., 712–13. Reagan (*An American Life*, 706) would later write in his memoir that when he had met Gorbachev for the first time, Gorbachev "made it plain he believed wholeheartedly in the Communist system of government." Reagan inferred from these remarks that Gorbachev intended to change the management style but not the system itself.

109. *PPP*, 1988, 1409.

110. Ibid., 1592–93.

111. For an excellent analysis of Reagan's personality traits that allowed him to revise his beliefs about the Soviet threat, see Barbara Farnham "Reagan and the Gorbachev Revolution: Perceiving the End of Threat," *Political Science Quarterly* 116, no. 2 (2001): 225–52. Emotional intelligence refers to a person's "ability to manage his emotions and turn them to constructive purposes, rather than being dominated by them and allowing them to diminish his leadership." Fred Greenstein, *The Presidential Difference: Leadership Styles from FDR to George W. Bush*, 2nd ed. (Princeton, NJ: Princeton University Press, 2004), 6. With respect to Reagan, see ibid., 157; Fred Greenstein, "Reckoning with Reagan," *Political Science Quarterly* 115 (Spring 2000): 121–22. On the connection between emotion and intuition, see Stanley A. Renshon and Deborah Welch Larson, *Good Judgment in Foreign Policy: Theory and Action* (Lanham, MD: Rowman and Littlefield, 2002), 10.

112. Farnham, "Reagan and the Gorbachev Revolution," 248.

113. Quoted in ibid.

114. George Breslauer and Richard Ned Lebow, "Leadership and the End of the Cold War: A Counterfactual Thought Experiment," in *Ending the Cold War: Interpretations, Causation, and the Study of International Relations*, ed. Richard K. Herrmann and Richard Ned Lebow (Basingstoke, UK: Palgrave Macmillan, 2004), 183.

115. Author's interview with Jack F. Matlock Jr.

116. Ibid.

117. Quoted in William C. Wohlforth, ed., *Witnesses to the End of the Cold War* (Baltimore: Johns Hopkins University Press, 1996), 46.

118. Quoted in ibid., 105.

119. Breslauer and Lebow, "Leadership and the End of the Cold War," 184. For a similar argument, see Fred I. Greenstein, "Ronald Reagan, Mikhail Gorbachev, and the End of the Cold War: What Difference Did They Make?" in *Witnesses to the End of the Cold War*, ed. William C. Wohlforth (Baltimore: Johns Hopkins University Press, 1996), 216.

120. *PPP*, October 24, 1985, 1287–88.

121. *PPP*, May 22, 1985, 650.

122. On other occasions, however, Reagan seemed to endorse the possibility that aggressive Soviet intentions depended on the Soviet Union's perceptions of its own capabilities. In 1986, Reagan claimed that when the Soviets perceived a change in the correlation of forces in their favor, they began to exhibit behavior that indicated their expansionist ambitions. Even in such instances, though, his inferences about intentions came primarily from a series of Soviet actions rather than its military strength per se. *PPP*, March 25, 1985, 343.

123. *PPP*, October 21, 1985, 1275.

124. Mark L. Haas, "The United States and the End of the Cold War: Reactions to Shifts in Soviet Power, Policies, or Domestic Politics?" *International Organization* 61, no. 1 (Winter 2007): 145–79. Political scientist John Mueller provides the strongest statement on the role of ideology: "The Soviet withdrawal from Afghanistan by early 1989 is properly taken as a 'costly signal' of Gorbachev's sincerity. But if that is so, it is because the signal was costly ideologically—a tangible admission that Gorbachev had abandoned Communist expansionary ideas. That is, had such deeds not been accompanied by indications of an ideological shift, they, like those of Khrushchev, would have been seen to be signaling simply that the Soviet Union was capable of pragmatic retreat from an overextended position." John Mueller, "What Was the Cold War About? Evidence from Its Ending," *Political Science Quarterly* 119, no. 4 (2004–5): 620.

125. *PPP*, September 22, 1986, 1230–31.

126. *PPP*, October 4, 1986, 1323. Communist ideology played a large role in how Reagan viewed the Soviet Union, but he placed a premium on the human factor, and believed in the ability of leaders and countries to change their behavior through communication. Author's interview with Jack F. Matlock Jr.

127. Haas, "The United States and the End of the Cold War," 175. These results are supported by Shimko (*Images and Arms Control*, 107), whose content analysis of Reagan's public statements reveals "a decreased emphasis on ideology as the source of Soviet behavior beginning in 1985."

128. Shultz, *Turmoil and Triumph*, 998.

129. Quoted in *DSB*, April 1985, 13.

130. *DSB*, December 1985, 33.

131. Shultz, *Turmoil and Triumph*, 1003.

132. Ibid., 987.

133. The Soviet acceptance of the zero option in the INF Treaty, by which the USSR agreed to eliminate many more warheads than the United States, is likely to have been viewed by Shultz as another critical indicator of Soviet willingness to improve relations with the United States and its European allies. Yet the documents currently available do not contain any explicit statements by Shultz linking the USSR's concessions on the INF with changes in perceptions of its intentions. It is difficult to

ascertain whether the absence of such evidence is an artifact of the declassification process or reflects Shultz's inference process. As for Soviet military doctrine, Shultz, like Reagan, made several references to Soviet doctrine, but never explicitly used it to draw conclusions about the Soviet Union's political intentions or inclination to use military force to achieve its objectives. See, for example, Shultz's testimony before Senate Committee on Appropriation, "Hearings on Foreign Assistance and Related Programs for FY1986," 99th Cong., 1st Sess., March 7, 1985, 58.

134. Author's interview with George Shultz, November 2009.

135. Shultz, *Turmoil and Triumph*, 780.

136. Ibid., 994.

137. Quoted in *DSB*, January 1988, 6–7.

138. Shultz, *Turmoil and Triumph*, 994.

139. Ibid., 986.

140. Ibid., 889.

141. Ibid., 990.

142. Shultz, *Turmoil and Triumph*, 987.

143. Ronald Reagan Oral History Project, *Interview with Caspar Weinberger*, November 19, 2002, 28–29, millercenter.org/president/reagan/oralhistory/caspar-weinberger (August 22, 2013).

144. See Garthoff, *The Great Transition*, 508–13; Fischer, *The Reagan Reversal*; Alexander Dallin and Gail Lapidus, "Reagan and the Russians: American Policy toward the Soviet Union," in *Eagle Resurgent? The Reagan Era in American Foreign Policy*, ed. Robert J. Lieber, Kenneth A. Oye, and Donald S. Rothschild (Boston: Little, Brown and Co., 1987), 193–254. Some trace the origins of that policy to mid- to late 1983. Others argue that the less confrontational policy became operational only from early 1984. See Garthoff, *The Great Transition*, 92–110, 118–41.

145. Matlock, *Reagan and Gorbachev*, 84.

146. See ibid., 74–76; Robert C. McFarlane, *Special Trust: Pride, Principle, and Politics Inside the White House* (New York: Cadell and Davies, 1994), 295.

147. Reagan, *An American Life*, 606.

148. Quoted in Garthoff, *The Great Transition*, 154.

149. Reagan later noted in his diary that the president of Yugoslavia told him that "coupled with their expansionist philosophy, they [the USSR] are also insecure and genuinely frightened of us," and "if we opened them a bit, their leading citizens would get braver about proposing change in their system." Then, Reagan (*An American Life*, 588–89) wrote, "I am going to pursue this."

150. NSC meeting, September 20, 1985, 4, www.foia.cia.gov/Reagan/19850920.pdf (accessed August 21, 2013).

151. These included the appointment of McFarlane as national security advisor in place of William P. Clark Jr. in late 1983 and replacement of the conservative Pipes as senior expert on Soviet affairs in the NSC with the more pragmatic Matlock. Together with Shultz, McFarlane and Matlock provided Reagan with a less confrontational view of US-Soviet relations that de-emphasized ideology.

152. Fischer (*The Reagan Reversal*, 102–43) claims that these events triggered Reagan to adopt a more conciliatory posture toward the Soviets in early 1984 in two ways. First, they "primed" Reagan to think about the devastating effects of a nuclear war. Second, these events created a scenario of nuclear war that was mentally "available," leading

Reagan to assign a greater probability to nuclear war than he had earlier. Reagan (*An American Life*, 582–87) also discusses these events in his memoir, and claims that they convinced him to work toward the elimination of nuclear weapons by negotiating with the Soviets and building a defensive shield (the SDI). Fischer (*The Reagan Reversal*, 16–40), too, argues that the new policy reflected an important change in Reagan's perceptions of the Soviet threat and intentions: during 1984–85, Reagan began to speak of "dangerous misunderstanding and miscalculations" that could lead to war as the primary source of threat. I think that this interpretation of Reagan's shift is exaggerated. Reagan did talk about mutual misunderstandings, and his opinion of Soviet motives might have changed somewhat, as he saw their aggressiveness as stemming from sense of insecurity. But Reagan and his advisers continued to assert in subsequent speeches their firm belief that Soviet intentions were expansionist.

153. Reagan, *An American Life*, 594; Dallin and Lapidus, "Reagan and the Russians," 230. Shultz also used this rationale when convincing Reagan to consider a change in policy toward the USSR in mid-1983. Shultz, *Turmoil and Triumph*, 267.

154. For a discussion on how Reagan's policies helped trigger the collapse of the Soviet Union, see Paul Kengor, *The Crusader: Ronald Reagan and the Fall of Communism* (New York: HarperCollins, 2006); Peter Schweizer, *Victory: The Reagan Administration's Secret Strategy That Hastened the Collapse of the Soviet Union* (New York: Atlantic Monthly Press, 1994).

155. Reagan's policy of supporting so-called freedom fighters in the third world was also known as the Reagan Doctrine. Garthoff, *The Great Transition*, 200.

156. Matlock, *Reagan and Gorbachev*, 114.

157. Renewed arguments over the administration's Soviet policy were also prompted by the approach of the end of the term of the (unratified) SALT II treaty. Members of the Reagan administration debated whether the United States should continue with "interim restraint" pending negotiation of a new treaty on strategic arms. Hard-liners in the administration asserted that it did not make sense for the United States to adhere to a flawed treaty after its expiration and following Soviet violations of it. Further, they advocated that Reagan commission the deployment of a new nuclear missile submarine without retiring any of the older Poseidon-type ones. If implemented, this move would have put the United States in clear violation of SALT II limits. Shultz and others in the administration urged pressuring the Soviets on their violations, but continuing to adhere to the treaty as long as doing so did not entail a military or security cost. After weeks of consultations, Reagan chose cooperation with the Soviets by staying within the SALT II limits. Yet this decision did not stem from a change in perceptions of Soviet intentions; instead, it sprang from a belief that treaty compliance was in the best interest of the United States. Matlock, *Reagan and Gorbachev*, 121–22; Shultz, *Turmoil and Triumph*, 569–70; Garthoff, *The Great Transition*, 229–30, 520–21.

158. Garthoff, *The Great Transition*, 230.

159. Around that time, Reagan issued National Security Decision Directive (NSDD) no. 166, which was intended to provide covert assistance to enable the rebels in Afghanistan to achieve "outright military victory" against the Soviets. This NSDD is still classified. For more on this, see Kengor, *The Crusader*, 232–33. To that end, Reagan sought to generate support for a then record $320 billion military budget. See Garthoff, *The Great Transition*, 271.

160. Reagan eventually declared that SALT II was "dead." Shultz had opposed this decision, but once the decision was made, he defended it. See Shultz, *Turmoil and Triumph*, 717; Garthoff, *The Great Transition*, 278; Matlock, *Reagan and Gorbachev*, 186.

161. According to Shultz, Reagan was afraid that any discussion with the Soviets about strategic nuclear weapons would be used as a way by the Soviets to scuttle the SDI. During NSC meetings and in public, he repeatedly declared that the SDI was not a bargaining chip. Shultz, *Turmoil and Triumph*, 718–27.

162. Shimko, *Images and Arms Control*, 246.

163. Even after Gorbachev accepted the zero option, some in the Republican Party were against the treaty, claiming that the United States needed intermediate-range nuclear missiles in Europe to provide a "ladder of escalation" in NATO's "flexible response doctrine." Shultz's (*Turmoil and Triumph*, 1082) response was that NATO would still have a robust deterrent against Soviet attack without relying exclusively on strategic systems.

164. Ibid., 879.

165. Ibid., 899.

166. See NSC, NSDD no. 288, "My Objectives in the Summit," November 10, 1987, 1–2, www.fas.org/irp/offdocs/nsdd/nsdd-288.htm (accessed July 14, 2010).

167. Quoted in ibid. See also Shultz's testimony before the Senate Foreign Relations Committee on January 1988, *DSB*, March 1988. Even Weinberger eventually believed that the INF was a triumph for Reagan's RS&D policy. See Caspar W. Weinberger, "Arms Reduction and Deterrence," *Foreign Affairs* 66, no. 4 (1988): 700–719.

168. Shimko, *Images and Arms Control*, 246–47.

169. NSDD no. 311, "US-Soviet Defense and Military Relations," July 28, 1988, www.fas .org/irp/offdocs/nsdd/ nsdd-311.htm (accessed July 14, 2010).

170. NSDD no. 305, "Objectives at the Moscow Summit," April 26, 1988, www.fas.org/ irp/offdocs/nsdd/ nsdd-305.htm (accessed July 14, 2010).

171. Garthoff, *The Great Transition*, 353, 372.

172. Shimko, *Images and Arms Control*, 246–47.

173. Other domestic political and strategic considerations were also important in shaping some of the specific policies Reagan adopted. For example, the Iran-Contra affair, according to Matlock (*Reagan and Gorbachev*, 246–47), impeded Reagan's ability to make progress on US-Soviet negotiations in early 1987, as did the fact that Carlucci and his successor as national security advisor later that year, Colin Powell, were new players who had not been intimately involved in the negotiations with the Soviets in Reykjavik. Crucially, Reagan continued to implement some anti-Soviet policies until shortly before he left office. NSDD no. 320, "National Policy on Strategic Trade Controls" (which is today still heavily redacted), for instance, contained calls to "restrict the transfer of strategic technologies to the Soviet Union and its allies whenever such transfers would make a significant contribution to Soviet bloc military capabilities that would prove detrimental to the national security of the United States and its allies." As Kengor (*The Crusader*, 281) argues, "NSDD-320 proved to be the last significant piece of anti-Soviet policy that Ronald Reagan implemented before leaving the White House." Since we know little about the conditions or debates that prompted this NSDD, it is hard to assess its significance, though.

174. I do not argue that Gorbachev's costly actions did not affect Reagan and Shultz's perceptions. Nevertheless, the evidence presented earlier in the chapter indicates that

the inference process of the three decision makers was at times sharply inconsistent with the logic of the behavior thesis. We should also explore whether Gorbachev's costly signaling induced a change in US perceptions, or whether Gorbachev had decided to make significant concessions after he had already come to view Reagan's intentions as cooperative. On that, see Ken Booth and Nicholas J. Wheeler, *The Security Dilemma: Fear, Cooperation, and Trust in World Politics* (Basingstoke, UK: Palgrave Macmillan, 2008), 155–56.

CHAPTER 10: THE US INTELLIGENCE COMMUNITY'S ASSESSMENTS OF SOVIET INTENTIONS: THE END OF THE COLD WAR

1. According to Douglas MacEachin, the director of SOVA in the 1980s, "Many of the people who had [earlier] expressed such criticism of our Soviet analysis moved into policy positions in the 1980s. Indeed, Mr. Casey made no secret of the fact that he had some of these same criticisms of CIA products—as did many CIA professionals." Quoted in "Nomination of Robert M. Gates to be Director of Central Intelligence: Report of the Select Committee on Intelligence, Together with Additional Views," 102nd Cong., 1st Sess., September–October 1991 (hereafter referred to as Gates Confirmation Hearings).
2. Raymond L. Garthoff, "Estimating Soviet Military Intentions and Capabilities," in *Watching the Bear: Essays on CIA's Analysis of the Soviet Union*, ed. Gerald K. Haines and Robert E. Leggett (Washington, DC: Center for the Study of Intelligence Publications, 2003), chapter 5. In this section, I track and analyze the conclusions expressed by the intelligence community about intentions in all available NIEs that provide any explicit statement about Soviet political and military objectives. For a list of the NIES, see www.foia.cia.gov/collection/declassified-national-intelligence-estimates-soviet-union -and-international-communism (accessed August 21, 2013).
3. Daniel Patrick Moynihan, quoted by Bill Gertz, *Washington Times*, May 21, 1992. Turner, head of the CIA from 1988–91, called the failure to forecast the magnitude of the Soviet crisis enormous, and said that he "never heard a suggestion from the CIA, of the intelligence arms of the departments of defense or state, that numerous Soviets recognized a growing systemic economic problem." See Stansfield Turner, "Intelligence for a New World Order," *Foreign Affairs* 71, no. 4 (1991): 151.
4. For studies on intelligence and the end of the Cold War, see Kirsten Lundberg for Ernest May and Philip Zelikow, *The CIA and the Fall of the Soviet Empire: The Politics of "Getting It Right,"* Case Study C16-94-1251.0, Intelligence and Policy Project, John F. Kennedy School of Government (Cambridge, MA: Harvard University, 1994); Gerald K. Haines and Robert E. Leggett, eds., *CIA's Analysis of the Soviet Union, 1947–91* (Washington, DC: Center for the Study of Intelligence Publications, 2001); Douglas MacEachin, "CIA Assessments of the Soviet Union: The Record versus the Charges," www.foia.cia.gov/Reagan/19960501.pdf (accessed August 21, 2013); Bruce Berkowitz, "US Intelligence Estimates of the Soviet Collapse: Reality and Perception," *International Journal of Intelligence and Counterintelligence* 21 (2008): 237–50.
5. Donald P. Steury, *Intentions and Capabilities: Estimates on Soviet Strategic Forces, 1950–1983* (Washington, DC: Central Intelligence Agency, 1996), 467.

6. George P. Shultz, *Turmoil and Triumph: My Years as Secretary of State* (New York: Charles Scribner's Sons, 1993), 691.

7. Robert M. Gates, *From the Shadows: The Ultimate Insider's Story of Five Presidents and How They Won the Cold War* (New York: Simon and Schuster, 1996), 201.

8. Memorandum to Holders of NIE 11-4-78, 3–5. The primary consumers of the NIEs were the major decision makers, including the president. The NIEs were typically produced to satisfy an explicit request by a decision maker, and were intended to report the best-available information on a given topic and provide some analysis of a set of policy options.

9. NIE 11-4-78.

10. SNIE 11-4/2-81, 5, 26–27.

11. According to this estimate, the balance of strategic intercontinental nuclear forces was a critical index for Moscow's assessment of the bilateral correlation of forces. NIE 11-4-82, 2.

12. Ibid., 7.

13. NIE 11-16-83, 1. Nevertheless, some in the intelligence community remarked that these arms control objectives were in fact similar to those of the United States, and that the Soviets, too, were interested in "reducing the risks of nuclear war and nuclear proliferation" as well as "fostering a more predictable basis for military planning, and a more predictable US-Soviet relationship." Others, including the DIA and military intelligence agencies, vehemently rejected such a comparison, claiming that "the Soviets seek to use arms control as a tool for shifting the 'correlation of forces' in their favor and for facilitating the attainment of superiority over the West, although they do seek to gain their objectives without a nuclear war." Ibid., 6n.

14. See, for instance, NIE 11-9-83 and SNIE 11-10-84.

15. See Ben B. Fischer, *A Cold War Conundrum: The 1983 Soviet War Scare* (Washington, DC: Center for Study of Intelligence Publications, 1997), https://www.cia.gov/csi/monograph/coldwar/source.htm (accessed July 14, 2008); John Prados, "The War Scare of 1983," in *The Cold War: A Military History*, ed. Robert Cowley (New York: Random House, 2005), 438–54. The NATO exercise Able Archer was intended to practice nuclear release procedures. It came at a moment of heightened stress in US-Soviet relations following Reagan's speeches announcing the SDI and calling the Soviet Union an evil empire (March 1983), and the Soviet shoot down of the civilian airliner KAL 007 (September 1983). Initially, Gates explains, the CIA did not quite grasp how alarmed the Soviets had been. After British intelligence reported the Soviet reaction, the US intelligence community decided to review its intelligence reporting. Gates, *From the Shadows*, 270–73.

16. NIE 11-10-84, iii.

17. According to Ermarth, the war scare had largely passed by May 1984. Fritz W. Ermarth, "Observations on the 'War Scare' of 1983 from an Intelligence Perch," Parallel History Project Working Paper, November 2003, kms2.isn.ethz.ch/serviceengine/Files/PHP/17325/ipublicationdocument_singledocument/D5125D02-AFCD-48ED-9DB4-BA4545DC87E8/en/ab_ar4.pdf (accessed July 14, 2008).

18. Ermarth based this on "the absence of forcewide combat readiness or other war preparation moves in the USSR, and the absence of a tone of fear or belligerence in Soviet diplomatic communications." The SNIE also claimed that if the Soviets had

been seriously considering military confrontation with the United States, the intelligence community would have seen "preparatory signs which the Soviets could not mask." SNIE 11-10-84, iii.

19. See ibid., 6.

20. Ibid.

21. Ermarth said this estimate was not controversial when it was first released. But in the late 1980s, the President's Foreign Intelligence Advisory Board directed a thorough, highly classified review of the case. Conducted by Nina Stewart, that review found that the SNIE authors had been "dangerously relaxed" and "not sufficiently alarmed" in estimating the Soviet threat. Author's interview with Fritz W. Ermarth. See also Ermarth, "Observations on the 'War Scare' of 1983."

22. SNIE 11-9-84, 1, 5, 12.

23. Gates, *From the Shadows*, 258, 273.

24. SNIE 11-16-85, 4–5.

25. NIE 11-3/8-85.

26. NIE 11-18-85.

27. Lundberg, *The CIA and the Fall of the Soviet Empire*, 12–14. In retrospect, the drafter of this NIE, Ermarth, expressed regret for not spelling out a prediction of the USSR's end in his estimate. But he believed that even if he had done so, none of the intelligence agencies would have agreed with him, particularly the DIA. Gates conceded that during this period the CIA was divided in its assessments of Gorbachev's motivation and foreign policy goals. Nevertheless, DCI Casey's views on the Soviet leader were unambiguous. In a 1985 memo to Reagan, Casey claimed that Gorbachev and those around him were neither reformers nor liberalizers in their domestic and foreign policy. According to Gates, Casey went beyond the CIA's assessments to urge Reagan to increase US military power, its alliance leadership, and its involvement in regional security matters. Gates, *From the Shadows*, 330–33.

28. SNIE 11-9-86, 4.

29. In retrospect, as Garthoff notes, "these judgments could not have been more wrong. Both domestic and foreign considerations led Gorbachev to adopt paradigm-breaking policies, and they involved not just compromises, but unilateral moves intended to change the basic equations involved in both arms control and regional security matters." See Douglas F. Garthoff, "Analyzing Soviet Politics and Foreign Policy," in *Watching the Bear: Essays on CIA's Analysis of the Soviet Union*, ed. Gerald K. Haines and Robert E. Leggett (Washington, DC: Center for the Study of Intelligence Publications, 2003), chapter 3, n71.

30. NIE 11-9-86, 5.

31. Numerous assessments by the INR during 1987 also indicate that the State Department shared these conclusions. See, for example, INR Intelligence Research Report, "What Does Gorbachev Want?" 3–4.

32. Gorbachev's goals were said by the NIE to include, first, constraining the growth of defense spending in order to rebuild Soviet economic strength so that in the long run, Soviet military requirements could be fulfilled; second, pursuing diplomatic efforts to restrict US military buildup, specifically the SDI; third, moving beyond former Soviet positions on arms control to achieve domestic and foreign policy goals; and finally, exploiting the new "favorable image" of the Soviet Union to reduce threat perceptions abroad and advance Soviet influence by political means. The DIA disagreed, claiming

that Gorbachev would "not be in a position to make an overall reduction in defense spending during the period of the Estimate." NIE 11-18-87, 3–4.

33. NIE 11-18-87.

34. In addition to a "rejuvenation of the existing system," the possibility of a "systemic reform" was assessed as having a relatively small chance, while a return to "Neo-Stalinism" was presented as remote. Ibid.

35. Ibid., 34.

36. Ibid., 9–10, 35.

37. Ibid., 11–12.

38. Memorandum by Robert Gates, "Gorbachev's Gameplan: The Long View," November 24, 1987. Gates had been acting DCI since December 1986. Casey, suffering from a brain tumor, resigned as DCI in January 1987, and Reagan nominated Gates as Casey's successor. During his confirmation hearings, however, allegations that Gates had been involved in the Iran-Contra affair ultimately led to the withdrawal of his nomination. FBI head Webster became the new DCI in May 1987, while Gates stayed on as deputy director. See Lundberg, *The CIA and the Fall of the Soviet Empire*, 19.

39. These traditional military considerations included improvement of the correlation of forces and reduction of NATO's capability to launch a surprise attack. Politically, the estimate concluded, Gorbachev sought to appeal to foreign and domestic audiences by projecting an image of the USSR as a "trustworthy, rational player in the international arena," with the hope that such a benign posture would make it difficult for NATO members to maintain or increase their defense spending. See NIE 11-16-88CX, iii–iv, 1–6; NIE 11-3-8-88, 16.

40. NIE 11-3-8-88, 16.

41. Ibid., iv, 12. Around the same time, the CIA's SOVA published a separate report on Soviet objectives in arms control negotiations that reiterated the conclusions reached in coordinated NIE 11-16-88. This showed that by the end of 1988, the CIA had not updated its assessment of Soviet motivations; it still asserted that Gorbachev's actions represented merely a change in tactics aimed at achieving long-held hostile objectives. See SOV 88-10073, 1.

42. Bob Blackwell, Transcript of the Soviet Task Force Proceedings before the Select Committee on Intelligence, December 7, 1988, quoted in Gates Confirmation Hearings 2:522.

43. Quoted in ibid., 520–21.

44. The breathing space thesis is essentially a thesis about motivation, attempting to explain why Gorbachev was seeking arms control negotiations, in turn to explain the discrepancy between his accommodating propaganda and the hostile long-term intentions that the United States attributed to the Soviet Union. This explanation diverges from the capabilities thesis, to some extent, in that the prospect of a change in the balance of power in favor of the United States (or USSR?) should have led the community to expect hostile Soviet intentions in the long run. The community, however, apparently reasoned that the Soviet Union was continuing to build and modernize its strategic arsenal, and therefore there was no change in its long-term intentions. This was not stated clearly in the NIEs, so the logic of what drove the community to attribute long-term hostile intentions to the Soviet Union is not entirely clear.

45. NIE 11-3/8-86, 5

46. NIE 11-3/8-85, 18. This line of reasoning was repeated in NIE 11-16-85, 3–9.

47. SNIE 11-9-86, 6.

48. See, for example, NIE 11-3/8-85, 17. For similar conclusions, see NIE 11-16-85.

49. NIE 11-18-85, 6.

50. In SNIE 11-9-86 (18), the community concluded that "foreseeable trends in Soviet internal affairs are unlikely to alter the main directions of Soviet policy toward the United States during the next two years."

51. Ibid., 7.

52. This, according to Gates (Confirmation Hearings, 3:129), "represented a continuing expansion of Soviet strategic capabilities."

53. In testimony in March 1986, Gates (ibid., 2:481) defended his position, saying, "Without any hint that such fundamental change is going on [in the Soviet Union], my resources do not permit me the luxury of sort of just idly speculating on what a different kind of Soviet Union might look like." Gates did acknowledge in October 1986 that a major change was taking place within the Soviet Union, but his beliefs about Soviet intentions did not change at all. Gates Confirmation Hearings, 3:129; November 25, 1986, speech titled "War by Another Name," quoted in ibid., 2:639–55.

54. NIE 11-3/8-86, 2, 18.

55. Garthoff, "Estimating Soviet Military Intentions and Capabilities."

56. The problem of overestimation remained, and it contributed to the pessimistic US judgments about Soviet policy under Gorbachev's premiership. In April 1989, the CIA issued a "print out" version of a project that had started in 1984 to determine why the intelligence community had overestimated Soviet strategic forces between 1975 and 1985 (as expressed in the NIE 11-3/8 reports) after having underestimated them prior to 1974. This paper explained that the overestimation of Soviet force modernization stemmed from a reliance on "ceteris paribus" assumptions about Soviet intentions (for example, "the Soviets will not attempt to achieve numerical equality," "the Soviets will be satisfied with parity," or "the Soviets are not seeking superiority"). Once these assumptions were made, MacEachin noted, analysts "were constrained from producing numerical projections that did not conform to the ceilings given in the assumptions." This situation led to exaggerated estimates of even the "low forces," which were accurate only for 1966 and 1970, when the Soviet economy was healthier. See Memorandum to Deputy Director of Intelligence (Richard J. Kerr) from Douglas J. MacEachin, Director, SOVA, "Force Projections," NIE 11-3/8, April 22, 1986, Records of the Directorate of Intelligence, job 90-60l35R, box 2, folder 20, 2–3.

57. NIE 11-18-88, 2.

58. NIE 11-3/8-86; NIE 11-3/8-88.

59. NIE 11-3/8-88, 15. For another example that supports this logic, see NIE 11-3/8-87W, 6.

60. When Gorbachev's economic plans revealed more about what he was actually doing, the NIEs shifted the focus from gauging his intentions to figuring out whether he would be able to retain power. The basis of this shift was the belief that even if Gorbachev had reformist objectives, the Soviet power structure as a whole did not.

61. The evolution in the intelligence community's understanding of the changes in Soviet military doctrine (strategic and conventional) is documented in chapter 8. Some have argued that its failure to understand the changes in Soviet doctrine constituted a major flaw in its analysis. For example, Garthoff ("Estimating Soviet Military Intentions and Capabilities") notes, "It should not have required Gorbachev's announce-

ment to alert the intelligence estimators to the changes under way in Soviet military doctrine and strategy and their implications not only for future Soviet capabilities but for already operative changed Soviet objectives and evaluations of the role of military power. In this respect, among others, the record shows that the analysts in [the] CIA's Directorate of Intelligence were well ahead of the Intelligence Community as a whole, and their published analyses were well in advance of the NIEs in predicting (or at least catching up with) Soviet actions based on these doctrinal and policy changes."

62. Ibid.

63. NIE 11-3/8-88, 3.

64. The CIA was referring to the Soviet doctrine that expected that any general war would remain conventional for an extended period or terminate without nuclear escalation.

65. SNIE 11-9-86, 16.

66. Ibid.

67. NIE 11-3/8-86, 16.

68. Ibid., 6–8.

69. The discussion section provided detailed evidence to support more specific objectives pertaining to Soviet military intentions. In this NIE (ibid., 13), for instance, Soviet force training and exercises were said to indicate that "the Soviets have become more realistic about the problem of conducting military operations in a nuclear environment, but the requirement to carry out nuclear combat operations as effectively as possible is still one of their highest priorities."

70. NIE 11-3/8-88, 3.

71. Ibid., 6.

72. Ibid., 18.

73. Garthoff, "Estimating Soviet Military Intentions and Capabilities."

74. See, for example, NIE 11-16-85, 12, 13.

75. NIE 11-18-87, 22.

76. NIE 11-3/8-88, 6.

77. Ibid., 22. Another example of this can be found in the discussion of Soviet defense policy where the particulars of Gorbachev's strategy appear to be inferred from his behavior and statements, while his foreign policy intentions and motivations were inferred from the USSR's capabilities relative to those of the United States. See ibid., 21. Similarly, in the following year, NIE 11-3/8-88 (6) acknowledged that "Soviet public statements" appeared to point to changes in Soviet strategic thought, including the acceptance of the concept of mutual assured destruction. Still, the intelligence community dismissed the importance of such statements. It instead inferred from Soviet procurement and modernization efforts that the Soviets were "continuing to build their forces on the premise that forces that are better prepared to effectively fight a nuclear war are also better able to deter such a war." Likewise, the intelligence community seriously doubted Soviet declaratory policy and actions in arms control, claiming that these "should not be taken as an indicator of whether or not they are implementing a fundamental change in their approach to nuclear war." See also NIE 11-16-88.

78. Melvin A. Goodman, "Ending the CIA's Cold War Legacy," *Foreign Policy* 106 (1997): 138.

79. Intelligence Assessment, "USSR: Domestic Fallout from the Afghan War," February 1987.

80. Quoted in Lundberg, *The CIA and the Fall of the Soviet Empire*, 23–24.
81. Gates, *From the Shadows*, 428–33; see also John Diamond, *The CIA and the Culture of Failure: U.S. Intelligence from the End of the Cold War to the Invasion of Iraq* (Stanford, CA: Stanford Security Studies, 2008), 97.
82. Garthoff, "Estimating Soviet Military Intentions and Capabilities."
83. Ibid.
84. Cited in Garthoff, "Estimating Soviet Military Intentions and Capabilities."
85. Gates was frustrated that members of the Reagan administration and beyond had unrealistic expectations of the CIA. "When this expectation is disappointed," Gates noted in 1988, "it often turns into skepticism that the agency can do much of anything." Robert Gates, "The CIA and Foreign Policy," *Foreign Affairs* 66, no. 2 (1987–88): 225–26.
86. Shultz, *Turmoil and Triumph*, 864; see also Ronald Reagan Oral History Project, *Interview with George Shultz*, December 18, 2002, 27. Shultz commented that he did not think the NIEs about the USSR were "interesting or informative" because they were lacking in useful insights. He found personal exchanges with Gates and other CIA analysts more useful since they presented different opinions.
87. Nevertheless, Matlock explained that Shultz was concerned that the NIEs' conclusions might undermine the public confidence of Reagan's attempts to cooperate with the Soviet Union.
88. Paul Pillar, *Intelligence and U.S. Foreign Policy: Iraq, 9/11, and Misguided Reform* (New York: Columbia University Press, 2011), 116. For a recent study of Reagan as a reader and consumer of intelligence that challenges the conventional wisdom, see Nicholas Dujmovic, *Ronald Reagan, Intelligence, William Casey, and CIA: A Reappraisal* (Washington, DC: Center for the Study of Intelligence Publications, April 2011), www.foia.cia.gov/Reagan/20110401.pdf (accessed August 21, 2013).
89. Author interview with Matlock.
90. Garthoff, "Estimating Soviet Military Intentions and Capabilities."

CHAPTER 11: SUMMARY AND IMPLICATIONS

1. Jonathan Mercer, "Emotional Beliefs," *International Organization* 64, no. 1 (2010): 14.
2. The evidence I have presented suggests that in neither of the Cold War episodes did US decision makers use the NIEs to derive conclusions about Soviet intentions. During the interwar period, British decision makers appeared to have relied on vivid reports on Hitler's mood and state of mind from human intelligence sources of the SIS, but much less on the COS strategic reports about German military power, to reach conclusions about Germany's intentions.
3. Systemic theories, such as structural realism (whether defensive or offensive), do not attempt to explain a state's foreign policy. Yet some debate exists on whether systemic theories could be refined and reformulated in order to account for such a dependent variable. See, for example, Thomas J. Christensen and Jack Snyder, "Chain Gangs and Passed Bucks: Predicting Alliance Patterns in Multipolarity," *International Organization* 44, no. 2 (1990): 137–68; John A. Vasquez, "The Realist Paradigm and Degenerative versus Progressive Research Programs: An Appraisal of Neotraditional Research on

Waltz's Balancing Proposition," *American Political Science Review* 91, no. 4 (1997): 899–912; Thomas J. Christensen and Jack Snyder, "Progressive Research on Degenerate Alliances," *American Political Science Review* 91, no. 4 (1997): 919–22; Randall L. Schweller, "New Realist Research on Alliances: Refining, Not Refuting, Waltz's Balancing Proposition," *American Political Science Review* 91, no. 4 (1997): 927–30.

4. Stephen M. Walt, *The Origin of Alliances* (Ithaca, NY: Cornell University Press, 1987). Other defensive realist scholars have also emphasized that states respond not only to the capabilities and behavior of other states but also to their motives. See, for instance, Charles L. Glaser, *Rational Theory of International Politics: The Logic of Competition and Cooperation* (Princeton, NJ: Princeton University Press, 2010).

5. From this study, it appears that the inference processes of intelligence organizations fit the predictions of both the capabilities thesis and selective attention theory's organizational expertise hypothesis. What remains unclear is whether intelligence organizations use military capabilities as an indicator of intentions because they operate more like realists in the sense that they believe intentions are reflected in or stem from military capabilities, because they follow the logic of costly signaling, or because of bureaucratic and practical reasons. Future studies, using surveys and experiments, might enable us to understand more clearly what truly guides intelligence organizations' inferences.

6. Technical expertise and training is required to decipher military doctrines. These difficulties in understanding an adversary's doctrines are compounded by the high degree of secrecy that generally surrounds them.

7. Christopher P. Twomey, *The Military Lens: Doctrinal Difference and Deterrence Failure in Sino-American Relations* (Ithaca, NY: Cornell University Press, 2010).

8. The formulation of indexes by Robert Jervis in *The Logic of Images in International Relations* (New York: Columbia University Press, 1989) was later picked up and reformulated a little differently in Michael Spence, "Job Market Signaling," *Quarterly Journal of Economics* 87, no. 3 (1973): 355–74.

9. Robert Jervis, "Signaling and Perception: Drawing Inferences and Projecting Images," in *Political Psychology*, ed. Kristen R. Monroe (Mahwah, NJ: Lawrence Erlbaum Associates, 2002).

10. This observation is similar to Sartori's discussion of how private diplomatic communications can become credible when states desire a bargaining reputation. In such a situation, states would avoid sending misleading signals lest they be caught in a bluff. See Anne E. Sartori, *Deterrence by Diplomacy* (Princeton, NJ: Princeton University Press, 2005).

11. Keren Yarhi-Milo, "Tying Hands Behind Closed Doors: The Logic and Practice of Secret Assurance," *Security Studies* 32 (2013): 405–35. See also Bahar Leventoglu and Ahmer Tarar, "Prenegotiation Public Commitment in Domestic and International Bargaining," *American Political Science Review* 99, no. 3 (2005): 419–33; Shuhei Kurizaki, "Efficient Secrecy: Public versus Private Threats in Crisis Diplomacy," *American Political Science Review* 101, no. 3 (2007): 543–58.

12. I find this proposition plausible but not convincing, primarily because both Vance and Weinberger continued to defend their assessments of Soviet intentions long after they had left office. There is no indication in their memoirs or later statements that their perceptions had changed after leaving their post.

13. Janice Gross Stein raises a similar point about Gorbachev. See Janice Gross Stein, "Political Learning by Doing: Gorbachev as Uncommitted Thinker and Motivated Learner," *International Organization* 48, no. 2 (1994): 155–83.

14. For a review of this episode, see Todd Hall and Keren Yarhi-Milo, "The Personal Touch: Leaders' Impressions, Costly Signaling, and Assessments of Sincerity," *International Studies Quarterly* 56, no. 3 (September 2012): 560–73.

15. Richard K. Betts, "Review of Sulmaan Wasif Khan's 'The Aesthetic of Analysis,'" *H-Diplo* 202 (November 28, 2008): 2, http://www.h-net.org/~diplo/reviews/PDF/Betts -Khan.pdf (accessed June 4, 2012).

16. Joshua Rovner, *Fixing the Facts: National Security and the Politics of Intelligence* (Ithaca, NY: Cornell University Press, 2011).

17. See interviews in Kenneth Lieberthal, "The U.S Intelligence Community and Foreign Policy: Getting the Analysis Right," Brookings Institute Report, September 2009.

18. Ibid., 16.

19. Ibid.

20. Richard Best, "Intelligence Estimates: How Useful to Congress?" Congressional Research Service Report, January 2011, 12.

Index

Aaron, David, 162
Able Archer exercise, 226, 337n15
ABM Treaty. *See* Antiballistic Missile (ABM) Treaty
abstract information. *See* colorless, abstract, or objective information
affective bias, 141
affective decision-making models, 3–4, 17
Afghanistan: Soviet invasion of, 123, 124, 136–38, 140–43, 146–47, 151, 153–57, 174, 206–8, 211–12, 246; Soviet withdrawal from, 39, 189–91, 202, 204, 212–14, 238; US invasion of (2001), 252; US support of (1980s), 216, 218
Africa, Soviet Union involvement in, 123, 124, 129–34, 140, 142–43, 146–47, 149–51, 155, 157, 164, 211, 238. *See also individual countries*
Air Intelligence Directorate (Britain), 48–49
Air Ministry (Britain), 48–49, 52
Allison, Graham, 24
Alsace-Lorraine, 72, 83
Anderson, George, 160
Andropov, Yuri, 195, 216, 228
anecdotal information, 20
Angola, 123, 143, 189, 206, 218, 220
Annual Reviews (Britain), 103–5, 295n1
Antiballistic Missile (ABM) Treaty, 193–94, 198, 218
appeasement, 6, 43, 74, 85–88, 91–100; Chamberlain and, 92, 97–98, 295n199; defined, 292n167; origins of, 92–93; revisionist interpretation of, 92
arc of crisis, 123
armor doctrine, 53

arms control agreements, 32–33
Austria, 50, 55, 63, 65, 68–70, 89, 97, 100, 105, 281n51

balance of power: in British-German case, 38–39, 48–49, 51–52, 106–8, 110, 112; capabilities thesis and, 29; in Carter-Soviet case, 117–19, 156, 157, 161, 165, 167, 169–71, 174–75; in Reagan-Soviet case, 183–84, 212. *See also* military capabilities
balance of threat theory, 247
Baldwin, Stanley, 58, 67
Beck, József, 88
behavior thesis: in British-German case, 55–57, 80, 113, 243; in Carter-Soviet case, 122–25, 139–42, 155–56, 173, 243; defined, 5; effectiveness of, 100, 156; overview of, 3, 31–34; predictions of, 36–37, 257; in Reagan-Soviet case, 188–91, 205–8, 211–12, 214, 221–22, 227, 237–39, 243; selective attention thesis compared to, 35; shortcomings of, 11–12, 243; and signaling, 5–6; support for, 205, 208, 221; unitary state assumed by, 6
Belgium, 55
belief change, 11, 192, 244–46, 249, 260n11; in British-German case, 99–100, 245–46; in Carter-Soviet case, 136, 140–42, 147–48, 154–57, 244–46, 310n86; in Reagan-Soviet case, 192, 199–200, 202–5, 214–17, 219–21, 244–46, 333n152
belief perseverance principle, 249
Berlin, Isaiah, 24
Berlin Wall, 180, 207, 208

110; image of Germany held by, 39; impression made by Hitler on, 45, 80, 87–88, 90, 101, 251–52; litmus tests of, 46; personal diplomacy of, 72–74
cheap talk/actions: in British-German case, 80, 85, 101; in Reagan-Soviet case, 188–89; reliance on, 11, 85, 101, 243, 248, 261n17; statements of peaceful intent as example of, 7; valuelessness of, 6, 33; vividness as, 248
Chernenko, Konstantin, 193, 195, 216
Chiefs of Staff (COS, Britain), 48–52, 70, 91, 98, 102–5, 107–8, 110–13, 299n45
China, US relations with, 2, 148–50, 153, 252–53
Christensen, Thomas, 53, 280n35
Christie, Malcolm Graham, 298n35
Churchill, Winston, 18, 282n1
CIA. See Central Intelligence Agency
CNA. See Comprehensive Net Assessment (CNA, United States)
cognitive bias, 141, 264n8
cognitive consistency principle, 20, 214, 249
cognitive decision-making models, 4
Colby, William, 158, 160
Cold War: behavior thesis and, 33, 39, 188; end of, 192, 205, 209, 210, 214–15, 220, 231; waning of, 178, 184
Collier, Laurence, 94
colorless, abstract, or objective information, 17, 20
Committee on Foreign Policy (Britain), 66, 70, 74, 82
Committee on German Rearmament (Britain), 59
comparative historical case study method, 38–39
Comprehensive Net Assessment (CNA, United States), 118, 157
congruence procedures, 40, 41
Consolidated Guidance (United States), 157
constructivism, 269n56
content analysis, 275n104
COS. See Chiefs of Staff (COS, Britain)
costless information. See cheap talk/actions
costly actions/information: characteristics of, 7–8; differentiation of, 10; Germany's, 55–57, 100; international institutions and, 273n80; in international relations theory, 248; interpretive value of, 5–6, 243, 248, 266n34; in security dilemma, 270n60; Soviet Union's, 122–24, 140–41, 178, 180, 188–90, 214, 221–22

Cuba, 124, 132–33, 135–36, 143, 146, 149, 152–53, 157, 206, 211, 220
current actions, in Carter-Soviet case, 142–43, 145–46, 173
current actions hypothesis, 33; in British-German case, 57, 80, 85, 113; in Carter-Soviet case, 124, 156–57; in Reagan-Soviet case, 190, 208, 212, 221, 229, 238, 239
Czechoslovakia: invasion of, 55–57, 61, 63, 65, 68, 70–74, 77, 87, 89, 97–98, 105, 107–9, 111, 299n47; reaction to invasion of, 52, 78–80, 89–92, 98–101

Daladier, Edouard, 73
Damasio, Antonio, 17
Danzig, 56
decision makers: in Britain, 58–101, 289n112; in Carter administration, 126–57; influence and impact of, 26, 43; intelligence organizations compared to, 34–35, 176; intelligence organizations' relations with, 25–26, 43, 240, 276n109; likelihood of change in assessments made by, 26; in Reagan administration, 192–223; reliability of statements by, 42–43; roles and affiliations of, 248–49, 251; selective attention thesis and, 16–23; similar processes of, 210, 246–47; subjective credibility hypothesis and, 20–23; theories favored by, 12; theories of, underlying thought and decisions of, 252; vividness hypothesis and, 16–20
Defense Requirements Committee (DRC, Britain), 59, 60–61, 63, 81, 92
defensive avoidance, 294n196
defensive doctrines, 30, 272n73
defensive forces/weapons, 28, 53, 270n59, 270n63, 270n64
defensive realism, 7, 27–30, 247
democratic peace theories, 31–32
détente, 116, 128, 130, 134, 138, 141–43, 149–50, 159–60, 163, 165, 173, 227, 229, 232–34
deterrence doctrines, 30, 272n74
deterrence dominance, 28, 29, 30, 119, 271n65
DIA. See US Defense Intelligence Agency
Disarmament Conference (1932–1937), 45, 55, 59, 80, 82, 93, 100
disconfirming evidence, 4, 23, 245
diversionary-war theory, 22